An Introduction to
STATISTICS

AN ACTIVE LEARNING APPROACH

Kieth A. Carlson
Jennifer R. Winquist

Valparaiso University

Los Angeles | London | New Delhi
Singapore | Washington DC

Los Angeles | London | New Delhi
Singapore | Washington DC

FOR INFORMATION:

SAGE Publications, Inc.

2455 Teller Road

Thousand Oaks, California 91320

E-mail: order@sagepub.com

SAGE Publications Ltd.

1 Oliver's Yard

55 City Road

London EC1Y 1SP

United Kingdom

SAGE Publications India Pvt. Ltd.

B 1/I 1 Mohan Cooperative Industrial Area

Mathura Road, New Delhi 110 044

India

SAGE Publications Asia-Pacific Pte. Ltd.

3 Church Street

#10-04 Samsung Hub

Singapore 049483

Acquisitions Editor: Reid Hester
Digital Content Editor: Lauren Habib
Editorial Assistant: Sarita Sarak
Production Editor: Jane Haenel
Copy Editor: QuADS
Typesetter: C&M Digitals (P) Ltd.
Proofreader: Barbara Johnson
Indexer: Will Ragsdale
Cover Designer: Bryan Fishman
Permissions Editor: Karen Ehrmann
Marketing Manager: Lisa Sheldon Brown

Copyright © 2014 by SAGE Publications, Inc.

Printed in the United States of America

Library of Congress Cataloging-in-Publication Data

Carlson, Kieth A.

An introduction to statistics : an active learning approach / Kieth A. Carlson, Jennifer R. Winquist.

p. cm.

Includes bibliographical references and index.
ISBN 978-1-4522-1743-7 (pbk.)

1. Social sciences—Statistical methods. 2. Statistics.
I. Winquist, Jennifer R. II. Title.

HA29.C288 2014

519.5—dc23   2012038266

This book is printed on acid-free paper.

13 14 15 16 17 10 9 8 7 6 5 4 3 2 1

Contents

Detailed Contents

3   Variability

6   Hypothesis Testing With *z* Scores   127

7   Hypothesis Testing Rules   153

12   One-Way Independent Measures ANOVA   325

13   Two-Factor Independent Measures ANOVA   373

14   Correlation and Regression   423

15   Goodness-of-Fit and Independence Chi-Square Statistics   473

16   Statistical Assumptions   505

Appendixes   519

Index   539

Preface

Several years ago, we attended a faculty teaching workshop in which the keynote speaker boldly stated that "most college courses are taught backwards." She explained that instructors often feel compelled to lecture on the most fundamental aspects of course readings, and consequently, they have less time for more challenging material. Students then must "figure out" the more challenging material to complete homework assignments. The speaker then asked, "Why are our courses structured so students must do the hard stuff at home alone? Wouldn't it make more sense if students came to class knowing the fundamentals (i.e., the easy stuff), then work on the hard stuff in class, when professors can answer their questions immediately?" Her description of "backward" accurately described our statistics courses. We assigned readings prior to class, we lectured in class, and students completed homework outside class. We both admitted that our students often commented, "I understand it in class, but when I try the homework, it doesn't make sense." We, very reluctantly, realized that our class structure was part of the problem.

"Of course," the speaker then acknowledged, "students have learned to operate (some even thrive) in this traditional structure. But what strategy have we taught them?" She pointed out that when students learn that a professor will lecture on the reading, they do the rational thing and stop reading before class. After all, in their busy lives, why should they spend time reading if the professor is going to give them the information? So the traditional lecture format actually reinforces *not* reading, which many professors respond to by lecturing *more*. Again, very reluctantly, we admitted that our students' end-of-course comments supported the speaker's premise. When evaluating the course text, both of our students frequently wrote, "As long as you pay attention to the lecture, you don't even have to read the text." For years, we had interpreted similar comments as evidence of our lecturing skills. However, the speaker made us recognize that we were inadvertently teaching our students that they didn't need to learn via reading. Wouldn't we be doing our jobs better if we taught students that reading was fundamental to learning? We concluded that the answer can only be "Yes."

The day after this workshop, we started restructuring our statistics courses. Our intent was to have students read the fundamentals prior to class and then use class time to work on more challenging concepts together. However, even though we were using excellent statistics texts, many of our students insisted that they needed lectures to help them understand the text. Finally, we decided to create our own readings, which covered only the fundamentals (i.e., the "easy" stuff). We embedded relatively easy reading questions to help students pick out the fundamentals before class. Then we developed activities to reinforce the fundamentals as well as cover the more challenging material (i.e., the "hard" stuff) in class. We worked with hundreds of students on these activities in class for several years.

Whenever students were confused, we assumed the problem was with the activity and revised it. We conducted item analyses on exams. When performance was low on particular items, we revised the exam items or the relevant activity and/or readings. Consequently, the readings, activities, and test items in this text have been refined across several years. Of course, not all our students master the course material. Student motivation still plays an important part in student learning.

Following the advice of experts in statistics education (e.g., American Statistical Association, 2006; Cobb, 1992; Garfield & Ben-Zvi, 2008), our primary goal when creating the activities was to encourage students to learn by doing. The most current, but unfortunate, label for this approach to teaching is "active learning." We say "unfortunate" because in our view all learning is active. There is no such thing as "inactive learning." Perhaps a better term for this text's approach would be "guided active learning." The text guides students' learning by providing carefully crafted tasks that require them to demonstrate their understanding of the fundamental concepts (e.g., the distribution of sample means) before they work with the more advanced topics (e.g., significance testing).

Most textbooks include problems at the end of the chapter to review the chapter content. This text is different in that the activities following the readings introduce new material. The activities require students to work with fundamental content as a way to learn more advanced concepts. To be clear, these activities were not designed to be fun demonstrations. Initially, we intended to make statistics more interesting to students by using fun demonstrations and data collection activities. Unfortunately, we found that our "fun activities" often unnecessarily confused students and sacrificed the course content. Based on our experience, in some cases, even "real-world" examples can add unnecessary confusion when students are first learning concepts. With this in mind, we used very basic examples to describe the fundamentals and shifted to more elaborate research scenarios after students have understood the basics. In all situations, we attempted to use empirically validated ways to increase long-term understanding and retention. For example, memory researchers have repeatedly demonstrated that students who study by answering questions outperform students who review notes or reread chapters. With this in mind, all of our activities are a series of carefully sequenced questions specifically designed to review the fundamentals as well as introduce new content.

We'll conclude by offering two observations about our transition to an active learning approach. First, our student evaluations have not changed relative to when we taught a lecture-based statistics course. Second, our new exams are more challenging, and yet student performance is higher on these, more difficult exams.

HOW TO USE THIS BOOK

This text certainly could be used in a lecture-based course, in which the activities would function as detailed, conceptually rich homework assignments. We also are confident that there are creative instructors and students who will find ways to use this text that we never considered. However, it may be helpful to know how we use this text. In our courses, students read the brief chapters and answer the reading questions prior to class. We begin classes with brief lectures (for about 15 minutes), and then students work alone or in groups (for the remaining 60 minutes) to complete the activities during class. There are a number of advantages to this approach. One advantage is that students do the easier work (i.e., reading the fundamentals) outside class and complete the more difficult work in class where an instructor can answer their questions. Another advantage is that students work at their own pace. We have used this approach for several years, with positive results. When we compared our students' attitudes toward statistics with those held by students taking more traditional courses, our students had substantially more positive attitudes (Carlson & Winquist, 2011).

In our courses, students answer the reading questions online prior to class. We allow students to take each reading quiz twice, and we score the average of their two attempts. This approach encourages students to review and correct any misunderstandings prior to class. We also encourage students to find and correct their mistakes on activities. Mistakes while completing the activities are inevitable and even desirable. After all, each mistake is an opportunity to learn. In our view, students should engage in the activities without concern about evaluation. Therefore, the final answers to all questions are provided on the book's website (www.sagepub.com/carlson). Students then focus on finding the answer, checking it, and then correcting their mistakes. In recent semesters, we have been confirming that students actually complete each assigned activity. We give points for completion (and showing work). Over the years, activity points have constituted between 7% and 17% of students' course grades. A simpler option we tried was to tell students that completing the activities is essential to success in the course and not confirm activity completion at all. When we did this, we found greater variability in activity completion and exam performance.

UNIQUE FEATURES OF THIS TEXT

By now you probably recognize that this is not a typical statistics text. For ease of review, we've listed and described the two most unique aspects of this text.

- *Embedded reading questions:* All 16 chapters contain embedded reading questions, which focus students' attention on the key concepts *as they read* each paragraph/ section of the text. Researchers studying reading comprehension report that such embedded questions help students with lower reading abilities achieve levels of performance comparable with that of students with greater reading abilities (Callender & McDaniel, 2007). The embedded questions encourage students to *read with purpose.*
- *Activity sections:* All 16 chapters contain active learning assignments, called "Activities." While the 16 chapters start by introducing foundational concepts, they are followed by activity sections, in which students *test or demonstrate their understanding of basic concepts while they read detailed explanations of more complex statistical concepts.* When using most traditional textbooks, students perform statistical procedures *after* reading multiple pages. This text adopts a workbook approach, in which students are actively performing tasks *while* they read explanations. Most of the activities are self-correcting, so if students misunderstand a concept, it is corrected early in the learning process. All answers to activity questions

are provided on the book's website, so students' goal is determining why a given answer is correct rather than just getting the right answer. After completing these activities, students are far more likely to understand the material than if they have simply *read* the material.

OTHER HELPFUL FEATURES

- *Learning objectives:* Each chapter and activity begins with clear learning objectives.
- *Practice problems:* All 16 chapters conclude with a set of practice problems for solidifying student learning.
- *SPSS:* All chapters contain detailed, step-by-step instructions for conducting statistical procedures with SPSS, as well as annotated explanations of SPSS output.
- *Emphasis on understanding:* The chapters use definitional formulas to explain the logic behind each statistical procedure and rely on SPSS for more advanced computations (e.g., factorial ANOVAs)
- *Writing results in APA format:* Many activity questions highlight how to write about statistical analyses in scholarly ways.

ANCILLARIES

The following student and instructor resources are available at www.sagepub.com/carlson:

Password-Protected Instructor Teaching Site

- Lecture Outlines
- Answers to activities and practice problems
- Empirically validated Test Bank questions

Open Access Student Study Site

- Answers to activities and practice problems
- Self quizzes

APPROPRIATE COURSES

This text is ideal for introductory statistics courses in psychology, sociology, and social work, as well as the health, exercise, and life sciences. The text would work well for any course intending to teach the statistical procedures of hypothesis testing, effect sizes, and confidence intervals that are commonly used in the behavioral sciences.

ACKNOWLEDGMENTS

We would like to thank Barbara E. Walvoord for inspiring us to write this text. We thank the many reviewers (listed below) who helped us improve the text with their insightful critiques and comments. We explicitly thank Nellie Laughlin and Jeff Sinn for their willingness to use an earlier version of this text in their statistics class.

Nancy Dorr
The College of Saint Rose

Bethany K. B. Fleck
Metropolitan State College of Denver

Tim Franz
St. John Fisher College

Robert A. Horn
Northern Arizona University

Nellie K. Laughlin
Carroll University

Damien Raftery
Institute of Technology Carlow

Bonnie L. Rosenblatt
Reading Area Community College

Elizabeth A. Sheehan
Georgia State University

Jeff Sinn
Winthrop University

Jeri J. Thompson
Hastings College

We greatly appreciate the invaluable feedback of our students, without whom this text would not have been possible.

Finally, we are grateful to SAGE Publications for giving us the opportunity to share this text with others.

REFERENCES

American Statistical Association. (2006). *Guidelines for assessment and instruction in statistics education (GAISE) college report*. Alexandria, VA: Author. Retrieved from http://www.amstat.org/education/gaise/GaiseCollege_Full.pdf

Callender, A. A., & McDaniel, M. A. (2007). The benefits of embedded question adjuncts for low and high structure builders. *Journal of Educational Psychology, 99*(2), 339–348.

Carlson, K. A., & Winquist, J. R. (2011). Evaluating an active learning approach to teaching introductory statistics: A classroom workbook approach. *Journal of Statistics Education, 19(1)*. Retrieved from http://www.amstat.org/publications/jse/v19n1/carlson.pdf

Cobb, G. (1992). Teaching statistics. In L. A. Steen (Ed.), *Heeding the call for change: Suggestions for curricular action* (pp. 3–34; MAA Notes No. 22). Washington, DC: Mathematical Association of America.

Garfield, J., & Ben-Zvi, D. (2008). *Developing students' statistical reasoning: Connecting research and teaching practice*. New York, NY: Springer.

About the Authors

Kieth A. Carlson received his Ph.D. in Experimental Psychology with an emphasis in Cognitive Psychology from the University of Nebraska in 1996. He is currently Associate Professor of Psychology at Valparaiso University. He has published research on visual attention, memory, student cynicism toward college, and active learning. He enjoys teaching a wide range of courses including statistics, research methods, sensation and perception, cognitive psychology, learning psychology, the philosophy of science, and the history of psychology. He was twice honored with the Teaching Excellence Award from the United States Air Force Academy.

Jennifer R. Winquist is currently Associate Professor of Psychology at Valparaiso University. She received her Ph.D. in Social Psychology from the University of Illinois at Chicago in 2000. She has published research on self-focused attention, group decision making, distributive justice, implicit attitudes, and active learning. Recently she has shifted her research program to focus on the teaching of statistics and research methods. She regularly teaches courses in introductory and advanced statistics and research methods.

CHAPTER 1

Introduction to Statistics and Frequency Distributions

LEARNING OBJECTIVES

After reading this chapter, you should be able to do the following:

- Explain how you can be successful in this course
- Explain why many academic majors require a statistics course
- Use common statistical terms correctly in a statistical context
  - Statistic, parameter, sample, population, descriptive statistics, inferential statistics, sampling error, and hypothesis testing
- Identify the scale of measurement of a variable (nominal, ordinal, or interval/ratio)
- Determine if a variable is discrete or continuous
- Create and interpret frequency distribution tables, bar graphs, histograms, and line graphs
- Explain when to use a bar graph, histogram, and line graph
- Enter data into SPSS and generate frequency distribution tables and graphs

HOW TO BE SUCCESSFUL IN THIS COURSE

Have you ever read a few pages of a textbook and realized *you were not thinking about what you were reading*? Your mind wandered to topics completely unrelated to the text, and you could not identify the point of the paragraph (or sentence) you just read. Most people will admit to having this experience, at least occasionally. It is easy to let your mind wander when you are not *reading with purpose*. Force yourself to read with purpose. As you read each paragraph ask, "What is the purpose of this paragraph?" or "What am I supposed to learn from this paragraph?" The sole purpose of reading a textbook is to extract information. If you don't remember what you've read, you've wasted your time. Most of us are too busy to waste time.

1

Reading Question

1. Reading with purpose means
   a. thinking about other things while you are reading a textbook.
   b. actively trying to extract information from a text.

Try to read the next four paragraphs with purpose. What are you supposed to learn from each paragraph?

This text is structured to make it easier for you to read with purpose. The short chapters have frequent reading questions embedded in the text that make it easier for you to remember key points from preceding paragraphs. Resist the temptation to go immediately to the reading questions and search for answers in the preceding paragraphs. *Read first, and then answer the questions*. Using this approach will increase your memory for the material in this text.

Reading Question

2. Is it better to read the paragraph and then answer the reading question or to read the reading question and then search for the answer? It's better to
   a. read the paragraph, then answer the reading question.
   b. read the reading question, then search for the question's answer.

This text also features "Activities," which present new material that is NOT covered in the short chapters. When completing these activities, you will demonstrate your understanding of basic material (by answering questions) before you learn more advanced topics. You will be provided with answers to every activity question. Therefore, your emphasis when working the activities should be on understanding your answers. If you generate a wrong answer, figure out your error. Every error is an opportunity to learn. If you find your errors and correct them, you will probably not repeat the error. Resist the temptation to "get the right answer quickly." It is more important that you understand why every answer is correct.

Reading Question

3. Which of the following best describe the activities in this book?
   a. Activities introduce new material that was not included in the chapter reading.
   b. All of the new material is in the reading. The activities are simply meant to give you practice with the material in the reading.

Reading Question

4. When completing activities, your primary goal should be to get the correct answer quickly.
   a. True
   b. False

At the end of each chapter, there are "Practice Problems." After you complete the assigned activities in a chapter (and you understand why every answer is correct), you should complete all of the practice problems. Most students benefit from a few repetitions of each problem type. The additional practice helps consolidate what you have learned so you don't forget it during tests. Finally, use the activities and the practice problems to study. Then, *after* you understand all of the activities and all of the practice problems, assess your understanding by taking a self-test. Try to duplicate a testing situation as much as possible. Just sit down with a calculator and have a go at it. If you can do the self-test, you should expect to do well on the actual exam. Taking a practice test days before your actual test will give you time to review material if you discover you did not understand something. Testing yourself is also a good way to lessen the anxiety that can occur during testing. Practice test questions are available on the SAGE website (www.sagepub.com/carlson).

Reading Question

5. How should you use the self-tests?

   a. Use them to study; complete them open-book so you can be sure to look up all the answers.

   b. Use them to test what you know days before the exam; try to duplicate the testing situation as much as possible.

MATH SKILLS REQUIRED IN THIS COURSE

Students often approach their first statistics course with some anxiety. The primary source of this anxiety seems to be a general math anxiety. The good news is that the math skills required in this course are fairly basic. You need to be able to add, subtract, multiply, divide, square numbers, and take the square root of numbers using a calculator. You also need to be able to do some basic algebra. For example, you should be able to solve the following equation for X: $22 = \dfrac{X}{3}$. [The correct answer is $X = 66$.]

Reading Question

6. This course requires basic algebra.

   a. True

   b. False

Reading Question

7. Solve the following equation for X: $30 = \dfrac{X}{3}$.

   a. 10

   b. 90

You will also need to follow the correct order of mathematical operations. As a review, the correct order of operations is (1) the operations in parentheses, (2) exponents, (3) multiplication or division, and (4) addition or subtraction. Some of you may have learned the mnemonic, Please Excuse My Dear Aunt Sally, to help remember the correct order. For example, when solving the following equation, $(3 + 4)^2$, you would first add $(3 + 4)$ to get 7 and then square the 7 to get 49. Try to solve the next more complicated problem. The answer is 7.125. If you have trouble with this problem, talk with your instructor about how to review the necessary material for this course.

$$X = \frac{(6-1)3^2+(4-1)2^2}{(6-1)+(4-1)}$$

8. Solve the following equation for X: $X = \frac{(3-1)4^2+(5-1)3^2}{(3-1)+(5-1)}$

   a. 11.33
   b. 15.25

You will be using a calculator to perform computations in this course. You should be aware that order of operations is very important when using your calculator. Unless you are very comfortable with the parentheses buttons on your calculator, we recommend that you do one step at a time rather than trying to enter the entire equation into your calculator.

9. Order of operations is only important when doing computations by hand, not when using your calculator.

   a. True
   b. False

Although the math in this course should not be new, you will see new notation throughout the course. When you encounter this new notation, relax and realize that the notation is simply a shorthand way of giving instructions. While you will be learning how to *interpret* numbers in new ways, the actual mathematical skills in this course are no more complex than the order of operations. The primary goal of this course is teaching you to use numbers to make decisions. Occasionally, we will give you numbers solely to practice computation, but most of the time you will use the numbers you compute to make decisions within a specific, real-world context.

WHY DO YOU HAVE TO TAKE STATISTICS?

You are probably reading this book because you are required to take a statistics course to complete your degree. Students majoring in business, economics, nursing, political science, premedicine, psychology, social work, and sociology are often required to take at least one statistics course. There are a lot of different reasons why statistics is a mandatory course for students in these varied disciplines, but the primary reason is that in every one of these disciplines people make decisions that have the potential to improve people's lives, and these decisions should be informed by data. For example, a psychologist may conduct a study to determine if a new treatment reduces the symptoms of depression. Based on this study, the researcher will need to decide if the treatment is effective or not. If the wrong decision is made, an opportunity to help people with depression may be missed. Even more troubling, a wrong decision might harm people. While statistical methods will not eliminate wrong decisions, understanding statistical methods will allow you to reduce the number of wrong decisions you make. You are taking this course because the professionals in your discipline recognize that statistical methods improve decision making. Statistics make us better at our professions.

Reading Question

10. Why do many disciplines require students to take a statistics course? Taking a statistics course
    a. is a way to employ statistics instructors, which is good for the economy.
    b. can help people make better decisions in their chosen professions.

STATISTICS AND THE HELPING PROFESSIONS

When suffering from a physical or mental illness, we expect health professionals (e.g., medical doctors, nurses, clinical psychologists, and counselors) to accurately diagnose us and then prescribe effective treatments. We expect them to ask us detailed questions and then to use our answers (i.e., the data) to formulate a diagnosis. Decades of research has consistently found that health professionals who use statistics to make their diagnoses are more accurate than those who rely on their personal experience or intuition.

For example, lawyers frequently ask forensic psychologists to determine if someone is likely to be violent in the future. In this situation, forensic psychologists typically review the person's medical and criminal records as well as interview the person. Based on the records and the information gained during the interview, forensic psychologists make a final judgment about the person's potential for violence in the future. While making their professional judgment, forensic psychologists weigh the relative importance of the information in the records (i.e., the person's behavioral history) and the information obtained via the interview. This is an extremely difficult task. Fortunately, through the use of statistics, clinicians have developed methods that enable them to optimally gather and interpret data. One concrete example is the Violence Risk Appraisal Guide (Harris, Rice, & Quinsey, 1993). The guide is a list of questions that the psychologist answers after reviewing someone's behavioral history and conducting an interview. The answers to the Guide questions are mathematically combined to yield a value that predicts the likelihood of future violence. Research indicates that clinicians who use statistical approaches like the Violence Risk Appraisal Guide make more accurate clinical judgments than those who rely solely on their own judgment. Today, statistical procedures help psychologists predict many things including violent behavior, academic success, marital satisfaction, and work productivity. Statistical approaches also help professionals determine which interventions are most effective.

Reading Question

11. Decades of research indicates that professionals in the helping professions make better decisions when they rely on
   a. statistics.
   b. their intuition and clinical experience.

HYPOTHESIS TESTING AND SAMPLING ERROR

The statistical decisions you will make in this course revolve around specific hypotheses. The primary purpose of this book is to introduce the statistical process of null hypothesis testing, *a formal multiple-step procedure for evaluating the likelihood of a prediction, called a null hypothesis*. Knowledge of null hypothesis testing, also called significance testing, is fundamental to those working in the behavioral sciences, medicine, and the counseling professions. In later chapters, you will learn a variety of statistics that test different hypotheses. All of the hypothesis testing procedures that you will learn are needed because of one fundamental problem that plagues all researchers, namely the problem of sampling error. For example, researchers evaluating a new depression treatment want to know if it effectively lowers depression in all people with depression, called the population of people with depression. However, researchers cannot possibly study every depressed person in the world. Instead, researchers have to study a subset of this population, perhaps a sample of 100 people with depression. *The purpose of any sample is to represent the population from which it came.* In other words, if the 100 people with depression are a good sample, they will be similar to the population of people with depression. Thus, if the average score on a clinical assessment of depression in the population is 50, the average score of a good sample will also be 50. Likewise, if the ratio of women with depression to men with depression is 2:1 in the population, it will also be 2:1 in a good sample. Of course, you do not really expect a sample to be exactly like the population. *The differences between a sample and the population create* sampling error.

Reading Question

12. All hypothesis testing procedures were created so that researchers could
   a. study entire populations rather than samples.
   b. deal with sampling error.

Reading Question

13. If a sample represents a population well, it will
   a. respond in a way that is similar to how the entire population would respond.
   b. generate a large amount of sampling error.

POPULATIONS AND SAMPLES

Suppose that the researcher studying depression gave a new treatment to a sample of 100 people with depression. Figure 1.1 is a pictorial representation of this research scenario. The large circle on the left represents a population, *a group of all things that share a set of characteristics*. In this case, the "things" are people, and the characteristic they all share is depression. Researchers want to know what the mean depression score for the population would be if all people with depression were treated with the new depression treatment. In other words, researchers want to know the population parameter, *the value that would be obtained if the entire population were actually studied*. Of course, the researchers don't have the resources to study every person with depression in the world, so they must instead study a sample, *a subset of the population that is intended to represent the population*. In most cases, the best way to get a sample that accurately represents the population is by taking a random sample from the population. When taking a random sample, *each individual in the population has the same chance of being selected for the sample*. In other words, while researchers want to know a population parameter, their investigations usually produce a sample statistic, *the value obtained from the sample*. The researchers then use the sample statistic value as an estimate of the population parameter value. The researchers are making an *inference* that the sample statistic is a value similar to the population parameter value based on the premise that the characteristics of those in the sample are similar to the characteristics of those in the entire population. *When researchers use a sample statistic to infer the value of a population parameter* it is called inferential statistics. For example, in Figure 1.1, the sample of 100 people with depression was given a new treatment. After the treatment, the average number of depressive symptoms from the sample was 8. If the researchers then inferred that the entire population of people with depression would have an average of 8 depressive symptoms after getting the new treatment, they would be basing their conclusion

| **Figure 1.1** | A pictorial representation of using a sample to estimate a population parameter (i.e., inferential statistics). |

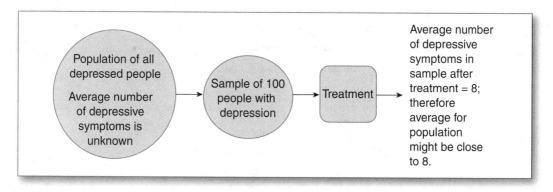

on inferential statistics. It should be clear to you that if the sample did not represent the population well (i.e., if there was a lot sampling error), the sample statistic would NOT be similar to the population parameter. In fact, sampling error is defined as *the difference between a sample statistic value and an actual population parameter value.*

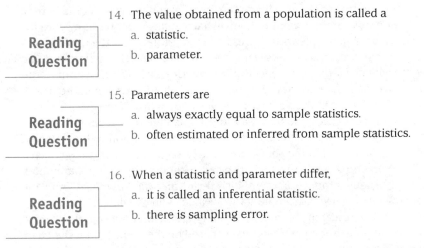

14. The value obtained from a population is called a

a. statistic.

b. parameter.

15. Parameters are

a. always exactly equal to sample statistics.

b. often estimated or inferred from sample statistics.

16. When a statistic and parameter differ,

a. it is called an inferential statistic.

b. there is sampling error.

The researchers studying depression were using inferential statistics because they were using data from a sample to infer the value of a population parameter. The component of the process that makes it inferential is that researchers are using data they actually have to estimate (or infer) the value of data they don't actually have. In contrast, researchers use descriptive statistics *when their intent is to describe the data that they actually collected.* For example, if a clinical psychologist conducted a study in which she gave some of her clients a new depression treatment and she wanted to describe the average depression score of only those clients who got the treatment, she would be using descriptive statistics. Her intent is only to describe the results she observed in the clients who actually got the treatment. However, if she then wanted to estimate what the results would be if she were to give the same treatment to additional clients, she would then be performing inferential statistics.

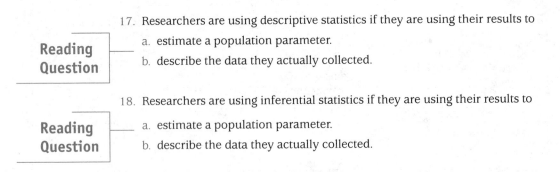

17. Researchers are using descriptive statistics if they are using their results to

a. estimate a population parameter.

b. describe the data they actually collected.

18. Researchers are using inferential statistics if they are using their results to

a. estimate a population parameter.

b. describe the data they actually collected.

INDEPENDENT AND DEPENDENT VARIABLES

Researchers design experiments to test if one or more variables cause changes to another variable. For example, if a researcher thinks a new treatment reduces depressive symptoms he could design an experiment to test this prediction. He might give a sample of people with depression the new treatment and withhold the treatment from another sample of people with depression. Later, if those who received the new treatment had lower levels of depression, he would have evidence that the new treatment reduces depression. In this experiment, the type of treatment each person received (i.e., new treatment vs. no treatment) is the independent variable (IV). In this study, the experimenter manipulated the IV by giving one sample of people with depression the new treatment and giving another sample of people with depression a placebo treatment that is not expected to reduce depression. In this experiment, the IV has two IV levels: (1) the new treatment and (2) the placebo treatment. The main point of the study is to determine if the two different IV levels were differentially effective at reducing depressive symptoms. More generally, *the IV is a variable with two or more levels that are expected to have different effects on another variable.* In this study, after both samples of people with depression were given their respective treatment levels, the amount of depression in each sample was compared by counting the number of depressive symptoms in each person. In this experiment, the number of depressive symptoms observed in each person is the dependent variable (DV). Given that the researcher expects the new treatment to work and the placebo treatment not to work, he expects the new treatment DV scores to be lower than the placebo treatment DV scores. More generally, *the DV is the outcome variable that is used to compare the effects of the different IV levels.*

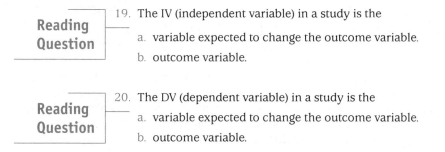

Reading Question

19. The IV (independent variable) in a study is the
    a. variable expected to change the outcome variable.
    b. outcome variable.

Reading Question

20. The DV (dependent variable) in a study is the
    a. variable expected to change the outcome variable.
    b. outcome variable.

The term *IV* is always used to refer to the variable being tested in a true experiment (i.e., studies in which the IV was manipulated by the researcher). However, in this text, we also use IV in a more general way. The IV is any variable predicted to influence another variable even when the IV was not manipulated. If you take a research methods course, you will learn an important distinction between manipulated IVs and *measured* IVs (sometimes called quasi-experimental variables or subject variables). Very briefly, the ultimate goal of science is to discover causal relationships, and manipulated IVs allow researchers to draw causal conclusions while measured IVs do not. You can learn more about this important distinction and its implications for drawing causal conclusions in a research methods course.

SCALES OF MEASUREMENT

All research is based on measurement. For example, if researchers are studying depression, they will need to devise a way to measure depression accurately and reliably. The way a variable is measured has a direct impact on the type of statistical procedures that can be used to analyze that variable. Generally speaking, researchers want to devise measurement procedures that are as precise as possible because more precise measurements enable more sophisticated statistical procedures. Researchers recognize four different scales of measurement: (1) nominal, (2) ordinal, (3) interval, and (4) ratio. Each of these scales of measurement is increasingly more precise than its predecessor, and therefore, each succeeding scale of measurement allows more sophisticated statistical analyses than its predecessor.

<table>
<tr><td>Reading
Question</td><td>21. The way a variable is measured

  a. determines the kinds of statistical procedures that can be used on that variable.

  b. has very little impact on how researchers conduct their statistical analyses.</td></tr>
</table>

For example, researchers could describe depression using a nominal scale by categorizing people with different kinds of major depressive disorders into groups, including those with melancholic depression, atypical depression, catatonic depression, seasonal affective disorder, or postpartum depression. Nominal scales of measurement *categorize things into groups that are qualitatively different from other groups*. Because nominal scales of measurement involve categorizing individuals into qualitatively distinct categories, they yield qualitative data. In this case, clinical researchers would interview each person and then decide which type of major depressive disorder each person has. With nominal scales of measurement, it is important to note that the categories are not in any particular order. A diagnosis of melancholic depression is not considered to be "more depressed" than a diagnosis of atypical depression. With all other scales of measurement, the categories are ordered. For example, researchers could also measure depression on an ordinal scale by ranking individual people in terms of the severity of their depression. Ordinal scales of measurement *rank order things*. In this case, researchers might interview people and diagnose them with a "mild depressive disorder," "moderate depressive disorder," or "severe depressive disorder." An ordinal scale clearly indicates that people *differ in the amount of something they possess*. Thus, someone who was diagnosed with mild depressive disorder would be less depressed than someone diagnosed with moderate depressive disorder. Although ordinal scales rank diagnoses by severity, they do not quantify how much more depressed a moderately depressed person is relative to a mildly depressed person. To make statements about how much more depressed one person is than another, an interval or ratio measurement scale is required. Researchers could measure depression on an interval scale by having people complete a multiple choice questionnaire that is designed to yield a score reflecting the amount of depression each person has. Interval scales of measurement *involve quantifying how much of something people have*. While the ordinal scale indicates that some people have more or less of something than others, the interval scale is more precise indicating exactly *how much* of something someone has. Another way to think about this is that for interval scales, the intervals are equivalent whereas for ordinal scales, the intervals are not equivalent. For example, on an ordinal scale, the interval (or distance) between a mild depressive disorder and a moderate depressive disorder may not be the same as the interval between a moderate depressive disorder and a severe depressive disorder. However, on an interval scale, the distances between values are equivalent. For example, if people completed a well-designed survey instrument that yielded a score between 1 and 50, the difference in the amount of depression between scores 1 and 2 would be the same as the difference in the amount of depression between scores 11 and 12. Most questionnaires used for research purposes yield scores that are measured on an interval scale of measurement. Ratio scales of measurement also *involve quantifying how much of something people have but a score of zero on a ratio scale indicates that the person has none of the thing being measured*. Because they involve quantifying how much of something an individual has, interval and ratio scales yield quantitative data. Interval and ratio scales are similar in that they both determine how much of something someone has but some interval scales can yield a negative number while the lowest score possible on a ratio scale is zero. Within the behavioral sciences, the distinction between interval and ratio scales of measurement is not usually very important. Researchers typically use the same statistical procedures to analyze variables measured on interval and ratio scales of measurement.

Although most variables can be easily classified as nominal, ordinal, or interval/ratio, there is one type of data that can be difficult to classify. Researchers often ask people to respond to questions using a Likert scale, where they are asked to indicate the extent to which they agree with a particular statement. For example, a professor may ask students at the end of the semester how much they agree with the statement, "I enjoyed taking this statistics course." Students may respond with 1 = *strongly agree*, 2 = *agree*, 3 = *neither agree nor disagree*, 4 = *disagree*, 5 = *strongly disagree*. Although there is not complete agreement among statisticians, most researchers classify these Likert questions as interval because there is evidence that people perceive the distance between categories as equivalent. Thus, in this course, responses to these types of questions will be considered interval/ratio data.

Reading Question

22. Researchers typically treat Likert scale responses (i.e., 1 = *strongly agree*, 2 = *agree*, etc.) as which scale of measurement?

   a. Nominal scale of measurement

   b. Ordinal scale of measurement

   c. Interval scale of measurement

When trying to identify the scale of measurement of a variable, it can also be helpful to think about what each scale of measurement allows you to do. For example, if you can only count the number of things in a given category, you know that you have a nominal scale.

Table 1.1 summarizes what you can do with each type of scale and provides examples of each scale of measurement:

Table 1.1   The four scales of measurement, what they allow, and examples.

Scale of Measurement	What the Scale Allows You to Do	Examples
Nominal	COUNT the number of things within different categories	Pets: 5 dogs, 12 cats, 7 fish, 2 hamsters
		Marital status: 12 married, 10 divorced, 2 separated
Ordinal	RANK some things as having more of something than others (but NOT QUANTIFY how much of it they have)	Annual income: above average, average, or below average
		Speed (measured by place of finish in a race): 1st, 2nd, 3rd, etc.
Interval	QUANTIFY how much of something there is but a score of zero does not mean the absence of the thing being measured	Temperature: −2° F, 98° F, 57° F; 0° F is not the absence of heat
Ratio	QUANTIFY how much of something there is and a score of zero means the absence of the thing being measured	Annual income: $25,048, $48,802, $157,435, etc.
		Number of text messages sent in a day: 0, 3351, 15, etc.

Reading Question

23. The scale of measurement that quantifies the thing being measured (i.e., indicates *how much* of it there is) is _____ scale(s) of measurement.

   a. the nominal

   b. the ordinal

   c. both the interval and ratio

Reading Question

24. The scale of measurement that categorizes objects into different kinds of things is _____ scale(s) of measurement.

   a. the nominal

   b. the ordinal

   c. both the interval and ratio

25. The scale of measurement that indicates that some objects have more of something than other objects but not how much more is _____ scale(s) of measurement

    a. the nominal

    b. the ordinal

    c. both the interval and ratio

DISCRETE VERSUS CONTINUOUS VARIABLES

Variables can also be categorized as discrete or continuous. A discrete variable *is measured in whole units rather than fractions of units.* For example, the variable "number of siblings" is a discrete variable because someone can only have a whole number of siblings (i.e., no one can have 2.7 siblings). A continuous variable *is measured in fractions of units.* For example, the variable "time to complete a test" is a continuous variable because someone can take a fraction of minutes to complete a test (i.e., 27.39 minutes). Nominal and ordinal variables are always discrete variables. Interval and ratio variables can be either discrete or continuous.

26. If a variable can be measured in fractions of units, it is a _____ variable.

    a. discrete

    b. continuous

GRAPHING DATA

The first step in all statistical analyses is to graph your data. Creating graphs gives you a picture of the data that you can inspect to "get a feel" for the data. For example, if you were looking at the number of siblings college students have, you could begin by looking at a graph to determine how many siblings most students have. Inspection of the graph also allows you to find out if there is anything odd in the data file that requires further examination. For example, if you graphed the data and found that most people reported having between 0 and 4 siblings but one person reported having 20 siblings, you should probably investigate to determine if that 20 was an error.

There are three basic types of graphs that we use for most data: (1) bar graphs, (2) histograms, and (3) line graphs. The names of the first two are a bit misleading because both are created using bars. The only difference between a bar graph and a histogram is that in a bar graph the bars do not touch while the bars do touch in a histogram. In general, bar graphs are used when the data are discrete or qualitative. The space between the bars of a bar graph emphasize that there are no possible values between any two categories. For example, when graphing the number of children in a family, a bar graph is appropriate because there is no possible value between any two categories (e.g., 1 and 2 children).

When the data are continuous, we use a histogram. The bars touch in a histogram to indicate that there are possible values between any two categories. For example, if we were graphing time to complete a test, the bars would touch to indicate that there are possible values between any two times (e.g., 27 and 28 minutes).

Reading Question 27. What type of graph is used for discrete data or qualitative data?
  a. bar graph
  b. histogram

Reading Question 28. What type of graph is used for continuous data?
  a. bar graph
  b. histogram

Reading Question 29. In bar graphs, the bars _____.
  a. touch
  b. don't touch

Reading Question 30. In histograms, the bars _____.
  a. touch
  b. don't touch

To create either a bar graph or a histogram, you should put categories on the x-axis and the number of scores in a particular category (i.e., the frequency) on the y-axis. For example, suppose we asked 19 students how many siblings they have and obtained the following responses:

0, 0, 0, 0, 1, 1, 1, 1, 1, 1, 2, 2, 2, 2, 2, 3, 4, 4, 6

To graph these responses, you would list the range of responses to the question "How many siblings do you have?" on the x-axis (i.e., in this case 0 through 6). The y-axis is the frequency within each category. For each response category, you will draw a bar with a height equal to the number of times that response was given. For example, in the bar graph (Figure 1.2), 4 people said they had 0 siblings and so the bar above the 0 has a height of 4.

Reading Question 31. Use the graph to determine how many people said they had 1 sibling.
  a. 4
  b. 5
  c. 6

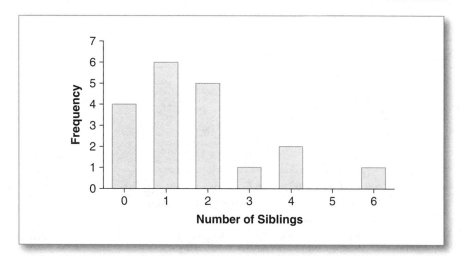

Figure 1.2   Bar graph of variable, number of siblings, collected from a sample of 19 students.

The procedure for creating a histogram is similar to that for creating a bar graph. The only difference is that the bars should touch. For example, suppose that you recorded the height of players on a volleyball team and obtained the following heights rounded to the nearest inch:

65, 67, 67, 68, 68, 68, 69, 69, 70, 70, 70, 71, 72

Height in inches is continuous because there are an infinite number of possible values between any two categories (e.g., between 68 and 69 inches). The data are continuous so we create a histogram (i.e., we allow the bars to touch) (Figure 1.3).

Whenever a histogram is appropriate, you may also use a line graph in its place. To create a line graph, you use dots to indicate frequencies and connect adjacent dots with lines (Figure 1.4).

Whether the data are discrete or continuous should determine how the data are graphed. You should use a bar graph for discrete data and a histogram or a line graph for continuous data. Nominal data should be graphed with a bar graph. Throughout the text we will use these guidelines, but you should be aware of the unfortunate fact that histograms and bar graphs are often used interchangeably outside of statistics classes.

Reading Question

32. Line graphs can be used whenever a _____ is appropriate.

a. histogram

b. bar graph

Figure 1.3   Frequency histogram of variable, height in inches, collected from a sample of 13 volleyball players.

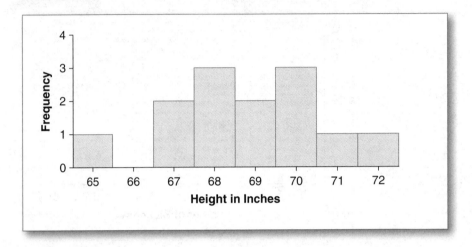

Figure 1.4   Frequency line graph of variable, height in inches, collected from a sample of 13 volleyball players.

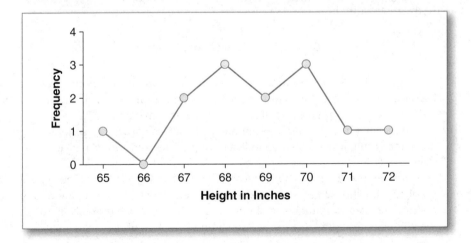

Reading
Question

33. What type of graph should be used if the data are measured on a nominal scale?

a. histogram

b. bar graph

FREQUENCY DISTRIBUTION TABLES

Graphing data is typically the best way to see patterns in the data and to look for potential problems. However, some precision is often lost with graphs. Therefore, it is sometimes useful to look at the raw data in a frequency distribution table. To create a frequency distribution table, you need to know the measurement categories as well as the number of responses within a given measurement category. For example, suppose that a market researcher asked cell phone users to respond to the following statement: "I am very happy with my cell phone service provider." People were asked to respond with 1 = *strongly agree*, 2 = *agree*, 3 = *neither agree nor disagree*, 4 = *disagree*, 5 = *strongly disagree*. The responses are listed below:

1, 1, 2, 2, 2, 2, 3, 3, 3, 3, 3, 3, 3, 4, 4, 4, 4, 4, 4, 5, 5, 5, 5

It is probably obvious that a string of numbers is not a particularly useful way to present data. A frequency distribution table organizes the data, so it is easier to interpret; one is shown in Table 1.2.

The first column (*X*) represents the possible response categories. People *could* respond with any number between 1 and 5, therefore the *X* column (i.e., the measurement categories) must include all of the *possible* response values, namely 1 through 5. In this case, we chose to put the categories in ascending order from 1 to 5, but they could also be listed in descending order from 5 to 1.

The next column (*f*) is where you record the frequency of each response. For example, 4 people gave responses of 5 (*strongly disagree*) and so a 4 is written in the "*f*" column across from the response category of 5 (*strongly disagree*).

Table 1.2   Frequency distribution table of the variable "I am very happy with my cell phone service provider."

	X	f
Strongly agree	1	2
Agree	2	4
Neither agree nor disagree	3	7
Disagree	4	6
Strongly disagree	5	4

Reading Question

34. The value for "*f*" represents the

    a. number of measurement categories.

    b. number of responses within a given measurement category.

Reading Question

35. In the above frequency table, how many people responded with an answer of 3?

    a. 2

    b. 4

    c. 7

SPSS

We will be using a statistical package called IBM SPSS to conduct many of the statistical analyses in this course. Our instructions and screenshots were developed with version 18. There are some minor differences between version 18 and other versions but you should have no difficulty using our instructions with other SPSS versions.

It is likely that your school has a site license for SPSS allowing you to access it on campus. Depending on your school's site license, you may also be able to access the program off campus. You may also purchase or "lease" a student or graduate version of SPSS for this course. Your instructor will tell you about the options available to you.

Data File

After you open SPSS, click on the Data View tab near the bottom left of the screen. Enter the data you want to analyze in a single column.

We have used the cell phone data from the previous page to help illustrate how to use SPSS. In the screen shot in Figure 1.5, a variable name "happycellphone" is shown at the top of the column of data. To add this variable name, double click on the blue box at the top of a column in the Data View screen. Doing so will take you to the Variable View screen. You can also access the Variable View screen by pressing the Variable View tab at the bottom left of the screen. In the first column and first row of the variable view screen, type the name of the variable you want to appear in the data spreadsheet (e.g., happycellphone—the variable name cannot have spaces or start with a number). To go back to the Data View, click on the blue Data View tab at the bottom left of the screen.

The data file you created should look like the screen shot in Figure 1.5. The exact order of the data values is not important, but all 23 scores should be in a single column. As a general rule, all of the data for a variable must be entered in a single column.

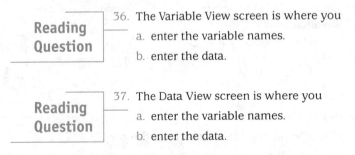

Reading Question

36. The Variable View screen is where you

   a. enter the variable names.

   b. enter the data.

Reading Question

37. The Data View screen is where you

   a. enter the variable names.

   b. enter the data.

Obtaining Frequency Distribution Tables and Graphs

SPSS can create frequency tables and graphs. To create a frequency graph of the data you just entered, do the following:

- From the Data View screen, click on Analyze, Descriptive Statistics, and then Frequencies.

- To create a graph, click on the Charts button and then choose the type of graph you want to create (Bar chart, Pie chart, or Histogram). Click on the Continue button.
- Be sure that the Display Frequency Tables box is checked if you want to create a frequency distribution table.
- Click on the OK button to create the frequency distribution table and graph.

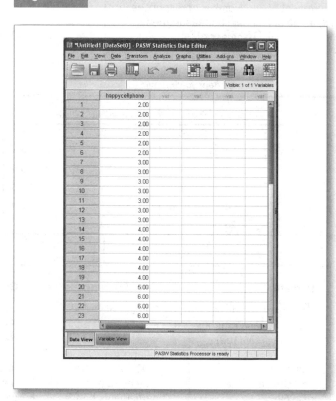

Figure 1.5   Screenshot of SPSS data entry screen.

Annotated Output

After performing the steps outlined above, a frequency distribution graph and table will appear in the SPSS output screen. Use the SPSS output provided in Figure 1.6 to answer the following three questions.

Reading Question

38. How many people responded with a 3 to the question "I am very happy with my cell phone provider?"

    a. 2

    b. 4

    c. 7

Figure 1.6   Annotated SPSS frequency table output.

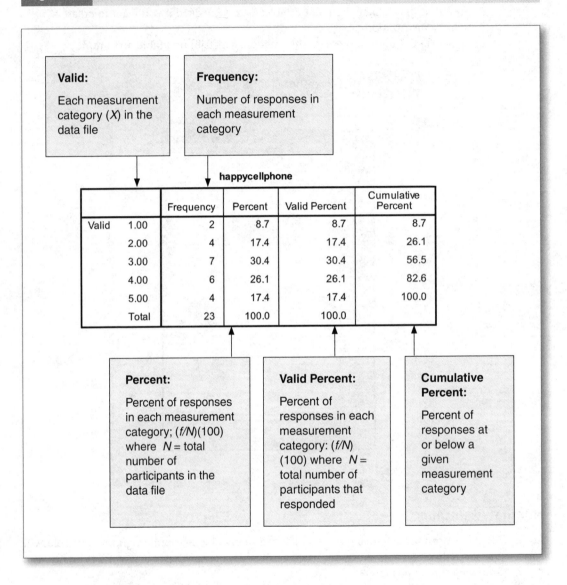

Valid:

Each measurement category (X) in the data file

Frequency:

Number of responses in each measurement category

happycellphone

		Frequency	Percent	Valid Percent	Cumulative Percent
Valid	1.00	2	8.7	8.7	8.7
	2.00	4	17.4	17.4	26.1
	3.00	7	30.4	30.4	56.5
	4.00	6	26.1	26.1	82.6
	5.00	4	17.4	17.4	100.0
	Total	23	100.0	100.0	

Percent:

Percent of responses in each measurement category; $(f/N)(100)$ where N = total number of participants in the data file

Valid Percent:

Percent of responses in each measurement category: (f/N) (100) where N = total number of participants that responded

Cumulative Percent:

Percent of responses at or below a given measurement category

---

Reading Question

39. What percentage of the respondents answered the question with a response of 4?

a. 30.4

b. 26.1

c. 17.4

Reading Question
40. What percentage of the respondents answered the question with a response of 4 or a lower value?

    a. 56.5

    b. 82.6

    c. 100

Use the histogram in Figure 1.7 to answer the following two questions.

Figure 1.7   Frequency histogram of "I am very happy with my cell phone service provider" data.

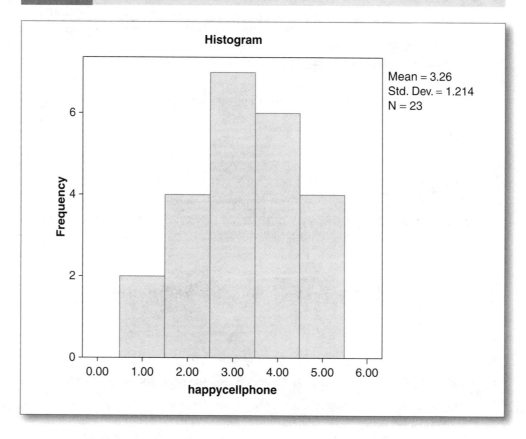

Reading Question
41. What is the most common response in the data?

    a. 2

    b. 3

    c. 4

    d. 5

Reading
Question

42. How many people responded with the most common response?

    a. 7

    b. 6

    c. 5

    d. 4

SPSS is a great tool for creating graphs to help you gain a better understanding of your data. However, it is not necessarily intended for creating presentation-quality graphs. You can customize graphs in SPSS by double clicking on the graph once you create it and then, once the image is open, double click on any aspect of the graph to change it. This is trickier than it sounds because there are a lot of options. We are not going to work on editing graphs in this course, but if you would like to edit graphs you can use the Help menu to obtain further information. There are several other ways to create more advanced graphs in SPSS. You can explore these options by clicking on Graphs menu.

Reading
Question

43. It is possible to change the appearance of graphs created by SPSS.

    a. True

    b. False

REFERENCE

Harris, G. T., Rice, M. E., & Quinsey, V. L. (1993). Violent recidivism of mentally disordered offenders: The development of a statistical prediction instrument. *Criminal Justice and Behavior, 20*, 315–335.

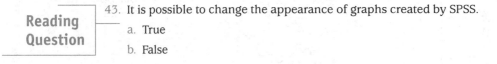

Activity 1-1:   Frequency Distributions

Learning Objectives

After reading the chapter and completing this activity, you should be able to do the following:

- Use common statistical terms correctly in a statistical context
- Construct a frequency distribution table from a bar graph
- Write a meaningful paragraph based on data in a frequency distribution
- Use SPSS to create a frequency table
- Interpret an SPSS frequency table
- Sketch a frequency distribution
- Identify distributions that are bell shaped, positively skewed, and negatively skewed

THERAPEUTIC TOUCH ACTIVITY

There is quite a bit of evidence that human touch is beneficial to our psychological and physical health. Hugs are associated with lower blood pressure, skin-to-skin contact can help preterm infants gain weight, and touch can improve immune system function. Although there is little doubt of the benefits of touch, a treatment known as "Therapeutic Touch" (TT) is far more controversial. Therapeutic touch involves no actual physical contact. Instead, practitioners use their hands to move "human energy fields" (HEFs) in an attempt to promote healing. Proponents of this approach claim that it can help with relaxation, reduce pain, and improve the immune system.

Emily Rosa (who was just 9 years old at the time) and her colleagues (including her parents) investigated the basis of these claims by putting a sample of actual TT practitioners to the test (Rosa, Rosa, Sarner, & Barrett, 1998). In their study, Rosa and colleagues designed a method to determine if TT practitioners could actually detect HEFs. As the figure to the right illustrates, individual practitioners sat at a table facing a large divider that prevented them from seeing their own hands or Emily. The practitioners placed both of their hands through the divider on the table, palms up. Practitioners were told to indicate whether Emily was holding her hand above their right or left hand. Emily began each trial by flipping a coin to determine where to place her hand. She then placed her hand 8 to 10 cm above one of the practitioner's hands. The practitioners had to "sense" the HEF allegedly emanating from Emily's hand to determine if Emily's hand was over their right hand or left hand. Each practitioner went through a total of 10 of these trials.

If the TT practitioners can actually sense HEFs they should be able to choose the correct hand 10 out of 10 times. However, if they really can't detect HEFs and the practitioners were guessing you would expect them to choose the correct hand 5 out of 10 times. Some may get more than 5 correct others may get less than 5 correct but the most common number of correct answers would be about 5 of 10, if the practitioners were guessing.

1. As mentioned previously, the researchers had a sample of TT practitioners participate in the experiment described above. They used the results from this sample to infer what the results would be if they had collected data from the entire population of TT practitioners. The purpose of their study was

   a. descriptive.

   b. inferential.

2. Use three of the following terms to fill in the blanks: parameters, statistics, inferential, descriptive, sampling error.

   If the sample of TT practitioners represented the population of TT practitioners well, the sample _____ would be similar to the population _____ and the study would have a relatively small amount of

   _____.

3. After the experiment was complete, the researchers counted the number of correct responses generated by each participant out of 10. The number of correct responses out of 10 ranged between a low of 1 correct to a high of 8 correct. The variable "number of correct responses out of 10 trials" is measured on which scale of measurement?

   a. Nominal

   b. Ordinal

   c. Interval/Ratio

4. Is the number of correct responses out of 10 a continuous or discrete variable?

   a. Continuous

   b. Discrete

The following bar graph is an accurate re-creation of the actual data from the experiment. The graph is a frequency distribution of the number of correct responses generated by each practitioner out of 10 trials. Use these data to answer the following questions:

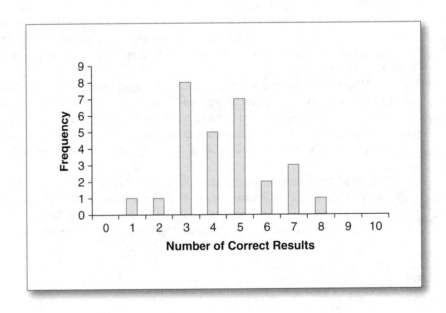

5. Use the data from the graph to complete the frequency table on the right.

X	f

6. How many practitioners were in the sample?

    a. 8

    b. 10

    c. 28

7. How many practitioners did *better* than chance (i.e., did better than 5 correct out of 10)?

    a. 3

    b. 6

    c. 13

8. What *percentage* of the practitioners performed *at or below* chance?

    a. 100

    b. 78.6

    c. 53.6

9. Compose several sentences that summarize the data. In other words, does the data support the conclusion that TT practitioners can detect HEFs or does the data support the conclusion that they cannot and instead are guessing? What evidence from the data supports your conclusion?

Every 2 years the National Opinion Research Center asks a random sample of adults in the United States to complete the General Social Survey (GSS). All of the GSS data are available at www.norc.org. You will be using a small portion of the GSS that we placed in a file titled "gss2010.sav." Your instructor will tell you how to access this file. Load this file into SPSS.

Part of the GSS assesses respondents' science knowledge. In 2010, respondents answered questions from a variety of different sciences, such as "True or False. Antibiotics kill viruses as well as bacteria" and "True or False. Lasers work by focusing sound waves." For this assignment, we created the variable "ScientificKnowledge" by summing the total number of correct answers each participant gave to 10 science questions. The resulting "ScientificKnowlege" variable was measured on a ratio scale and had a possible range of 0 to 10 correct answers.

Use SPSS to create a frequency distribution table and graph of "ScientificKnowledge" scores. To create a frequency distribution table and graph, do the following:

- From the Data View screen, click on Analyze, Descriptive Statistics, and then Frequencies.
- Move the variable(s) of interest into the Variable(s) box. In this case, you will move "ScientificKnowledge" into the Variable(s) box.

- Make sure the Display Frequency Tables box is checked.
- To create a graph, click on the Charts button and then choose Bar chart. Click on the Continue button.
- Click on the OK button to create the frequency distribution table and graph.

10. Use the frequency distribution table you created in SPSS to determine how many people responded to the "ScientificKnowledge" questions.

11. How many people got all 10 questions right?

12. What *percentage* of people got all 10 questions right?

13. How many people got all 10 questions wrong?

14. What *percentage* of people got all 10 questions wrong?

15. All of the questions had just two response options. Thus, if people answered every question and they were *guessing* on every question, we would expect them to get 50% of the questions correct. What percentage of people got exactly 5 of the 10 questions correct?

16. What percentage of people scored at or below chance (i.e., 5 correct responses out of 10) on this test?

17. After taking standardized tests you typically get a raw score as well as a percentile rank, *the percentage of scores a given score is higher than*. For example, if you scored at the 95th percentile you would know that you scored as well or better than 95% of the people who took the test. The same thing can be done for this data file by using the cumulative percent column of the frequency distribution table? What Science Knowledge test score is at the 95th percentile?

18. What Science Knowledge test score is at the 9th percentile?

19. What is the percentile rank for a Science Knowledge test score of 7?

20. What is the percentile rank for a Science Knowledge test score of 3?

21. On the GSS, people were asked how many years of school they completed. Before you graph the data in SPSS, what two responses to this question do you think will

be the most common in the United States? Explain why you think these answers would be given frequently.

22. Create a bar graph of the YearsofEducation variable. What was the most frequently occurring response?

23. What percentage of the respondents completed exactly 12 years of school?

24. What percentage of the respondents completed 16 or more years of school?

25. What percentage of the respondents completed fewer than 12 years of school?

26. As you work with data throughout this course you will find that frequency distribution graphs (i.e., bar graphs and histograms) can look quite different for different variables. By far, the most commonly seen shape in statistics courses is a bell-shaped distribution. For example, the Science Knowledge scores that you graphed above are approximately bell shaped. Sketch a bar graph of the Science Knowledge scores below:

This **bell shape** occurs when most of the scores are concentrated around the mean of the scores, and there are fewer and fewer scores the further you get from the mean. For example, the average score on the Scientific Knowledge test was 5.95, and most of the scores are very close to 5.95. The further a score is from 5.95, the less frequently it occurred. If you look at the Scientific Knowledge graph closely, you will see that it is not perfectly bell shaped because it is not perfectly symmetrical. The right and left sides of the distribution do not look exactly alike. Statisticians often refer to the declining slopes to the right and left of a distribution's peak as "tails." When the right tail is longer than the left tail, the distribution is **positively skewed**. Conversely, when the left tail is longer than the right tail the distribution is **negatively skewed**. Therefore, if the right tail (which is over the larger numbers) is longer, the distribution is positively skewed. Conversely, if the left tail (which is over the smaller numbers) is longer, the distribution is negatively skewed.

27. Is the graph of the number of hours people report watching TV each day positively or negatively skewed?

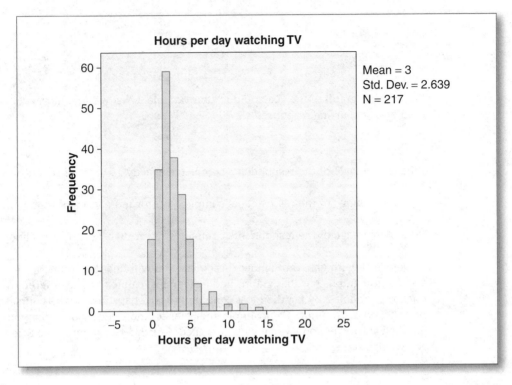

28. Make a rough sketch of a frequency distribution graph that is negatively skewed.

29. On the GSS, respondents were asked how old they were when their first child was born (variable is named AgeFirstChildBorn). Use SPSS to create a histogram for this variable. Does the data look to be positively skewed, negatively skewed, or bell shaped?

30. As part of the GSS, respondents were given a vocabulary test that consisted of 10 words. Create a bar chart of the number of correct words on the vocabulary test (VocabTest). Do the data look to be positively skewed, negatively skewed, or bell shaped?

31. If a test is relatively easy and most people get between 90% and 100%, but a few people get low scores (10–20%), would that data be positively skewed or negatively skewed?

    a. Positively skewed

    b. Negatively skewed

32. A recent study revealed that the brains of new mothers grow bigger after giving birth. The researchers performed MRIs (magnetic resonance imagings) on the brains of 19 women and found that the volume of the hypothalamus was greater after giving birth than prior to giving birth. Circle the scale of measurement used for each of the variables listed below:

    a. Volume of the hypothalamus: Nominal   Ordinal   Interval/ratio

    b. Before and after birth: Nominal   Ordinal   Interval/ratio

33. A researcher designs a study in which participants with low levels of HDL (high-density lipoprotein) cholesterol are randomly assigned to exercise for 0 minutes, 30 minutes, 60 minutes, or 90 minutes a day. After 3 months, HDL levels are measured. Women and men often react differently to treatments, and so the researcher also records the gender of each participant. Circle the scale of measurement used for each of the variables listed below:

    a. Amount of exercise   Nominal   Ordinal   Interval/ratio
        (0, 30, 60, or 90 minutes a day):

    b. HDL cholesterol levels: Nominal   Ordinal   Interval/ratio

    c. Gender of the participants: Nominal   Ordinal   Interval/ratio

34. A researcher used government records to classify each family into one of seven different income categories ranging from "below the poverty line" to "more than $1 million dollars a year." The researcher used police records to determine the number of times each family was burglarized. Circle the scale of measurement used for each of the variables listed below:

    a. Income category: Nominal   Ordinal   Interval/ratio

    b. Number of times burglarized: Nominal   Ordinal   Interval/ratio

REFERENCE

Rosa, L., Rosa, E., Sarner, L., & Barrett, S. (1998). A close look at therapeutic touch. *Journal of the American Medical Association, 279*(13), 1005–1010.

Activity 1-2:   Practice Problems

1. Practice determining if variables are continuous or discrete.

    a. Weight of a rat in ounces   Continuous   Discrete

    b. Number of heart attacks   Continuous   Discrete

    c. Grade point average   Continuous   Discrete

    d. The number of students in a class   Continuous   Discrete

    e. Percent body fat   Continuous   Discrete

2. Practice identifying the scale of measurement as nominal, ordinal, or interval/ratio.

   a. Weight of a rat in ounces   Nominal   Ordinal   Interval/ratio
   b. Number of heart attacks   Nominal   Ordinal   Interval/ratio
   c. Football jersey number   Nominal   Ordinal   Interval/ratio
   d. Grade point average   Nominal   Ordinal   Interval/ratio
   e. Class standing (freshmen, sophomore, etc.)   Nominal   Ordinal   Interval/ratio
   f. Percent body fat   Nominal   Ordinal   Interval/ratio
   g. Military rank (private, corporal, etc.)   Nominal   Ordinal   Interval/ratio
   h. Student identification number   Nominal   Ordinal   Interval/ratio
   i. The number of students in a class   Nominal   Ordinal   Interval/ratio

3. True or False. Interval/Ratio data are always continuous.

4. A student distributes a questionnaire to 21 students in her statistics course. On this questionnaire, people are asked to indicate the extent to which they agree with this statement: "I am happy with my life." Responses were made using a 7-point Likert scale, where 1 = *strongly disagree* and 7 = *strongly agree*. The data she obtained are as follows: 7, 7, 7, 7, 6, 6, 6, 6, 6, 6, 6, 6, 6, 5, 5, 5, 5, 4, 3, 3, 1

   a. What scale of measurement is this variable measured on (i.e., nominal, ordinal, interval/ratio)?

   b. Create a frequency table for these data.

   c. Use your frequency distribution table to determine how many people had scores of 4. Don't just count from the raw data. Make sure you understand the table.

   d. Enter the data into SPSS and create a frequency distribution table. What percentage of people had scores of 4?

   e. What percentage of people had scores of 4 or below?

   f. Create a histogram of these data by hand and using SPSS.

   g. Is this distribution best described as bell shaped, positively skewed, or negatively skewed?

5. A political pollster asked voters to indicate the degree of their agreement with the following question: "Global warming is real and is at least partially caused by human activity." The voters responded using the following scale: 1 = *strongly disagree* to 5 = *strongly agree*. The SPSS output for the pollster's data are presented below.

globalwarming

		Frequency	Percent	Valid Percent	Cumulative Percent
Valid	1.00	5	21.7	21.7	21.7
	2.00	7	30.4	30.4	52.2
	3.00	1	4.3	4.3	56.5
	4.00	4	17.4	17.4	73.9
	5.00	6	26.1	26.1	100.0
	Total	23	100.0	100.0	

a. How many people responded to this survey question?

b. How many people *strongly agreed* with the statement?

c. What percentage of people *strongly disagreed* with the statement?

d. What percentage of the sample disagreed with the statement about global warming (i.e., gave an answer of 2 or lower)?

e. What score is at the 74th (73.9) percentile?

f. What is the percentile rank for a score of 3?

g. Are these data normally distributed (i.e., bell shaped)?

h. Suppose that these scores came from all of the students in a political science class. If these data were being used to describe the class, would you use descriptive or inferential statistics?

i. If these data were intended to represent all voters, would you use descriptive or inferential statistics?

6. A chair of a foreign languages department is interested in determining the language background of incoming freshmen. She asks a random sample of freshmen to report the number of languages they speak fluently. The following data were obtained:

1, 1, 1, 1, 1, 1, 1, 1, 2, 2, 2, 2, 2, 2, 3, 5

a. What scale of measurement is this variable measured on (i.e., nominal, ordinal, interval/ratio)?

b. Are these data discrete or continuous?

c. Create a frequency table for these data.

d. Create an appropriate graph for these data.

e. Enter the data into SPSS and create a frequency distribution table. What percentage of students report that they speak two languages fluently?

f. What percentage of students report that they speak two or fewer languages fluently?

g. Is this distribution best described as bell shaped, positively skewed, or negatively skewed?

C H A P T E R 2

Central Tendency

LEARNING OBJECTIVES

After reading this chapter, you should be able to do the following:

- Compute the mean, median, and mode
- Identify when to use the mean, median, or mode when describing a distribution's central tendency

CENTRAL TENDENCY

You are probably already familiar with the notion of central tendency. For example, if your five history exam scores for a semester were 33%, 81%, 86%, 96%, and 96%, the "center" of these scores summarizes your academic performance in history. However, did you know that your history instructor could use the mean, median, or mode to find the center of your scores? If your instructor used the *arithmetic average* (i.e., the mean, 78.4%) you would get a C. Although the mean is the most common measure of central tendency, there are other options. She could use the *middle test score* (the median, 86%), and you would get a B. She could also use the *most frequently occurring test score* (the mode, 96%), and you would get an A. Clearly, the mode gives the most favorable picture of your performance, but which measure of center gives the most accurate picture? Researchers frequently must summarize large data sets by presenting a single measure of their center, and every time they do so, they must determine whether the mean, the median, or the mode offers the most accurate summary of the data. It should be clear from the history exam example that one's choice of statistic can dramatically change the interpretation of the data. Luckily, there are rules of thumb that help researchers decide when to use the mean, median, and mode.

The mean is the arithmetic average (the sum of the scores divided by the number of scores). While the mean is the most common measure of a data set's center, there are situations when it cannot be used. For example, *when the data being summarized are nominal, the mean cannot be used.* Suppose we recorded the academic majors of students in a class

33

and 17 responded psychology, 9 nursing, 7 sociology, and 8 social work. These academic majors are categories, not values; one cannot compute the average academic major. In other words, academic major is a nominal variable. In this case, psychology is the most frequently reported academic major, and therefore it is the center of the data. *When the data are nominal (i.e., when the data are categories rather than values), you must use the mode to summarize the center.*

Reading Question

1. What measure of central tendency is used when data are measured on a nominal scale?

   a. Mean

   b. Median

   c. Mode

While the mode is the only option when data are nominal, *the median is the best option when data are ordinal.* The median of a distribution of scores is the value at the 50th percentile, which means that half of the scores are below this value and half are above it. For example, suppose we wanted to know the center class rank of students in a statistics course with five freshmen, seven sophomores, four juniors, and three seniors. We could assign ordinal positions to each class rank so that freshman = 1, sophomore = 2, junior = 3, and senior = 4. This would result in the following distribution of scores: 1, 1, 1, 1, 1, 2, 2, 2, 2, 2, 2, 2, 3, 3, 3, 3, 4, 4, 4. Although we used numbers to represent the ordinal positions, it would not make mathematical sense to compute the mean of class rank (i.e., freshmen, sophomores, juniors, seniors). Class rank is an ordinal variable, and you cannot compute the mean of ordinal data. Hence, in this case we would report the median. The median is the score with exactly the same number of scores above it and below it. In this distribution, there are 19 scores, so the 10th highest score would have 9 scores above it and 9 scores below it. For this set of data, the 10th highest score would be a 2: 1, 1, 1, 1, 1, 2, 2, 2, 2 , 2, 2, 2, 3, 3, 3, 3, 4, 4, 4. Thus, the median value, or center value, is sophomore. If a data set has an even number of scores, you find the median by computing the average of the middle 2 scores.

Reading Question

2. What is the median for this set of scores? 3, 3, 3, 4, 4, 5, 5, 5

   a. 3

   b. 4

   c. 5

Reading Question

3. What measure of central tendency should be used with ordinal data?

   a. Mean

   b. Median

   c. Mode

When working with interval or ratio data, you need to choose between the mean and the median to represent the center. In general, you should use the mean to summarize interval or ratio data; however, if the data set contains one or more "extreme" scores that are very different from the other scores, you should use the median. For example, if you wanted to summarize how many text messages you typically send/receive during a typical hour-long class, you could use the mean or the median because the number of texts sent/received in a class is ratio data. Suppose that during your last seven classes you sent/received the following numbers of messages: 7, 9, 38, 6, 7, 8, and 7. The mean number of text messages would be 11.7, but this is not really a typical value for you. During the vast majority of classes (i.e., six of your last seven classes) the number of messages you sent was less than 11.7. The mean does not represent the center of these data very well because a single extreme score is inflating the mean, "pulling" it away from the center. Statisticians would consider the 38 value an outlier because it is *a very extreme score compared with the rest of the scores in the distribution*. The median is far less affected by extreme scores. The median would be 7, and this would be a much better summary of your in-class texting habits.

Reading Question

4. What measure of central tendency is obtained by adding all of the scores and then dividing by the number of scores?

a. Mean

b. Median

c. Mode

Reading Question

5. What measure of central tendency is the value that has half of the scores above it and half of the scores below it?

a. Mean

b. Median

c. Mode

Reading Question

6. What measure of central tendency should be used when the data are interval and there are extreme scores in the distribution?

a. Mean

b. Median

c. Mode

Reading Question

7. Extreme scores are also called

a. modes scores.

b. outliers.

Another situation in which you should use the median even though you have interval or ratio data is when the distribution is asymmetrical, or skewed. A distribution of scores is skewed if the "tail" on one side of the distribution is substantially longer than the tail on the other side. The bar graph in Figure 2.1 is the one you created in the previous chapter using Vocabulary Test data from the 2010 General Social Survey. This distribution is roughly symmetrical, and therefore the mean should be used to summarize the center of these data. Although the Vocabulary Test scores were symmetrical, the Age When First Child Was Born responses were positively skewed. The tail on the right side of the distribution is substantially longer than the tail on the left. When a distribution looks like this, you should use the median rather than the mean to summarize its center. It is worth noting that when a distribution is bell shaped (or close to being bell shaped) the mean, median, and mode are all very similar in value. However, when a distribution is very asymmetrical, the mean, median, and mode are dramatically different. In asymmetrical distributions, the mean is "pulled" away from the center toward the distribution's longer tail. This fact is illustrated by the Age When First Child was Born distribution in Figure 2.1.

| Figure 2.1 | A bar graph of roughly symmetrical data (Vocabulary test) and a histogram of positively skewed data (Age when first child born). |

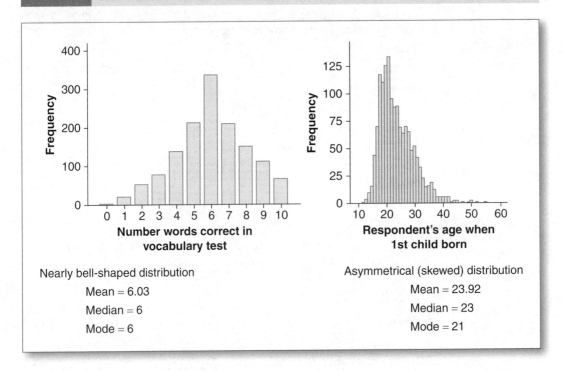

Nearly bell-shaped distribution

Mean = 6.03

Median = 6

Mode = 6

Asymmetrical (skewed) distribution

Mean = 23.92

Median = 23

Mode = 21

Reading Question

8. What measure of central tendency should be used when a distribution of scores measured on the interval or ratio scale of measurement is skewed?

    a. Mean

    b. Median

    c. Mode

9. When a distribution of scores is skewed, the median and mean will be similar.

   a. True

   b. False

COMPUTING THE MEAN

To compute the mean of the following sample of scores, you would add up the scores and then divide by the number of scores. If you do these calculations, you will find that the mean is 73:

100, 70, 80, 90, 50, 60, 70, 80, 90, 40.

Although this is probably something that you already know how to do without referring to a formula, you will need to be familiar with the following notation in order to understand the more complicated statistical formulas covered in later chapters. The formula for computing the mean (*M*) of sample data is

$$M = \frac{\Sigma X}{N}.$$

The numerator of the formula (ΣX) is using statistical notation to indicate that the scores should be added. The *X* refers to scores, and the sigma (Σ) means to sum. Therefore, when you see ΣX (read as "sum of *X*"), you need to sum all of the scores. The *N* in the denominator of the formula refers to the size of the sample, or the number of scores. Thus, the statistical formula for the mean is literally a set of instructions telling you to add the scores and then divide them by the number of scores. In this case, the sum of the *X*s (ΣX) is 730, the *N* is 10, and therefore the mean is 73:

$$M = \frac{\Sigma X}{N} = \frac{100+70+80+90+50+60+70+80+90+40}{10} = \frac{730}{10} = 73$$

In subsequent chapters, we will be learning statistical procedures that are more complicated than the mean. Understanding and computing these more advanced statistics will be much easier if you learn to read statistical notations (e.g., ΣX). In the long run, learning to read statistical formulas will be much easier than trying to memorize the exact order of multiple mathematical operations.

10. What does ΣX tell you to do?

    a. Compute the mean

    b. Sum the scores (*X*s)

Reading
Question

11. What does *N* represent?

    a. The number of scores

    b. Measurement categories

Reading
Question

12. A statistical formula is

    a. a helpful set of instructions indicating how to compute something.

    b. a bunch of meaningless symbols I should skip when I'm reading.

Table 2.1	Frequency distribution table of variable scores.

X	f
100	1
90	2
80	2
70	2
60	1
50	1
40	1

You will also need to be able to compute the mean from data presented in a frequency distribution table. For example, the test scores listed above could be presented in a frequency distribution table, as in Table 2.1.

The frequency distribution indicates that there is one person with a score of 100, two people with scores of 90, two people with scores of 80, and so forth. To obtain the sum of the scores, you could add each individual number, like you did previously, but with larger data sets it is more efficient to work with the data as they are presented in the table. There is just one person with a score of 100, and so we will include just one score of 100. However, there are two people with a score of 90. Rather than put two 90s into the equation, you can multiply 90 by 2. More generally, you will need to multiply each score by the number of people who had that score. This is illustrated below:

$$\Sigma X = 100(1) + 90(2) + 80(2) + 70(2) + 60(1) + 50(1) + 40(1) = 730.$$

Of course, the sum of scores is identical to what you computed above. As before, you must divide the sum of scores by the number of scores (*N*) to find the mean. The *N* of a frequency table is the sum of the frequencies. In this case, $N = 10$, and so the mean is computed as

$$M = \frac{\Sigma X}{N} = \frac{730}{10} = 73$$

In this case, it does not save a lot of time computing the sum of scores this way, but it would save quite a bit of time with a larger data set. For example, suppose that you had test scores from a larger sample of people (Table 2.2).

As before, the sum of scores should be computed by multiplying each score by its frequency and then summing the products:

$$\Sigma X = 100(5) + 90(7) + 80(8) + 70(10) + 60(6) + 50(9) + 40(3)$$
$$= 500 + 630 + 640 + 700 + 360 + 450 + 120 = 3400$$

Once you have computed the sum of the scores, you need to divide by the total number of scores (N). The frequency table indicates that there are 5 people with scores of 100, 7 people with scores of 7, and so forth. Therefore, to determine the total number of scores, you sum the frequencies. In this case, there are 48 scores ($5 + 7 + 8 + 10 + 6 + 9 + 3 = 48$). The mean test score for this sample is

Table 2.2	Frequency distribution table for a larger set of scores.

X	f
100	5
90	7
80	8
70	10
60	6
50	9
40	3

$$M = \frac{\Sigma X}{N} = \frac{3400}{48} = 70.83.$$

Reading Question

13. Which of the following is the correct way to compute the sum of scores for the following frequency distribution table?

X	f
3	4
2	7
1	5

a. $\Sigma X = 3(4) + 2(7) + 1(5)$

b. $\Sigma X = 3 + 2 + 1$

c. $\Sigma X = (3 + 2 + 1) + (4 + 7 + 5)$

The data in the previous problems came from samples. The computations are identical when you are working with a population. As with the sample, you will sum the scores and divide by N. However, the notation is a bit different. Greek letters are used to represent population parameters (i.e., μ, pronounced "myoo," represents a population mean), while Arabic letters are used to represent sample statistics (i.e., M represents a sample mean). The formula for the population mean (μ) is provided below, but you should note that it is computed in exactly the same way as the sample mean (M):

$$\mu = \frac{\Sigma X}{N}$$

14. The sample mean is represented by

    a. *M*.

    b. μ.

    c. both *M* and μ.

15. The population mean is represented by

    a. *M*.

    b. μ.

    c. both *M* and μ.

FIND THE MEDIAN

The median is the midpoint of a distribution of scores. When working with a list of scores, you begin by putting the scores in order from lowest to highest (or highest to lowest). For example, the test scores 100, 70, 80, 90, 50, 60, 70, 80, 90, and 40 would be ordered as follows:

40, 50, 60, 70, 70, 80, 80, 90, 90, 100

The median is the middle score in the list. In this case, there are an even number of values, and so there is not one middle score but two. The two middle scores are 70 and 80. To find the median, compute the average of the two middle scores. Thus, the median would be 75. When the number of scores is odd, the median is the one value that is the exact center of the list. For example, for the following list of scores, the median would be 6:

7, 7, 6, 6, 6, 5, 4, 3, 1

Part of the work is done for you when you work with a frequency distribution table. The scores are already in order. You just have to find the middle score. In Table 2.3, there are 48 scores ($\Sigma f = 48$), and so the midpoint would be between the 24th and 25th scores. You can work from either the top or the bottom of the table to find the 24th and 25th scores. If you start from the bottom, you will see that there are 3 people with scores of 40. There are 9 people with scores of 50, and so there are 12 people with scores of 50 or below. If we continue up the table, we see that there are 18 people with scores of 60 or below and 28 people with scores of 70 or below. Thus, the 24th and 25th scores are both 70, and so the median is 70.

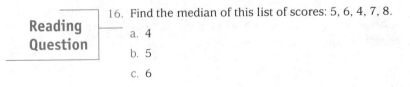

16. Find the median of this list of scores: 5, 6, 4, 7, 8.

    a. 4

    b. 5

    c. 6

	Table 2.3	Frequency distribution table for a larger set of scores with median identified.

X	f
100	5
90	7
80	8
70	10
60	6
50	9
40	3

The 24th and 25th scores are in this group of 10 scores.

Reading Question

17. Find the median of this frequency table of scores:

X	f
3	4
2	7
1	5
0	1

a. 1
b. 2
c. 3

FIND THE MODE

The mode is the most frequently occurring score in a distribution. To locate the mode in the frequency distribution table, you look for the measurement category (X value) with the highest frequency. In Table 2.4, the mode would be 70 because 10 people had scores of 70.

Reading Question

18. Find the mode of this set of scores:

X	f
3	4
2	7
1	5
0	1

a. 1

b. 2

c. 3

Table 2.4	Frequency distribution table for a larger set of scores, with the mode bolded.

X	f
100	5
90	7
80	8
70	**10**
60	6
50	9
40	3

SPSS

Data File

To compute measures of central tendency, you will need to begin by entering the data. As described in Chapter 1, all of the scores for a particular variable should be entered in one column. You cannot enter a frequency distribution table but instead need to enter individual scores. For example, to enter the scores from Table 2.5, you would need to enter 100 once, 90 twice, and so forth.

When you are done, your data file should look like the one in Figure 2.2. The exact order of the values is not important, but you should be sure that all 10 scores are entered in a single column.

Table 2.5	Frequency distribution table of the variable called scores.

X	f
100	1
90	2
80	2
70	2
60	1
50	1
40	1

Reading Question

19. When entering data into SPSS, you can enter a frequency table of the data; you do not have to enter each score individually.

a. True

b. False

Obtaining Measures of Central Tendency Using SPSS

Do the following to generate measures of central tendency using SPSS:

- Click on the Analyze menu. Choose Descriptive Statistics and then Frequencies.
- Move the variable(s) of interest into the Variable(s) box.
- Make sure the Display Frequency Tables box is checked if you want a frequency distribution table. Uncheck the box if you do not want a frequency table.
- Click on the Statistics button.
- Click on the boxes for mean, median, and mode, and then click on the Continue button.
- Click OK.

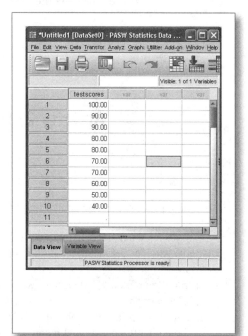

Figure 2.2 SPSS screenshot of the data entry screen of the variable labeled test scores.

Output

Your output file should look similar to that in Figure 2.3. Note that this data file had multiple modes because three different test scores

Figure 2.3 SPSS output for the central tendency of the variable score.

Statistics

testscores

N	Valid	10
	Missing	0
Mean		73.0000
Median		75.0000
Mode		70.00ᵃ

a. Multiple modes exist. The smallest value is shown

testscores

		Frequency	Percent	Valid Percent	Cumulative Percent
Valid	40.00	1	10.0	10.0	10.0
	50.00	1	10.0	10.0	20.0
	60.00	1	10.0	10.0	30.0
	70.00	2	20.0	20.0	50.0
	80.00	2	20.0	20.0	70.0
	90.00	2	20.0	20.0	90.0
	100.00	1	10.0	10.0	100.0
	Total	10	100.0	100.0	

each had a frequency of 2. SPSS only tells you one mode, but it does make a note that there are additional modes. To find the other modes, you need to look at the frequency distribution table.

Reading
Question

20. What was the mean of these data?

a. 73.0

b. 75

c. 70

Activity 2-1:   Central Tendency

Learning Objectives

After reading the chapter and completing this activity, you should be able to do the following:

- Compute the mean, median, and mode for data presented in a frequency table
- Identify whether the mean, median, or mode best represents the center of a given distribution of data
- Recognize from a graph when data will produce a misleading mean, median, or mode
- Create a frequency distribution that has a given mean
- Use deviation scores to change an existing frequency distribution into a new frequency distribution with a designated mean

COMPUTING THE MEAN, MEDIAN, AND MODE

A student at a Midwestern college asked 10 fellow statistics students how many courses they were taking this semester. He organized their answers into the following frequency table:

X: Number of Courses Taken	f: Number of People Taking X Courses
5	1
4	3
3	3
2	2
1	1

1. In the space provided above, create a frequency bar graph of the "Number of Courses" data.

2. Compute the mean, median, and mode for the data in the frequency table.

3. Which measure of central tendency would be the best in this situation?

You should have found that the mean and median were 3.1 and 3, respectively. There were two modes, 3 and 4. When it comes to choosing the best measure of central tendency, some statisticians would say that the number of courses is discrete and therefore the mean should not be used. They would argue that the value of 3.1 is not a good measure of central tendency because no one can ever take 3.1 courses. However, other statisticians would argue that as long as you remember that no one actually takes 3.1 courses, the mean of 3.1 is a more accurate measure of the center than 3.

CHOOSING MEASURES OF CENTRAL TENDENCY

For the following problems, determine which measure of central tendency is the most appropriate. Be sure to consider the scale of measurement as well as the shape of the distribution.

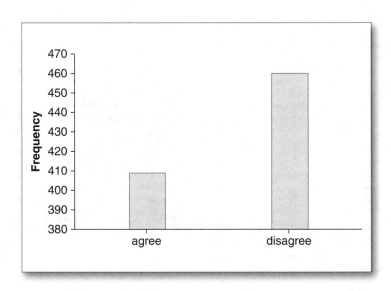

4. These data came from clinical psychologists who were attending a professional conference. They responded to the question "Do you agree that patients' memories of past events are improved by hypnosis?" What is the best measure of central tendency for these data and why?

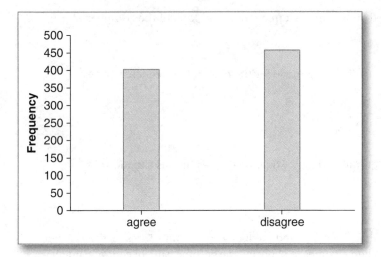

5. This graph presents the same data that were presented in the above graph. Why do the graphs look so different? Which do you think is a more accurate representation of the data and why? It is important to note that memories are *not* improved by hypnosis. Finally, do you think that someone could create graphs in ways that might be misleading in order to achieve mischievous goals? Explain your answer.

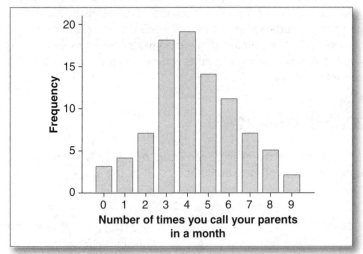

6. These data came from a sample of college students who attend college at least 100 miles away from their parents. They were asked how many times they called their parents in a typical month. The mean, median, and mode were 4.34, 4, and 4, respectively. Which measure of central tendency should be used and why?

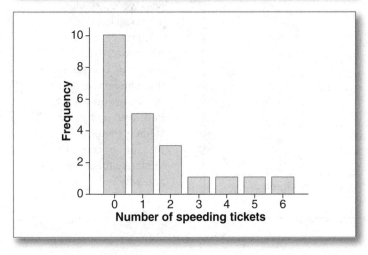

7. These data came from people attending a stock car race in Indiana. They were asked how many speeding tickets they had received in the previous 2 years. The mean, median, and mode were 1.45, 1, and 0, respectively. Which measure of central tendency should be used and why?

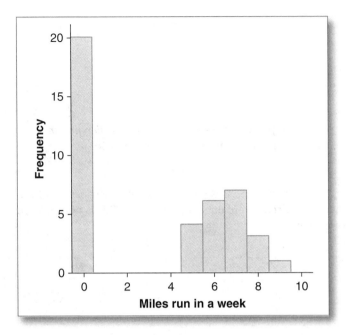

8. These data were obtained from a sample of people in the supermarket. They were asked how many miles they ran in the current week. The mean, median, and mode were 3.37, 5, and 0, respectively. In this case, no one number accurately describes the distribution of scores. In fact, one could argue that presenting only a measure of central tendency would be misleading. Accurately summarize these data.

UNDERSTANDING THE MEAN

Using Deviation Scores to Understand the Mean

The mean, median, and mode are all used to represent the center of scores. However, the preceding questions made it clear that each of these statistics defines "center" differently. The mode defines the center as the most common score. The median defines the center as the middle score. Both of these definitions of "center" are easy to understand. The mean defines the center in a more sophisticated way. In this activity, we are going to use frequency histograms to explain how the mean defines the center of scores.

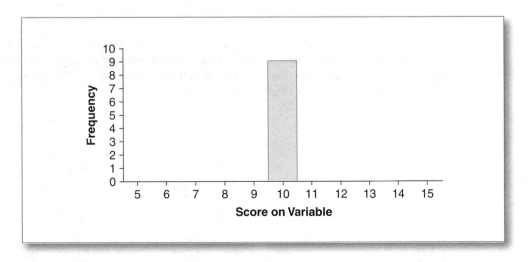

9. In the above distribution of scores, _____ people have a score of _____. (Fill in the blanks with numbers.)

10. What is the mean of the above distribution?

11. If you had to add another score to the above distribution *without changing the mean of the distribution*, what would the additional value have to be?

In the above distribution of scores, there is no variability in the data because all of the scores are equal and therefore all of the scores are equal to the mean. This is not the case in the following distribution of scores.

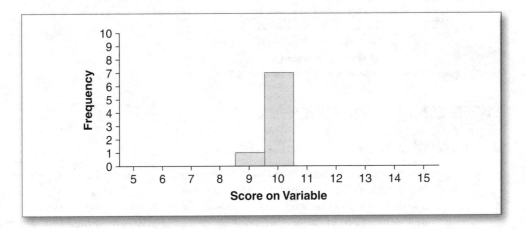

12. There is one value missing in the above frequency histogram. What must the missing value be if the mean of all the values is 10?

You should have found that the missing value had to be 11. You could have solved the previous problem using the formula for the mean and substituting the mean and N into the equation. If $M = 10$ and $N = 9$ (the eight values in the graph plus the missing value), the missing value would have to be 11. For example,

$$M = \frac{\Sigma X}{N}$$

$$10 = \frac{\Sigma X}{9}$$

$$90 = \Sigma X$$

Given that all nine scores must sum to 90 and the eight known scores sum to 79, the ninth missing score must be the difference between 90 and 79, or 11:

$$90 - 79 = 11$$

In addition to using algebra to solve for the ninth score, you could also use a deviation score method. Every value in a distribution is a certain distance from the mean; this distance from the mean is the value's deviation score $(X - M)$. In a distribution in which the mean is $M = 10$ and all scores are $X = 10$, all of the X values have deviation scores of 0, because the X score of 10 is 0 units away from the mean of 10. The questions that follow will help you discover how to use deviation scores to determine a missing score's value.

13. In the data graphed below, there are 7 scores of 10 and 1 score of 9. What is the deviation score $(X - M)$ for a score of 10, assuming that the mean is 10?

14. What is the deviation score, $(X - M)$, for a score of 9, assuming that the mean is 10?

The deviation scores and their frequencies are displayed in the following graph. There are 7 deviation scores equal to 0 and 1 deviation score equal to −1.

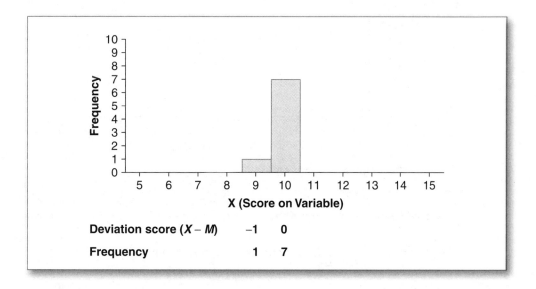

Deviation score ($X - M$)	−1	0
Frequency	1	7

15. One very important characteristic of the mean is that the sum of the positive and negative deviations from the mean will ALWAYS "balance out." In other words, the sum of the deviations above the mean is equal to the sum of the deviations below

the mean. Assuming that the mean of all nine scores is 10, what is the sum of the deviation scores below the mean (i.e., the sum of the negative deviation scores)?

16. You should have found that the sum of the negative deviation scores was −1. Based on this information, what does the sum of the positive deviation scores have to equal?

17. You found that the deviation score $(X - M)$ for the one missing value had to be +1; given that the mean of all nine scores is 10, what is the value of the last missing score (X)?

18. What score could be added to the data below such that the mean would equal 10? Compute the deviation scores for each score, and write them on the lines below the graph.

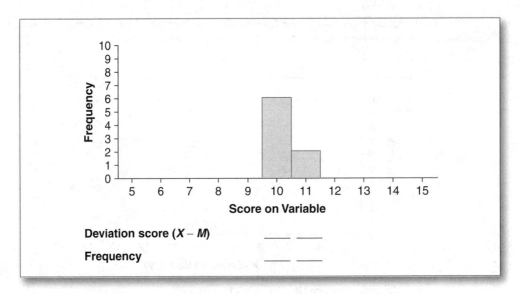

Deviation score $(X - M)$ ____ ____

Frequency   ____ ____

19. What is the sum of the deviation scores above the mean?

20. What does the sum of the deviation scores below the mean have to equal?

21. What score would result in a mean of 10?

22. Use deviation scores to determine what the one missing value must be. The mean of all 16 values for this distribution is 10. What must the missing 16th value be?

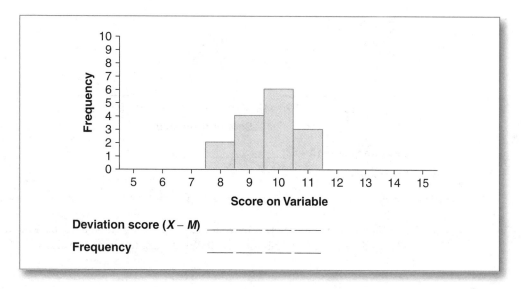

Deviation score (X – M) ____ ____ ____ ____

Frequency ____ ____ ____ ____

23. Use deviation scores to determine what the one missing value must be. The mean of all 25 values for this distribution is 10. What must the missing 25th value be?

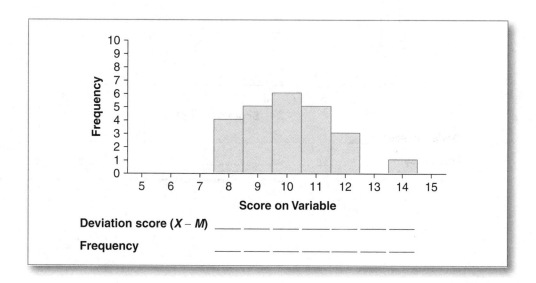

Deviation score (X – M) ____ ____ ____ ____ ____ ____ ____

Frequency ____ ____ ____ ____ ____ ____ ____

24. Use deviation scores to determine what the one missing value must be. The mean of all 25 values for this distribution is 20. What must the missing value be?

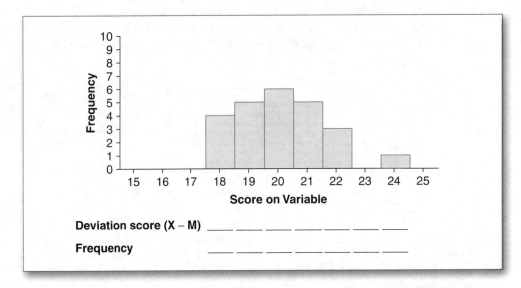

Deviation score (X – M) ___ ___ ___ ___ ___ ___ ___

Frequency ___ ___ ___ ___ ___ ___ ___

25. Use deviation scores to determine what the one missing value must be. The mean of all 28 values for this distribution is 20. What must the missing value be?

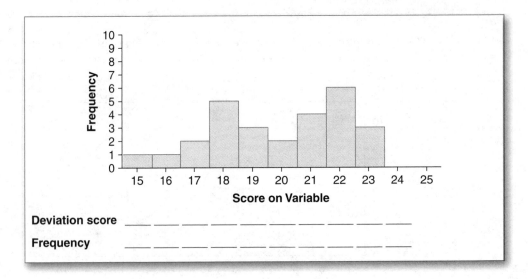

Deviation score ___ ___ ___ ___ ___ ___ ___ ___

Frequency ___ ___ ___ ___ ___ ___ ___ ___

26. Which of the following statements about the mean is true? (Choose all that apply.)
    a. The mean is ALWAYS the exact point at which the sum of positive and negative deviation scores balance out.
    b. The mean is ALWAYS the score with the highest frequency.
    c. The mean is ALWAYS equal to the median.
    d. The mean is ALWAYS equal to the mode.
    e. The mean is NEVER equal to the median.
    f. The mean is NEVER equal to the mode.

Create Frequency Distributions

27. Use the space below to draw two frequency histograms such that
    - both histograms have 7 values,
    - both histograms have a mean of 10,
    - one frequency histogram has less spread and the other histogram has more spread, and
    - *neither* graph is symmetrical—that is, the right and left sides of both graphs should not look exactly alike.

28. You should have found that it was important to pay attention to the distance of each X value from the mean value of 10. Explain how this helped you keep the mean equal to 10.

Compute Deviation Scores

A deviation score represents the distance and direction by which an individual score varies from the mean. It is the number of units to the left or right of the mean that each score is located. Deviations to the left of the mean are negative, and deviations to the right are positive. [*Note:* deviation score = $(X - M)$.]

29. Use the first distribution you created for Question 27 to answer this question. Write the values and the deviation scores of each value into the table provided below. Sum the deviation scores. [*Note:* Sum of all deviation scores $= \Sigma(X - M)$. What value do you get for the sum of the deviation scores?]

Score	Deviation Scores: (X − M)
	$\Sigma(X - M) =$

30. Use the second distribution you created for Question 27 for this question. Write the values and the deviation scores into the provided table, and sum the deviation scores.

Score	Deviation Scores: (X − M)
$\Sigma(X - M) =$	

You should have found that the sum of the deviation scores, $\Sigma(X - M)$, for both distributions is exactly 0. In your answer to Question 27, you intentionally created these distributions to be different. The fact is, no matter what data you are working with, $\Sigma(X - M)$ will always equal 0.

SUMMARY POINTS

31. Suppose someone told you that the average (mean, *M*) age of students in this class is 21 years. What does knowing the mean age tell you about the *distribution* of ages? (*Hint:* Are all students 21 years old?) Explain.

32. How does having a lot of deviation or a little bit of deviation (i.e., having a lot of large or a lot of small deviation scores) influence an accurate interpretation of the mean? Use this information to describe why the mean alone cannot accurately describe a distribution of scores.

33. One of the key points of this activity is that the sum of the distances from the mean (i.e., the deviation scores) ALWAYS equals 0. This means that the positive and negative deviations will ALWAYS balance out. This balancing of *distances* will ALWAYS occur even when the *number* of positive and negative deviations is unequal. Which of the following statements is always true about the mean? (Choose all that apply.)

    a. The mean will always be the middle score; it will have the same number of scores above it and below it.

    b. The mean will always be the most common score in a distribution.

    c. The mean is the only value that exactly balances the distances of the deviations to the left and right of the mean.

Activity 2-2: Practice Problems

SCENARIO 1: FREQUENCY DISTRIBUTIONS AND CENTRAL TENDENCY

A political pollster asked voters to respond to the following statement: "Global warming is at least partially caused by human activity." Voters responded using the following scale: 1 = *strongly disagree* to 5 = *strongly agree*. The pollster's data are given below:

X	f
5	6
4	2
3	4
2	1
1	1

1. Compute the mean, median, and mode for this distribution of scores.

2. Are the above data nominal, ordinal, or interval/ratio?

3. Build a histogram from the above data.

4. What measure of central tendency should be used to summarize these data?

SCENARIO 2: DEVIATION SCORES AND THE MEAN

A data set has six scores. The mean of all six scores is 102. Five of the six scores are displayed below:

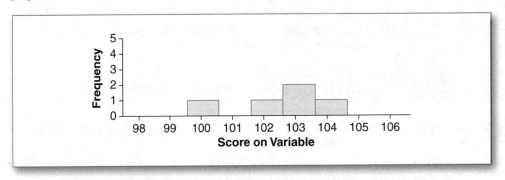

5. If the mean of a set of scores is 102, what is the deviation score for the value of 103?

6. Compute the deviation scores for each of the values displayed above. Assume the mean of all six scores is 102. What does the *deviation score* of the sixth missing score have to be?

7. What does the value of the sixth missing score have to be? What is the sum of the deviation scores?

SCENARIO 3: DEVIATION SCORES AND THE MEAN

A data set has seven scores. The mean of all seven scores is 14. Six of the seven scores are displayed below:

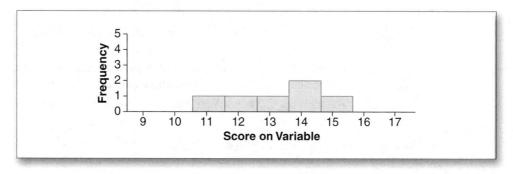

8. If the mean of a set of scores is 14, what is the deviation score for the value of 12?

9. Compute the deviation scores for each of the values displayed above. What does the *deviation score* of the seventh missing value have to be if the mean of all seven scores is 14?

10. What does the value of the seventh missing score have to be?

SCENARIO 4: FREQUENCY DISTRIBUTIONS AND CENTRAL TENDENCY

A yoga teacher wants to know how relaxed students feel after her class. Following one class, she asks students to rate their level of relaxation using a scale in which 7 indicates *very relaxed* and 1 indicates *very tense*.

X	f
7	2
6	5
5	7
4	9
3	5
2	3
1	1

11. How do you compute the sum of X (i.e., ΣX) when the data are in a frequency table?

   a. To obtain the sum of the scores, multiply each score (i.e., X) by the number of people who reported that score (i.e., f), and then sum all of the products.

   b. Add up all the scores (i.e., Xs), add up all the frequencies (i.e., fs), and multiply the two numbers together.

12. For the data presented in Scenario 4, $\Sigma X = $ _____.

13. How do you compute the mean (i.e., M) when the data are in a frequency table?

   a. Divide the sum of the scores, ΣX, by N. In this case, $N = 7$.

   b. Divide the sum of the scores, ΣX, by N. In this case, $N \neq 7$; N equals the sum of the frequencies.

14. For the data presented in Scenario 4, $M = \dfrac{\Sigma X}{N}$ _____.

15. For the data presented in Scenario 4, what is the median?

16. For the data presented in Scenario 4, what is the mode?

CHAPTER 3

Variability

LEARNING OBJECTIVES

After reading this chapter, you should be able to do the following:

- Explain what the standard deviation measures
- Compute the variance and standard deviation for a population using a calculator
- Compute the variance and standard deviation for a sample using a calculator and SPSS

POPULATION VARIABILITY

You have already learned that the mean is commonly used to summarize the center of a distribution of scores measured on an interval or ratio scale. While the mean does a good job describing the center of scores, it is often also necessary to describe how "spread out from center" scores are. To illustrate this point, consider two students who both work an average of 3 hours a day to help pay their college expenses. George works exactly 3 hours every day of the week. George's work hours are 3, 3, 3, 3, 3, 3, and 3, for Monday through Sunday. Morgan's daily work schedule is more variable. Her Monday through Sunday work hours are 2, 2, 5, 2, 6, 4, and 0. Even though the centers of these two data sets are identical (i.e., $\mu = 3$ for both), the two work schedules are very different. Thus, we need some way to describe the variability of these different work schedules, or *"spread" of each distribution*. There are a number of ways to describe the variability of interval/ratio data. The easiest measure of variability is the range, which is *the difference between the highest and lowest scores*. The range is a poor measure of variability because it is very insensitive. By insensitive, we mean the range is unaffected by changes to any of the middle scores. As long as the highest score (i.e., 6) and the lowest score (i.e., 0) do not change, the range does not change. A sensitive measure of variability changes if any number in the distribution changes. Researchers value this sensitivity because it allows them describe the variability in their data more precisely. The most common measure of variability is the standard

59

deviation. *The standard deviation tells you the typical, or standard, distance each score is from the mean.* Therefore, the standard deviation of George's daily work hours is 0 because all of the scores are exactly equal to the mean. In other words, George's daily work hours have zero variability. Morgan's daily work hours do vary, and therefore, the standard deviation of her data is larger (i.e., 1.96, you will learn to compute this below).

Reading Question

1. Why is the range a poor measure of variability?

   a. It uses only two values rather than all of the values in the distribution.

   b. It is overly sensitive to changes in the data.

Reading Question

2. What characteristic of a distribution of scores does a standard deviation describe?

   a. How far scores are from the mean

   b. How spread out the scores are

   c. The variability of scores in a distribution

   d. All of the above

Reading Question

3. The smallest standard deviation that is possible is _____ because this would mean that _____.

   a. −1; all of the scores are negative

   b. 0; all of the scores are the same

   c. 1; all of the scores are positive

STEPS IN COMPUTING A POPULATION'S STANDARD DEVIATION

We are going to use Morgan's daily work hours to illustrate how to compute the standard deviation. The lengths of Morgan's workdays in hours are 2, 2, 5, 2, 6, 4, and 0. We are going to consider these seven scores to be a population because we are only interested in describing this 1 week of work. Computing the standard deviation of this population consists of five steps. Focus on understanding what you are trying to do at each step rather than simply doing the calculations.

Step 1: Compute the Deviation Scores ($X - \mu$)

The standard deviation measures the standard (or typical) distance each score is from the mean. Thus, to compute the standard deviation, you first need to determine how far each score is from the mean. The distance each score is from the mean is called a *deviation score* and is computed as $X - \mu$, where X is the score and μ is the mean of the population. For example, this small population of seven scores (2, 2, 5, 2, 6, 4, 0) has a mean of $\mu = 3$. Table 3.1 displays a deviation score for each of the seven scores in the population.

Reading Question

4. A deviation score measures

    a. the typical distance all of the scores are from the mean.

    b. the distance of an individual score from the mean.

Table 3.1	Computing deviation scores, Step 1.

Score (X)	Step 1: Deviation Score $(X - \mu)$
2	2 − 3 = −1
2	2 − 3 = −1
5	5 − 3 = 2
2	2 − 3 = −1
6	6 − 3 = 3
4	4 − 3 = 1
0	0 − 3 = −3

Step 2: Square the Deviation Scores $(X - \mu)^2$

One logical way to find the typical deviation of scores from a mean is finding the average deviation score of a distribution. One could sum the deviation scores and divide their sum by the number of deviation scores, in this case 7. However, if you sum the deviation scores *of any distribution*, you get 0. Of course, if summing deviation scores always yields zero, this approach doesn't help us differentiate between distributions with different amounts of variability. So we need some way to combine deviation scores without losing the variability among the scores. There are a number of ways to avoid this problem, but the one that statisticians use when computing the standard deviation is to square the deviation scores first and then to sum the squared deviation scores. The deviation scores have been squared in Table 3.2.

Table 3.2	Computing deviation scores, Step 2.

Score (X)	Step 1: Deviation Score $(X - \mu)$	Step 2: Squared Deviation Score $(X - \mu)^2$
2	2 − 3 = −1	1
2	2 − 3 = −1	1
5	5 − 3 = 2	4
2	2 − 3 = −1	1
6	6 − 3 = 3	9
4	4 − 3 = 1	1
0	0 − 3 = −3	9

Reading Question

5. Statisticians square each deviation score so that

    a. when they sum them they will not sum to zero.

    b. the standard deviation will be larger.

Step 3: Compute the Sum of the Squared Deviation Scores $SS = \sum (X - \mu)^2$

Our goal is to compute the typical deviation score. To do this, our next step is to compute the sum of the squared deviation scores (*SS*). To compute the *SS*, you simply add (i.e., sum) the squared deviation scores as was done in Table 3.3.

Table 3.3   Computing deviation scores, Step 3.

Score (X)	Step 1:Deviation Score (X − μ)	Step 2: Squared Deviation Score (X − μ)²
2	2 − 3 = −1	1
2	2 − 3 = −1	1
5	5 − 3 = 2	4
2	2 − 3 = −1	1
6	6 − 3 = 3	9
4	4 − 3 = 1	1
0	0 − 3 = −3	9
		$\Sigma(X - \mu)^2 = 26$

$$SS = \Sigma(X - \mu)^2 = 1 + 1 + 4 + 1 + 9 + 1 + 9 = 26.$$

Reading Question

6. *SS* stands for the

 a. standard deviation.

 b. sum of the squared deviation scores.

 c. sum of the deviation scores.

Step 4: Compute the Population Variance (σ^2)

Again, our goal is to compute the typical, or standard, deviation of the scores. We cannot compute the average deviation score because their sum is always zero. So instead we compute the average squared deviation score, which is called the variance (σ^2, lowercase sigma squared). When computing any mean, we divide the sum of values by the number of values. Therefore, in this case, we divide the sum of the squared deviation scores by the number of squared deviations (i.e., N). The result is the mean of the squared deviation scores, the variance.

$$\text{Population variance: } \sigma^2 = \frac{\Sigma(X-\mu)^2}{N} = \frac{SS}{N} = \frac{26}{7} = 3.71$$

Reading Question ——— 7. The variance (σ^2) is the

    a. average squared deviation from the mean.

    b. average deviation from the mean.

Step 5: Compute the Population Standard Deviation (σ)

We squared the deviation scores before we summed them and then divided the sum by N to get the variance. This means that the variance is the average *squared* deviation of all the scores from the mean. While informative, the average *squared* deviation from the mean is not very intuitive to think about. It is much easier to think about the typical deviation of scores from the mean. Therefore, we convert the typical *squared* deviation into the typical deviation by taking the square root of the variance. The square root of the variance is the typical or standard deviation of scores from the mean.

$$\text{Population standard deviation: } \sigma = \sqrt{\sigma^2}$$

or

$$\text{Population standard deviation: } \sigma = \sqrt{\frac{\Sigma(X-\mu)^2}{N}} = \sqrt{\frac{SS}{N}} = \sqrt{\frac{26}{7}} = \sqrt{3.71} = 1.93$$

The standard deviation tells us the standard (or typical) distance of all the scores from the mean. In this population, the typical distance of all the scores from the mean is 1.93.

Reading Question ——— 8. The standard deviation (σ) is

    a. how far all of the scores are from the mean.

    b. the *typical* distance of all the scores from the mean.

The five steps to computing the standard deviation of a population are listed in Table 3.4. It is worth familiarizing yourself with the verbal labels as well as their symbolic equivalents because we will be using both in future chapters. You should notice that there are two SS formulas. While these formulas are mathematically equivalent (meaning they yield the same answer), researchers use the second formula when working with larger data sets. This computational formula is much easier to use with large data sets than the first definitional formula. You will use both of these equations in a future activity.

| Table 3.4 | Summary of five steps to computing a population's standard deviation. |

Population Standard Deviation			
Step	Verbal Label	Symbolic Equivalent	Equation
1	Deviation score		$(X - \mu)$
2	Square the deviation scores		$(X - \mu)^2$
3	Sum of squared deviation scores	SS	Definitional: $SS = \sum (X - \mu)^2$ Computational: $SS = \sum X^2 - \dfrac{(\sum X)^2}{N}$
4	Population variance	σ^2	$\sigma^2 = \dfrac{SS}{N}$
5	Population standard deviation	σ	$\sigma = \sqrt{\dfrac{SS}{N}}$

Reading Question

9. What symbol represents the standard deviation of a population?

   a. SS

   b. σ

   c. σ^2

Reading Question

10. Which equation defines the sum of the squared deviation scores?

   a. $\sum (X - \mu)^2$

   b. $\sum (X - \mu)$

   c. $\sqrt{\sigma^2}$

Reading Question

11. What does SS stand for?

   a. Sum of the scores

   b. Sum of the squared scores

   c. Sum of the squared deviation scores

Once you have computed the standard deviation, you should interpret it in the context of the data set. For this population of daily work hours, the number of hours worked each day varied. In other words, not all workdays were equally long. The standard deviation indicates how much the length of the workdays differed. Specifically, the standard deviation of 1.93 hours means that the typical distance of all the scores from the mean was 1.93 hours. With a mean of only 3 hours worked each day, a standard deviation of 1.93 hours suggests that the number of hours Morgan works each day varies quite a bit (e.g., 2, 2, 5, 2, 6, 4, 0).

It may help you understand that the standard deviation is actually measuring the distance of all the scores from the mean if we very briefly consider a completely new data set. Suppose Morgan's mom works an average of 9 hours each day. Specifically, the number of hours she works on Monday through Sunday is 8, 8, 11, 8, 12, 10, and 6. Even though her mom works a lot more hours on every day of the week, the standard deviation of her mom's work hours would also be 1.93. The standard deviations of these two data sets are identical because both data sets vary equally around their respective means of 3 and 9. Use the space in Table 3.5 to compute the standard deviation of the new data to confirm that it is 1.93.

Table 3.5	Example table for computing a population standard deviation.

Score (X)	Step 1: Deviation Score (X − μ)	Step 2: Squared Deviation Score (X − μ)²
8		
8		
11		
8		
12		
10		
6		
		$SS = \Sigma(X - \mu)^2 =$

Population variance: $\sigma^2 = \dfrac{\Sigma(X-\mu)^2}{N} = \dfrac{SS}{N} =$

Population standard devation: $\sigma^2 = \sqrt{\dfrac{\Sigma(X-\mu)^2}{N}} = \sqrt{\dfrac{SS}{N}} =$

12. In order for two data sets to have the same standard deviation, they must have the same mean.

    a. True

    b. False

SAMPLE VARIABILITY

Computing the variability of a sample of scores is very similar to computing the variability of a population of scores. In fact, there is only one computational difference that arises when you compute the variance. To highlight the difference between the sample and population formulas, we will analyze the same scores we analyzed above (i.e., 2, 2, 5, 2, 6, 4, 0) as if they came from a sample rather than a population.

In the above example, we used the number of hours Morgan worked on each day of a week as if it were a population because we were only trying to describe the variability of Morgan's workdays for that week. We were doing descriptive statistics because we were working with data from an entire population. If we wanted to describe the variability of Morgan's work schedule during all of last year, but we did not have the data from all of last year, we could use the week's data we have as a sample to estimate the standard deviation of her work hours for last year. In this scenario, the week of data we have is a sample from Morgan's entire population of workdays last year. In this new scenario, we would be doing inferential statistics, and therefore, there is one small change to how we compute the standard deviation. The reason for the change is that we are using a sample to infer or estimate the value of the population's standard deviation and the change helps correct for sampling error.

13. When you are using a sample to estimate a population's standard deviation you are doing _____ statistics.

    a. descriptive

    b. inferential

14. When computing a sample's standard deviation there _____ to the computation process relative to when you are computing a population's standard deviation.

    a. are many changes

    b. is one change

STEPS IN COMPUTING A SAMPLE'S STANDARD DEVIATION

Steps 1 Through 3: Compute the Sum of the Squared Deviation Scores $SS = (X - M)^2$

Computing the deviation scores and the sum of the squared deviation scores (*SS*) is identical for a sample and population. The only difference is in the notation. Population parameters are represented with Greek letters (e.g., μ represents a population mean) and sample statistics are represented by Arabic letters (e.g., M represents a sample mean). Because we are now working with a sample, we replace μ in the deviation score and SS formulas with M but the computations are the same.

$$SS = \Sigma(X - M)^2 = 1 + 1 + 4 + 1 + 9 + 1 + 0 = 17$$

Reading Question
15. Population parameters are represented by_____ letters and sample statistics are represented by _____ letters.
    a. Greek; Arabic
    b. Arabic; Greek

Reading Question
16. The SS is computed in exactly the same way for a sample and a population.
    a. True
    b. False

Step 4: Compute the Sample Variance (SD^2)

However, there is a difference between the computation of a sample variance and a population variance. To compute the *population variance*, you divided the SS by N. To compute the *sample variance*, you divide the SS by N − 1. This is the only difference between the computation of a variance for a sample and a population.

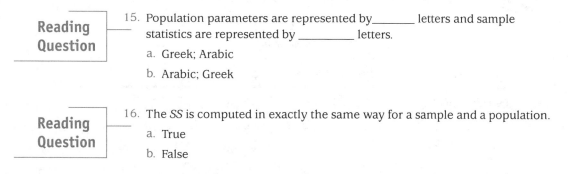

$$\text{Sample variance: } SD^2 = \frac{\Sigma(X - M)^2}{N - 1} = \frac{SS}{N - 1} = \frac{26}{6} = 4.33$$

Why we divide by N − 1 rather than N is a somewhat complicated issue. The simplest explanation is that samples are less variable than populations. This is a problem if we are trying to use a sample to estimate a population's standard deviation. If we don't fix this systematic problem, we will tend to underestimate the variability of the population. We correct the underestimation problem by dividing by N − 1 rather than N.

Reading Question
17. The variance of a sample is computed by dividing the SS by N − 1 rather than N to correct for a sample's tendency to
    a. overestimate the variability of a population.
    b. underestimate the variability of a population.

Step 5: Compute the Sample Standard Deviation (SD)

Take the square root of the sample variance.

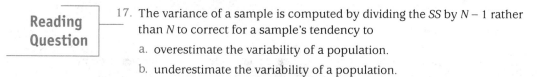

$$\text{Sample standard deviation: } SD = \sqrt{\frac{\Sigma(X - M)^2}{N - 1}} = \sqrt{\frac{SS}{N - 1}} = \sqrt{\frac{26}{6}} = \sqrt{4.33} = 2.08$$

The verbal labels corresponding to each computational step for a sample's standard deviation are identical to those used when computing a population's standard deviation. However, as indicated above, the sample's symbolic equivalents are Arabic letters rather than Greek letters (Table 3.6).

Table 3.6   Summary of five steps to computing a population's standard deviation.

	Sample Variability		
Step	Verbal Label	Symbolic Equivalent	Equation
1	Deviation score		$(X - M)$
2	Square the deviation scores		$(X - M)^2$
3	Sum of squared deviation scores	SS	Definitional: $SS = \Sigma(X - M)^2$ Computational: $SS = \Sigma X^2 - \dfrac{(\Sigma X)^2}{N}$
4	Sample variance	SD^2	$SD^2 = \dfrac{SS}{N - 1}$
5	Sample standard deviation	SD	$SD = \sqrt{\dfrac{SS}{N - 1}}$

18. What symbol represents the standard deviation of a sample?

    a. *SD*

    b. *SD²*

    c. *SS*

19. When computing the variance for a population you divide the *SS* by ___; when computing the variance for a sample you divide the *SS* by ____.

    a. *N, N − 1*

    b. *N − 1; N*

SPSS

Data File

You can compute the standard deviation and variance of a *sample* (not a population) using SPSS. Begin by entering the sample scores (2, 2, 5, 2, 6, 4, 0) into one column in SPSS. This is what your data file should look like when it is done (Figure 3.1):

Obtaining Measures of Variability

- Click on the Analyze menu. Choose Descriptive Statistics and then Frequencies.
    - You can obtain descriptive statistics (e.g., mean, standard deviation) in a lot of different ways in SPSS. We are only showing you one way here but if you explore the menus you can find other ways to obtain the same statistics.
- Move the variable(s) of interest into the Variable(s) box.
- Make sure the Display frequency tables box is unchecked if you do not want a frequency distribution table.
- Click on the Statistics button.
- Click on the boxes for mean, standard deviation, variance, minimum, and maximum, and then click on the Continue button, and then click OK.
- Important Note: SPSS computes the sample standard deviation and variance, NOT the population values.

Output

Your output file should look similar to the one below. Note that the results are the same as what you did by hand (Figure 3.2).

Figure 3.1   SPSS screenshot of data entry screen.

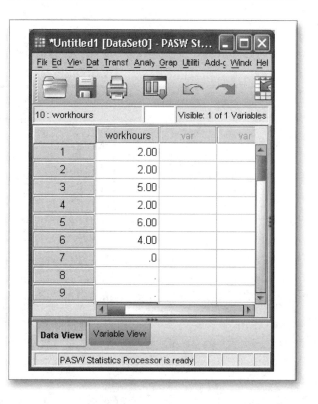

| Figure 3.2 | SPSS output for standard deviation. |

Statistics

workhours

N	Valid	7
	Missing	0
Mean		3.0000
Median		2.0000
Mode		2.00
Std. Deviation		2.08167

Reading
Question

20. What is the standard deviation of these data?

    a. 3

    b. 2

    c. 2.08

Activity 3-1:   Variability

Learning Objectives

After reading the chapter and completing this activity, you should be able to do the following:

- Recognize how measurement error, individual differences, and treatments can create variability
- Determine which of two distributions has a higher standard deviation by comparing histograms
- Explain what the standard deviation is to someone who has not taken a statistics course
- Compute the standard deviation for population or sample data presented in a histogram or frequency table
- Use the definitional and computational formula to compute the SS
- Use the statistics mode on your calculator to find the $\sum X^2$ and the $\sum X$

CONCEPTUAL UNDERSTANDING OF VARIABILITY

The physical development of infants is carefully tracked during the child's first year of life. At every doctor's visit, the child's height, weight, and head circumference are measured, typically by nurses. Consequently, nursing students are often taught how to take these measurements accurately. During one lesson an instructor brought a 1-year-old infant to class and had each student measure the circumference of the infant's head in centimeters. The 18 students' measurements are graphed below.

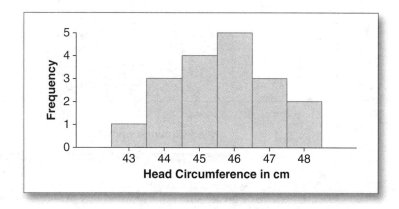

1. Given that all students were measuring the same head and that the head did not change size during the 50-minute class session, all of the head circumference measurements should be the same. In other words, there should be no variability in the measurements. However, the above graph clearly illustrates that there was variability in the measurements. Explain why there was variability in the measurements of the infant's head circumference.

2. In the above question, all of the variability in scores was created by **measurement error** because everyone was measuring the same thing and, therefore, should have obtained the same score. Unfortunately, measurement error is always present. No matter what you are measuring you will never be able to measure it perfectly every time. You can however reduce the amount of measurement error. In the context of measuring an infant's head circumference, how could the instructor and/or nursing students reduce the variability in scores created by measurement error (i.e., what could they do to increase the accuracy/reliability of each measurement)?

The following week each student went to a pediatrician's office at different times. They each measured the head circumference of one or more infants during their respective times at the office. The head circumference measurements for 35 *different* infants are graphed below:

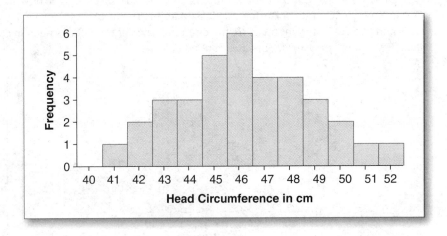

3. Did measurement error create some of the variability in scores collected from the doctor's office? Explain your answer.

4. In addition to measurement error, something else is also creating variability in the distribution of 35 scores (i.e., head circumferences). Besides measurement error, what is another reason for the variability in the above distribution of 35 infants' head circumferences?

In the previous question, the variability in head circumferences was created by both *measurement error*, which is always present, and the fact that the 35 infants' heads actually varied in size. Researchers refer to this second source of variability as being created by individual differences. The fact that people are different from each other creates variability in their scores.

5. Using highly standardized measurement procedures can reduce the amount of variability created by _____.

a. individual differences

b. measurement error

6. In which of the following distributions of scores would there be *more* variability created by individual differences?

   a. The heights of fifty 1st graders

   b. The heights of fifty elementary school children (1st through 5th graders)

It should be clear to you that researchers need to understand the variability in their data and what is creating it. Researchers view measurement error variability as "bad" and attempt to *minimize* it. Researchers also recognize that individual differences variability will always create variability in their data, and they try to control this variability with carefully designed experiments. Additionally, in many research situations, researchers actually want to *generate* variability by creating different kinds of treatments.

For example, suppose that a researcher thought that physically touching prematurely born infants would increase their growth. To test this hypothesis, the researcher could conduct a study with two samples of prematurely born infants. All of the infants in Group 1 could be touched with skin-to-skin contact for at least 6 hours a day. All of the infants in Group 2 could be touched only by someone wearing gloves. After 4 weeks of these differing treatments, the circumferences of the babies' heads could be compared.

7. In this study, there are three things creating variability in infant's head circumference. The fact that measuring an infant's head circumference is hard to do accurately contributes to the amount of _____ in this study.

   a. treatment differences variability

   b. individual differences variability

   c. measurement error variability

8. The fact that researchers gave some infants 6 hours of skin-to-skin touch a day and some other infants no skin-to-skin touch contributes to the amount of _____ in this study.

   a. treatment differences variability

   b. individual differences variability

   c. measurement error variability

9. The fact that infants naturally differ from each other in head size contributes to the amount of _____ in this study.

   a. treatment differences variability

   b. individual differences variability

   c. measurement error variability

10. If we measured each of the following variables for every person in this class, which variables would have the MOST *measurement error variability*?

    a. Students' report of their parents' annual income

    b. Parents' annual income recorded from official tax forms

11. If we measured each of the following variables for every person in this class, which variables would have the LEAST *individual differences variability*?

   a. Number of siblings a person has

   b. Number of fingers a person has

12. Understanding variability is important because some variables simply have more variability than others. For example, in high school students, which of the following variables would have the largest standard deviation?

   a. Annual income of parents

   b. Age

13. Which of the following variables would have the smallest standard deviation for high school students?

   a. Number of phone calls made in a day

   b. Number of phones owned

The figure below displays the head circumferences of 70 premature infants. Half of the infants were only touched by someone wearing gloves (*the darker bars*). The other half of the infants were only touched by someone who was not wearing gloves (*the lighter bars*).

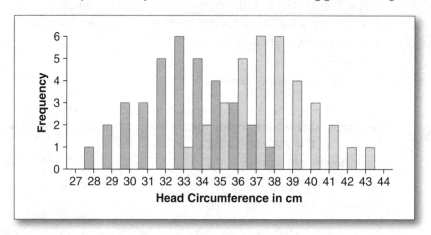

14. In the above figure, the variability created by the different treatments (i.e., touching infants while wearing gloves vs. touching infants while not wearing gloves) is depicted by the fact that

   a. all of the infants who were touched while wearing gloves do not have the same head circumference.

   b. all of the infants who were touched while not wearing gloves do not have the same head circumference.

   c. the infants who were touched without wearing gloves (*lighter bars*) tended to have larger head circumferences than infants who were touched while wearing gloves (*darker bars*).

15. In most research situations, there will be variability that is created by *measurement error*, *individual differences*, and *differing treatments*. In the study described above, the researchers expect that touch would result in faster growth. Thus, the researcher compares the mean head circumference for a sample of the premature babies who were touched with direct skin contact to the mean head circumference for a sample of the premature babies who were only touched by someone wearing gloves. Suppose that the mean head circumference for the direct touch sample was 38 cm, and the mean for the other sample was 33 cm. Explain why we cannot just look at those two numbers and conclude that direct skin touching facilitated infant growth. In other words, the variability between the two sample means *may* have been created by the treatment but it might also have been created by what other potential sources of variability?

A primary goal of this course is to teach you how researchers determine if the variability you see in data (e.g., the difference between the head circumferences of infants who were touched in different ways) was likely created by a treatment difference or if the variability was likely created by individual differences and/or measurement error.

16. State in your own words the primary goal of this course that is articulated in the previous paragraph.

As you know from the reading on variability, the standard deviation is commonly used to measure the amount of variability in a set of scores. Computing the standard deviation will NOT enable you to determine if the variability in the scores is created by treatment differences, individual differences, or measurement error. The standard deviation reveals the typical variability of scores from their mean. Later in the course we will learn how to use other statistics to help us determine if treatment differences created variability in scores.

17. The standard deviation is a measure of

   a. treatment variability in scores.

   b. individual differences variability in scores.

   c. typical distance of scores (i.e., variability) from the mean score.

If you understand the concept of variability, you should be able to "read" histograms. Specifically, you should be able to determine which of two histograms has more variability (i.e., a higher standard deviation).

For example, suppose that a professor asked students at the end of the semester how much they agree with the statement, "I enjoyed taking this course." Students may respond with 1 = *strongly agree*, 2 = *agree*, 3 = *neither agree nor disagree*, 4 = *disagree*, 5 = *strongly disagree*. Distributions from two of his classes are displayed below. The first graph is from a research methods course, and the second graph is from a statistics course.

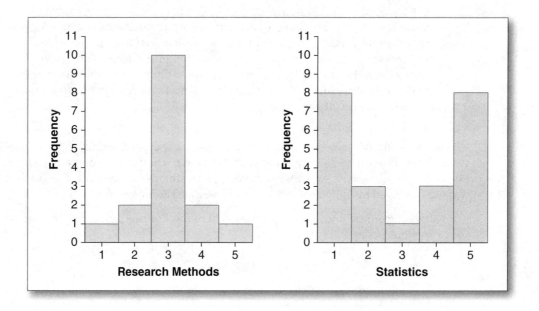

18. You should note that the mean rating for both courses was 3 (*neither agree nor disagree*). Which of the courses had more scores closer to its mean?

19. Given that the standard deviation measures the typical distance of scores from the mean, which course has the *smaller* standard deviation? (*Hint*: Both distributions have a mean of 3.)

There is far less variability in the research methods course than in the statistics course. In the research methods course, the majority of students responded with a 3, and most responses were very close to the mean. However, in the statistics course, most people responded with either a 1 or a 5, and most responses were relatively far from the mean. In other words, in the research methods course, most students gave the same answer (i.e., there was little variability in their responses). However, in the statistics course, there were greater differences of opinion (i.e., there was a lot of variability in responses). In general, *graphs with a lot of data points "piled up" close to the mean (like the research methods distribution) have less variability than graphs with a lot of data points "piled up" further from the mean (like the statistics distribution).*

While there are other factors to consider looking at where the scores are piled relative to the mean is a good way to start "reading" the variability in a distribution of scores. Use this rule to "read" the variability in the following pairs of graphs.

For Questions 20–22, determine if Graph A has more variability, Graph B has more variability, or if they have similar amounts of variability.

20.

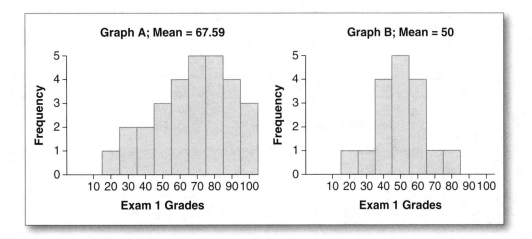

Explain your choice:

21.

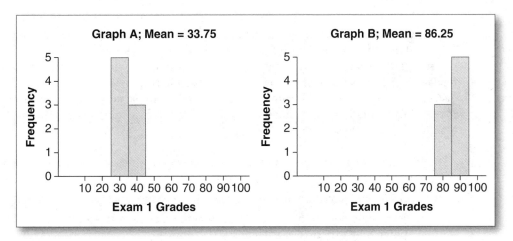

Explain your choice:

22.

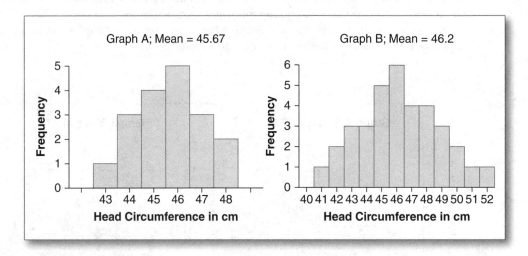

Explain your choice:

23. If a histogram has many scores piled up close to the mean value, the data set will tend to have

a. a large standard deviation.

b. a small standard deviation.

You should also note that there is no cutoff value for large or small standard deviations. In this case, the standard deviation for the research methods course was $SD = 0.89$, and the standard deviation for the statistics course was $SD = 1.78$. We can say that the standard deviation for the statistics class was relatively large because a standard deviation of 1.78 is large when the range of possible responses is only between 1 and 5. A typical distance of 1.78 from the mean on a 5-point scale is quite large. However, if teaching evaluations were made on a 50-point scale, a standard deviation of 1.78 would be quite small.

24. Which of the following standard deviations would represent greater variability relative to the range of possible scores?

a. A standard deviation of 2.51 for a variable measured with a 1 to 7 Likert scale

b. A standard deviation of 2.51 for a 5th-grade spelling test (scores could potentially vary between 0 and 100)

COMPUTING THE STANDARD DEVIATION

A group of four students reports their heights in inches as follows: 68, 61, 72, 70.

25. Use the table below to help you compute the *SS* (sum of the squared deviation scores) using the definitional formula:

$$SS = \Sigma(X - M)^2$$

Score (X)	(X – M)	(X – M)²
68		
61		
72		
70		
		$SS = \Sigma(X - M)^2 =$

You should find that the *M* is 67.75 and the *SS* is 68.75.

26. Although the definitional formula makes intuitive sense, it is not an easy formula to work with when you have a large set of scores. Is it far easier to compute the *SS* using the computational formula:

$$SS = \Sigma X^2 - \frac{(\Sigma X)^2}{N}$$

These definitional and computational *SS* formulas will yield identical values. To avoid a common error when using the computational formula, be sure you understand the distinction between ΣX^2 and $(\Sigma X)^2$. To compute ΣX^2 you should square each score first, then sum them ($\Sigma X^2 = 68^2 + 61^2 + 72^2 + 70^2$). To compute $(\Sigma X)^2$ you should sum all the scores

Score (X)	X²	
68		$SS = \Sigma X^2 - \frac{(\Sigma X)^2}{N}$
61		
72		
70		
$\Sigma X =$	$\Sigma X^2 =$	

first, then square the sum $((\sum X)^2 = (68 + 61 + 72 + 70)^2)$. The N is the number of scores. Use the table below to help you compute the SS using the computational formula.

This is a very small data set, so it is probably not obvious that the computational formula for the SS can save you quite a bit of time. When working with large data sets or when the mean of the data is not a whole number, the definitional formula takes longer and the final answer is likely to have rounding error. Another advantage to using the computational formula is that even cheap statistics calculators will compute the $\sum X^2$ and $\sum X$ for you. Therefore, if you learn how to use your statistics calculator, computing the SS will become quite easy. You can simply substitute the values of $\sum X$ and $\sum X^2$ into the computational formula. Try to use the statistics mode on your calculator to find the $\sum X^2$ and $\sum X$.

27. Use the SS you computed in Number 26 above to compute the standard deviation, assuming the data came from a sample. *You will use the following equation whenever you are analyzing data from a sample.* You should get 4.79.

$$SD = \sqrt{\frac{SS}{N-1}}$$

28. Now use the SS you computed in Number 26 above to compute the standard deviation, assuming that the data came from a population. *You will use the following equation whenever you are analyzing data from an entire population.* You should get 4.15.

$$\sigma = \sqrt{\frac{SS}{N}}$$

Figure out how to use the statistics mode on your calculator to compute the standard deviation of a population and a sample. There should be one button you can push or one line in a display that shows you the sample and population standard deviation.

29. Compute the *SS* and the standard deviation for the following *sample* of five scores: 5, 6, 3, 2, 7.

Compute the SS using the definitional formula		
Score (X)	(X − M)	(X − M)²
5		
6		
3		
2		
7		
		$SS = \Sigma(X - M)^2 =$

Confirm that you obtain the same results using the computational formula:

$$SS = \Sigma X^2 - \frac{(\Sigma X)^2}{N}$$

Compute the standard deviation:

$$SD = \sqrt{\frac{SS}{N-1}}$$

30. Compute the SS and the standard deviation for the following population of five scores: 1, 3, 3, 5, 7.

Compute the SS using the definitional formula		
Score (X)	(X − M)	(X − M)²
1		
3		
3		
5		
7		
		$SS = \Sigma(X - M)^2 =$

Confirm that you obtain the same results using the computational formula:

$$SS = \sum X^2 - \frac{(\sum X)^2}{N}$$

Compute the standard deviation:

$$\sigma = \sqrt{\frac{SS}{N}}$$

31. The graph from the Research Methods course described above is reproduced below. Create a frequency distribution table from this *population* data and then compute the standard deviation of the ratings.

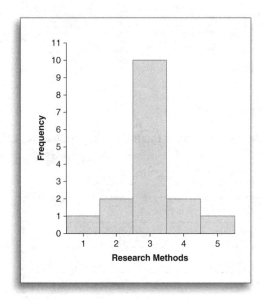

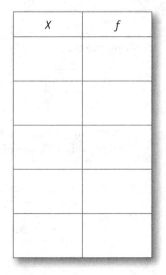

32. You should have found that the standard deviation was 0.87. Explain what 0.87 means in the context of this set of data.

33. After computing the standard deviations for the Research Methods course, the instructor realizes that some students did not complete the rating form, and so it was a sample not an entire population. Recompute the standard deviation of the course as if it came from a sample.

Activity 3-2:   Practice Problems

SCENARIO 1: COMPUTING Σ FROM FREQUENCY DISTRIBUTION TABLE

The values to the right are POPULATION data with a mean of $\mu = 5$ and $\sigma = 1.81$. You should note that the data are presented in a frequency table. This means there are zero 1s, two 2s, etc. Be sure to keep that in mind when you compute ΣX and ΣX^2.

1. Compute the SS. You should get 62.

2. Compute the standard deviation for this population using the SS you computed above.

3. Compute the mean for this population: $\mu = \Sigma X/N$.

4. Enter the data into the statistics mode of your calculator and confirm that the standard deviation and mean are equal to $\mu = 5$ and $\sigma = 1.81$.

X	f
1	0
2	2
3	4
4	1
5	2
6	6
7	3
8	1
9	0
10	0

SCENARIO 2: COMPUTING SD FROM FREQUENCY DISTRIBUTION TABLE

5. The values to the right are SAMPLE data. Compute the mean and the standard deviation. If you compute them correctly, you will find that $M = 6$ and $SD = 1.60$ (rounded up from 1.595).

X	f
1	0
2	0
3	1
4	1
5	3
6	1
7	4
8	2
9	0
10	0

SCENARIO 3: COMPUTING Σ FROM FREQUENCY DISTRIBUTION GRAPH

6. The values below are POPULATION data. Compute the mean and the standard deviation. It may be helpful to create a frequency distribution table as a first step. If you compute them correctly, you will find that μ = 4 and σ = 1.41.

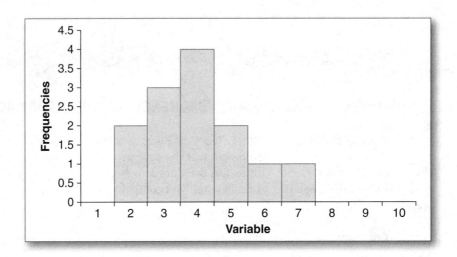

SCENARIO 4: COMPUTING *SD* FROM FREQUENCY DISTRIBUTION GRAPH

7. The values below are SAMPLE data. Compute the mean and the standard deviation. It may be helpful to create a frequency distribution table as a first step. If you compute them correctly, you will find that *M* = 7 and *SD* = 1.79 (rounded up from 1.789).

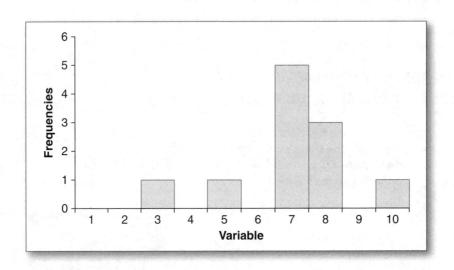

SCENARIO 5: COMPUTING *SD* FROM FREQUENCY DISTRIBUTION TABLE

A political pollster asked a SAMPLE of voters to indicate the degree of their agreement with the following question: "Global warming is real and is at least partially caused by human activity." The voters responded using the following scale: 1 = *strongly disagree* to 5 = *strongly agree*. The pollster's data are listed below.

X	f
5	6
4	2
3	4
2	1
1	1

8. Use the *computational formula* to determine the sum of the squared deviation scores (i.e., *SS*), the variance, and the standard deviation of these sample data.

SCENARIO 6: COMPUTING Σ FROM RAW DATA

A coach records the number of times players on a very small team (*N* = 6) miss practice in one season. The data from this POPULATION of scores are below.

5, 2, 1, 3, 8, 5

9. What scale of measurement is the variable measured on (i.e., nominal, ordinal, interval/ratio)?

10. What are the mean, median, and mode of these data?

11. What is the deviation score for a value of 8?

12. What is the squared deviation score for a value of 1?

13. Use the *definitional formula* to determine the sum of the squared deviation scores (*SS*), the variance (σ^2) and the standard deviation (σ) for these population data.

14. Which of the following is the correct way to enter these data into SPSS?

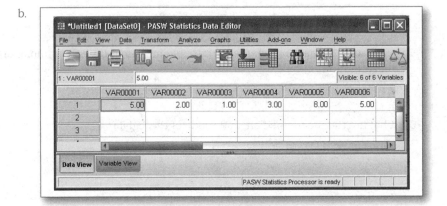

a.

b.

15. The values SPSS produces for the standard deviation and variance are the correct values for a

   a. population.

   b. sample.

CHAPTER 4

z Scores

LEARNING OBJECTIVES

After reading this chapter, you should be able to do the following:

- Compute and interpret a z score for a given raw score
- Solve for X if given a z score
- Explain what the sign of a z score indicates
- Explain what the value of a z score indicates
- Locate a z score within a distribution
- Use a unit normal table to determine the proportion of scores above or below any given z score

z FOR A SINGLE SCORE

In Chapter 2, you learned that the mean perfectly balances the positive and negative deviation scores of a distribution. In other words, when you compute each score's distance from the mean, the sum of the positive deviation scores will ALWAYS equal the sum of the negative deviation scores. In Chapter 3, you learned that the standard deviation describes how much variability there is in a set of numbers. Together the mean and the standard deviation help you interpret a distribution of scores by telling you the "center" of the scores and how much scores vary around that center.

In a very similar way, the mean and the standard deviation can also help you interpret an individual score in a distribution. For example, suppose your score on the American College Test (ACT) was 25. This score alone doesn't tell you much about your performance, but if you knew that the mean ACT score was 21 with a standard deviation of 4.7, you could interpret your score. Your score of 25 was 4 points better than the population mean. The population standard deviation was 4.7; this means that your score of 25 (i.e., a + 4 deviation from the mean) deviated less from the mean than was typical. So you did better than average but only a little better because your score was less than 1 standard deviation above the mean.

Clearly, knowing your score's deviation from the mean, whether that deviation is positive or negative and whether the deviation is smaller or larger than the standard deviation, helps you interpret your ACT score. In this chapter, you will learn to use the z for a single score. This statistical procedure is the mathematical equivalent of using the mean and the standard deviation of a distribution to help you interpret an individual score. As is often the case with mathematical procedures, it has the advantage of being more precise than the logical analysis provided in the previous paragraph.

Reading Question

1. The z for a single score is a procedure that
   a. tells if a score is above or below a population mean.
   b. informs whether a score's deviation from the mean is relatively large or relatively small compared with the deviations of the rest of the data.
   c. both of the above.

The z for a single score is useful for two purposes. First, as described above, it is used to locate a score in a distribution of scores. A z score will indicate if a given score is very good (far above the mean), very bad (far below the mean), or average (close to the mean). For example, when looking at ACT scores, larger positive z scores represent better performance and larger negative z scores represent worse performance. In the following section, you will learn how to compute and interpret z scores so you can evaluate an individual's performance. Second, a z for a single score can help you compare two scores from *different* distributions. For example, the z for a single score can help you compare scores on the ACT and Scholastic Aptitude Test (SAT) even though the maximum score on the ACT is 36 and the maximum score on the math and verbal sections of the SAT is 1,600. The z for a single score "corrects" for the differences in scale. Therefore, z scores can reveal if a score of 22 on the ACT was better than a score of 1,100 on the SAT.

Reading Question

2. The z for a single score can be used to
   a. locate a specific score in a distribution of scores and compare scores from different distributions.
   b. locate a sample mean in a distribution of means and compare means from different distributions.

Computing a z for an Individual Score

To compute a z for a single score, you need to know the score (X), the mean of the population (μ), and the standard deviation of the scores. While the z for a single score can be computed with either the population standard deviation (σ) or a sample standard deviation (SD), the sample standard deviation is used only when the population standard deviation is not known. Likewise, the sample mean (M) is used only when the population mean (μ) is not known. For example, suppose that a student took the ACT and obtained a score of 22.

The mean for this test is $\mu = 21$, with a standard deviation of $\sigma = 4.7$. To compute the z score, you first compute the deviation between the score and the population mean $(X - \mu)$. You then divide this difference by the standard deviation—in this case the population standard deviation (σ):

$$z = \frac{X - \mu}{\sigma} = \frac{22 - 21}{4.7} = 0.21$$

Interpreting the z for a Single Score

The z score is positive because the student's score of 22 was above the mean ACT score of 21. The numerator of the z formula is a deviation score $(X - \mu)$. It indicates how far the given score is above or below the population mean. Thus, whenever a raw score is above the mean you will obtain a positive z score, and whenever a raw score is below the mean you will obtain a negative z score.

The denominator of the z formula is the population standard deviation, σ. The standard deviation is the typical distance scores are from the mean in the population. Using the population standard deviation as the denominator of the z score equation means that z scores should be interpreted as the number of standard deviation units a given raw score is away from the mean of the distribution.

So, as described above, the z score reveals two really important bits of information. First, if it is positive, the given score was above the average score. Additionally, the farther the absolute value of the z score is from 0, the more the score deviates from the mean. A z score with an absolute value of 1 indicates that the score is 1 standard deviation from the mean. The standard deviation is the typical distance of scores from the mean. Thus, if the z score is greater than 1 (or less than −1), then the score deviates from the population mean more than is typical. In this case, the student's score of +0.21 was above average but only slightly so.

Reading Question

3. If a given z score is negative, then the raw score it is representing was
   a. above the population mean.
   b. below the population mean.
   c. at the population mean.

Reading Question

4. Which of the following z scores represents a raw score that is the most atypical (i.e., farthest from the mean)?
   a. −3.1
   b. +2.2
   c. −0.81
   d. +0.47

Reading
Question

5. A z score of +1.90 is above the mean less than is typical.

   a. True

   b. False

Reading
Question

6. A z score of +1 is above the population mean by exactly 1 standard deviation.

   a. True

   b. False

USING X TO FIND IMPORTANT "CUT LINES"

In some situations, you might be interested in identifying the specific score that is well above (or below) the average so you can use that score as a "cut line." For example, perhaps you are interested in identifying students who score "far above average" on the ACT so you can invite them to join an honors program. You might decide that you want to know what score represents performance that is 2 standard deviations above the average score of 21 on the ACT. You could do this by using the z formula, inserting 2 for z and 21 for μ. You would also have to know the standard deviation (i.e., σ or *SD*).

Here is an example of solving for the raw score when given that $z = 2$, $\mu = 21$, and $\sigma = 4.7$:

$$z = \frac{X - \mu}{\sigma}$$

$$2 = \frac{X - 21}{4.7}$$

$$9.4 = X - 21$$

$$X = 30.4$$

A raw score of 30.4 on this test represents performance that is 2 standard deviations above the population mean (i.e., very good performance!). This value could be used to identify very motivated students who score far above average.

z SCORES AND PROBABILITY

As mentioned above, z scores reveal if a score is above or below a population mean and if a score's deviation from the mean is greater than typical or less than typical. While knowing if a score's deviation is more or less than typical is useful, *if the set of scores being analyzed is normally distributed*, we can use z scores to make precise probability statements about a raw score's location relative to other scores. For example, you can determine what proportion of scores is higher than or lower than a particular z score. Similarly, if you randomly select one score from a distribution, you can determine the probability of selecting a z score of that size or larger from the distribution.

Reading Question

7. z scores can be used to make precise probability statements about the location of a raw score relative to other scores only if the scores are normally distributed.

   a. True

   b. False

Any distribution of scores can be converted into a z distribution simply by converting the raw scores into z scores using the z for a single score formula (e.g., $z = (X - \mu)/\sigma$). If you convert all of the raw scores in a distribution into z scores, you will end up with a distribution that has a mean of 0 and a standard deviation of 1.

Reading Question

8. If you convert an entire distribution of raw scores into z scores, the distribution of z scores will have a mean equal to _____ and a standard deviation equal to _____.

   a. 1, 0

   b. 0, 1

Although you can compute z scores from any set of scores, you can only determine the probability of obtaining a particular score if the raw scores are normally distributed. If the scores are normally distributed, the distribution of z scores will be a normal curve with a mean of 0 and a standard deviation of 1.

As you can see in Figure 4.1, a normally shaped frequency histogram, there are many z scores close to 0 (the mean z score) and fewer z scores that are far from 0. The "peak" of the curve is over 0 (the mean z score), and the height of the curve decreases as you move farther away from 0. Scores that are common (e.g., 0) have a lot of "area" under the curve. Conversely, scores that are rare (e.g., −3 and + 3) have very little area under the curve. It is possible to get z scores that are farther from 0 than −3 and +3, but as the curve implies, this is rare. In fact, the normal curve allows us to say *exactly* how rare.

Figure 4.1   A frequency histogram of z scores for a normally shaped distribution.

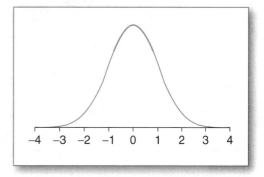

Reading Question 9. In a normal distribution of z scores, the most common z score value is

a. 1.

b. −1.

c. 3.

d. −3.

e. 0.

The following three problems exemplify how you can use z scores to determine the exact probability of any given score.

POSITIVE z SCORE EXAMPLE

To make a precise statement about the location of a score in a distribution, begin by computing a z for a single score, as you did above. For example, suppose Harriet wanted to know what proportion of all the students who took the ACT scored *lower* than her score of 22. In other words, she wanted to know her percentile rank. The first step would be to compute the z score for her ACT score of 22. As you may recall, the population mean score on the ACT is $\mu = 21$, with a standard deviation of $\sigma = 4.7$.

Compute the z Score

This is exactly what you did at the beginning of this chapter.

$$z = \frac{X-\mu}{\sigma} = \frac{22-21}{4.7} = 0.21.$$

Figure 4.2 A z distribution with the target area below z = 0.21 shaded.

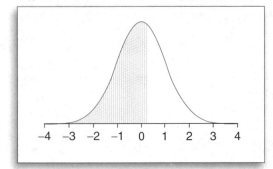

Draw a Normal Distribution, and Shade in the Area You Are Interested In

In this problem, we want to find the percentile rank, or the percentage of z scores *less than* a z score of 0.21, and so we shade in the area in the curve that is below +0.21 on the z score number line. An example is shown in Figure 4.2. After you have drawn a figure similar to the one shown in Figure 4.2, you will determine the exact proportion of the curve's area that is shaded by using a unit normal table in Appendix A.

Use a Unit Normal Table to Find the Area of the Shaded Portion of the Curve

- If the shaded area is MORE than 50% of the distribution, use the BODY column in the table.
- If the shaded area is LESS than 50% of the distribution, use the TAIL column in the table.

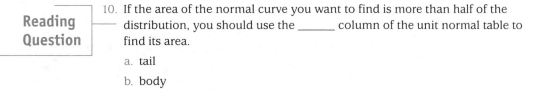

Reading Question

10. If the area of the normal curve you want to find is more than half of the distribution, you should use the _____ column of the unit normal table to find its area.

   a. tail

   b. body

Find the *z* score of 0.21 in the left most column of the normal unit table. Then find the value in the BODY column of the table, because the shaded area is more than half of the distribution. The BODY column indicates that the proportion of scores below a *z* score of +0.21 is .5832. Therefore, 58.32% of the population of students who took the ACT had scores that were lower than Harriet's ACT score of 22. In other words, Harriet is at the 58.32nd percentile. This 58.32% is based on the assumption that the population of students' ACT scores is normally distributed. If the population distribution is not normal in shape, the 58.32% value would be inaccurate.

NEGATIVE *z* SCORE EXAMPLE

Antonio took the SAT. He wants to know the percentile rank of his combined math and verbal score on the SAT, which was 1,005 (i.e., *X* = 1005). The mean combined math–verbal score on the SAT is μ = 1008, with a standard deviation of 114. Again, the first step is to compute the *z* score for a combined SAT score of 1,005. This is done below:

$$z = \frac{X - \mu}{\sigma} = \frac{1005 - 1008}{114} = -0.026$$

Draw a Normal Distribution, and Shade in the Area You Are Interested In

The next step is to draw the distribution of combined SAT scores, locate the *z* score of –0.026, and shade the area under the curve that is below the *z* score of –0.026. This is done in Figure 4.3.

Use a Unit Normal Table to Find the Area That Is Shaded In

For this example, you want to know the proportion of *z* scores that are below –0.026. Note that the normal unit table does not include negative values. Therefore, you will

Figure 4.3	A z distribution with the target area below $z = -0.026$ shaded.

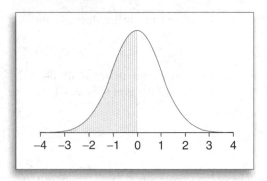

always look up the absolute value of the z score you compute (i.e., in this case, you would look up 0.026) and then decide if you should use the BODY or the TAIL column based on your sketch. If the shaded area is more than half of the distribution, use the BODY column. If the shaded area is less than half of the distribution, use the TAIL column. In this case, less than half of the distribution is shaded, so we use the TAIL column for the z score of 0.026. The table in this book only goes two places past the decimal, so you should round 0.026 to 0.03. If you look up 0.03, you will find that the proportion of scores in the TAIL column is .4880. Therefore, approximately 48.80% of the students who took the SAT had combined math–verbal SAT scores that were lower than Antonio's score of 1,005.

If you wanted to compare Antonio's SAT performance (i.e., 1,005) with Harriet's ACT performance (i.e., 22), the raw scores are not very helpful. However, Antonio's and Harriet's z scores of −0.026 and 0.21, respectively, make it clear that Antonio scored slightly below the SAT mean and Harriet scored slightly above the ACT mean. If you wanted to be even more precise in your comparison, you could use the percentile ranks associated with each z score. Antonio's SAT performance was better than 48.80% of the SAT scores, and Harriet's ACT performance was better than 58.32% of the ACT scores.

Reading Question

11. When finding the area of the distribution that is above or below a negative z score, you

   a. need a different z table with negative values in it.

   b. simply look up the absolute value of the z score and then determine if you need to use the tail or body column of the table.

PROPORTION BETWEEN TWO z SCORES EXAMPLE

Professor Jones wanted to know the proportion of students with ACT scores between 1 standard deviation above the mean (i.e., a z score of +1) and 1 standard deviation below the mean (i.e., a z score of −1). The first step in this problem is to draw the distribution of ACT scores and sketch in the area you are trying to find. This has been done below.

Draw a Normal Distribution, and Shade in the Area You Are Interested In

Figure 4.4   A z distribution with the target area between $z = -1$ and $z = +1$ shaded.

In this example, you are trying to find the proportion of students in the middle of the curve, with z scores between -1 and $+1$. The area between the z scores of -1 and $+1$ has been shaded in Figure 4.4.

Use a Unit Normal Table to Find the Area That Is Shaded In

There are a number of correct ways to do this problem. One would be to determine the entire area greater than -1. Because this is greater than 50% of the distribution, we look in the BODY column for the z score of 1 and find .8413. However, we aren't interested in everything greater than -1. Specifically, we want to exclude that area beyond the z score of $+1$, or the area in the TAIL for a z score of 1, which is .1587. Therefore, the area that we're interested in the area between the z scores of -1 and $+1$, is $.8413 - .1587 = .6826$. Look at the figure above, and confirm that you understand why we had to subtract the positive tail to get our answer.

The proportion of ACT scores between the z scores of -1 and $+1$ was .6826. Therefore, 68.26% of all ACT scores are between 1 standard deviation below the population mean and 1 standard deviation above the population mean. In other words, most people (approximately 68% of them) have ACT scores between 16.3 (i.e., $24 - 4.7$) and 25.7 (i.e., $24 + 4.7$).

Reading Question

12. If you want to determine the area of the normal curve that is between any two z scores, you will need to

a. use a different normal unit table.

b. sketch the area you need and then add two areas together or subtract one area from another.

Activity 4-1:   z Scores

Learning Objectives

After reading the chapter and completing this activity, you should be able to do the following:

* Identify likely and unlikely body temperatures by using z scores
* Explain why a sample mean is likely to be less extreme than an individual score

BODY TEMPERATURE

Almost all of us have had our body temperature measured at the doctor's office. Not only is temperature an indicator of physical health, but it is also associated with psychological health. For example, research has shown that people with major depression tend to have higher body temperatures than people who are not depressed (Rausch et al., 2003). Conventional wisdom is that the average human body temperature is 98.6°F. This value seems to have originated from Carl Wunderlich's 1868 publication, in which he says that he measured the body temperatures of approximately 25,000 patients. However, more recent research (Mackowiak, Wasserman, & Levine, 1992) has revealed that the average body temperature (taken orally) of healthy adults is $\mu = 98.2$, with a standard deviation of $\sigma = 0.6$. The graph below is a frequency distribution of body temperatures.

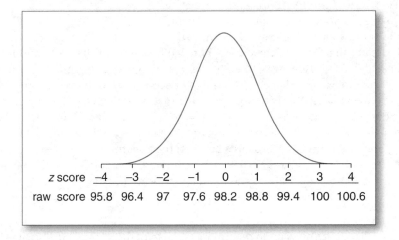

1. Locate the following individual body temperatures on the graph: 98.0°F, 97.5°F, 97.0°F, 96.5°F. Put an "x" on the graph for each temperature.

2. Which of the four body temperatures in the preceding question are rare or unusual?

3. Explain how you used the frequency distribution histogram of the population's body temperatures to determine which of the preceding temperatures are unusual or rare.

In the previous questions, you visually inspected a frequency distribution graph to determine whether certain body temperatures were unusual. While this technique is informative, it is not very precise. You can use *z* scores to determine the exact probability of obtaining any particular range of scores in a distribution. As you know from the reading on *z* scores, you need to know the population mean (μ) and population standard deviation (σ) for all body temperatures to compute the *z* score for any given body temperature. We will use $\mu = 98.2$ and $\sigma = 0.6$.

4. Find *z* scores for the body temperatures listed below. Then find the probability of having each temperature or a more extreme temperature (i.e., lower).

Test Score	98.0°F	97.5°F	97.0°F	96.5°F
z score: $z = \dfrac{X - \mu}{\sigma} =$				
Probability of a *z* score or a more extreme *z* score(sketch the distribution, shade in the area you are interested in, and then look up the *z* score in the unit normal table)				

5. Find *z* scores for the body temperatures listed below. Then find the probability of having each temperature or a more extreme temperature (i.e., higher).

Test Score	98.4°F	98.9°F	99.4°F	99.9°F
z score: $z = \dfrac{X - \mu}{\sigma} =$				
Probability of a *z* score or a more extreme *z* score (sketch the distribution, shade in the area you are interested in, and then look up the *z* score in the unit normal table)				

Once the probability of a *z* score or a more extreme *z* score is found, you will still need to determine if that probability is small enough to be considered *unlikely.* Researchers frequently use a 2.5% cutoff, meaning that if the probability of obtaining a given *z* score or a more extreme *z* score is less than 2.5% it is considered rare or uncommon.

6. Find the *z* score cutoff that separates the top 2.5% from the rest of the distribution. Then find the *z* score cutoff that separates the bottom 2.5% from the rest of the distribution. Draw a vertical line at *each* cutoff point. Find the location of these lines by finding the *z* score (Appendix A) that has .025 in the tail column.

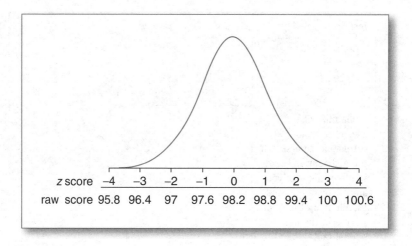

z score	−4	−3	−2	−1	0	1	2	3	4
raw score	95.8	96.4	97	97.6	98.2	98.8	99.4	100	100.6

7. Label each of the three sections that you created for the previous question as "likely scores" or "unlikely scores." Two of the sections will be labeled as "unlikely scores."

8. After you have the positive *and* negative *z* scores from Question 6 above, find the body temperature that corresponds to the positive *z* score and the body temperature that corresponds to the negative *z* score by using the *z* score formula.

The positive *z* score = _____; temperature = _____.

The negative *z* score = _____; temperature = _____.

COMPARING THE VARIABILITY OF INDIVIDUALS WITH THE VARIABILITY OF RANDOM SAMPLES

9. If you took a *random sample* of 10 students ($N = 10$), you would expect their mean body temperature to be *close to* what value?

10. Suppose you took another random sample of 10 different students. While you should still expect this second sample of 10 people to have a mean body temperature *close to* 98.2, you should not expect the second sample's mean to be *exactly* the same as the first sample's mean. Explain why not.

11. Suppose you took five random samples of 10 students each and computed each sample's mean body temperature. What value would you expect for the mean of the five sample means?

    The mean of the five sample means would be close to _____.

12. Which would you expect to be closer to 98.2, a mean from a randomly selected sample or a randomly selected individual score? Why?

13. Suppose you took five random samples of 100 students and computed each sample's mean body temperature. Which would you expect to be closer to 98.2, the sample means based on 10 scores or the sample means based on 100 scores? Why?

14. Generally speaking, how does increasing the sample size change a sample mean's probable deviation from the population's mean body temperature of 98.2?

15. In Question 4 above, you determined that the probability of randomly sampling an *individual* with a body temperature of 97.5° or lower is .1210. Would the probability of getting a *sample mean* of 97.5° or lower be higher, lower, or about equal to .1210? Explain.

SIMULATING THE IMPACT OF INCREASING THE SAMPLE SIZE ON SAMPLING ERROR

Now we are going to use SPSS to simulate what would happen if we took random samples of different sizes from a population (parts of this exercise were created by Garfield, Zieffler, & Lane-Getaz, 2005). Open SPSS, and then open "bodytempdata.sav." In the data file, there are 3,998 hypothetical body temperatures taken from every student attending a Midwestern college. These values will serve as the population from which researchers could take a sample. The researchers want to get a sample that has a body temperature mean that is representative of the population body temperature mean (i.e., they want their sample's mean, M, to be close to the population's mean, μ). They want to have a small amount of sampling error.

Use SPSS to obtain a random sample of 10 body temperatures. Then use SPSS to compute the mean of this sample. To do this, open the data file, and follow these steps:

- Click on the Data menu, and then choose Select Cases.
- Click on Random Sample of Cases, and then click on the Sample button.
- A new window will open. Select the Exactly option.
- In the first box, enter the number 10.
- In the second box, enter 3998 (the total number of cases).
- Click on Continue and then OK.
- If you look at the data file, you will see that all but 10 cases have a diagonal line through their case number. To obtain a mean for the 10 cases that were randomly selected, click on the Analyze menu. Choose Descriptive Statistics and then Descriptives.
- Move bodytempdata into the Variables box.
- Click on OK.
- Record the sample mean in the first box below.

Following the above steps, select a new random sample four more times, and record the sample mean each time in the boxes provided below (five sample means when $N = 10$):

Now use SPSS to obtain a random sample of 100 body temperatures, and then use SPSS to compute the mean. As above, perform this procedure five times, and record the five sample means below (five sample means when $N = 100$).

16. Compare the sample means obtained when $N = 10$ and when $N = 100$. As the sample size was increased, what happened to the variability of the sample means from the population mean of 98.2? Did the variability tend to increase or decrease as the sample size increased?

17. If researchers want to decrease sampling error, what should they do with their sample size? Explain your answer.

REFERENCES

Garfield, J., Zieffler, A., & Lane-Getaz, S. (2005). EPSY 3264 Course Packet, University of Minnesota, Minneapolis.

Mackowiak, P. A., Wasserman, S. S., & Levine, M. M. (1992). A critical appraisal of 98.6 degrees F, the upper limit of the normal body temperature, and other legacies of Carl Reinhold August Wunderlich. *Journal of the American Medical Association, 268,* 1578–1580.

Rausch, J. T., Johnson, M. E., Corley, K. M., Hobby, H. M., Shendarkar, N. N., Fei, Y. Y., . . . Leibach, F. H. (2003). Depressed patients have higher body temperature: 5-HT transporter long promoter region effects. *Neuropsychobiology, 47*(3), 120–127.

Activity 4-2:   Introduction to Distributions of Sample Means

Learning Objectives

After reading the chapter and this activity, you should be able to do the following:

- Describe a distribution of sample means
- Explain how a distribution of raw scores is different from a distribution of sample means that is created from those raw scores
- Find the mean and the standard deviation of a distribution of sample means
- Explain what the standard error of the mean measures
- Compute the sampling error
- Describe how the standard error of the mean can be decreased
- Explain why you would want the standard error of the mean to be minimized
- State the central limit theorem and why it is important

DISTRIBUTION OF SAMPLE MEANS AND SAMPLING ERROR

1. Why are researchers frequently forced to work with samples when they are really interested in populations?

2. When researchers work with samples, there is always the risk of large amounts of sampling error (i.e., getting a sample that does not represent the population accurately). Why is sampling error a problem for researchers?

If a study has too much sampling error, its results can be misleading to researchers. In your last activity, you learned that increasing the sample size decreases sampling error. In this activity, you will learn *why* increasing the sample size decreases sampling error. You must understand the distribution of sample means if you hope to understand the more advanced topics presented later in this course.

A distribution of sample means is defined as all possible random sample means of a given sample size (*N*) from a particular population.

In this activity, you are going to "build" a distribution of sample means and then use it to calculate the average amount of sampling error researchers should expect to have in their study. Working with a very small population is probably the easiest way to start. Thus, you are going to work with a population of just four people. Researchers are usually interested in much larger populations, but it is much easier to illustrate what a distribution of sample means is by working with a very small population.

Suppose there is a very small population of 4 billionaires who live in a small country. Further suppose that the data below represent the number of years of college/graduate school each billionaire completed:

$$2, 4, 6, 8$$

3. What is the mean for this population? $\mu =$ _____.

4. What is the standard deviation for this population? $\sigma =$ _____.

Because there is just one of each score, the frequency distribution bar graph would be quite simple:

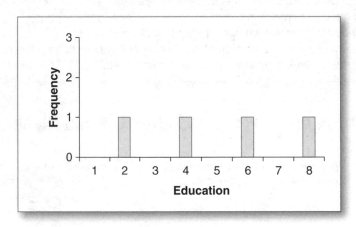

To create a distribution of sample means, we need to obtain ALL possible RANDOM samples of a given size from this population. For this example, we are going to use a sample size of $N = 2$. Because the samples must be random, we must be sure to sample with replacement. Thus, you would choose one score at random, put it back in the population, and then choose again at random.

All possible random samples with $N = 2$ are listed below. The 16 samples below are ALL of the possible combinations of two scores from the population of four billionaires.

5. Complete the following table by finding the mean for each of the 16 possible samples:

Sample	First Score	Second Score	Mean
1	2	2	2 −3 9
2	2	4	3 −2 4
3	2	6	4 −1 1
4	2	8	5 0 6
5	4	2	3 −2 4
6	4	4	4 −1 1
7	4	6	5 0 0
8	4	8	6 1 1
9	6	2	4 −1 1
10	6	4	5 0. 6
11	6	6	6 1 1
12	6	8	7 2 4
13	8	2	5 0 0
14	8	4	6 1 1
15	8	6	7 4 16
16	8	8	8 3

6. The means you computed above are ALL of the means that are possible when researchers take a sample of two scores from the population of four people. Collectively, the means are a *distribution of sample means*. Draw a frequency distribution graph of ALL THE POSSIBLE SAMPLE MEANS in the space below.

$$\rho^2 = \frac{58}{16} = 3.6$$

Mean $= 5$ $80/16 = 5$

$s = 1.89$

7. You should know that some samples represent the population better than other samples and therefore have less *sampling error* than others. Each of the above sample means that are not exactly equal to the population mean of 5 ($\mu = 5$) have *sampling error.* Which samples have the most sampling error?

8. You should also know that ALL of the above sample means are possible when the researcher randomly selects a sample from the population. Looking at the distribution of sample means, imagine that you randomly pick one sample mean from all the possible sample means. Which sample mean are you most likely to pick and why?

9. How does the graph of the distribution of sample means (the frequency distribution you created in 6 above) *differ* from the graph of the original data (the frequency distribution under 4 above)?

10. Although the graphs look very different, there is one similarity between the graphs. Which of the following is identical for the two graphs?

   a. Central tendency (i.e., mean)

   b. Spread (i.e., variability)

   c. Shape

11. Compute the mean and the standard deviation of the distribution of sample means. You should be able to use the Statistics mode on your calculator to obtain these numbers.

   a. The mean of ALL POSSIBLE sample means = ____5____.

   b. The size of each sample = ____2____.

   c. The standard deviation of ALL POSSIBLE sample means = ____1.6____.

CAUTION: When computing the standard deviation of all sample means, N is the number of sample means (i.e., 16), NOT the size of each sample (i.e., 2). Also, because you have the population of all possible sample means, you should treat the set of all possible sample means as a population.

12. How does the mean of the distribution of sample means compare with the mean of the population?

13. The standard deviation of the distribution of sample means is ~~larger~~ *Smaller* than the *population* standard deviation because ___b___.

    a. larger; sample means are *less* variable than individual scores in the population

    b. smaller; sample means are *less* variable than individual scores in the population

    c. larger; sample means are *more* variable than individual scores in the population

    d. smaller; sample means are *more* variable than individual scores in the population

14. The exact relationship between the *population* standard deviation (σ) and the standard deviation of the distribution of sample means (abbreviated SEM_p, called the standard error of the mean) is

$$SEM_p = \frac{\sigma}{\sqrt{N}} \cdot$$

$$SEM = \frac{2.24}{\sqrt{4}}$$

$$= \frac{2.24}{2} = 1.12$$

   (*Note:* N is the size of each sample, not the number of samples taken from the population.)
   Verify that this relationship is true by computing the standard deviation of the distribution of sample means (i.e., the standard error of the mean) from the population standard deviation and N. Compare this answer with the value you computed for the standard deviation of ALL sample means in 11c above.

15. The *population* standard deviation of σ = 2.24 tells us that the typical distance the individual scores are away from the population mean (μ = 5) is 2.24. What does the standard deviation of the distribution of sample means tell us? Explain how it is related to sampling error.

      ?

16. How could we make the standard error smaller?
      Increase Sample size

17. Why would we want to make the standard error smaller?
      More confidence in our sample mean estimate

CENTRAL LIMIT THEOREM

18. We are usually interested in larger populations and use larger samples than those used in this example. A population of 4 people and a sample size of 2 generated 16 possible random samples (and 16 possible sample means). Imagine how many different samples would be possible if you were interested in a large population of

100,000 scores and a large sample of 100 scores. It would be *extremely* impractical to actually build the distribution of sample means every time you conducted a study. Fortunately, the same general principles (and the formula) apply to larger data sets. Based on what you did above, describe the characteristics of all distributions of sample means. Collectively, these principles are called the **central limit theorem**. This is a really important concept.

a. The *shape* of the distribution of sample means will be _Normal_.

b. The *mean* of the distribution of sample means will be _equal_. to the population

c. The *standard deviation* of the distribution of sample means will be _____.

19. Explain how you can use the central limit theorem to compute the amount of sampling error expected in a given study.

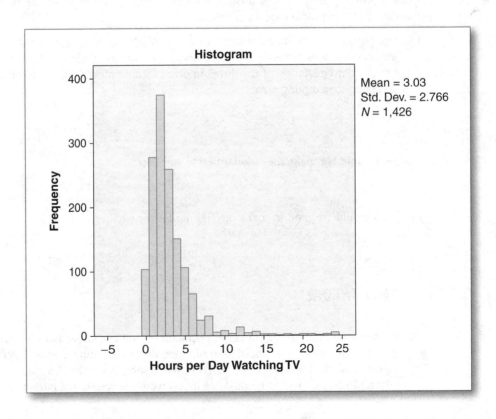

Histogram

Mean = 3.03
Std. Dev. = 2.766
N = 1,426

Hours per Day Watching TV

Frequency

20. Suppose that you took a random sample of 1,000 scores from the TV-watching population. Sketch what the frequency distribution would look like.

21. Suppose that you created a distribution of sample means from this population using a sample size of 50. Sketch what the *shape* of the frequency distribution would look like.

22. What would be the *center* of the distribution of sample means in Question 21?

23. What would be the *spread* of the distribution of sample means in Question 21 (i.e., the *SEM*)?

24. Even if a parent population's distribution is skewed, the distribution of the sample means is approximately _____ and becomes even more so as the sample size _____.

25. If a distribution of sample means has a normal shape, what does that allow you to do?

26. The *SEM* is the typical distance that all possible sample means differ from the population   mean . (two words).

Activity 4-3:   Practice Problems

1. A student took the SAT and received a score of 1,100 (verbal + math). The mean for this test is $\mu = 1020$, with a standard deviation of $\sigma = 100$. What was this student's *z* score?

2. Did this student do better, worse, or the same as the person who took the received a *z* score of 0.21?

3. A student received a *z* score of –3 on a test, with a mean of $\mu = 100$ and a standard deviation of $\sigma = 4$. What was this student's raw score (i.e., *X*)?

4. A student received a score of 85 on a test, which corresponds to a *z* score of –0.80. Given that the mean for this test was 90, what was the standard deviation of the test?

5. Which of the following is the best interpretation of a *z* score of –2?

    a. The raw score was 2 below the mean.

    b. The raw score was 2 above the mean.

    c. The raw score was 2 standard deviations below the mean.

    d. The raw score was 2 standard deviations above the mean.

The cost of living varies dramatically across the United States. For example, living in Chicago, Illinois, is much more expensive than living in Wahoo, Nebraska. If Susan was being offered a sales position in Chicago and a sales position in Wahoo, she could use *z* scores to compare the "relative salaries" being offered by the two jobs. Use the information below to determine which position was offering her a higher relative salary (i.e., how each salary compares with the mean salary in the respective cities).

6. The mean salary for sales positions in Chicago is $35,000, with a standard deviation of $3,000. Susan is being offered $37,000 to work in Chicago. The mean salary for sales positions in Wahoo is $20,000, with a standard deviation of $5,000. She is being offered $25,000 to work in Wahoo. Use *z* scores to determine which job is offering Susan the higher "relative salary."

    $$\frac{2000}{3000} = 0.66 \qquad 50 + 34\% = \text{Top } 64 \checkmark$$

    $$z = 0.66$$

7. Suppose Susan was being offered $34,000 for the Chicago job and $24,000 for the Wahoo job. Assuming the rest of the information is the same as in the previous question, which job has the higher "relative salary"?

For each of the following problems, it is a good idea to (a) sketch a normal distribution, (b) locate the z score(s) on your sketch, (c) shade the area of the curve that you are interested in, and (d) use the unit normal table to determine the precise size of the shaded area.

For the next 10 problems, determine the proportion of the normal distribution that is

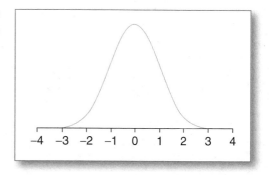

8. greater than +1.04.

9. greater than −0.80.

10. less than 1.9.

11. between−1.5 and +1.5.

12. between−1.0 and +2.2.

13. greater than −0.91.

14. greater than +1.80.

15. less than −0.95.

16. between −0.75 and +0.75.

17. between −0.5 and +1.3.

For each of the following situations, use z scores and the unit normal table (Appendix A) to gain useful information:

18. A psychology instructor wants to know the proportion of students at his university who have ACT scores at or below 20. The average ACT score at his university is 24.3, with a standard deviation of 5.2. Based on this information, what proportion of the students attending this university have ACT scores at or below 20?

19. The scholarship committee is trying to determine which of two students applying to their university will receive a $3,000 stipend. One of the criteria they are using is academic performance in high school. The problem is that the two students come from different high schools, with very different mean Grade Point Averages (GPAs). Student A has a GPA of 3.89 while attending a school with a mean GPA of 3.11 and a standard deviation of 1.01. Student B has a GPA of 3.75 while attending a school with a mean GPA of 2.75 and a standard deviation of 1.23. Use z scores to help the committee determine which of these two students exhibited better academic performance relative to their peers at their respective high schools.

NOTES

The Distribution of Sample Means and *z* for a Sample Mean

LEARNING OBJECTIVES

After reading this chapter, you should be able to do the following:

- Explain how a distribution of sample means is created
- Explain how a random sample is obtained
- Determine the mean and standard deviation of a distribution of sample means
- Explain what the standard error of the mean measures
- Explain the central limit theorem and why it is important
- Explain the law of large numbers
- Compute a *z* for a sample mean
- Use the *z* for a sample mean and a unit normal table to determine how likely a given sample mean is to occur

DISTRIBUTION OF SAMPLE MEANS

The last activity you completed introduced distributions of sample means. You learned that a distribution of sample means contains all possible random samples of a given size (*N*) drawn from a population. You also learned that the mean of the distribution of sample means is always equal to the population mean (μ), and the standard deviation of the distribution of sample means is always equal to the standard error of the mean $\left(SEM_p = \dfrac{\sigma}{\sqrt{N}} \right)$.

You were able to directly compute μ and *SEM* in the last activity because you worked with a very small population of just four scores. With such a small population of four scores, you were able to create an entire distribution of sample means with a sample size (*N*) of 2. In actual practice, researchers rarely have access to every individual in a population. Even if

111

researchers did have access to every individual in a population, it is very unlikely that they would be able to obtain all possible random samples of a given size from that population. Fortunately, it is not necessary to actually create a distribution of sample means because all distributions of sample means behave in very predictable ways. According to the central limit theorem, all distributions of sample means have three characteristics in common. A distribution of sample means will (1) approach a normal shape as the sample size (N) increases, (2) have a mean equal to the population mean (μ), and (3) have a standard deviation equal to the standard error of the mean $\left(SEM_p = \dfrac{\sigma}{\sqrt{N}} \right)$.

The amazing thing about this theorem is that it describes all distributions of sample means for populations of all shapes and sizes. Regardless of what the population distribution of scores looks like, the distribution of sample means will always have a predictable shape, mean, and standard deviation.

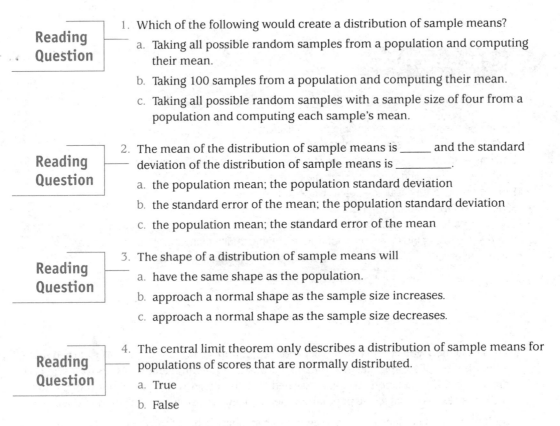

Reading Question

1. Which of the following would create a distribution of sample means?
   a. Taking all possible random samples from a population and computing their mean.
   b. Taking 100 samples from a population and computing their mean.
   c. Taking all possible random samples with a sample size of four from a population and computing each sample's mean.

Reading Question

2. The mean of the distribution of sample means is _____ and the standard deviation of the distribution of sample means is _____.
   a. the population mean; the population standard deviation
   b. the standard error of the mean; the population standard deviation
   c. the population mean; the standard error of the mean

Reading Question

3. The shape of a distribution of sample means will
   a. have the same shape as the population.
   b. approach a normal shape as the sample size increases.
   c. approach a normal shape as the sample size decreases.

Reading Question

4. The central limit theorem only describes a distribution of sample means for populations of scores that are normally distributed.
   a. True
   b. False

The central limit theorem tells us that the standard deviation of the distribution of sample means is equal to the standard error of the mean $\left(SEM_p = \dfrac{\sigma}{\sqrt{N}} \right)$. When we are working with a distribution of scores, the standard deviation tells us the typical distance each score is from the mean. Similarly, when we are working with a distribution of sample means, the standard deviation tells us the typical distance each sample mean is from the population mean. In other words, the standard error of the mean is a measure of the typical distance between all possible sample means and the population mean.

Another way to think about the standard error of the mean is that it measures the typical amount of sampling error. In Chapter 1, we defined sampling error very broadly as the discrepancy between a sample statistic and its corresponding population parameter. The standard error of the mean allows us to compute the typical deviation between all possible sample means of a given size and the population mean (μ).

Reading Question

5. The standard error of the mean (SEM_p) is the
   a. discrepancy between a single score and a sample statistic.
   b. typical discrepancy between all possible sample means of a given size and the population mean.

Reading Question

6. The typical amount of sampling error can be computed as the
   a. standard deviation of the distribution of sample means.
   b. standard error of the mean.
   c. Both of the above.

Reading Question

7. Which of the following is the best description of the standard error of the mean?
   a. The distance between a sample mean and all other possible sample means.
   b. The typical distance between all possible scores and the sample mean.
   c. The typical distance between all possible sample means of a given size and the population mean.

It should be clear that we want the standard error of the mean to be small because we want there to be as little sampling error as possible. Based on the formula $\left(SEM_p = \dfrac{\sigma}{\sqrt{N}} \right)$, you can deduce that there are two ways to reduce sampling error. One option is to reduce the population standard deviation (σ), but this option is rarely possible. You can't usually just make scores less variable. A much more feasible option is to increase the size of the sample. As N increases, the overall standard error of the mean will decrease. This means that sample means based on larger sample sizes will tend to deviate less from the population mean than sample means based on smaller sample sizes. This is a specific example of the *law of large numbers: As N increases, the sample statistic (i.e., the sample mean) is a better estimate of the population parameter (i.e., the population mean).*

Reading Question

8. Which of the following will *reduce* the standard error of the mean?
   a. Increasing N
   b. Decreasing N
   c. Both increasing and decreasing N can reduce the standard error of the mean.

9. According to the law of large numbers, as sample size increases, the sample mean tends to get closer to the population mean.

    a. True

    b. False

z FOR A SAMPLE MEAN

The central limit theorem allows us to compute the mean and standard deviation of any distribution of sample means. It also tells us that the distribution of sample means will become more normal (i.e., more bell shaped) as the sample size increases. Practically, this means that we can now compute z scores for sample means, locate those means in a distribution, and use a unit normal table to determine probabilities associated with any given sample means.

The formula for a z for a sample mean is very similar to the formula for a z for a single score. Both formulas are below.

$$z \text{ for an individual score formula: } z = \frac{X - \mu}{\sigma}$$

$$z \text{ for a sample mean formula: } z = \frac{M - \mu}{SEM_p}, \text{ where } \left(SEM_p = \frac{\sigma}{\sqrt{N}} \right)$$

For both formulas, the numerator is simply the observed difference between the score and the population mean ($X - \mu$) or the sample mean and the population mean ($M - \mu$). For both formulas, the denominator is the typical amount of variability that is expected due to sampling error. For the individual score formula, σ is the typical distance of all possible individual scores from the population mean. For the sample mean formula, the standard error of the mean (SEM_p) is the typical distance of all possible sample means of a given size from the population mean. Thus, for both formulas, the obtained z score is a ratio of the observed difference over the difference expected by sampling error. For both, a z score close to zero means that the observed deviation (i.e., the numerator) was small compared with the deviation expected by sampling error (i.e., the denominator). In other words, if the z score is "close" to zero the score (i.e., X) or the sample mean (i.e., M) was "close" to the population mean. However, a z score of 2 means that the observed deviation (i.e., the numerator) was two times as large as the deviation expected by sampling error (i.e., the denominator). In other words, if the z score is far from zero, the score (i.e., X) or the sample mean (i.e., M) was "unexpectedly far" from the population mean. Large z scores often indicate that something other than sampling error variability caused the score (i.e., X) or the sample mean (i.e., M) to be very far from the population mean.

10. When computing a z for a sample mean, if the z score is close to zero the sample mean was

    a. not very different from the population mean and the difference was probably due to sampling error.

    b. very different from the population mean and the difference was probably created by something other than sampling error.

<table>
<tr><td>

Reading Question

</td><td>

11. When computing a z for a sample mean, if the z score is far from zero the sample mean was

   a. not very different from the population mean and the difference was probably due to sampling error.

   b. very different from the population mean and the difference was probably created by something other than sampling error.

</td></tr>
</table>

COMPUTING AND INTERPRETING THE z FOR A SAMPLE MEAN: EXAMPLE

A federal investigator found evidence that loan officers at a large banking conglomerate participated in an illegal mortgage fraud scheme. As a result, 16 employees were fired. Loan officers at this bank were paid partly on commission, and so these illegal activities may have raised their income. By looking at the company records, the investigator finds that the mean income of loan officers in the company prior to the firings was $\mu = 50,000$ with a standard deviation of $\sigma = 12,000$. Furthermore, the mean income for the 16 people who were fired was $55,000. They want to know the probability of obtaining a sample mean of $55,000 or greater due to chance (i.e., sampling error). Was the fact that the fired employees' mean income was $55,000 (i.e., $5,000 higher than the company mean income) merely a coincidence (i.e., due to sampling error)?

Step 1: Compute the Observed Deviation

Find the deviation between the sample mean (M) and the population mean (μ).

$$(M - \mu) = (55,000 - 50,000) = 5,000$$

Step 2: Compute the Deviation Expected by Sampling Error

Next, compute the standard error of the mean.

$$SEM_p = \frac{\sigma}{\sqrt{N}} = \frac{12,000}{\sqrt{16}} = 3,000$$

In this case, the standard error of the mean is 3,000. This means that when $N = 16$, the typical distance that all possible sample means are from the population mean is 3,000. When the sample size is 16, this is the amount of deviation we expect between any sample mean and the population mean due to sampling error.

Step 3: Compute the Ratio Between Observed and Expected Deviation

To compute the z for a sample mean, divide the observed mean difference by the expected amount of sampling error (i.e., the standard error of the mean).

$$z = \frac{M - \mu}{SEM_p} = \frac{55,000 - 50,000}{3,000} = 1.67$$

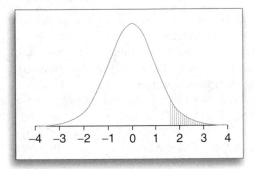

Figure 5.1 A z distribution with the target area z > 1.67 shaded.

The z of 1.67 tells us that the observed deviation was 1.67 times greater than the deviation expected by sampling error.

Step 4: Locate the z Score in the Distribution

Once you have computed the z score (i.e., 1.67), locate it on a z curve. To determine which area to shade in, you need to consider the question being asked. For this example, the federal investigator wants to know the probability of obtaining a sample of 16 people with a mean of $55,000 or higher. Therefore, we would shade in everything higher than the z score of 1.67; this is done in Figure 5.1.

Step 5: Look Up the z Score

Use the unit normal table (Appendix A) to determine the probability of obtaining a z score of 1.67 or higher due to chance. Because less than half of the distribution is shaded, we look at the TAIL column for the z of 1.67 and find .0475.

Step 6: Interpret z Score

When the sample size is 16, the probability of getting a sample mean income of $55,000 or greater is .0475. Another way of saying this is that 4.75% of all possible sample means based on 16 people have a mean equal to or greater than $55,000. It is possible that the salaries of the 16 people who were fired for illegal activities were higher than the company mean income merely due to chance or coincidence, but it is not likely. Specifically, we would only expect to obtain a random sample mean of $55,000 or higher 4.75% of the time. Therefore, the fact that the mean income of the 16 fired employees was higher than the companies mean income was unlikely to be due to chance or sampling error. Perhaps the employees' illegal activities were in some way increasing their salaries.

Reading Question

12. This example illustrates that the z for a sample mean procedure

   a. can be used to identify if the discrepancy between a sample mean and a population mean is likely or unlikely to be due to sampling error.

   b. is only useful in a controlled laboratory setting.

   c. Both a and b are correct.

EXACT PROBABILITIES VERSUS PROBABILITY ESTIMATES

The previous example illustrates that the *z* for a sample mean statistical procedure can be useful outside of controlled laboratory settings. There are many situations in which an investigator of some kind might want to know the probability that something is happening due to chance or sampling error. The central limit theorem enables us to compute the sampling error we expect. We can then compute the obtained *z* score and determine the probability of obtaining a score that extreme or more extreme due to chance. We noted previously that the central limit theorem is based on random sampling. However, researchers are rarely able to obtain truly random samples. Therefore, researchers are most often working with nonrandom samples. The result of working with nonrandom samples is that any probability statements based on nonrandom samples are *estimates* rather than exact probabilities. Thus, the probability of .0475 in the previous example is an estimate. The real probability could be a bit more or a bit less. As we matriculate through this course, try to remember that most (if not all) probability statements derived from research are *estimates*, and as a result, the actual probability might be a bit higher or a bit lower. Although researchers are usually creating probability estimates, the estimates are usually very good estimates.

Reading Question	13. The probabilities produced by most research studies are considered estimates (i.e., not exact probabilities) because

   a. most research studies do not use truly random samples.

   b. most research studies use samples that are too small.

Activity 5-1:   Central Limit Theorem

Learning Objectives

After reading the chapter and completing the homework, you should be able to do the following:

- Determine when to use the two different *z* score formulas
- Define sampling error and the standard error of the mean
- Compute and interpret the standard error of the mean
- Explain the difference between raw scores and *z* scores
- Compute and interpret the *z* score for a sample mean

DESCRIBING SAMPLING ERROR

1. In words, sampling error is the difference between a _____ and a _____?

2. In words, what is the standard error of the mean? (Your answer should include a description of what a distribution of sample means is.)

3. What is the relationship between sampling error and the standard error of the mean?

COMPUTING SAMPLING ERROR

The next several questions are working with body temperature data in which the population mean (μ) is 98.2 and the population standard deviation (σ) is 0.6.

Compute the standard error of the mean for each of the following situations and use it to help you complete the x-axes below. The standard error of the mean is equal to the standard deviation divided by the square root of N. Therefore, when $N = 9$, the standard error of the mean is 0.2 $\left(SEM_p = \dfrac{\sigma}{\sqrt{N}} = \dfrac{.6}{\sqrt{9}} = 0.2 \right)$. Thus, the standard deviation of the distribution of sample means is 0.2. You should also complete the number lines by filling in any values missing from the x-axes. The first one is started for you.

Each raw score can also be converted into z scores. For example, a sample mean of 98.4 can be converted into a z by using the z for a sample mean formula $z = \dfrac{M - \mu}{SEM_p} = \dfrac{98.4 - 98.2}{.2} = 1$. You should also complete the number lines by filling in any missing z scores.

4. Distribution of sample means when sample size (N) is 9 people: $\mu = 98.2$, $\sigma = 0.6$, $N = 9$.

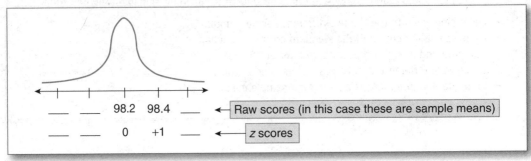

5. Distribution of sample means when sample size (N) is 36 people: μ = 98.2, σ = .6, N = 36.

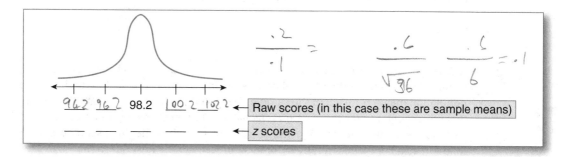

$$\frac{.2}{.1} = \qquad \frac{.6}{\sqrt{36}} \qquad \frac{.6}{6} = .1$$

962 962 98.2 |00 2 102 2 ← Raw scores (in this case these are sample means)

____ ____ ____ ____ ____ ← z scores

6. Distribution of sample means when sample size (N) is 100 people: μ = 98.2, σ = 0.6, N = 100.

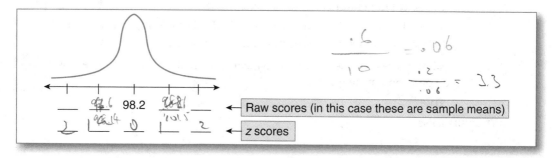

$$\frac{.6}{10} = .06 \qquad \frac{.2}{.06} = 3.3$$

____ 98.6 98.2 98.81 ____ ← Raw scores (in this case these are sample means)

2 9814 0 101.5 2 ← z scores

7. Each of the examples above come from the same population with μ = 98.2 and σ = 0.6. Because of the way we have drawn the graphs, the distributions may look similar. However, there is one important difference between these three graphs that is created by the different sample sizes. If you look at the range of possible sample means on the axes of the graphs, you will notice that they are dramatically different. Which of the following best summarizes the differences between the graphs?

   a. When the sample size is larger, the standard error is smaller.

   b. When the sample size is larger, the standard error is larger.

8. If all of the graphs above were created using the same range of values on the x-axis (e.g., 93–102), which sample size would produce the most "spread out" distribution of sample means. In other words, which sample size produces the most sampling error?

9

9. What is the probability of obtaining a *z* for a sample mean between −1 and +1? Note that this answer will be the same regardless of sample size. (Use the unit normal table, Appendix A, to answer this question.)

68.27.

10. A different sample size was used in each of the examples above. The size of the sample directly affects the probability of obtaining a sample mean close to the population mean. For each of the sample sizes listed below, write the sample means that correspond to *z* scores of −1 (*first blank*) and +1 (*second blank*). Refer back to Questions 4, 5, and 6 to do this. After you complete each of the three sentences that follow, read all of them carefully before you proceed to the next question.

   a. When the sample size is 9, 68.26 % of all possible sample means are between the body temperatures of _____ and _____.

   b. When the sample size is 36, 68.26 % of all possible sample means are between the body temperatures of __98.2__ and __100.2__.

   c. When the sample size is 100, 68.26 % of all possible sample means are between the body temperatures of _____ and __101.5__.

11. As sample size increases, the sample mean you are likely to get will be closer to the population mean (μ).

   a. True

   b. False

DETERMINING THE PROBABILITY OF A GIVEN SAMPLE

12. Researchers take a sample of 27 toddlers who were all born prematurely and score them on visual acuity. They want to know how this sample compares with the mean visual acuity score of the population of toddlers who were carried to full term: $\mu = 45$, $\sigma = 6$, $N = 27$, $M = 44$. What is the probability of obtaining a sample mean of 44 or lower? Is this sample mean likely or unlikely *to have come from the target population of full-term toddlers*?

$$\frac{45-44}{6} = \frac{1}{6} \qquad \frac{6}{\sqrt{44}} = 0.91 \qquad \frac{1}{0.9} = 1.09 \qquad = 16.1.$$

13. Researchers take a sample of 100 adult males from northwest Indiana and measure their cholesterol. They want to know how this sample compares with the national average cholesterol score for adult males: $\mu = 208$, $\sigma = 15$, $N = 100$, $M = 205$. What is the probability of obtaining a sample mean of 205 or lower? Is this sample mean likely or unlikely *to have come from the target population*?

14. An exercise instructor takes a sample of 105 middle school students all of whom are participants in a team sport and measure each student's "athletic aptitude." They want to know if this sample's "athletic aptitude" is different from the national average athletic aptitude for middle school students: $\mu = 1{,}003$, $\sigma = 25$, $N = 105$, $M = 1004.5$. What is the probability of obtaining a sample mean of 1004.5 or higher? Is this sample mean likely or unlikely *to have come from the target population*?

15. Explain why the probabilities you computed in the examples above are estimates rather than precise values.

PICKING THE CORRECT STATISTIC

For each of the following problems, choose if a researcher should use a *z* for an individual score or a *z* for a sample mean. Just choose which statistic is appropriate. Do not compute the *z* yet.

16. A school psychologist wants to identify students who may need extra help in their math course and so gives the students a standardized math test. The scores are normally distributed and have a mean of 500 and a standard deviation of 100. Students who score below 400 are given additional tutoring. What percentage of students would you expect to receive scores at or below 400? Choose the correct statistic.

    a. *z* for an individual score   b. *z* for a sample mean

17. A car seat manufacturer develops a seat that is safest for people who are between 62 inches and 68.5 inches. If the average height of women in the United States is 64 inches with a standard deviation of 2 inches, what percentage of women fall outside of the safest range? Choose the correct statistic.

    a. *z* for an individual score   b. *z* for a sample mean

18. A researcher knows that poverty is often associated with poor nutrition. The researcher wants to determine if poverty is also related to height. To test this association, he obtains a sample of 25 women who have incomes below the

poverty line. Assuming that the average height of women is 64 inches with a standard deviation of 2 inches, what is the probability that sampling error would result in obtaining a sample mean that is below 63 inches for a sample of 25 women? Choose the correct statistic.

a. *z* for an individual score   b. *z* for a sample mean

19. The average worker in a manufacturing plant produces 27 units every hour with a standard deviation of 2.9. The manager of the plant took a sample of 25 workers and gave them special training designed to increase their productivity. After the special training was complete, the 25 workers produced 28.2 units every hour. What is the probability of randomly sampling 25 workers from the general population and their mean productivity being 28.2 or higher? Choose the correct statistic.

a. *z* for an individual score   b. *z* for a sample mean

20. The manager of the manufacturing plant is responsible for distributing bonuses based on each worker's productivity. The mean productivity for all workers in the plant is 27 units per hour with a standard deviation of 2.9. The manager wants to give every worker in the top third a $200 bonus and every worker in the middle third a $100 bonus. The workers in the bottom third will get no bonus. What is the number of units produced per hour that separates those in the top third from those in the middle third? What is the number of units produced per hour that separates those in the middle third from those in the bottom third? Choose the correct statistic.

a. *z* for an individual score   b. *z* for a sample mean

21. Once you are sure that you have chosen the correct statistic, do the computations for Questions 16–20.

22. After you complete the computations for each problem, try to write a problem that would require researchers to use a *z* for an individual score and a different problem that would require researchers to use a *z* for a sample mean.

Activity 5-2:   Practice Problems

SCENARIO 1: z FOR A SAMPLE MEAN AND SAMPLING ERROR

The scores on a shyness questionnaire are normally distributed with a mean of 100 and a standard deviation of 15. A researcher asks a sample of 25 college students to complete the shyness questionnaire. What percentage of all possible sample means of this sample size have a mean greater than 103?

1. What is the observed deviation between the sample mean and the population mean (i.e., $M - \mu$)?

2. What is the deviation expected due to sampling error $\left(i.e., SEM_p = \dfrac{\sigma}{\sqrt{N}} \right)$?

3. What is the ratio between the observed deviation and the deviation expected due to sampling error $\left(i.e.,\ \text{what is the } z \text{ for the sample mean, } z = \dfrac{M - \mu}{SEM_p} \right)$?

4. Sketch a normal distribution and locate the z score in the distribution. Is this sample mean in the right or left half of the distribution?

5. What percentage of all possible sample means of this sample size have a mean greater than 103 (i.e., what is the probability of getting this z score or a larger z score due to sampling error)?

6. Why is the percentage in the previous question an estimate rather than an exact percentage?

7. Suppose that a different researcher did a study using the same population but had a sample size of 60. Would this study have more or less sampling error than the original study with $N = 25$? Explain your reasoning.

SCENARIO 2: z FOR A SAMPLE MEAN AND SAMPLING ERROR

The scores on a shyness questionnaire are normally distributed with a mean of 100 and a standard deviation of 15. This time a researcher asks a random sample of 100 college students (rather than 25 students as in the previous example) to complete the questionnaire. What percentage of all possible sample means *of this size* are greater than 103?

8. Compute the z for the sample mean, $z = \dfrac{M - \mu}{SEM_p}$.

9. Is the z score for this sample mean in the right half or left half of the distribution?

10. What percentage of ALL POSSIBLE sample means *of this sample size* (i.e., $N = 100$) have a mean greater than 103 (i.e., what is the probability of getting this z score or a more extreme z score due to sampling error)?

11. The z score associated with the sample mean of 103 (when the sample size was 100) was

    a. very likely to have occurred due to sampling error.

    b. pretty unlikely to have occurred due to sampling error.

12. What effect did increasing the sample size from 25 to 100 have? (Compare the results from Scenario 1 and Scenario 2.)

    a. It decreased the sampling error and therefore increased the z score.

    b. It increased the sampling error and therefore decreased the z score.

SCENARIO 3: CENTRAL LIMIT THEOREM

Two different psychologists were each studying trust by using a scale designed to assess how much individuals trust other people. This particular scale is positively skewed with a mean of $\mu = 65$ with a standard deviation of $\sigma = 11$. Researcher A obtained scores from a sample of 40 participants while Researcher B obtained scores from a sample of 138 participants.

13. According to the central limit theorem, what is the mean of the distribution of sample means for Researcher A and Researcher B, respectively?

14. According to the central limit theorem, what is the standard deviation of the distribution of sample means for Researcher A and Researcher B, respectively?

15. According to the central limit theorem, will the distribution of sample means for Research A be normal or positively skewed? What about for Researcher B?

16. Which researcher is more likely to obtain a sample mean that is closer to the population mean? Explain your reasoning.

NOTES

Hypothesis Testing With z Scores

INTRODUCTION TO HYPOTHESIS TESTING

In the previous chapter, you learned to compute a *z* for a sample mean and to locate a particular sample mean within a distribution of sample means. At this point, you may be wondering why you would ever want to do that. The short answer is that being able to determine how likely you are to obtain a particular sample mean from a population will allow you to test hypotheses.

For example, suppose that a teacher reads a study reporting that frequent testing helps improve recall of information and so she redesigns her history course such that students are required to take frequent quizzes (two quizzes per chapter) prior to taking exams. After one semester, using this new approach, the mean score on the final exam for the 25 students in her course was $M = 80$. This same teacher is extremely organized and knows that the mean score on this same final exam for *all* students who took the course with her before she required frequent quizzing was 75 points with a standard deviation of 10 points ($\mu = 75$, $\sigma = 10$).

The teacher has every reason to believe that the 25 students in the new history course are similar to all the students she has taught in the past. So, logically, all the past students are considered a population and the 25 new students are considered to be a sample. Although these 25 new students were not literally taken from the past population, it is reasonable to expect them to score similarly to all previous students who have taken this same exam. Therefore, you can determine if frequent quizzing is associated with better test scores by comparing the mean test score for the 25 new students who take frequent quizzes to the mean test score for all students who took the exam without taking frequent quizzes.

Obviously, the sample mean of 80 is *numerically* greater than the population mean of 75. The teacher's question is whether the deviation between the sample mean of 80 and the population mean of 75 is likely or unlikely to have occurred due to sampling error. You can use the z for a sample mean procedure you learned in the previous chapter to determine if the 5-point difference between the sample mean and the population mean is likely to be due to sampling error or if the 5-point difference is likely to have been created by the new frequent quizzing process. The computations are exactly the same as what you did in the previous chapter. However, there are quite a few concepts that we need to introduce in order to evaluate hypotheses. These new concepts are described below in a series of steps required for hypothesis testing.

HYPOTHESIS TESTING WITH z FOR A SAMPLE MEAN (ONE-TAILED)

A teacher suspects that frequent quizzing before taking a test will *improve* test scores. For the population of students who have taken the test without frequent quizzes, the population mean is $\mu = 75$, and the standard deviation is $\sigma = 10$. A sample of 25 students takes frequent quizzes on the material before taking the final, and they have a mean score of $M = 80$. Is it likely that the difference between the population mean of 75 and the sample mean of 80 is due to sampling error or is it likely that frequent quizzing actually improves test scores?

Step 1: State the Null and Research Hypotheses Symbolically and Verbally

The first step in hypothesis testing is to set up the null and research hypotheses. In this example, the teacher predicts that frequent quizzing will *increase* test scores. Thus, her research hypothesis states that the students who take frequent quizzes will have a higher mean than the population of students who do not take frequent quizzes prior to the final. The formal symbolic representation of her research hypothesis in terms of population parameters is $\mu_{quiz} > 75$.

The research hypothesis predicts that frequent quizzing will increase final exam scores. It is possible, however, that the quizzing will *not* increase exam performance. This second possibility is called the null hypothesis, and it is always the *opposite of the research hypothesis*. In this case, the null hypothesis is that frequent quizzing will either have no effect on final exam scores or it will decrease them. The formal symbolic representation of the null hypothesis is $\mu_{quiz} \leq 75$. Note that the null hypothesis includes the equal sign while the research hypothesis does not.

You should recognize that the null and research hypotheses are opposites and, therefore, mutually exclusive. They collectively encompass all possible outcomes. Only one of these hypotheses can be correct. The entire point of doing the significance test is to determine which of these two hypotheses is most likely to be true. The symbolic and verbal representations of both hypotheses are presented in Table 6.1.

Table 6.1 Symbolic and verbal representations of the null and research hypotheses for the *z* for a sample mean.

Hypothesis Type	Symbolic	Verbal
Research hypothesis	$\mu_{quiz} > 75$	Frequent quizzing *does* increase test scores.
Null hypothesis	$\mu_{quiz} \leq 75$	Frequent quizzing *does not* increase test scores.

Reading Question

1. The research hypothesis states that
   a. frequent quizzes will increase final exam scores.
   b. frequent quizzes will either have no effect on final exam scores or will decrease them.

Reading Question

2. The null hypothesis states that
   a. frequent quizzes will increase final exam scores or will decrease them.
   b. frequent quizzes will either have no effect on final exam scores or will decrease them.

Reading Question

3. The fact that the null and research hypotheses are mutually exclusive means that
   a. if the null is true, the research hypothesis must also be true.
   b. if the null is true, the research hypothesis can be true or false.
   c. if the null is true, the research hypothesis must be false.

Some students find the symbolic notation of the null and research hypotheses a bit confusing because we are trying to determine whether or not $\mu_{quiz} > 75$, and we already know that $M = 80$ and $\mu = 75$, based on the information given in the problem. However, it is important to note the subscript in $\mu_{quiz} > 75$. The subscript "quiz" refers to those who take frequent quizzes before completing the final exam. We do NOT know what the mean test score would be if the entire population of students took quizzes before the test (i.e., we don't know μ_{quiz}). We know that the population mean is 75 when students take the test WITHOUT previously taking quizzes. The research question is whether taking frequent quizzes would create a population mean that is greater than 75.

Therefore, the research hypothesis is predicting that if there were a population of students who took the final exam after taking frequent quizzes on the material, their population test mean (μ_{quiz}) would be greater than 75 (i.e., the mean of those who did not take frequent quizzes before the final exam). In contrast, the null hypothesis is predicting that if there were a population of students who took the final exam after frequent quizzing, their population test mean (μ_{quiz}) would be equal to or less than 75 (i.e., the mean of those who did not take frequent quizzes before taking the final).

Reading Question

4. In this research situation, μ_{quiz} represents

    a. the population's mean test score.

    b. what the population's mean test score would be if all students took quizzes before taking the test.

Step 2: Define the Critical Region

The second new concept in the hypothesis testing process is the critical region. To understand the critical region, we need to return to the distribution of sample means.

Figure 6.1 is the distribution of sample means for all samples of size $N = 25$ taken from the population of students who took the final exam without completing frequent quizzes. The central limit theorem tells us that the mean of this distribution is 75, and the standard error of the mean is 2 $\left(SEM = \dfrac{\sigma}{\sqrt{N}} = \dfrac{10}{\sqrt{25}} = 2 \right)$. Thus, the distribution is labeled with a mean of 75 and a standard deviation of 2. Ultimately, we will be working with z scores, and so we have also converted each of the possible sample mean values on the x-axis into z scores using the z for a sample mean formula $\left(e.g., z = \dfrac{M - \mu}{SEM} = \dfrac{77 - 75}{2} = 1 \right)$.

Figure 6.1	A distribution of sample means with a z number line *(top)* and a sample mean number line *(bottom)*.

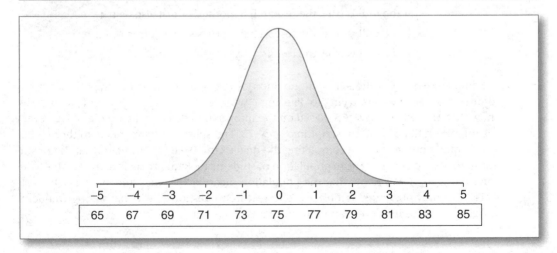

If frequent quizzing has no effect on performance, you would expect a *z* score of 0 because *M* and μ would be expected to be identical (i.e., they would both be expected to be 75). Therefore, the numerator of the *z* formula would be $M - \mu = 0$. But, even if the null hypothesis were true, the numerator of the *z* formula may not be exactly 0 because there is likely to be some sampling error. For example, because of sampling error, you wouldn't be surprised to get a *z* score of 0.2, even if quizzing has no effect on performance. You would, however, be surprised to get a *z* score of 2.9 if quizzing has no effect on performance.

Figure 6.1 is shaded to indicate the *z* scores that are unlikely if the **null** hypothesis is true. The lighter the shading, the more likely it is that the deviation between the sample and population means is due to sampling error. The further the *z* score is from zero, the more likely it is that frequent quizzing had an effect on test scores.

Reading Question

5. If the null hypothesis is true, you should expect a *z* score that is close to

   a. 0.

   b. 1.

   c. −1.

   d. 2.9.

Reading Question

6. Even if the null hypothesis is true, you should not be surprised if the *z* score resulting from a significance test is not the exact value you selected above because of _____ .

   a. a nonspecific research hypothesis

   b. sampling error

Reading Question

7. If the null hypothesis is true, *z* scores close to zero are _____ .

   a. likely

   b. unlikely

Figure 6.1 gives you a general idea of how likely particular *z* scores are if the null hypothesis is true. You can also use the unit normal table (Appendix A) to determine how likely a particular *z* score is to occur. For example, the probability of obtaining a sample mean with a *z* score of 1 or higher is .1587 (i.e., the tail area of $z = 1$) if the null hypothesis is true. The probability of obtaining a sample mean with a *z* score of 2.5 or higher is .0062 if the null hypothesis is true. Clearly, a *z* score of 2.5 is less likely than a *z* score of 1. However, we need to decide on a cutoff that will tell us how to distinguish between likely and unlikely *z* scores. The most commonly used cutoff is .05. Thus, *z scores with probabilities of .05 or lower are considered unlikely to occur if the null hypothesis is true.* Extremely low *z* scores are likely to be due to something other than sampling error (e.g., frequent quizzing improving test scores). Any *z* scores with probabilities higher than .05 are considered likely to occur if the null hypothesis is true and are likely to be due to sampling error.

It is important to remember that you could obtain a *z* score with a probability less than the .05 cutoff simply due to sampling error. In fact, *if the null were true*, you would have a 5% chance of getting an extreme *z* score, which would lead you to incorrectly conclude

that the frequent quizzing improved test scores. When you decide to use .05 as a cutoff *and the null hypothesis is actually true*, there is a 5% chance that you are going to get an extreme z score simply due to sampling error.

Reading Question

8. If you look up a z score of 2.2 in the unit normal table, you will find that the probability of obtaining a z score of 2.2 or higher if the null hypothesis is true is .0139. Is this a likely or unlikely outcome if we use a cutoff of .05?

   a. Likely

   b. Unlikely

Reading Question

9. If a researcher obtains a z score of 2.2, you can be absolutely confident that the observed difference between the sample mean and the population is not due to sampling error.

   a. True

   b. False

The *.05 value we are using as a cutoff for likely and unlikely sample means* is referred to as an **alpha (α) level**. The .05 probability cutoff can also be converted into a z score cutoff by using the unit normal table; this has been done in Figure 6.2. If you look in the tail column of the unit normal table for .05, you will see that it corresponds to a z score of 1.65 (it is actually between 1.64 and 1.65 and so we rounded up to obtain a more conservative value). This z score cutoff of 1.65 is known as the **critical value**. z Scores that are equal to or more extreme (i.e., further into the tail of the distribution) than the critical value (1.65) are considered unlikely to occur if the null hypothesis is true. In contrast, z scores that are closer to zero than the critical value (1.65) are considered more likely to occur if the null hypothesis is true.

It is important to note that the research hypothesis for the frequent quizzing example predicts that scores will be more extreme when using frequent quizzing than when not using frequent quizzing. Because we expect the sample mean to be greater than the population mean, we expect the z score to be positive. However, if we predict that the sample mean will be less than the population mean, we expect the obtained z score to be negative.

Figure 6.2   The critical value that defines the critical region when the alpha value is .05.

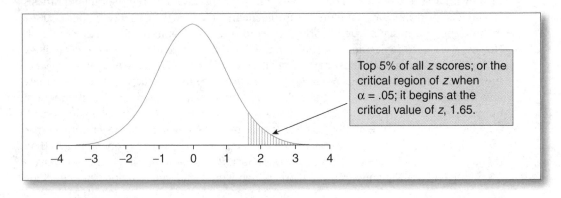

Top 5% of all z scores; or the critical region of z when α = .05; it begins at the critical value of z, 1.65.

Therefore, the critical region would be on the negative tail of the above distribution of sample means and obtained *z* scores less than or equal to − 1.65 are considered unlikely.

Reading Question

10. When the researcher hypothesizes that the sample mean will be lower than the population mean, the critical region will be on the _____ side of the distribution because they are expecting that the obtained *z* score will be _____.

    a. positive; positive

    b. negative; positive

    c. negative; negative

Reading Question

11. The alpha (α) level determines the location of the

    a. *z* score.

    b. *z* score cutoff that starts the critical region (i.e., the critical value of *z*).

The critical value separates the distribution into two regions: (1) *z* scores that are likely to occur if the null hypothesis is true and (2) *z* scores that are unlikely to occur if the null hypothesis is true. For this example, *z* scores that are greater than 1.65 are unlikely to occur if the null hypothesis is true. Thus, if you obtain a *z* score that is in this critical region (i.e., greater than 1.65) you will reject the null hypothesis. This critical region is also called the "region of rejection" because if the *z* score is in the critical region, you should reject the null hypothesis. If the *z* score is not in the critical region, you will fail to reject the null hypothesis. We will talk more about this decision in Step 4 below.

Reading Question

12. The critical value defines the "decision point" for

    a. determining if the null hypothesis should be rejected or not.

    b. determining if the research hypothesis should be rejected or not.

Reading Question

13. If the obtained *z* score is in the critical region you will

    a. reject the null hypothesis.

    b. fail to reject the null hypothesis.

Reading Question

14. If the obtained *z* score is NOT in the critical region you will

    a. reject the null hypothesis.

    b. fail to reject the null hypothesis.

Step 3: Compute the Test Statistic

Step 3a: Compute the Observed Deviation Between the Sample Mean and the Population Mean

Find the deviation between the sample mean and the population mean.

$$(M - \mu) = (80 - 75) = 5$$

Step 3b: Compute the Deviation Expected Due to Sampling Error

Compute the expected amount of sampling error given the sample size.

$$SEM_p = \frac{\sigma}{\sqrt{N}} = \frac{10}{\sqrt{25}} = 2$$

In this case, the standard error of the mean is 2. This means that when $N = 25$, the typical distance that all possible sample means are from the population mean is 2. This is the amount of deviation we expect between any sample mean and the population mean due to sampling error (i.e., the difference expected by chance).

Step 3c: Compute the z for a Sample Mean

Compute the obtained z score associated with the obtained sample mean.

$$z = \frac{M - \mu}{SEM_p} = \frac{80 - 75}{2} = 2.5$$

The obtained z score value associated with the sample mean of 80 is 2.5. Because the obtained z score of 2.5 is more extreme than the critical value of 1.65, this z score is located in the region of rejection (i.e., the critical region). As a result, the researchers can conclude that the z score of 2.5 is unlikely to be due to sampling error and that the unexpectedly high z score results from frequent quizzing *improving* test scores. To review the logic of this significance test again briefly, the obtained z score should have been close to 0 if the null was true. The z score was not close to 0 (close being defined as closer to 0 than the critical region starting at $+1.65$), and so the null hypothesis is probably false. Therefore, the researchers conclude that the research hypothesis is probably true. In other words, they conclude that frequent quizzing *improved* test scores because the z score was in the critical region.

Reading Question

15. If a z score is in the critical region, the null hypothesis is probably _____ and the research hypothesis is probably _____.

   a. false; true
   b. true; false

Reading Question

16. If a z score is beyond a critical value (further into the tail of the distribution), the researcher should

   a. fail to reject the null hypothesis.
   b. reject the null hypothesis.

Step 4: Compute an Effect Size, and Describe It

The purpose of significance testing is to decide whether the difference between a sample mean and a population mean can be attributed to a treatment effect or if it is due to sampling error. If the null hypothesis is rejected, the researcher is saying that the observed difference is most likely due to a treatment effect and not sampling error. A related but different topic is the size of the difference between the sample mean and the population mean. For example, the researcher in this example concluded that frequent quizzing does improve test scores but *how much* did frequent quizzing improve test scores? This question cannot be answered with significance testing. Rather this question requires another statistic called an effect size.

Effect size is an index of the size of the difference between the sample mean and the population mean. In this case, the effect size indicates how large the difference is between the mean for the sample that took frequent quizzes compared with the mean for the population that did not take frequent quizzes. The effect size statistic typically used when comparing two means is Cohen's *d*. The numerator for the *d* is the same as the *z* for a sample mean (i.e., the difference between the means). The denominator, however, is different. When computing the *z* for a sample mean, you divide the deviation between the sample mean and the population mean by the standard error of the mean (i.e., typical sampling error). When computing Cohen's *d*, you divide the deviation by the population standard deviation. The computations for this problem are shown below.

$$\text{Cohen's } d = \frac{Observed\ deviation\ between\ the\ means}{Standard\ deviation} = \frac{M - \mu}{\sigma} = \frac{80 - 75}{10} = 0.50$$

By computing *d*, researchers can describe the relative size of the deviation between the sample mean and the population mean. A *d* = .5 means that the sample mean was a half of a standard deviation higher than the population mean. Interpreting *d* is a bit more complicated. Is a *d* = .5 good? The best way to interpret any effect size is comparing it with the effect sizes produced by similar studies in the research literature. For example, if most studies investigating ways to improve science test scores in the literature report effect sizes of *d* = .25 and your study had a *d* = .5 you should be pretty excited because your effect size is double of that frequently reported in the literature. Relative to other similar studies, your study created an impressively larger effect. However, it is not always possible to compare your effect size with that reported in the literature. If you can't find similar studies in the literature to provide a reference, it is helpful to have general guidelines for interpreting effect sizes. Table 6.2 contains the general guidelines suggested by Cohen *when you don't have a research context*:

Table 6.2	General guidelines for interpreting Cohen's *d*.
d	*Estimated Size of the Effect*
Close to .2	Small
Close to .5	Medium
Close to .8	Large

Cohen's *d* values close to .2 are small, those close to .5 are medium, and those close to .8 are large. This means that a *d* of .35 is a "small-medium effect." Again, these general guidelines are intended to aid interpretation when a larger context is not provided by studies in the relevant research literature.

In the present example, we do not have similar studies to provide specific guidelines for interpreting our *d* of .50. Therefore, we use general guidelines and conclude that the size of the difference between the quiz and no quiz means was medium. As stated above, *d* of .50 indicates that the mean for those who took frequent quizzes is .50 standard deviations above the mean for the population, which did not take frequent quizzes.

Reading Question

17. An effect size of *d* = .35 is

   a. small.

   b. small-medium.

   c. medium.

   d. medium-large.

   e. large.

Reading Question

18. An effect size of .3 indicates that the sample and population means were different by

   a. .3 of a standard deviation.

   b. .3%.

In this example, we rejected the null hypothesis and found that the size of the effect frequent quizzing had on the test scores was medium. We will address the important differences between significance testing and effect size in an activity. One very important difference between the two statistical concepts is that significance testing is heavily influenced by sample size and effect size is not.

Step 5: Interpret the Results of the Hypothesis Test

For the rest of the semester, you will be computing statistical tests, interpreting the results, and then writing summary statements about the results of the tests. These summary statements need to be in a very specific format. The following is a summary statement about the above statistical test.

The exam scores of students who took frequent quizzes over the material ($M = 80$) were significantly higher than the scores of those who did not take frequent quizzes ($\mu = 75$), $z = 2.50, p < .05, d = .50$.

In this case, we would write "$p < .05$" because the null hypothesis was rejected using an alpha value of .05. If you fail to reject the null hypothesis, we would write "$p > .05$."

ERRORS IN HYPOTHESIS TESTING

Whenever you make a decision regarding a null hypothesis, there is a chance that you made an error. More specifically, there are two types of errors that statisticians have labeled Type I and Type II. For both types of errors, the decision made about the null was wrong. Specifically, a Type I error occurs *when you incorrectly reject the null*. Therefore, a Type I error can only occur when you reject the null. A Type II error occurs *when you incorrectly fail to reject the null*. Therefore, a Type II error can only occur when you fail to reject the null.

Reading Question

19. If you reject the null, there is some probability that you have made a

    a. Type I error.

    b. Type II error.

Reading Question

20. If you fail to reject the null, there is some probability that you have made a

    a. Type I error.

    b. Type II error.

Of course, your decision about the null might be correct. In hypothesis testing, there are two types of correct decisions. Researchers can either correctly reject the null or correctly fail to reject the null. A study that has a high probability of *correctly rejecting the null* is said to have high statistical power.

Reading Question

21. Statistical power refers to

    a. correctly rejecting the null.

    b. correctly failing to reject the null.

Table 6.3 may help you understand the relationship between specific decisions regarding the null hypothesis and the occurrence of Type I errors, Type II errors, and statistical power.

Unfortunately, you can never be certain if you made a correct or an incorrect decision. After all, if you knew the "True State" of the null, there would be no need to conduct a hypothesis test. However, we can estimate the probability that we made a Type I or Type II error. Additionally, researchers frequently compute the probability that they correctly rejected the null (i.e., statistical power) because doing so, among other things, helps them assess the quality of their study. A study with low statistical power (i.e., a value far below .80) is deemed less reliable by researchers. We will discuss the interrelationships among Type I error, Type II error, and statistical power in this chapter's activities. For right now, your goal is simply to know the definitions of these terms.

Reading Question

22. Once you have failed to reject the null, you can be certain that a Type II error occurred.

    a. True

    b. False

Table 6.3   Situations defining Type I error, Type II error, and statistical power.

		True State of Null	
		Null Is False	Null Is True
Statistical decision	Reject null	Correct decision; statistical power	Type I error
	Fail to reject null	Type II error	Correct decision

An example may help you think about these terms. A researcher conducted a study evaluating the impact of frequent quizzing on students' grades. Because the researcher rejected the null we know that there is some probability that he made a Type I error. In other words, he concluded that quizzing worked, but it is possible that quizzing really did not improve exam scores and instead the result was due to sampling error. There is also some probability that he correctly rejected the null (i.e., statistical power). There is *zero* probability that he made a Type II error because you must fail to reject null in order to make a Type II error.

The language of hypothesis testing can be a bit tricky because of double negatives (e.g., "fail to reject the null"). We will explain why the double negative language is necessary in the next chapter. Table 6.4 summarizes a variety of correct ways to describe Type I error, Type II error, and statistical power.

Table 6.4   Various correct ways of describing Type I error, Type II error, and statistical power.

Statistical Term	Way of Describing #1	Way of Describing #2	Way of Describing #3
Type I error	Rejecting the null when you should not reject it	Saying the treatment works when it does not work	Rejecting a true null
Type II error	Failing to reject the null when you should reject it	Saying the treatment does not work when it does work	Not rejecting a false null
Statistical power	Rejecting the null when you should reject it	Saying the treatment works when it does work	Rejecting a false null

Reading Question

23. If a researcher concludes that a treatment did not work, but it really did work, what type of error did she make?

   a. Type I
   b. Type II

Reading Question

24. Rejecting a false null hypothesis is called

   a. Type I error.
   b. Type II error.
   c. statistical power.

Reading
Question

25. Concluding that a treatment does not work when it does work is called

    a. Type I error.

    b. Type II error.

    c. statistical power.

Reading
Question

26. Rejecting the null hypothesis when you should not reject it is called

    a. Type I error.

    b. Type II error.

    c. statistical power.

Activity 6-1:   Hypothesis Testing

Learning Objectives

After reading the chapter and completing this activity, you should be able to do the following:

- Write null and research hypotheses using population parameters or words
- Create a distribution of sample means assuming the null hypothesis is true and assuming the research hypothesis is true
- Explain why the null hypothesis is necessary
- Define a critical region and use it to identify "likely" and "unlikely" sample means assuming the null hypothesis is true
- Compute a *z* for a sample mean and determine if you should reject or fail to reject the null hypothesis
- Compute and interpret an effect size (*d*)
- Define statistical power, Type I error, and Type II error and locate them on a graph of the sampling distributions for the null and research hypotheses
- Determine if a given study had sufficient statistical power
- Explain why a larger sample size is usually preferable to a smaller sample size
- Distinguish between significance testing, effect size, and the practical usefulness of a treatment

HYPOTHESIS TESTING (SIGNIFICANCE TESTING) EXAMPLE

Researchers want to increase the science test scores of high school students. Based on tremendous amounts of previous research on science education using a national science test, researchers know that the mean science test score for ALL senior high school students in the United States is 50 with a standard deviation of 20. In other words, *50 and 20 are the known population parameters for the mean and the standard deviation, respectively* (i.e., $\mu = 50$, $\sigma = 20$). In the following scenario, the researchers take a sample of high school seniors, tutor them for 2 months, and then give them the national science test to determine if the test scores of those who had the tutoring were higher than the national average science test score of 50 (i.e., $\mu = 50$). After the tutoring, the mean test score of the sample was $M = 58$. The researchers want to determine if the difference between the sample's mean of 58 and the population mean of 50 is likely to be due to sampling error or if the tutoring improved the sample's science test score.

Because the researchers are only interested in adopting the tutoring if it *increases* science test scores, they will be using a one-tailed hypothesis test. They also chose to use a .05 alpha value (i.e., $\alpha = .05$).

Understanding the Null and Research Hypotheses

1. State the null and research hypotheses using symbolic notation.

   Null hypothesis (H_0):

   Research hypothesis (H_1):

2. State the null and research hypotheses in words.

   Null hypothesis (H_0):

   Research hypothesis (H_1):

3. Each of the above hypotheses makes an explicit statement about the entire *population* of senior students after tutoring. Of course, only a sample of the population actually received tutoring. Researchers use the sample to infer what the entire population *would be like* if it had received tutoring. What is it called when researchers use a sample to represent a population and infer that the sample results represent what the population *would be like* if the entire population was treated like the sample was treated? Choose from the options provided below:

   (a) Descriptive statistics   (b) Inferential statistics

   (c) Sample statistics   (d) Population statistics

4. Whenever researchers use a sample to represent a population, the researcher's sample probably does not represent the population *perfectly*. Which of the following is created when a sample does not represent the population perfectly?

   (a) Statistical error   (b) Parameter error

   (c) Inferential error   (d) Sampling error

   (e) Research error   (f) Population error

5. **Assuming the null hypothesis that tutoring does NOT work at all**, what precise value would you *expect* from the *sample* of seniors that received tutoring?

   Precise expected value for sample mean = _____.

6. Even if you assume that tutoring does NOT work at all, given that the study used a sample, you should not be surprised if the sample mean was not *exactly* the value you indicated above. Why not? Explain your answer.

7. The term for your explanation of Question 6 above (and the answer to Question 4 above) is "sampling error." In fact, you know exactly how to compute sampling error. Assume that the study sampled 16 senior students. What is the value for sampling error in this scenario? (*Hint 1*: What is the formula for sampling error? *Hint 2*: the σ = 20.)

8. Which of the following describes how you should interpret the sampling error value you computed above?

    a. The typical distance of all possible sample means from the population mean (when N = 16) is 5 points.

    b. All possible means will be within 5 points above the population mean and 5 points below the population mean.

    c. Every time a sample of 16 people is taken it will be exactly 5 points away from the population mean.

    d. A sampling error of 5 is large.

9. Assuming that tutoring does NOT work at all (i.e., assuming the null hypothesis is true), use the curve provided below to complete the distribution of sample means that you would expect. The sample size is N = 16. The area under the curve represents the frequency (or probability) of each possible sample mean. The center or peak of this distribution should be located over the sample mean you expect if the null hypothesis is true. Use the value you computed for sampling error to compute at least 3 "standard errors" to the right and the left of center. (*Hints*: What value do you expect for the sample mean [i.e., what value should be under the peak]? The sampling error expected tells you how large to make the "steps" to the right and left of center.)

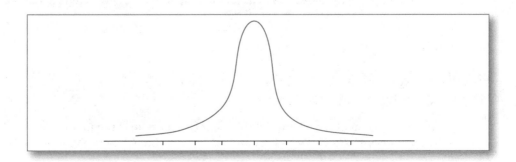

Defining the Critical Region

10. Use the z for a sample mean formula to "re-label" the distribution of sample means you created above. Do this by converting each sample mean on the distribution into a z score. Then, draw a vertical line at the critical value of z and shade in the critical region of z. You may need to consult your reading to remind yourself how to locate the critical value of z.

11. Look at the distribution of sample means you just created. Assuming that the null hypothesis is true, researchers use the above distribution to determine if a sample mean is likely or unlikely. Unlikely sample means cause researchers to reject the null hypothesis. The critical value of z determines where the "cut line" between *likely* and *unlikely* sample means is located. Which of the following statements is most accurate?

    a. The cut line's location is determined by the sample size.

    b. The cut line's location is determined by the standard deviation of the population.

    c. The cut line's location is determined by the population mean.

    d. The cut line's location is determined by the alpha value.

12. The z score located exactly on the cut line is called the

    a. absolute value.

    b. critical value.

    c. significant value.

    d. immaculate value.

Evaluating the Likelihood of the Null Hypothesis

13. Now that the critical region of z is determined, researchers can find the z score associated with the sample mean and determine if it is in the critical region (also known as the *region of rejection*). If the sample mean was 54, what should the researchers conclude about the null hypothesis and why?

14. If the sample mean was 58, what should the researchers conclude about the null hypothesis and why?

Why Must We Assume the Null Hypothesis Is True?
Why Do We Need a Null Hypothesis?

15. Go back to the second page of this exercise and re-read the null and research hypotheses. (*No, really go back and read them!*) You will notice that the null

hypothesis is very specific. In this case, when we assume that tutoring does NOT work at all, we can then *expect a very specific value* for the sample mean. What value does the null hypothesis say we should expect for the sample mean?

The null hypothesis tells us that we should expect the sample mean to be =

_____ .

16. In contrast to the very specific prediction of the null hypothesis, the research hypothesis is vague. In this case, if we assume that the one-tailed research hypothesis is true (i.e., that tutoring *increases* science test scores) can we expect any *specific* value or can we expect only a score in a *range* of values?

    The research hypothesis tells us that we should expect the sample mean to be (*choose one*)

    a. a specific value.

    b. a value in a general range.

17. Given your answer to the previous question, explain why assuming that tutoring does *not* work (i.e., the sample mean should be 50) and then computing the probability of getting a different sample mean due to sampling error is necessary for the processes of hypothesis testing. (*Hint*: Can you compute a probability if you don't know what sample mean to expect?)

Type I Errors, Type II Errors, and Statistical Power

18. BEFORE collecting data from the sample that received tutoring, researchers can't locate the center of the distribution of sample means if the research hypothesis is true. However, AFTER they have the data from the sample they do have *an idea* of where the research hypothesis distribution of sample means is located. What could they use to estimate the location of this distribution? Provide a specific value. (*Hint*: What value might represent what the population's science score would be if they all received tutoring?)

    Specific value for the center of the research hypothesis distribution of sample means = _____ .

19. The research hypothesis distribution of sample means represents ALL possible sample means if the research hypothesis is true. For this one study, we have just one sample mean. Therefore, if a different sample of people participated in the study, it would likely produce a different sample mean. Suppose that another study was done with 16 different people and the sample mean was $M = 61$ rather

than 58. How would the research hypothesis distribution of sample means for this second study differ from that of the first study?

  a. It would be more spread out than when the sample mean was 58.

  b. It would be centered on 61 rather than 58 and more spread out.

  c. It would be centered on 61 rather than 58 but its spread would be the same.

20. Your answer to Question 18 above is considered to be an *estimate* of the mean of the research distribution of sample means. Explain, in your own words, why we have to estimate the mean of the research distribution of sample means.

21. Even though the center of the research hypothesis distribution of sample means is based on an estimate, if the sample's size was sufficiently large it can be thought of as a close estimate. Which of the following explains why a larger sample size would improve one's confidence in the estimate?

  a. A larger sample size increases the standard error of the mean.

  b. A larger sample size reduces the amount of sampling error we expect a sample mean to have.

22. Explain why the answer you choose for 21 is correct.

   A major benefit of locating the center of the research hypothesis distribution of sample means, even if it is an *estimated* center, is that it allows researchers to quantify several other very important statistical concepts. This quantification process can be illustrated by "building a distribution." You have already built one of the distributions that are necessary in 9 above. As you know from Question 9 above, the null hypothesis distribution of sample means is centered at a raw score of 50 and a z score of 0. You also know that the spread of this null hypothesis distribution is determined by the standard error of the mean, $\sigma/\sqrt{N}$. You created this distribution in Question 9 above. This distribution is re-created for you below

23. The second distribution we need to build is the distribution of the sample means if the research hypothesis is true. As mentioned above, the center of this distribution is determined by the actual mean of the sample. In this case, the actual sample mean was 61, meaning that the center of this distribution of sample means is at 61 on the raw score number line (and at the z score associated with a sample mean of 61, or 2.2). Draw a vertical line on this figure at $+2.2$ to represent the center of the distribution of sample means if the research hypothesis is true. Remember that the only reason we can locate this curve's center is because we know the actual mean of the sample that received tutoring. We can't know this *before* we collect data.

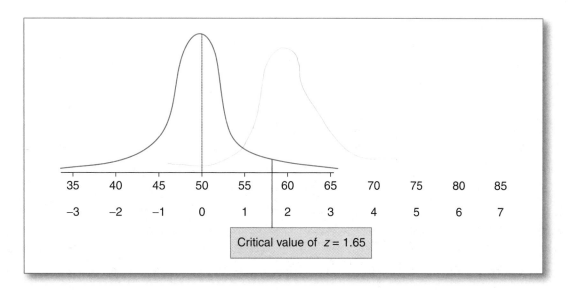

| 35 | 40 | 45 | 50 | 55 | 60 | 65 | 70 | 75 | 80 | 85 |
| -3 | -2 | -1 | 0 | 1 | 2 | 3 | 4 | 5 | 6 | 7 |

Critical value of *z* = 1.65

24. The spread of this new distribution *is assumed* to be the same as that of the null distribution of sample means. This assumption simply means that we assume the variability around center after receiving tutoring is the same as it was without receiving tutoring. Sketch in the distribution of sample means if the research hypothesis is true. (Just try to duplicate the null curve's shape and spread but have it centered at + 2.2 on the *z* score number line rather than at 0 where the null curve is centered.)

    After you have completed sketching in the research hypothesis distribution of sample means, turn the page and confirm that your figure looks like the figure on the next page.

    If your figure does not look like this one, determine what is wrong and fix it. Be sure you understand why the figure looks as it does.

    Previously, we said that "locating the center of the distribution of sample means **if the research hypothesis is true** allows researchers to quantify several other very important statistical concepts." Now, it's time to reap the benefits of locating the research distribution of sample means. To reap these benefits, you need to realize that both of the above curves are frequency histograms and the areas under each respective curve represent all possible outcomes. The null distribution of sample means represents all possible outcomes (i.e., all possible sample mean values) if the null hypothesis is true. The research distribution of sample means represents all possible outcomes (i.e., all possible sample mean values) if the research hypothesis is true. By "cutting" these curves into different sections at the critical value of *z*, we can determine the probability of (a) rejecting a false null (i.e., statistical power), (b) failing to reject a false null (i.e., Type II error), (c) rejecting a true null (i.e., Type I error), and (d) failing to reject a true null. In the figure on page 147, there is a distribution of sample means for the null hypothesis and a distribution of sample means for the research hypothesis. The two curves have been "separated" so that it is easier to see the

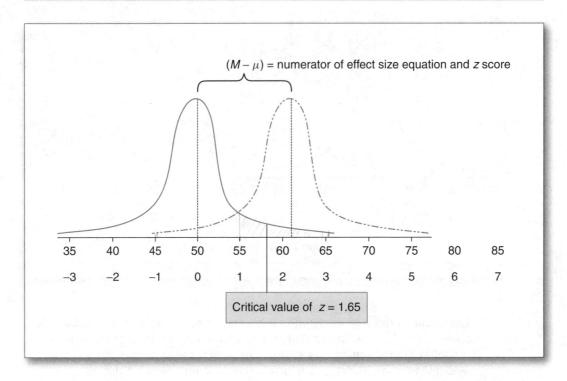

distinct sections of each curve. The areas under each of these respective curves represent statistical power, Type II errors, Type I errors, and failing to reject a true null. Try to determine which areas under each curve below represent (a) rejecting a false null (i.e., statistical power), (b) failing to reject a false null (i.e., Type II error), (c) rejecting a true null (i.e., Type I error), and (d) failing to reject a true null.

25. Match the area to the statistical outcome

    Type I error (rejecting a true null):   Area _____34-1._____

    Type II error (failing to reject a false null):   Area _____2.5·/._____

    Statistical power (rejecting a false null):   Area _____

    Failing to reject a true null: Area _____

Effect Size

In the above figure, the mean difference between the peak of the "null" and "research" distributions of sample means represents the size of the effect that the IV (independent variable) had on the DV (dependent variable). In this case, it is the size of the effect that tutoring had on science test scores. As mentioned above, the size of the IV's effect is very important information when evaluating whether or not an IV is worth implementing.

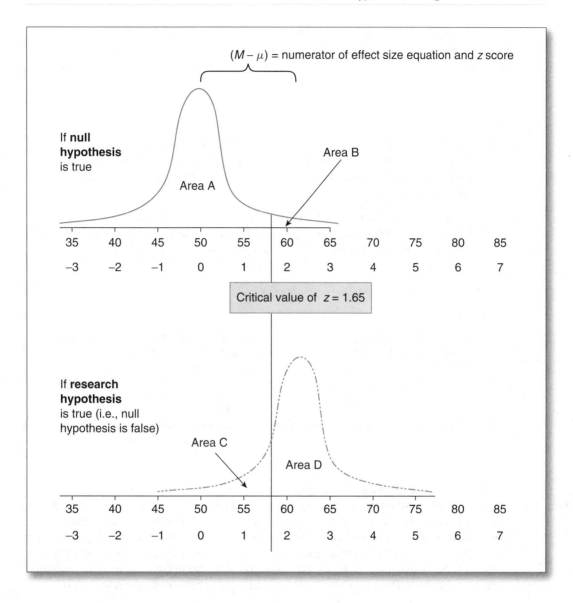

$(M - \mu)$ = numerator of effect size equation and z score

If **null hypothesis** is true

Area A

Area B

| 35 | 40 | 45 | 50 | 55 | 60 | 65 | 70 | 75 | 80 | 85 |
| -3 | -2 | -1 | 0 | 1 | 2 | 3 | 4 | 5 | 6 | 7 |

Critical value of $z = 1.65$

If **research hypothesis** is true (i.e., null hypothesis is false)

Area C

Area D

| 35 | 40 | 45 | 50 | 55 | 60 | 65 | 70 | 75 | 80 | 85 |
| -3 | -2 | -1 | 0 | 1 | 2 | 3 | 4 | 5 | 6 | 7 |

Researchers often want to quantify precisely how effective IVs are so that the relative effectiveness of different IVs can be compared. Comparing the relative effectiveness of IVs across different experiments is difficult for many reasons. For example, experiments often differ in their DVs (e.g., ACT or SAT scores) and/or their sample sizes. These differences make it impossible to compare the "difference between the peaks" or $(M - \mu)$ across experiments. Instead, researchers correct for these differences by computing d, a measurement of effect size that is not affected by differences in DVs or differences in sample size.

$$d = \frac{(M - \mu)}{\sigma}$$

You should notice that the numerator is the "difference between the peaks." Dividing this difference by the standard deviation of the population in the study creates a common metric on which effect sizes can be compared across experiments with different DVs and/or different sample sizes.

26. In the above scenario, the sample mean was 61. Use this information and the fact that the population mean and standard deviation were 50 and 20, respectively, to compute the effect size of tutoring. (*Note*: You should get $d = .55$.)

$$\frac{66-50}{20} = \frac{14}{20} \ .55$$

27. Use the information from your reading to interpret the effect size of tutoring using terms like small, small-medium, medium, medium-large, or large.

28. Interpret the effect size in terms of standard deviation units.

The process of significance testing yields only a decision as to whether the null hypothesis or the research hypothesis is more likely to be true. It does NOT indicate how effective the IV was in affecting the DV. In the above scenario, if the null hypothesis was rejected, the researchers would only know that tutoring increased science test scores but they would not know how effective the tutoring actually was. In many cases, the size of the IV effect is very important for researchers to know. For example, if the tutoring only increases science scores a very small amount, it might not be worth giving tutoring to the population.

29. Assume the effect of tutoring is small, try to identify a situation in which it would NOT be worth implementing it in the entire population even though the effect is statistically significant.

30. Assume the effect of tutoring is small, try to identify a situation in which it WOULD be worth implementing it in the entire population. (*Hint*: Think practically—when might it be worth using a program that works "a little bit"?)

Activity 6-2: Practice Problems

SCENARIO 1: ONE-TAILED *z* FOR A SAMPLE MEAN

A researcher studying self-esteem and depression in children obtains a sample of 25 children with low self-esteem and gives them a standardized test for depression. The average score for the group is $M = 93.3$. For the general population, scores on the depression test form a normal distribution with a mean of $\mu = 90$ and a standard deviation of $\sigma = 15$. Do children with low self-esteem show significantly higher levels of depression than other children? Use a one-tailed test with $\alpha = .05$.

1. State the null hypothesis in terms of population parameters (LSE = low self-esteem).
   a. $\mu_{LSE} \leq 93.3$
   b. $\mu_{LSE} < 93.3$
   c. $\mu_{LSE} < 90$
   d. $\mu_{LSE} \leq 90$ ✓

2. State the null hypothesis in words.
   a. The mean depression score of low self-esteem children will be the same or less than the mean depression score of the general population.
   b. The mean depression score of low self-esteem children will be higher than the mean depression score of the general population.

3. State the research hypotheses in terms of population parameters (LSE = low self-esteem).
   a. $\mu_{LSE} > 93.3$
   b. $\mu_{LSE} > 90$ ✓
   c. $\mu_{LSE} \geq 93.3$
   d. $\mu_{LSE} \geq 90$

4. State the research hypotheses in words.
   a. The mean depression score of low self-esteem children will be the same or less than the mean depression score of the general population.
   b. The mean depression score of low self-esteem children will be higher than the mean depression score of the general population.

5. What critical value defines the critical region for this one-tail, $\alpha = .05$ z for a sample mean test?

   1.65

6. What is the z score for this sample mean $\left(\text{i.e., } z = \dfrac{M - \mu}{SEM_p}\right)$? $\dfrac{93.3 - 90}{\cancel{90}} = \dfrac{3.3}{3}$

7. What is the effect size for this study $\left(\text{i.e., } d = \dfrac{M - \mu}{\sigma}\right)$? $\dfrac{15}{5} = \dfrac{3}{z=}$ $\boxed{= 1.1}$

8. Is the effect size (i.e., d) for this study small, small-medium, medium, medium-large, or large?

9. Which of the following statements best summarizes the results of the study?

   a. The mean depression score of the students with low self-esteem ($M = 93.3$) was significantly higher than the mean depression score of the general population ($\mu = 90$), $z = 1.1, p > .05, d = .22$.

   b. The mean depression score of the students with low self-esteem ($M = 93.3$) was not significantly different from the mean depression score of the general population ($\mu = 90$), $z = 1.61, p > .05, d = .47$.

   c. The mean depression score of the students with low self-esteem ($M = 93.3$) was significantly higher than the mean depression score of the general population ($\mu = 90$), $z = 1.1, p > .05, d = .61$.

   d. The mean depression score of the students with low self-esteem ($M = 93.3$) was not significantly different from the mean depression score of the general population ($\mu = 90$), $z = 1.1, p > .05, d = .22$. ✓

SCENARIO 2: ONE-TAILED z FOR A SAMPLE MEAN

Disc golf is a game in which participants try to throw plastic discs into targets called baskets in as few throws as possible. A statistician who plays disc golf wants to know if a new disc that is being advertised as the best long distance driver will enable him to throw a greater distance. His average long distance throw is 300 feet with a standard deviation of 11.3 feet. He threw the new disc 10 times and measured the distance of each throw. The average distance for these 10 throws was 315 feet.

10. State the one-tailed null and research hypotheses for this study.

11. What is the critical value for this study? Use $\alpha = .05$.

12. Compute the test statistic for these data.

13. Compute the effect size for this study and interpret it as small, small-medium, and so on.

14. Write an APA-style summary of this analysis.

SCENARIO 3: ONE-TAILED *z* FOR A SAMPLE MEAN

An educational psychologist wants to know if taking practice ACT tests helps improve one's score on the ACT test. The mean score on the ACT is 21 with a standard deviation of 4.7. The psychologist obtained a sample of 9 students and had each one take two ACT practice tests before they took the actual ACT test. The mean ACT scores for the 9 students in the sample are 21, 22, 19, 23, 25, 20, 22, 22, 20. Does taking practice ACT tests help increase performance on the actual ACT test?

15. State the one-tailed null and research hypotheses for this study.

16. What is the critical value for this one-tailed study? Use $\alpha = .05$.

17. Compute the test statistic for these data.

18. Compute the effect size for this study and interpret it as small, small-medium, and so on.

19. Write an APA-style summary of this analysis.

NOTES

CHAPTER 7

Hypothesis Testing Rules

LEARNING OBJECTIVES

After reading this chapter, you should be able to do the following:

- Provide a detailed description of a p value, critical value, and obtained value
- Explain what a p value means in a specific research context
- Explain the relationship between a p value, critical value, and obtained value and how this relationship determines whether the null hypothesis would be rejected

HYPOTHESIS TESTING RULES

In the previous chapter, you learned that the process of hypothesis testing is nothing more than a formal set of rules that researchers use to determine if the null hypothesis (H_0) is likely or unlikely to be true. If the null hypothesis is true, the researchers expect the computed statistic to be close to a specific value. When performing a z for a sample mean, researchers expect the z score to be close to 0 *if the null hypothesis is true*. Every z score has some probability of occurring. *If the null hypothesis is true*, z scores close to 0 have a high probability and z scores far from 0 have a low probability. If the probability of a z score is low enough, researchers reject the null hypothesis. The logic of this decision is that if a z score has a low probability *if the null is true* and that z score still happens, then the null hypothesis probably is *not* true. But how low does the probability of a z score have to be before the null hypothesis is rejected? Researchers typically use one of two different probability "cut lines," either .05 (5%) or .01 (1%). In other words, researchers agree that if they obtain a statistical result (e.g., a z score) that is expected to happen less than 5% or 1% of the time *assuming the null is true*, they conclude that the null is probably *not* true.

Reading
Question
1. If the null hypothesis is true, you should expect the z score to be close to

    a. the population mean.

    b. 0.

    c. 0.05.

Reading
Question
2. When you reject the null hypothesis, you are concluding that the null hypothesis is

    a. definitely not true.

    b. probably not true.

Reading
Question
3. You reject the null hypothesis if the z score has a low probability if the null hypothesis is

    a. true.

    b. false.

Reading
Question
4. How low does the probability of a z score have to be before a researcher can reject the null hypothesis?

    a. Less than .95

    b. Less than .05

The previous paragraph describes the decision-making process that underlies hypothesis testing in a general way. The next paragraph describes the same hypothesis testing process with a specific example that you are familiar with.

In Figure 7.1 we have reproduced the null distribution of sample means from a previous activity. In the scenario, the researchers attempted to increase science test scores by tutoring students. If tutoring did not have any effect on the science scores, the researchers expected to obtain a z value "close to 0." The researchers decided on a one-tailed alpha value of .05. They used this information to look up the critical z score (i.e., the critical value) in the unit normal table and found that it was +1.65. The obtained z value of +2.2 was greater than the critical value, so the researchers rejected the null hypothesis. Getting a z value of +2.2 or larger if the null were true would be "unlikely." In fact, you can determine precisely how unlikely. Use the unit normal table (Appendix A) to look up *the probability of getting a z value of +2.2 or larger if the null were true*. You should find that the probability or p value is .0139. This means that only 1.39% of all z values are larger than +2.2 if you assume the null hypothesis is true. The probability of a z score being +2.2 or larger is .0139, which is less than the alpha value of .05 or 5%, therefore the researchers rejected the null hypothesis.

Reading
Question
5. A researcher is expecting the sample mean to be greater than the population mean and so does a one-tailed test with an alpha of .05. What is the critical value for this test?

    a. 0.05

    b. 1.65

    c. 2.22

Reading Question

6. How do you obtain the critical value?

    a. Look up .05 in the TAIL column of the unit normal table.

    b. Look up .05 in the BODY column of the unit normal table.

Reading Question

7. In this problem, what percentage of z scores are equal to or greater than the critical value?

    a. 5 ✓

    b. 95

Reading Question

8. To determine if the null hypothesis should be rejected, the researcher compared the computed z score with the critical value. The null hypothesis was rejected because the obtained (i.e., calculated) z score was _____ than the critical value.

    a. less extreme

    b. more extreme

Reading Question

9. In addition to rejecting or failing to reject the null, researchers can state the probability of obtaining a particular z score if the null hypothesis is true. This probability is obtained by looking up the value in the TAIL column of the unit normal table across from the _____.

    a. alpha level

    b. obtained (i.e., calculated) z score

    c. critical value

WHAT IS A p VALUE?

A p value *is the probability of getting an obtained value or a more extreme value assuming the null hypothesis is true.* It is used by researchers to determine whether or not they should reject a null hypothesis.

Figure 7.1 may help you visualize how obtained z values, critical values, and p values are related.

We will be performing several different statistical procedures in this book (e.g., z, t, r, and F). For every one of these statistical tests, the basic rules of hypothesis testing are the same. *If the calculated statistical value (called the obtained value) is more extreme than the critical value, you should reject the null hypothesis.* Additionally, *if the p value for an obtained value is less than or equal to the alpha value (usually .05 or .01), you should reject the null hypothesis.*

Whenever you are confronted with a hypothesis testing situation and you need to determine whether or not you should reject the null hypothesis, you can use *either* one of the following two rules:

1. If the obtained value is more extreme than the critical value, you should reject the null hypothesis.

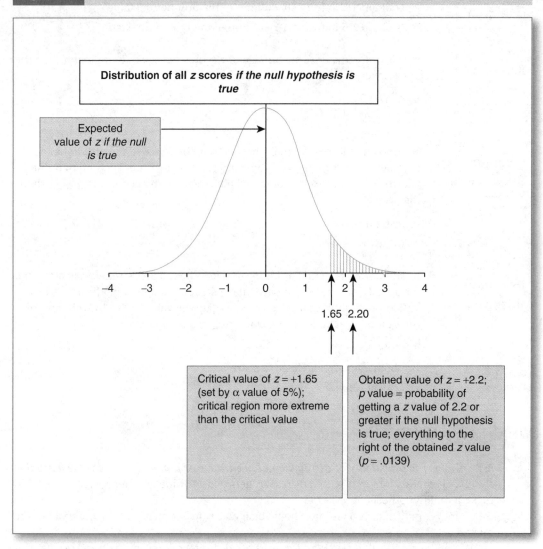

Figure 7.1   The relationship between obtained *z* values, critical values, and *p* values.

2. If the *p* value is less than the alpha value, you should reject the null hypothesis.

Rule 1 will always lead to the same decision as Rule 2, and vice versa. These two rules are completely dependent. They are analogous to two different paths to the same location. It doesn't matter which of these two paths you take—you will always end up in the same place (i.e., the same statistical decision).

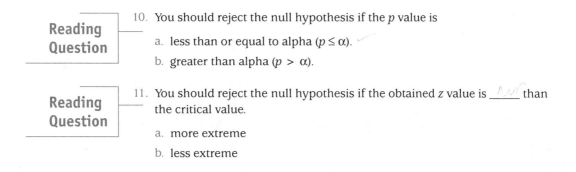

Reading Question

10. You should reject the null hypothesis if the *p* value is

    a. less than or equal to alpha ($p \leq \alpha$).

    b. greater than alpha ($p > \alpha$).

Reading Question

11. You should reject the null hypothesis if the obtained *z* value is _____ than the critical value.

    a. more extreme

    b. less extreme

WHY STATISTICIANS "FAIL TO REJECT THE NULL" RATHER THAN "ACCEPT THE NULL"

Students often wonder why statisticians use the confusing double negative "fail to reject the null" instead of the easier to understand "accept the null." We'll offer two related explanations. The first will be in the context of a specific research example. The second will be a more abstract logical argument.

A researcher testing the effectiveness of a program intended to reduce math anxiety administers the program to a sample of $N = 25$ people. After the participants complete the program, the researcher compares their mean anxiety score ($M = 55$) with the known population parameter ($\mu = 58$, $\sigma = 10$). The resulting *z* score for the sample mean of -1.5 is not farther from 0 than the critical value of -1.65, so he *fails to reject the null hypothesis*. The null states that the program is not effective. By failing to reject this hypothesis, the researcher is saying that the present study gave no reason to reject it. However, he is also acknowledging the possibility that the null hypothesis might not have been rejected because of one or more possible problems with the study. For example, a false null might not be rejected for a large number of reasons, including sampling error, if the program needed more time to be effective, or if there were any number of methodological problems with the study. By "failing to reject the null," the researcher is acknowledging all of these possibilities. In contrast, the phrase "accept the null" ignores these possibilities, implying a final, definitive conclusion that belies most research situations. Ignoring alternative possibilities is not consistent with the cautious nature of scientific conclusions.

The second explanation for why researchers do not "accept the null" is related to an inherent limitation of inductive reasoning. For example, suppose you have a hypothesis that all swans are white. You could test your hypothesis by going to a local pond. If you find that all swans at that pond are indeed white, does your visit to the local pond mean you should "accept" the hypothesis that *all swans* are white? No, it is possible that there is a different pond that does have at least one black swan. Even if you visit 1, 3, or 10 additional ponds and at every one you see only white swans, you cannot rule out the possibility that somewhere in the world there exists a pond with at least one black swan. In other words, you would not "accept" the hypothesis that all swans are white. Instead, you could only say that after many, many attempts to refute your hypothesis that all swans are white you have "failed to reject" it every time. You might be very confident in your hypothesis, but scientifically you have to acknowledge that a black swan is possible. Similarly, when a researcher conducts many experiments (i.e., visits many ponds) and all "fail to reject the null," he is acknowledging that another study could potentially reject that same null hypothesis.

Scientifically speaking, failing to reject the null hypothesis is usually an uninformative outcome. If you take a research methods course, you will learn potential reasons why a study might fail to reject the null hypothesis. Only *one* of these reasons is that the null hypothesis is actually true.

Reading Question

12. Failing to reject the null hypothesis is the same as accepting the null hypothesis.

    a. True

    b. False

Reading Question

13. A researcher may fail to reject the null hypothesis because

    a. the treatment really did not work.

    b. of sampling error.

    c. the study was poorly designed.

    d. All of the above.

Reading Question

14. Statisticians do not "accept" the null hypothesis because

    a. doing so fails to recognize the possibility of problems in their study.

    b. they don't not like speaking in double negatives.

Activity 7-1:   Statistical Power, Type I Error, and Type II Error

Learning Objectives

After reading the chapter and completing this activity, you should be able to do the following:

- Use two distributions of sample means to make probability statements about statistical power, Type I error, the probability of rejecting a false null, and Type II error
- Define statistical power, Type I error, the probability of rejecting a false null, and Type II error
- Describe how changing each of the following affects statistical power, Type I error, the probability of rejecting a false null, and Type II error:

  - Effect size of a treatment
  - Sample size of a study
  - Alpha level
  - Variability in a sample

- Apply the above relationships to novel scenarios and determine if researchers are being "dishonest" when presenting their statistical results
- Determine whether an alpha level of .05 or .01 is more appropriate by considering whether a Type I error or a Type II error is more "costly"
- Use the available statistics to determine which of several studies has produced the most promising results

DETERMINING IF A NEW DRUG WORKS: EXAMPLE

A pharmaceutical company has developed a drug (New Drug) to help treat depression. Clinically depressed people on medication often have difficulty concentrating, and so the pharmaceutical company has developed this New Drug to increase depressed people's ability to concentrate. Currently, another drug (Old Drug) dominates the market. Suppose that it is known that people with depression who use the Old Drug have an average score of $\mu = 50$ on a mental concentration inventory, with a standard deviation of $\sigma = 10$. To test the effectiveness of the New Drug, a sample of 25 people with depression are given the New Drug, and their mental concentration inventory scores are recorded. Higher scores reflect greater mental concentration.

WISE Statistical Power Applet

Go to the website http://wise.cgu.edu/, and then click on "Statistical Power" under the WISE Applet heading on the left side of the page.

In the Power Applet, type the following values into the boxes: $\mu_0 = 50$, $\mu_1 = 56$, $\sigma = 10$, $N = 25$, $\alpha = .05$. **Be sure to hit the ENTER key after typing EACH value.** When you are done, your graphs should look like those below.

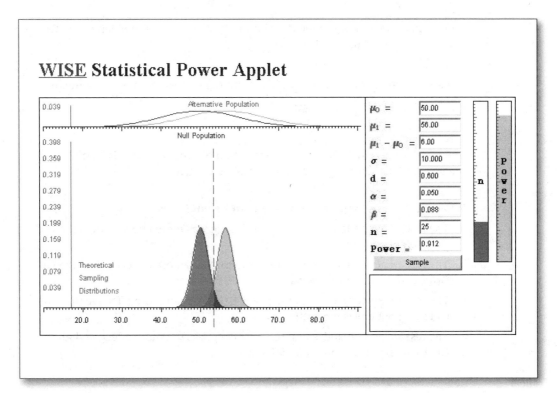

Source: ©WISE Team. Used with permission.

1. The two population distributions at the top of the graphic represent the two populations of people who got the Old Drug (*blue line*) and the New Drug (*red line*). Researchers would not normally know the precise location of the New Drug population distribution, but it is provided here for teaching purposes. The two curves at the bottom represent the distribution of sample means if the null is true (*blue histogram*) and the distribution of sample means if the null is false (*pink histogram*). These are the two curves you created during the previous activity on hypothesis testing. Notice how much narrower the *sample mean* distributions are relative to the *original population* distributions, which are displayed at the top of the graphic. Explain why this is not at all surprising.

Blue Curve

The shaded blue curve represents the sampling distribution assuming the null hypothesis is true (i.e., the New Drug did not increase mental concentration). The dark blue area shows the critical region for a one-tailed test. Because we selected an alpha of .05, the critical region is exactly 5% of the null hypothesis distribution.

2. What is the mean of this sampling distribution?   58

3. The mean of the null sampling distribution is the same as the mean of the Old Drug population. True or false?   True

4. What is the standard deviation of this sampling distribution (i.e., the standard error of the mean)? $\left(Hint: SEM = \dfrac{\sigma}{\sqrt{N}} \right)$

5. The standard deviation of the null distribution of sample means is smaller than the standard deviation of the population. True or false?

6. What happens if a Type I error occurs in this study?
   a. The researcher concludes that the New Drug was more effective than the Old Drug, but it was not more effective.
   b. The researcher concludes that the New Drug was more effective than the Old Drug, and it was more effective.
   c. The researcher concludes that the New Drug was not more effective than the Old Drug, but it was more effective.
   d. The researcher concludes that the New Drug was not more effective than the Old Drug, and it was not more effective.

7. Which area of the graph represents the probability of making a Type I error?
   a. Light blue
   b. Dark blue

8. Which area of the graph represents the probability of correctly failing to reject the null hypothesis?
   a. Light blue
   b. Dark blue

9. For this study, if the researchers failed to reject the null hypothesis, what conclusion would they draw about the New Drug?
   a. It was not effective.
   b. It was effective.

Red Curve

The red curve represents the sampling distribution *assuming the null hypothesis is false* (the New Drug did increase mental concentration). For now, we've set the mean of this distribution as 56. As was explained in the previous activity, the precise location of this distribution is based on a single sample mean, and therefore the location should be considered an estimate. This distribution represents all possible sample means if the New Drug increases mental concentration to 56. You can see that the mean of this distribution is 56 and the standard deviation of this distribution is $10/\sqrt{25} = 2$ (the standard error of the mean).

10. What is statistical power in the context of this study?
    a. The probability of correctly concluding that the New Drug WAS more effective than the Old Drug
    b. The probability of correctly concluding that the New Drug WAS NOT more effective than the Old Drug
    c. The probability of incorrectly concluding that the New Drug WAS more effective than the Old Drug
    d. The probability of incorrectly concluding that the New Drug WAS NOT more effective than the Old Drug

11. Which area of the graph represents statistical power?
    a. Everything to the right of the red line (*pink*)
    b. Everything to the left of the red line (*red*)

12. What happens if a Type II error occurs in this study?
    a. The researcher concludes that the New Drug was more effective than the Old Drug, but it was not more effective.
    b. The researcher concludes that the New Drug was more effective than the Old Drug, and it was more effective.

    c. The researcher concludes that the New Drug was not more effective than the Old Drug, but it was more effective.

    d. The researcher concludes that the New Drug was not more effective than the Old Drug, and it was not more effective.

13. Which area of the graph represents the probability of making a Type II error?

    a. Red

    b. Dark blue

The Curves and Numerical Values

In addition to showing the distributions graphically, the Applet also gives you exact numerical values for Type I error, Type II error, and statistical power. You can find these values listed on the right side of the display.

- The total area under each curve is equal to 1.
- Type I error is set by alpha (α). We set α at .05, and so we set Type I error at .05.
- Type II error is sometimes called beta error (β). For this study, it is .088.
- Statistical power is labeled "Power," and it is .912. Note that Power = $1 - \beta$.
- The effect size is d, and it is the difference between μ_0 and μ_1 divided by σ. (Note that this is similar to the d you calculated on previous activities.)

Hypothesis Testing

14. The hypothesis testing process is frequently used to determine whether a treatment is effective. As you learned in the previous activity, hypothesis testing is based on evaluating a null hypothesis. The null hypothesis states that the treatment will NOT work at all, and therefore the null hypothesis predicts that

    a. those who receive the treatment will have higher scores than the population who did not receive the treatment.

    b. those who receive the treatment will have lower scores than the population who did not receive the treatment.

    c. those who receive the treatment will have the same scores as the population who did not receive the treatment.

15. If the mean of those who receive the treatment (i.e., the sample mean) is NOT exactly the same as the population mean, there are two possible explanations for the difference: (1) sampling error created the difference or (2) the treatment created the difference. If sampling error created the difference, the _____ would be true.

    a. research hypothesis

    b. null hypothesis

16. If the treatment created the difference the _____ would be true.
    a. research hypothesis
    b. null hypothesis

17. The sole purpose of hypothesis testing is to determine whether the observed difference between the sample mean and the population mean was created by sampling error or by the treatment. How do researchers make this decision?
    a. If the z score for the sample mean is in the critical region, they conclude that the difference was created by sampling error.
    b. If the z score for the sample mean is in the critical region, they conclude that the difference was NOT created by sampling error and therefore it must have been created by the treatment.

In this problem, researchers are trying to determine if a new depression drug leads to higher mental concentration scores than another drug. Clinically depressed people who are using the Old Drug have a mental concentration score of 50 (i.e., $\mu = 50$), with a standard deviation of 10 (i.e., $\sigma = 10$). To test the New Drug, the researchers have to decide how much of the drug they should give to the people in the sample they selected ($N = 25$). Suppose they decided to give each person in the sample 80 mg of the New Drug each day. Further suppose that after taking the drug the mean mental concentration score for those in the sample was 52 (i.e., $M = 52$).

18. Obviously, the sample mean of 52 is different from the population mean of 50. The question is whether this difference was likely to have been created by sampling error. Compute the z for the sample mean of 52 when $\mu = 50$, $\sigma = 10$, and $N = 25$.

19. Locate the z score you just computed on the figure below.

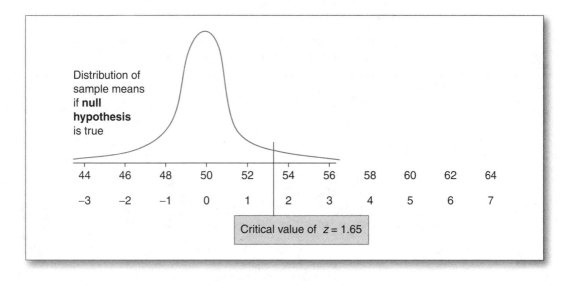

Distribution of sample means if **null hypothesis** is true

| 44 | 46 | 48 | 50 | 52 | 54 | 56 | 58 | 60 | 62 | 64 |
| −3 | −2 | −1 | 0 | 1 | 2 | 3 | 4 | 5 | 6 | 7 |

Critical value of $z = 1.65$

20. Would you reject or fail to reject the null hypothesis in this situation?

   a. Reject the null (i.e., the difference is probably NOT due to sampling error)

   b. Fail to reject the null (i.e., the difference is probably due to sampling error)

21. When $\mu = 50$, $\sigma = 10$, and $N = 25$, obtaining a sample mean of 52 (i.e., $M = 52$) leads to the conclusion that the treatment did not work because the difference between the sample mean and the population mean ($M - \mu = 2$) led to a z score of 1, which was small enough to have resulted from sampling error. However, it is also *possible* that the small difference was actually created by the treatment (i.e., the treatment worked just not very well). If the treatment really did work but the researcher mistakenly concluded that it did not work, the researcher would have committed a

   a. Type I error.

   b. Type II error.

   c. Type III error.

After conducting a study in which the null hypothesis was NOT rejected, it is a good idea for researchers to recognize that they may have made a Type II error. Many researchers will want to estimate the probability that they made a Type II error. If the probability is too high, they may decide that it is necessary to conduct an additional study. While you will be using computers to perform the computations, it is important that you have a conceptual understanding of Type II errors.

To determine the probability that a Type II error was made (i.e., that researchers concluded the treatment did NOT work when it really did work), a second distribution of sample means is created. This second distribution of sample means is centered on the mean of the sample from the study; in this case, the sample mean was 52. If the treatment really improves mental concentration by 2 from 50 to 52 and we built a distribution of sample means *for those receiving the treatment*, it would be centered on 52. This second distribution is the research hypothesis distribution of sample means. The research hypothesis distribution of sample means has been added to the null distribution of sample means below.

22. Look at the figure below. Which curve is the null hypothesis curve, and which curve is the research hypothesis curve? Explain your reasoning.

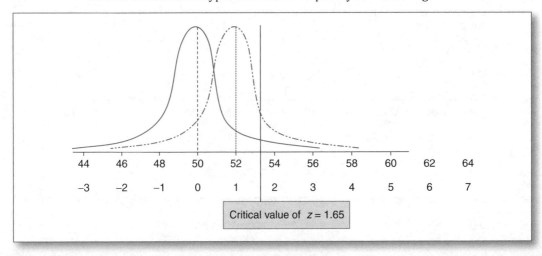

Critical value of $z = 1.65$

23. The null hypothesis curve represents
    a. all possible sample means if the treatment does not work at all.
    b. all possible sample means if the treatment improves mental concentration by 2.
    c. all possible sample means.

24. The research hypothesis curve represents
    a. all possible sample means if the treatment does not work at all.
    b. all possible sample means if the treatment improves mental concentration by 2.
    c. all possible sample means.

25. If the treatment really improves mental concentration by 2 and you randomly selected a sample from the *research hypothesis distribution of sample means*, what sample mean would you expect for the sample? I would expect a sample mean of _____, which corresponds to a *z* score of _____.

26. If the sample you selected had the mean you expected above, would the *z* score corresponding to that mean lead you to reject the null hypothesis or fail to reject the null hypothesis?
    a. To reject the null because the *z* score would be in the critical region
    b. To fail to reject the null because the *z* score would NOT be in the critical region

At this point, you should notice that even if the treatment really does improve mental concentration by 2, most samples in the research hypothesis distribution of sample means would result in researchers failing to reject the null hypothesis, which would be a Type II error if the treatment really works.

27. This unfortunate fact is illustrated by the above figure, because most of the possible samples in the *research hypothesis curve* are located
    a. to the left of the critical value.
    b. to the right of the critical value.

28. The proportion of the *research hypothesis curve* that is to the left of the critical value is equal to the probability of committing a
    a. Type I error.
    b. Type II error.

29. The proportion of the *research hypothesis curve* that is to the right of the critical value is equal to the probability of
    a. *correctly* concluding that a treatment works, known as statistical power.
    b. *correctly* concluding that the treatment does NOT work.
    c. making a Type I error.

30. Enter the following values into the Power Applet ($\mu_1 = 52$, $\mu_0 = 50$, $\sigma = 10$, and $N = 25$). You will find that when the treatment effect is an improved mental concentration of 2, the probability of committing a Type II error is _____ and statistical power is _____.

31. When you add the probability of a Type II error and the value for statistical power together, you will always get exactly 1. Explain why this is true.

Factors That Influence the Hypothesis Testing Process

Generally speaking, *researchers like their studies to have statistical power values of at least .80 and Type II error values less than .20.* The research study you just worked with had too little statistical power and a Type II error rate that was too high. As a consequence, the researchers decided to design a new study that might have more statistical power. Researchers can increase a study's statistical power by changing several things about the study. In this activity, you will learn how changing (a) the size of the treatment effect, (b) sample size, (c) alpha level, and (d) amount of variability created by measurement error each influences statistical power and Type II error rate.

Size of the Treatment Effect

One possible way researchers could increase the statistical power is to *increase the size of the treatment effect.* It is possible that if they gave the people in their sample 200 mg/day of the new antidepression drug rather than 80 mg/day, the treatment effect might be greater than the 2-point improvement. Suppose the higher dosage was given to a new sample, and further suppose that the sample's mean mental concentration was 56 rather than the population average of 50. The new research hypothesis distribution of sample means for this study is shown below:

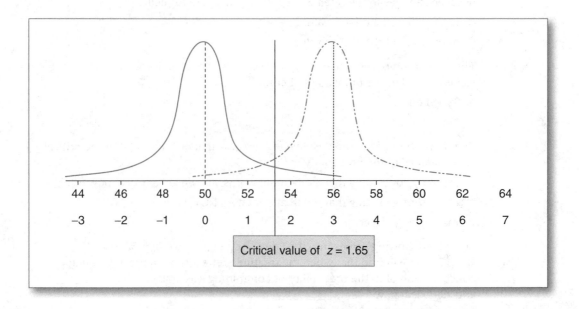

32. What impact did increasing the treatment effect from 2 (52 − 50 = 2) to 6 (56 − 50 = 6) have on the proportion of the *research hypothesis curve* that was to the right of the critical value?

    a. It increased the statistical power.

    b. It decreased the statistical power.

33. In the Power Applet, change μ_1 from 52 to 56, and then record the exact values for statistical power and Type II error rate.

    The statistical power changed from .26 to _____.

    The Type II error rate changed from .74 to _____.

34. Summarize how increasing and decreasing the treatment effect affects each of the following by completing the following table:

If the Treatment Effect Is	Statistical Power Will (increase/ decrease/not change)	Type II Error Will (increase/decrease/ not change)
Increased		
Decreased		

Increasing Sample Size

Of course, researchers cannot always increase the treatment effect. Suppose that the New Drug has too many negative side effects when taken at 200 mg/day. Another way researchers can increase the statistical power of a study is to increase the sample size of the study. Reset the values in the Power Applet to $\mu_0 = 50$, $\mu_1 = 52$, $\sigma = 10$, and $N = 25$. Record the values for statistical power and Type II error rate below.

35. The statistical power was _____, and the Type II error rate was _____. Be sure to look at the figure produced by the Applet. You will need to determine how the figure changes when N is increased.

36. Now change the sample size so $N = 100$, and compute the z score for a sample mean of 52 (i.e., the expected value if the improvement in mental concentration is 2). When the sample size was 25, the z score for a sample mean of 52 was 1. However, when the sample size is 100, the z score for a sample mean of 52 is _____.

37. The figure that reflects the change in sample size is given below. (Note that the values on the *x*-axis are different from those when $N = 25$; the graphs in the Applet are more accurate than those in this workbook.) You should notice that when the sample size is increased from 25 to 100, most of the sample means in the *research hypothesis curve* would lead researchers to

    a. reject the null hypothesis.

    b. fail to reject the null hypothesis.

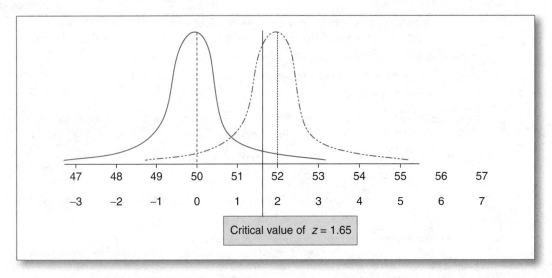

Critical value of $z = 1.65$

38. Increasing the sample size will _____ the statistical power.
    a. increase
    b. decrease

39. Increasing the sample size will _____ the Type II error rate.
    a. increase
    b. decrease

40. Use the equation for the z for the sample mean to *explain* how increasing the sample size of a study will affect that study's statistical power. (*Hint*: What impact does increasing the sample size have on the size of the standard error of the mean?)

41. Now enter the values for this study into the Power Applet, and record the exact values for statistical power and Type II error rate when the sample size is 100 rather than 25.

    When $N = 25$, statistical power is _____, and when $N = 100$, it is _____.

    When $N = 25$, Type II error rate is _____, and when $N = 100$, it is _____.

42. Summarize how increasing and decreasing the sample size affects each of the following by completing the following table:

If the Sample Size Is	Statistical Power Will (increase/ decrease/not change)	Type II Error Will (increase/decrease/not change)
Increased		
Decreased		

Changing the Alpha Level

Sometimes it is not possible to increase the sample size. Another way researchers can change the statistical power and Type II error rate of a study is by changing the alpha (α) level of the study. Essentially, this means that the researcher changes the size of the critical region on the *null hypothesis curve*. If $\mu_0 = 50$, $\mu_1 = 52$, $\sigma = 10$, $N = 25$, and $\alpha = .05$, the distribution of sample means for the null hypothesis curve would look like the top curve below. The area to the right of the critical value in this curve is 5% of the overall curve. The distribution of sample means for the research curve would look like the bottom curve below.

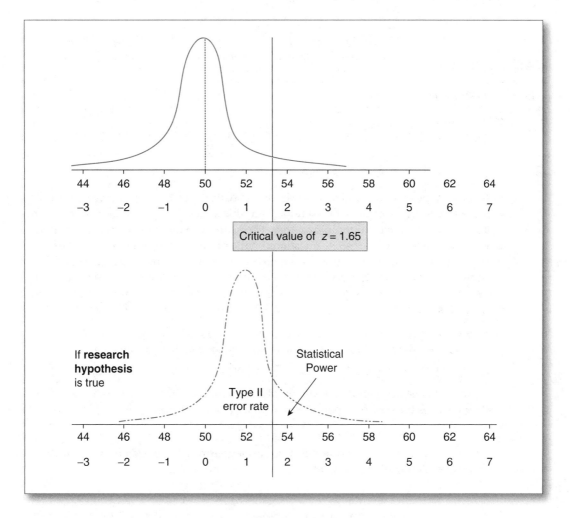

43. If researchers decreased the α level from .05 to .01 (i.e., moved the critical value line to the right), what impact would it have on the study's statistical power?

    a. It would increase the statistical power.

    b. It would decrease the statistical power; therefore, in this situation the researchers would probably leave the α level at .05.

44. Researchers in psychology usually choose between α levels of .05 and .01. The α level the researchers choose has a direct impact on the Type I error rate. An α level of .05 has a 5% Type I error rate, and an α level of .01 has a 1% Type I error rate. What is a Type I error?

   a. A Type I error is saying the treatment works when it does work.

   b. A Type I error is saying the treatment works when it does NOT work.

45. Summarize how increasing and decreasing the α level affects each of the following by completing the following table:

If the α Level Is	Statistical Power Will (increase/decrease/not change)	Type I Error Will (increase/decrease/ not change)	Type II Error Will (increase/decrease/not change)
Increased to .05 from .01			
Decreased to .01 from .05			

Reducing Variability by Reducing Measurement Error

Another way researchers could increase the statistical power of a study would be to improve the accuracy of their measurement. In this study, the dependent variable is the score on a mental concentration inventory. The scores are computed based on patients' answers to questionnaires. If some questions on the original questionnaire were confusing to the patients, it would produce measurement error. If the confusing questions were rewritten so that they are less confusing, it would reduce the measurement error, resulting in less variability in the study. In other words, the standard deviation of the population would be less, and the statistical power and Type II error rates would be affected.

46. Set the values for this research scenario at $\mu_0 = 50$, $\mu_1 = 52$, $\delta = 10$, $N = 25$, and a =.05. Record the values for statistical power and Type II error rate below:

   Statistical power is _____; Type II error rate is _____.

47. Now change the standard deviation of the population from $\delta = 10$ to $\delta = 5$. Record the values for statistical power and Type II error rate below:

   Statistical power is _____; Type II error rate is _____.

48. Summarize how decreasing the measurement error affects each of the following by completing the following table:

If the Measurement Error Is	Statistical Power Will (increase/decrease/not change)	Type II Error Will (increase/decrease/not change)
Decreased		

Putting It All Together

49. The pharmaceutical company that developed the New Drug has invested many years and millions of dollars in developing this New Drug. Financially, it is very important that it brings this drug to market. Obviously, it is easier to convince doctors to prescribe this drug if the company can present scientific evidence that the New Drug is more effective than the Old Drug. Unfortunately, Phase I clinical trials suggest that the New Drug is only slightly more effective than the Old Drug. How could the sample size be manipulated to maximize the likelihood that their drug would be found to be "significantly better," even if the drug's actual effectiveness is only slightly better than that of the competitor's drug?

50. Suppose you work for the company that manufactures the Old Drug and you find out that the above pharmaceutical company manipulated the sample size. You are still convinced that the Old Drug is a better option because it costs almost 75% less than the New Drug. How could you convince doctors that the difference between the effectiveness of the Old Drug and that of the New Drug is not really important, even though it was statistically significant in the studies conducted by the above pharmaceutical company?

51. Suppose a pharmaceutical company has developed a new drug to treat a severe mental disorder that currently has no effective drug treatment available. The statistician responsible for analysis of the data suggests that they use an alpha level of .10 rather than .05 or .01. Explain why this is a legitimate option in this case. Be sure to talk about Type I and Type II errors.

52. A researcher in another company reads the above study and sees that they used an alpha of .10 and decides to use an alpha of .10 in a study his company is currently conducting to test the effectiveness of a new cough drop. Is this a legitimate option in this case? Explain your answer by talking about Type I and Type II errors.

Suppose that the National Institute of Mental Health has the money to fund two research programs. Although there is only money to fund two research programs, more than 30 research teams have applied for this grant money. A group of experts read all the grant applications and narrow it down to the five best ones. A number of factors are being considered, but one factor is the researchers' past success in developing treatments. Each of the researchers submitted information about the type of mental disorder and population they have studied, the sample size, the result of the significance test, and the effect size. Use the information provided in the chart below to answer the next question:

Study Number	Type of Cancer/Population	N	Significance	d
1	Depression in teenagers	500	$p < .05$ Reject H_0	0.25
2	Obsessive compulsive disorder in adults	15	$p < .05$ Reject H_0	0.92
3	Anxiety disorder in the elderly	210	$p < .05$ Reject H_0	1.2
4	Bipolar disorder in adults	430	$p < .05$ Reject H_0	0.57
5	Antisocial disorder in teenagers	9	$p > .05$ Fail to reject H_0	0.67

53. Based on these data, which two researchers would you recommend receive the research grant? Explain your answer using effect sizes, sample sizes, and the results of the hypothesis test.

Activity 7-2:   Hypothesis Testing and Effect Size

Learning Objectives

After reading the chapter and completing this activity, you should be able to do the following:

- Conduct a hypothesis test using the z for a sample mean
- Distinguish between Type I errors and Type II errors
- When the null hypothesis is not rejected, use effect size to plan your future research
- When the null hypothesis is rejected, use effect size to determine the practical importance of a treatment

SCENARIO 1: WHAT TO CONSIDER WHEN YOU FAIL TO REJECT THE NULL

College students frequently ask their professors how they should study for exams. Research on human memory and learning suggests that taking practice tests is a very effective learning strategy. In fact, several research studies suggest that taking practice tests is a more effective strategy than rereading chapters or reviewing class notes. However, one of the obstacles to using the practice test strategy is that students don't always have access to practice tests. A college professor wondered if he could teach his students to test themselves while studying for exams. To answer this question, the college professor taught students to test themselves while they studied for his exams. For example, he taught students to test themselves by trying to summarize paragraphs they read and by explaining why each answer on previously completed classroom activities was correct. He taught these studying techniques to all 33 of his students (i.e., $N = 33$) and encouraged them to use these studying strategies to prepare for the exams in his course. The average score on the first exam in the course was $M = 76$, with a standard deviation of $SD = 11.7$. The professor wanted to know if his students' performance on this first exam was significantly better than the mean performance of his students from previous semesters on the same test. The mean score of his previous students on the test was $\mu = 74$, with a standard deviation of $\sigma = 10.9$.

1. State the one-tailed null and research hypotheses for this professor's research question. Write the hypotheses verbally and using symbolic notation.

   Null hypothesis:

   Research hypothesis:

2. Determine the critical value for this one-tailed z for a sample mean test (use $\alpha = .05$).

   $74 \times 1.65 \; SEM$

3. Compute the z for the sample mean test.

   Expected sampling error: $SEM_p = \dfrac{\sigma}{\sqrt{N}}$

   $\dfrac{11.7}{\sqrt{33}} = \dfrac{c}{\partial \!\!\!\! \diagdown 5}$

   Obtained z score statistic: $z = \dfrac{M - \mu}{SEM_p}$

   $76 - 74 = \dfrac{2}{6} = 0.33$

4. Based on the critical value of z and the obtained z score, the null hypothesis should
   a. be rejected because the obtained z score is greater than the critical value.
   b. be rejected because the obtained z score is less than the critical value.
   c. not be rejected because the obtained z score is greater than the critical value.
   d. not be rejected because the obtained z score is less than the critical value.

5. Which of the following is the best interpretation of these results?
   a. The null hypothesis is definitely true.
   b. There is insufficient evidence to reject the null.

6. Which of the following is the best summary of these results?
   a. The self-testing study strategy did not lead to significantly higher exam performance than that produced by previous students.
   b. The self-testing study strategy did lead to significantly higher exam performance than that produced by previous students.

7. You should have failed to reject the null hypothesis and concluded that the self-testing strategy did not lead to significantly better performance than in previous semesters. Whenever you *fail to reject a null hypothesis*, you should stop to consider the possibility that you *might* have committed a _____.
   a. Type I error
   b. Type II error

8. A Type II error occurs when a researcher concludes that the null hypothesis is _____ when the null hypothesis is _____.
   a. true; actually false
   b. true; actually true
   c. false; actually false
   d. false; actually true

9. Which of the following is the best description of a Type II error in this research scenario?
   a. Concluding that teaching students to self-test does increase exam scores when in fact it does not.
   b. Concluding that teaching students to self-test does increase exam scores when in fact it does.
   c. Concluding that teaching students to self-test does not increase exam scores when in fact it does not.
   d. Concluding that teaching students to self-test does not increase exam scores when in fact it does.

The purpose of hypothesis testing is to decide if you should reject or fail to reject the null hypothesis. Every time you make a decision about a null hypothesis, it is important to recognize that you might have made an error (i.e., your decision about the null hypothesis might have been incorrect). It is important to recognize that *whenever you fail to reject the null hypothesis you might have made a Type II error*. In this specific case, a Type II error would be concluding that the self-test study strategy did not improve test scores when in fact it did actually improve test scores.

If a Type II error were made in this study, it could have occurred because of any one of four possible reasons: (1) we might have, simply by chance, gotten a nonrepresentative sample, (2) there may have been too much measurement error in the experimental procedure, (3) the treatment effect may not have been sufficiently powerful, or (4) the sample size may not have been sufficiently large. Any one of these things can cause a Type II error. While you can never know for sure if you have made a Type II error, by carefully evaluating the effect size (i.e., *d*) of your study, you may be able to determine if a Type II error was likely to have occurred.

10. Which of the following can cause a Type II error? (Choose all that apply.)
    a. A nonrepresentative sample
    b. Rejecting the null hypothesis
    c. Too much measurement error
    d. A treatment that is not sufficiently powerful
    e. A sample size that is too small

11. When you fail to reject the null hypothesis, you should compute an effect size
    a. to help you determine if a Type II error was likely in your study.
    b. to determine how much sampling error was there in your study.

12. Compute the effect size for the professor's study, and determine if it is small, small-medium, and so on.

$$\text{Cohen's } d = \frac{M - \mu}{\sigma} = \frac{2}{10.9}$$

13. Interpret the effect size in terms of standard deviation units.

You should have found *d* to be .18, which is a small effect size. Now that you know the observed effect size was small, you can consider whether the null hypothesis was not rejected because the null was actually true and the treatment really was not effective (i.e., you made a correct decision about the null) or if the null was not rejected because something caused you to make a Type II error. The table below lists the potential reasons for failing to reject a null, when each is more likely to occur, and what researchers can to do to address each potential problem. You can use this table whenever you fail to reject a null, to help you plan your next research study.

Reasons Leading to Failing to Reject a Null	Problem Is More Likely When	Research Recommendations
The null was actually true		
A nonrepresentative sample was created by sampling error	σ (or *SD*) is relatively large, and *N* is small	Collect a different sample and do the study again
There was too much measurement error	σ (or *SD*) is relatively large	Increase procedural control and/or measurement precision in the study
The treatment was too weak	*d* is small	Make the treatment more powerful in the next study
The sample size was too small	*d* is large	Use more participants in the next study

The professor was disappointed that the result of the significance test (i.e., Questions 3–6) indicated his self-testing strategy did not seem to help his students perform better. However, because he was a careful researcher, he wanted to make sure he had not made a Type II error, so he planned to perform the study again. However, he wanted to strengthen the design of his next study by addressing as many of the potential problems that may have created a Type II error in his previous study as possible. Carefully examine the table above before you answer the following questions:

14. The professor could improve his future study by *decreasing the measurement error and/or increasing the procedural control*. Which of the following would accomplish this goal?

    a. He could grade the exams himself rather than having many different teaching assistants (TAs) grade the exams; doing so would reduce the "bad variability" in his study.

    b. He could continue to teach his students to use the self-test studying strategy in the hope that with more practice using the strategy the students would get better at it.

    c. He could make his exams easier, so that his current students' scores would be higher than his previous students' scores.

    d. He could increase the number of students enrolled in his class.

15. The professor could improve his future study by *making the treatment more powerful*. Which of the following would accomplish this goal?

    a. He could grade the exams himself rather than having many different TAs grade the exams; doing so would reduce the "bad variability" in his study.

    b. He could continue to teach his students to use the self-test studying strategy in the hope that with more practice using the strategy the students would get better at it.

    c. He could make his exams easier, so that his current students' scores would be higher than his previous students' scores.

    d. He could increase the number of students enrolled in his class.

The professor graded all of the future exams himself, and he continued to teach his students how to test themselves for the next 3 weeks. He also spent time encouraging them to use the self-test studying strategy outside class. After 3 weeks, he gave his current 33 students Exam 2, which was the same test he had given his previous students during previous semesters. The mean score of his current students on Exam 2 was $\mu = 81$, with a standard deviation of $SD = 11.3$. The mean score of his previous students on Exam 2 was $\mu = 77$, with a standard deviation of $\sigma = 10.4$.

16. State the one-tailed null and research hypotheses for the professor's second study.

    Null hypothesis:

Research hypothesis:

17. Determine the critical value for this one-tailed z for a sample mean test.

18. Compute the z for the sample mean test.

    Expected sampling error: $SEM_p = \dfrac{\sigma}{\sqrt{N}}$

    Obtained z score statistic: $z = \dfrac{M - \mu}{SEM_p}$

19. Based on the critical value of z and the obtained z score, the null hypothesis should
    a. be rejected.
    b. not be rejected.

20. Which of the following is the best interpretation of these results?
    a. The null hypothesis is definitely false.
    b. There is sufficient evidence to reject the null.

21. Which of the following is the best summary of these results?
    a. The test-yourself study strategy did not lead to significantly higher exam performance than that produced by previous students.
    b. The test-yourself study strategy did lead to significantly higher exam performance than that produced by previous students.

22. This time you should have rejected the null hypothesis and concluded that those using the self-test strategy did have significantly better performance than the previous students who did not use the strategy. Whenever you *reject a null hypothesis*, you should stop to consider the possibility that you *might* have committed a _____.
    a. Type I error
    b. Type II error

23. Which of the following best describes what a Type I error would be in this study?
    a. Saying that the self-testing strategy does not improve test scores when it does improve test scores
    b. Saying that the self-testing strategy does not improve test scores when it does not improve test scores
    c. Saying that the self-testing strategy does improve test scores when it does not improve test scores
    d. Saying that the self-testing strategy does improve test scores when it does improve test scores

As mentioned above, the purpose of hypothesis testing is to decide if you should reject or fail to reject the null hypothesis. Every time you make a decision about a null hypothesis, it is important to recognize that you might have made an error (i.e., your decision about the null hypothesis might have been incorrect). *If you rejected the null hypothesis, you might have made a Type I error.* In this specific case, a Type I error would be concluding that the self-test study strategy improves test scores when in fact it does not improve test scores.

Type I errors are generally less common than Type II errors. Assuming the null hypothesis is actually true, the probability of a Type I error is always equal to alpha (i.e., α). Before a study starts, researchers typically set the alpha value at .05 or .01, which means that the probability of a Type I error is 5% or 1%, respectively. If the alpha level is $\alpha = .05$ and the null hypothesis is actually true, 5 times out of 100 a researcher will conclude that a treatment works when it really does not work (i.e., the researcher will make a Type I error). Unlike Type II errors, which can be created in many different ways, Type I errors are generally thought of as being created by sampling error. Consequently, the only way to assess if you have made a Type I error is to run the same study a second time. If you replicate a study (i.e., run it a second time) and reject the null hypothesis both times, it is very unlikely that both of your studies produced Type I errors. The table below displays potential causes of Type I and Type II errors.

Error Type	List of Potential Causes for Each Type of Error
Type I	Sampling error
Type II	Large amounts of measurement error, a weak treatment, or a small sample size

24. If the null hypothesis is actually true, the probability of a Type I error is always equal to the
   a. critical value.
   b. obtained value.
   c. *p* value.
   d. alpha value.

25. When the null hypothesis is actually true and the α level is .05, researchers will make a _____ error _____ of the time.
   a. Type II; 5%
   b. Type I; 5%
   c. Type II; 1%
   d. Type I; 1%

26. _____ errors are thought of as being primarily caused by sampling error.
   a. Type II
   b. Type I

27. After rejecting a null hypothesis, careful researchers recognize that they might have made a Type I error. What should researchers do if they suspect that they rejected a null hypothesis due to a Type I error?

28. A Type I error can be caused by sampling error. What can researchers do to reduce the potential problem of sampling error in their future studies? (*Hint*: You should mention both items in the formula for sampling error.)

There is a very important addition to the above table. When you take your research methods course, you will learn that *confounds can also create both Type I and Type II errors*. For example, if the exam that the professor gave to his students this semester was easier (or harder) than the exam he gave to his previous students, the difference in exam difficulty would be a confound. If the current semester's exam was easier, this confound might create a Type I error (i.e., concluding that the studying strategy worked, when his current students' scores were actually higher because this semester's exam was easier than the previous semesters' exams). On the other hand, if the current semester's exam was harder, this confound might create a Type II error (i.e., concluding that the studying strategy did not work, when his current students' scores were actually lower because this semester's exam was harder than the previous semesters' exams). You will learn about the many ways in which researchers try to eliminate potential confounding variables when you take a research methods course. Essentially, researchers try to ensure that their study is "fair" by ensuring that some participants do not have an advantage over others.

29. *Confounding variables can cause both Type I and Type II errors*. Very briefly, describe what the professor probably did in an attempt to make his study "fair" (i.e., to guard against potential confounding variables).

Our professor rejected the null hypothesis in his second study. The next step in the hypothesis testing procedure is to compute an effect size. If you reject a null hypothesis, you will want to compute the effect size of the study so that you can determine the *practical significance* of the treatment. In other words, computing the effect size will help you determine if the treatment worked very well, moderately well, or only a little. Cohen's d $\left(\text{i.e., } \dfrac{M-\mu}{\sigma} \right)$ indicates how well a treatment works. If d is close to .2, the treatment is described as having a small effect (i.e., it works "only a little"). If d is close to .5, the treatment is described as having a medium effect (i.e., it works "moderately well"). And if d is close to .8, the treatment is described as having a large effect (i.e., it works "very well").

More generally, a d equal to 1 indicates that the treatment improved scores by an entire standard deviation, while a d equal to .5 indicates that the treatment improved scores by half a standard deviation.

30. Compute the effect size for the professor's second study, and determine if it is small, small-medium, and so on.

$$\text{Cohen's } d = \frac{M - \mu}{\sigma} =$$

31. You should have found d to be .38, which is a small to medium effect size. Which of the following is the best interpretation of this effect size?

    a. Those students using the self-test studying strategy had scores that were .38 points better than those who did not use this strategy.

    b. Those students using the self-test studying strategy had scores that were .38 of a standard deviation higher than those who did not use this strategy.

32. The professor wanted to share his latest results with a colleague. Which of the following summaries (Option A or Option B) is the correct summary of his results? After you choose which one is correct, fill in the missing statistical values from his second study.

    Option A: The Exam 2 scores for the current students who were trained to test themselves while studying for exams ($M =$ _____) were significantly higher than the exam scores of the previous students who did not receive the training ($\mu =$ _____, $\sigma =$ _____), $z =$ _____, p __ .05, $d =$ _____. However, it is worth noting that there was no difference between the students' scores on Exam 1. It is possible that the current students needed more practice using the self-testing strategy than they had prior to Exam 1.

    Option B: The Exam 2 scores for the current students who were trained to test themselves while studying for exams ($\mu =$ _____) were *not* significantly higher than the exam scores of the previous students who did not receive the training ($\mu =$ _____), $\sigma =$ _____, $z =$ _____, p __ .05, $d =$ _____. It is worth noting that there was also no difference between the students' scores on Exam 1.

SCENARIO 2: WHAT TO CONSIDER WHEN YOU REJECT THE NULL

This second scenario involves a different college professor who was also interested in helping her students study and learn more effectively. She taught a large introductory psychology course with 312 students (i.e., $N = 312$). The professor wanted to try a new online introductory psychology textbook this semester to see if it would increase her students' scores relative to her previous students' scores on her comprehensive final exam. After the course was over, she compared the final exam scores. The mean final exam score of the current students who used the online text was $M = 74$, with a standard deviation of $SD = 13.5$. The mean final exam score of the previous students who used the traditional text was $\mu = 73$, with a standard deviation of $\sigma = 9.3$. Use $\alpha = .05$.

33. State the one-tailed null and research hypotheses for this professor's study.

    Null hypothesis:

    Research hypothesis:

34. Determine the critical value for this one-tailed z for a sample mean test.

35. Compute the z for the sample mean test.

    Expected sampling error: $SEM_p = \dfrac{\sigma}{\sqrt{N}}$

    Obtained z score statistic: $z = \dfrac{M - \mu}{SEM_p}$

36. Based on the critical value of z and the obtained z score, the null hypothesis should

    a. be rejected.

    b. not be rejected.

37. Which of the following is the best interpretation of these results?

    a. The null hypothesis is definitely false.

    b. There is sufficient evidence to reject the null.

38. Which of the following is the best summary of these results?

    a. The students using the online text did not have significantly higher exam performance than those using the traditional text.

    b. The students using the online text did have significantly higher exam performance than those using the traditional text.

39. Compute the effect size for the professor's study, and determine if it is small, small-medium, and so on.

    Cohen's $d = \dfrac{M - \mu}{\sigma} =$

40. You should have found d to be .11, which is a small effect size. Which of the following is the best interpretation of this effect size?

    a. Those students using the online text had scores that were .11 points better than those using the traditional text.

    b. Those students using the online text had scores that were .11 of a standard deviation higher than those using the traditional text.

The results of the significance test (i.e., Questions 32–38) indicate that the 1-point difference between the students using the online text and the students using the traditional text was unlikely to be due to sampling error (i.e., if the null hypothesis is actually true, there is only a

5% chance of the 1-point difference occurring due to sampling error). So, assuming that there is no confounding variable operating, this decision is probably not a Type I error. The online text probably is better than the traditional text. However, the effect size you computed (i.e., $d = .11$) indicates that the online text is *only slightly better* than the traditional text. *Whenever you reject the null hypothesis and the effect size is small, you need to consider if the treatment is practically significant.* In other words, you need to consider if the treatment's effect is so small that it is not worth using. For example, suppose the online text costs $250 while the traditional text costs $50. While the significance test indicates that the online text is statistically better, the effect size indicates that it is only slightly better. Is having students perform .11 of a standard deviation better (i.e., in this case 1 point better) worth the additional $200 in cost? If your answer is "no," then you are saying that the treatment is not worth using. In terms of cost, the slightly better performance is not worth the substantially higher monetary cost. However, if the online text and the traditional text both cost $50, then you would probably decide that the online text is the better choice (i.e., the treatment is worth using). Depending on the practical costs, a small treatment effect can be very useful or not at all useful.

41. In your own words, describe how it is possible that a treatment can actually be better than an alternative treatment but still not be worth using. How can you decide if a treatment is worth using or not?

Significance testing (also called hypothesis testing) and effect sizes have different purposes. The purpose of significance testing is to determine if a treatment works. Effect size determines the practical usefulness of a treatment. This distinction is important because many students ask, "Why do we need significance testing at all? Why don't we just use effect size?" Significance testing helps prevent us from adopting treatments that only appear to be better than other treatments due to sampling error. The following table may help you remember the different purposes of significance testing and effect size:

Statistical Procedure	Purpose
Null hypothesis significance testing	To determine if a given result is likely to have occurred due to sampling error; to determine if the null hypothesis is likely to be true or false
Effect size	To determine if a treatment was very effective, moderately effective, or only slightly effective

42. In your own words, explain why researchers need both significance testing and effect size estimates. That is, what is the purpose of each statistical procedure?

43. Another important distinction between significance testing and effect size is that one of them is greatly influenced by sample size while the other is not. Which statistical procedure is influenced by sample size? (*Hint*: Look at the equations.)

44. Explain how it is possible to fail to reject the null in one study when an effect size is large and to reject the null in another study when the effect size is small.

POST HOC VERSUS A PRIORI STATISTICAL POWER

The distinction between post hoc and a priori statistical power analysis is an important one. In Activity 7-1, you performed post hoc power analyses. (Look over Activity 7-1 to remind yourself what you did.) You used the data from a current study (i.e., the sample mean) to estimate the power of a study that was already conducted. *The purpose of post hoc power analysis is to help researchers interpret the results of studies they have already conducted.* For example, if a given study failed to reject the null and the post hoc power was only .60, researchers should recognize that their failure to reject the null could well be a Type II error. More precisely, if the sample mean was a good estimate of the population parameter, then a Type II error would result 40% of the time (1 − Power = Type II error rate, i.e., 1 − .60 = .40). The key point here is that post hoc power analysis helps researchers estimate the probability that they have made a Type II error. It is not a great estimate, but it is better than nothing.

A priori power analysis has a completely different purpose. Its goal is to help researchers plan their future research so that it has sufficient statistical power. *The purpose of a priori power analysis is to determine the correct sample size for studies that researchers are planning to run in the future.* For example, if researchers expect their treatment to have a medium effect, a priori power analysis will reveal how many participants researchers should use in their future study to achieve sufficient statistical power (i.e., .80 statistical power).

Several statisticians have pointed out that it is inappropriate to use post hoc power analyses for a priori purposes (i.e., to plan future studies). Post hoc power analyses rely solely on a single sample, which can be highly variable due to sampling error. Therefore, using post hoc power values to estimate the power of future studies is strongly discouraged by statisticians. In contrast, a priori power analysis uses the observed effect sizes of several studies, which is much more reliable than using any single study. The moral of the story is that post hoc power should only be used to help you understand the study you just completed running.

45. SPSS sometimes provides the analysis option of "Observed power." Checking the appropriate box will provide a specific value for observed power alongside the results of a significance test. Based on the two paragraphs above, is SPSS providing a post hoc power analysis or an a priori power analysis? Explain your reasoning.

46. Again, based on the two paragraphs above, the observed power value provided by SPSS is best used to estimate the

a. sample size needed for future research.

b. probability that the current study may have resulted in a Type II error.

Activity 7-3: Practice Problems

p VALUES, ALPHA LEVELS, AND CRITICAL VALUES

Determine if you should *reject* or *fail to reject* the null hypothesis.

1. The $\alpha = .05$. The p value is .04.

2. The $\alpha = .05$. The p value is .08.

3. The $\alpha = .01$. The p value is .04.

4. The $\alpha = .01$. The p value is .02.

5. The critical value of the statistic is 1.65. The obtained value is 1.85.

6. The critical value of the statistic is 1.65. The obtained value is 1.55.

7. The critical value of the statistic is 1.96. The obtained value is 1.85.

8. The critical value of the statistic is 1.96. The obtained value is 1.97.

9. A researcher performed a statistical test with an alpha value of .05. The obtained value had a p value of .02. The obtained value in this study must be _____ the critical value.

a. more extreme than

b. less extreme than

c. equal to

d. There is no way to tell.

10. A researcher performed a statistical test with an alpha value of .01. The obtained value had a p value of .02. The obtained value in this study must be _____ the critical value.

a. more extreme than

b. less extreme than

c. equal to

d. There is no way to tell.

11. A researcher performed a statistical test with a critical value of +1.65. The obtained value was 1.70. The p value in this study must be _____ the alpha value.

   a. greater than

   b. less than

   c. equal to

   d. There is no way to tell.

12. A researcher performed a statistical test with a critical value of +1.65. The obtained value was 1.5. The p value in this study must be _____ the alpha value.

   a. greater than

   b. less than

   c. equal to

   d. There is no way to tell.

POWER AND ERROR RATES

Suppose researchers gave a sample of students an online tutoring program in the hope that it would raise their reading comprehension scores. The researchers computed a z for a sample mean to compare the mean of the sample with the known reading comprehension score for the population, μ_{RC}. The obtained z value for the study was +1.71, and the p value was .0436. Use the unit normal table (Appendix A) to confirm that you can find the p value. The critical value was 1.65 using an alpha of .05.

13. What does the p value of .0436 mean in this study?

   a. The probability of obtaining a z value of 1.71 or higher is .0436.

   b. The probability of obtaining a z value of 1.71 or higher is .0436 assuming the null hypothesis is true.

   c. The probability of obtaining a z value of 1.71 or higher is .0436 assuming the research hypothesis is true.

14. You can use the p value (.0436) and the alpha level (.05) to determine if you should reject the null. In this case, should the researcher reject the null?

   a. Yes, the p value is less than alpha.

   b. No, the p value is less than alpha.

15. You can also use the obtained z (1.71) and the critical value (1.65) to determine if you should reject the null. In this case, should the researcher reject the null? Your decision whether to reject the null should be the same as it was in the previous question.

   a. Yes, the obtained value is farther from 0 than the critical value.

   b. No, the obtained value is farther from 0 than the critical value.

16. What type of error could you make if you reject the null hypothesis?

17. What type of error could you make if you fail to reject the null hypothesis?

18. What must you do to sample size to increase statistical power?

19. What must you do to measurement error to increase statistical power?

20. Which has a higher Type I error rate, $\alpha = .05$ or $\alpha = .01$?

21. Which has more statistical power, $\alpha = .05$ or $\alpha = .01$?

22. If you fail to reject the null and you have a large effect size, what does this probably mean?

23. Why does replicating a result make a researcher more confident that he or she did not make a Type I error?

C H A P T E R   8

Single Sample *t* Test

SINGLE SAMPLE *t* TEST

In the last two chapters, you learned to use the *z* for a sample mean statistic to test a null hypothesis. Specifically, you learned how to use the sample size and the population standard deviation to compute the average sampling error. You then determined if the deviation between the sample mean and the population mean was likely or unlikely to have resulted from sampling error by computing a *z* for a sample mean statistic and comparing the *z* with a critical value. In most research situations, the standard deviation of the population is not known and therefore you cannot use the *z* for a sample mean statistic to test your null hypothesis. In this chapter, you will learn how to use the single sample t statistic when you don't know the population standard deviation, σ.

Like the z for a sample mean, the single sample t statistic is used to determine if a sample mean is significantly different from a population mean, however, because the population standard deviation is not known, the single sample t test uses the standard deviation of the sample (SD) to compute an estimate of the typical amount of sampling error. *Almost* everything else is the same between the single sample t and the z for a sample mean.

<table>
<tr><td>

**Reading
Question**

</td><td>

1. One of the differences between a z for a sample mean test and a single sample t test is that

   a. the z for a sample mean is used when you don't know the population standard deviation.

   b. the single sample t test uses the sample standard deviation to compute an *estimate* of the typical amount of sampling error.

</td></tr>
</table>

You can also use this statistic when you need to determine if a sample mean is significantly different from any number that is of "theoretical" interest. For example, you could compare the average amount of weight that a group of people lost while on a weight loss program to 0, which would represent no weight loss at all. In the weight loss example, the comparison value of 0 has a theoretical rationale because if a group of dieters' average weight loss does not exceed 0 pounds the program would not work. The single sample t test can be used to evaluate whether the weight loss program produced significantly more weight loss than 0 pounds. In this case, 0 pounds would be the value expected if the weight loss program did not work at all. It would be the value expected if the null hypothesis were true.

<table>
<tr><td>

**Reading
Question**

</td><td>

2. A researcher wants to assess people's knowledge of a topic by using a 10-question True/False test. Which value could be of theoretical interest to this researcher and, therefore, function as a null hypothesis test value?

   a. The researcher might compare the mean number of correct answers to 10, the number that represents perfect performance on the test.

   b. The researcher might compare the mean number of correct answers to 5, the average number of correct answers people would get if they were simply guessing on every question of the test.

   c. The researcher could use either "10" or "5" in this situation because both values represent a level of performance that might be of theoretical interest to the researcher.

</td></tr>
</table>

Conceptual Information

The single sample t test is logically identical to the z for a sample mean. Both tests compute the deviation between a sample mean and some expected value, which is usually a population mean (or a value of theoretical interest to the researcher). This deviation between the sample mean and population mean is the numerator of both the z test and the t test. The denominator of both tests is a value representing "typical sampling error."

The minor computational difference between the *z* test and *t* test is in the computation of typical sampling error. Table 8.1 highlights the similarities and differences between these two significance tests.

Table 8.1   Similarities and differences between the *z* test and *t* test.

	z Test	*t* Test
Formula	$z = \dfrac{M - \mu}{SEM_p}$	$t = \dfrac{M - \mu}{SEM_s}$
Computation of sampling error (standard error of the mean)	$SEM_p = \dfrac{\sigma}{\sqrt{N}}$	$SEM_s = \dfrac{SD}{\sqrt{N}}$

When using the *z* test, the standard deviation of the population is used to compute the expected amount of sampling error (i.e., the denominator of the test, which is often called the **error term**). Specifically, sampling error is computed using the formula for the standard error of the mean $\left(SEM_p = \dfrac{\sigma}{\sqrt{N}} \right)$. In some situations, however, researchers may not know σ, the population's standard deviation. In these situations, researchers compute the standard deviation of the **sample** data and use it to compute an **estimate** of expected sampling error. This procedure is one of the ways the single sample *t* test differs from the *z* test. Specifically, sampling error is computed using the formula for the estimated standard error of the mean $\left(SEM_s = \dfrac{SD}{\sqrt{N}} \right)$ when using a sample *t* test.

Reading Question

3. The only computational difference between the *z* for a sample mean formula and the single sample *t* formula is the way
   a. the numerator is computed.
   b. typical sampling error is computed.

You should recall that critical regions define which values (*z* or *t* values) result in rejecting the null hypothesis. Another difference between *z* and *t* tests is the critical values used for each test. While the critical values for *z* tests are ALWAYS the same, the critical values for *t* tests change based on sample size. For example, the critical value for a one-tailed *z* test with α = .05 is ALWAYS +1.65 *or* −1.65. Stated differently, the *z* scores of +1.65 *or* −1.65 will always be the points that "cut" the 5% of the *z* scores in the critical region from the 95% of *z* scores in the body of the *z* distribution. Conversely, the critical values for a one-tailed *t* test with α = .05 will change based on how many people are in the sample. The reason for this is that the distribution of *t* values is not always normal in shape. When the sample size is small (*N* is less than 30), the curve of *t* values is not shaped like a normal curve. In fact, *the shape of the curve is different for every sample size*. Figure 8.1 illustrates how the shape of the *t* curve changes with sample size by displaying three different *t* curves, each one created by a different sample size. The important consequence of the *t* curves' frequent "shape shifting" as the sample size changes is that the critical values that "cut" the 5% of the *t* scores in the critical region from the 95% of *t* scores in the body of the *t* distribution are different for different sample sizes (i.e., *N*). Therefore, studies with different sample sizes will have different critical values even if both use one-tailed tests with α = .05. As *N* increases, the critical value is closer to zero.

Figure 8.1   The shape of the *t* distribution for three different sample sizes.

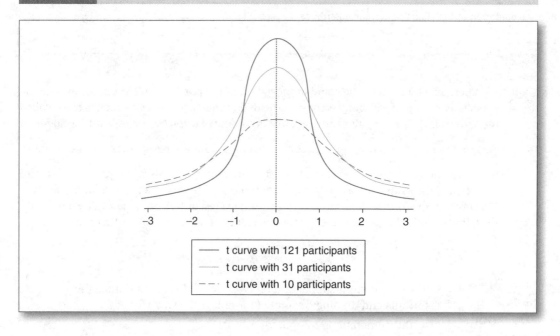

— t curve with 121 participants
--- t curve with 31 participants
— - · t curve with 10 participants

Reading Question

4. The critical value for a one-tailed *z* test with α = .05 is always

a. + 1.65 or −1.65.

b. 0.

c. + 1.96 or −1.96.

Reading Question

5. The critical value for a one-tailed *t* test with α = .05

a. is the same as the critical value for a similar *z* test.

b. changes based on the size of the sample (i.e., *N*) being used.

Reading
Question
6. The critical value for a *t* test will get _____ as sample size increases.
   a. farther from zero
   b. closer to zero

Reading
Question
7. As the sample size increases, the critical region for a *t* test
   a. gets larger (more than 5% of the distribution).
   b. gets smaller (less than 5% of the distribution).
   c. stays the same size (equal to 5% of the distribution), but its location changes.

The reason why the *t* curve changes shape so readily as sample size changes is related to the fact that random sampling error changes so readily with sample size. Intuitively, it probably makes sense to you that larger random samples have less sampling error than smaller random samples. After all, larger samples contain more of the population in them and that implies less of a difference between the sample and the population.

Reading
Question
8. When performing a *t* test, increasing the sample size will _____ the amount of sampling error expected. This means the denominator of the *t* test will be _____ .
   a. increase; smaller
   b. increase; larger
   c. decrease; smaller
   d. decrease; larger

ONE-TAILED SINGLE SAMPLE *t*-TEST EXAMPLE

A researcher asks you to help her evaluate the effectiveness of a new physical education program for elementary school children. The program is designed to increase physical fitness. A sample of 15 children is selected and placed in the new program. After 3 months, each child is given a physical fitness test. The test consists of running, doing sit-ups, and doing push-ups. Performance on these three activities is compiled into one score of physical fitness with higher scores indicating greater fitness. For the general population of elementary school children, the scores on the physical fitness test form a normal distribution with a mean of 100. The scores of the 15 students in the new physical education program are as follows: 105, 98, 101, 110, 96, 103, 104, 101, 99, 105, 112, 95, 105, 100, and 109. The program is designed to *increase* students' physical fitness so the researcher uses a one-tailed test. She also chooses an alpha of .05. You need to help her determine if this program increases kids' physical fitness.

Step 1: State the Research Hypothesis and Null Hypothesis Symbolically and Verbally

In a one-tailed significance test, the researchers make a specific prediction about whether the program will increase or decrease the dependent variable (i.e., physical fitness score), and therefore, there is one critical region. In this case, the *research hypothesis* would be that *the program increases physical fitness scores* and therefore the critical region would be on the positive side of the distribution. The *null hypothesis* would be that *the program does not increase physical fitness*. The null and research hypotheses will always be mutually exclusive and will cover all possible outcomes.

Reading Question

9. One-tailed significance tests

   a. have one critical region that is either on the positive or negative side of a distribution.

   b. have two critical regions one on the positive side and one on the negative side of a distribution.

Reading Question

10. When using a one-tailed significance test, if the research hypothesis predicts an increase (or positive change), the critical region will be on the _____ side of the distribution.

   a. negative

   b. positive

You should notice two things about the null and research hypotheses for a one-tailed significance test. First, because they are mutually exclusive, one of them has to be correct. Second, the one-tailed hypotheses indicate that researchers will only reject the null hypothesis if the *t* value is far from zero AND if it is in the direction stated in the research hypothesis. In this case, the researchers would only reject the null hypothesis if the *t* value is far from zero on the positive side of the *t* distribution. A *t* value in a positive critical region would indicate that the new program improved physical fitness scores. In this example, a *t* value that is far from zero in the negative direction would result in failing to reject the null hypothesis. The symbolic and verbal representations of the research and null hypotheses are presented in Table 8.2.

Table 8.2   Symbolic and verbal representations for one-tailed research and null hypotheses for single sample *t* test.

	Symbolic	Verbal
Research hypothesis (H_1)	$H_1 : \mu_{\text{new program}} > 100$	The physical fitness scores of the students in the new physical fitness program *are higher* than the average physical fitness scores in the population.
Null hypothesis (H_0)	$H_0 : \mu_{\text{new program}} \leq 100$	The physical fitness scores of the students in the new physical fitness program *are not higher* than the average physical fitness scores in the population.

Step 2: Define the Critical Region

In the previous discussion about critical regions you learned that as sample size increases, the critical value gets closer to zero. To locate the critical region, you will use a table of critical *t* values (Appendix B). Most tables of critical *t* values are organized around the degrees of freedom (*df*) for the specific statistical test rather than sample size (*N*). Therefore, in order to determine the critical region you will need to compute the *df* for the statistical test you are using. For the single sample *t* test the *df* formula is $df = N - 1$. So, in this case,

$$df = N - 1 = 15 - 1 = 14.$$

Use the table of *t* critical values in Appendix B to find the specific *t* critical value when $df = 14$. In this case, find the *df* in the left most column and then find the value in that row under the one-tailed .05 heading. You should find that when $df = 14$, the critical value is 1.761. The research hypothesis predicted that our sample mean would be greater than our population mean (i.e., a positive difference for $M - \mu$). Thus, the critical region is on the positive side of the distribution, and the critical region is defined by +1.761. Therefore, the null hypothesis should be rejected if $t \geq +1.761$.

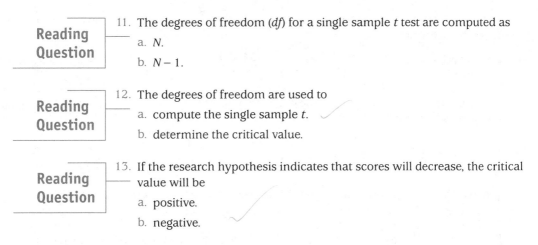

Reading Question

11. The degrees of freedom (*df*) for a single sample *t* test are computed as
    a. *N*.
    b. *N* − 1.

Reading Question

12. The degrees of freedom are used to
    a. compute the single sample *t*.   ✓
    b. determine the critical value.

Reading Question

13. If the research hypothesis indicates that scores will decrease, the critical value will be
    a. positive.
    b. negative.   ✓

Step 3: Compute the Test Statistic

Step 3a: Compute the Deviation Between the Sample Mean and the Population Mean

Begin by computing the deviation between the sample mean and the population mean.

$$(M - \mu) = (102.87 - 100) = 2.87$$

In this case, the observed deviation is 2.87.

Step 3b: Compute the Average Sampling Error Expected

To interpret the observed deviation of 2.87, you need to determine how much of a difference you would expect between M and μ due to sampling error. Sampling error is estimated by computing the estimated standard error of the mean $\left(SEM_s = \dfrac{SD}{\sqrt{N}} \right)$. To compute sampling error, you need to know the standard deviation of the sample (SD) and the size of the sample (N). In this problem, the standard deviation of the sample is not given to you. Therefore, you must compute it from the sample data. As you may recall from Chapter 3, computing the SS (i.e., the sum of squared deviations) is the first step to computing SD. The computational formula for SS is $SS = \Sigma X^2 - \dfrac{(\Sigma X)^2}{N}$. You need to sum all of the scores to find ΣX. Then, you need to square every score and sum all of the squared scores to find ΣX^2. In this example, $\Sigma X = 1543$, and the $\Sigma X^2 = 159073$. There were 15 scores, so $N = 15$. Therefore, the SS is computed as shown below.

$$SS = \Sigma X^2 - \frac{(\Sigma X)^2}{N} = 159073 - \frac{(1543)^2}{15} = 159073 - 158723.267 = 349.73$$

The standard deviation is computed by dividing the SS by $N - 1$ and taking the square root of the quotient.

$$SD = \sqrt{\frac{SS}{N-1}} = \sqrt{\frac{349.73}{14}} = 5$$

And finally, the standard error of the mean is computed by dividing the standard deviation by the square root of the sample size.

$$SEM_s = \frac{SD}{\sqrt{N}} = \frac{5}{\sqrt{15}} = 1.29$$

In this case, the typical amount of sampling error was computed to be 1.29. In this case, sample means will typically be 1.29 away from the population mean due to sampling error.

Reading Question

14. For this example, the observed difference between the sample mean and the population mean was _____ ; the difference expected due to sampling error was _____ .

    a. 1.29; 2.87

    b. 2.87; 1.29

Step 3c: Compute the Test Statistic (Single Sample t Test)

Dividing the observed difference between the sample mean and the population mean by the estimate of typical sampling error yields the obtained t value.

$$t = \frac{M - \mu}{SEM_s} = \frac{102.87 - 100}{1.29} = 2.22$$

To determine if you should reject or fail to reject the null hypothesis, you compare the obtained *t* value (2.22) to the critical value. In this case, the obtained *t* value associated with the sample mean of 102.87 (i.e., 2.22) was in the critical region. In other words, 2.22 is further from zero than the critical value of 1.761. This means that there is less than a 5% chance that the mean of 102.87 is due to random sampling error. Therefore, we reject the null hypothesis in favor of the research hypothesis and conclude that the program seems to have improved physical fitness scores in this sample of 15 children.

Reading Question

15. If the obtained *t* value is further from zero than the critical value, you should

 a. reject the null hypothesis.

 b. fail to reject the null hypothesis.

Step 4: Compute an Effect Size, and Describe It

As with the *z* for a sample mean, careful researchers compute effect sizes for single sample *t* tests so they can determine if the "treatment" was only slightly, moderately, or very beneficial. The effect size estimate for the single sample *t* test is computed in the same way it was for the *z* for a sample mean except the sample standard deviation (i.e., *SD*) is the denominator rather than the population standard deviation (i.e., σ).

$$\text{Cohen's } d = \frac{\text{Observed deviation between the means}}{\text{Standard deviation}} = \frac{M - \mu}{SD} = \frac{102.87 - 100}{5} = .57$$

The effect size computation means that the size of the difference between the physical fitness scores of children who experience the new physical fitness program and those who did not experience the program is .57 standard deviations. The same effect size guidelines are used for *z* and *t*, namely, *d*'s close to .2, .5, and .8 are small, medium, and large, respectively. In this case, the effect size of .57 is medium.

Reading Question

16. When computing an effect size for a single sample *t* test, the denominator is

 a. the sample standard deviation.

 b. the population standard deviation.

Step 5: Interpret the Results of the Hypothesis Test

As before with the *z* for the sample mean, the final step of the hypothesis testing procedure is to summarize the results by indicating if the fitness program worked or not. The summaries must also include the mean of the sample and population, the *df*, the obtained *t* value, if the *p* value was less than or greater than the alpha value and the computed effect size. Psychologists report the statistical information in a very specific format. An example APA summary statement is shown below.

The average physical fitness score for the students in the new physical education fitness program (*M* = 102.87, *SD* = 5.00) is significantly higher than the population mean (μ = 100), *t*(14) = 2.22, *p* < .05, *d* = .57.

17. The number in the parentheses in the character string "$t(14) = 2.22$, $p < .05$, $d = .57$" is the

    a. number of participants in the study.

    b. degrees of freedom.

    c. critical t value.

TWO-TAILED SINGLE SAMPLE t-TEST EXAMPLE

In the previous example, we used a one-tailed t test (also known as a directional test) to test the null hypothesis. It is also possible to use a two-tailed t test (also known as a nondirectional test). For example, suppose that a different researcher was also interested in the effects of the physical fitness program on children. However, this researcher was interested in the effect that this program might have on the self-esteem of the children. To determine the effect of this program on self-esteem, a different sample of 15 children is selected and placed in the physical fitness program. After 3 months, each child is given a standardized self-esteem test. The researcher is not sure if the program will increase or decrease the children's self-esteem, so she correctly chose to do a two-tailed test rather than a one-tailed test.

In two-tailed hypothesis tests, the researcher does not have a specific directional prediction concerning the treatment. Therefore, the two-tailed research hypothesis states that the fitness program will *either increase or decrease* the children's self-esteem. Thus, two-tailed research hypotheses have two critical regions, one in the positive tail and one in the negative tail. If the obtained t value were in the positive critical region, the researcher would conclude that the program increases children's self-esteem. Conversely, if the obtained t value were in the negative critical region, the researcher would conclude that the program decreases children's self-esteem. Finally, if the obtained t value were "close to zero" (i.e., between the positive and negative critical values), the researcher would fail to reject the null hypothesis.

The choice between a one- and two-tailed test can have a dramatic impact on the critical region(s), and therefore, your decision about whether to use a one- or two-tailed test can influence whether or not you reject the null hypothesis. For example, if your sample has 15 people and you conduct a one-tailed test with $\alpha = .05$, you would reject the null if your obtained t value was $+1.8$. However, if you analyzed the same data but chose to conduct a two-tailed test you would fail to reject the null if your obtained t value was $+1.8$. Figure 8.2 below makes this point visually. The reason for the different conclusion is that the one-tailed test critical value is closer to zero than the two-tailed critical values. For both types of tests, 5% of the distribution is in a critical region. With a two-tailed test, this means that 2.5% of the sample means are in each tail of the distribution. With a one-tailed test, 5% of the sample means are in one tail of the distribution. This means that the critical value will be closer to zero for a one-tailed test than a two-tailed test. Therefore, if your research hypothesis is directional, it is to your advantage to use a one-tailed test rather than a two-tailed test. This point is made visually in Figure 8.2.

Figure 8.2   Two-tail and one-tail test examples.

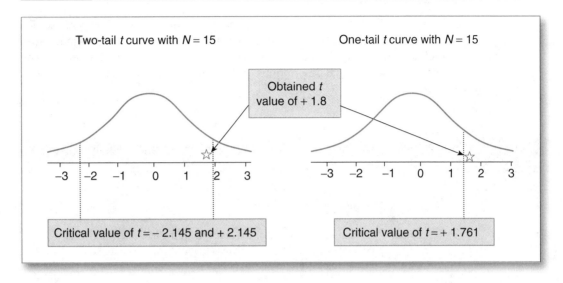

Two-tail *t* curve with *N* = 15

One-tail *t* curve with *N* = 15

Obtained *t*
value of + 1.8

–3 –2 –1   0   1   2   3   –3 –2 –1   0   1   2   3

Critical value of *t* = – 2.145 and + 2.145

Critical value of *t* = + 1.761

Reading Question

18. Why is your decision to conduct a one-tailed rather than a two-tailed test potentially important?

    a. One- and two-tailed tests have different critical regions and therefore may lead to different conclusions about the null hypothesis.

    b. One- and two-tailed tests will produce different obtained *t* values.

Reading Question

19. When should you conduct a one-tailed test?

    a. Conduct a one-tailed test when the research hypothesis sets up two critical regions.

    b. Conduct a one-tailed test when the research hypothesis sets up one critical region.

The program described above was designed to increase physical fitness, but researchers are also concerned about what effect this program might have on the self-esteem of children. A different sample of 15 children is selected and placed in this program. After 3 months, each child is given a standardized self-esteem test. For the general population of elementary school children, the scores on the self-esteem test form a normal distribution with a mean of 50. The scores of the 15 students in the new physical fitness program are as follows: 55, 48, 51, 60, 66, 53, 54, 49, 47, 51, 41, 47, 61, 58, and 45. The researcher is not sure what effect the physical fitness program will have on self-esteem, so she correctly chooses to do a two-tailed test rather than a one-tailed test. She used an alpha of .05.

Step 1: State the Research Hypothesis and Null Hypothesis Symbolically and Verbally

The null and research hypotheses for two-tailed tests are different from the hypotheses for one-tailed tests. For a two-tailed test, the *null hypothesis* is always that the treatment does not have an effect. The *research hypothesis* is that the treatment does have an effect. The symbolic notation and the verbal descriptions of the null and research hypotheses for this study are presented in Table 8.3.

Table 8.3	Symbolic and verbal representations for two-tailed research and null hypotheses for a single sample *t* test.

	Symbolic	Verbal
Research hypothesis (H_1)	$H_1: \mu \neq 50$	The self-esteem scores of the students in the new physical fitness program *are* significantly different from the average self-esteem scores in the population.
Null hypothesis (H_0)	$H_0: \mu = 50$	The self-esteem scores of the students in the new physical fitness program *are not* significantly different from the average self-esteem scores in the population.

Always use the "not equal" sign for a two-tailed research hypothesis. This indicates that you are predicting that the sample mean will be different from the population mean. You are not specifying whether the sample mean will be higher or lower than the population mean, just that it will be different.

Reading Question

20. Which of the following symbols should be used to represent a two-tailed research hypothesis?

   a. $\leq$

   b. $>$

   c. $=$

   d. $\neq$

Step 2: Define the Critical Regions

The formula for *df* is the same for one- and two-tailed tests. As was the case in the one-tailed example, the *df* here is

$$df = N - 1 = 15 - 1 = 14.$$

Now you will use the table of critical values of *t* in Appendix B to determine the critical value for a two-tailed test when the *df* = 14. In this case, find the *df* in the left most column and then find the value in that row under the two-tailed .05 heading. You should find the critical value of *t* with 14 degrees of freedom to be 2.145. Therefore, the two cut lines that define the positive and negative critical regions are located at +2.145 and −2.145, respectively. Figure 8.3 will help you visualize these two critical regions on the distribution of *t* values.

Step 3: Compute the Test Statistic

Step 3a: Compute the Deviation Between the Sample Mean and the Population Mean

This step is identical to a one-tailed test.

$$(M - \mu) = (52.4 - 50) = 2.4$$

Step 3b: Compute the Typical Sampling Error Expected

This step is identical to a one-tailed test. As in the previous example, the standard deviation of the sample (i.e., *SD*) is not given to you in the problem, so you must compute it from the sample data. If you are not sure how this is done, you should review the previous example. In this problem, the standard error of the mean is defined by

$$SEM_S = \frac{SD}{\sqrt{N}} = \frac{6.74}{\sqrt{15}} = 1.74.$$

In this case, the typical amount of sampling error was computed to be 1.74. In this case, all of the possible sample means are, on average, 1.74 away from the population mean due to sampling error.

Step 3c: Compute the Test Statistic (Single Sample *t* Test)

The computation of the test statistic is also identical for one- and two-tailed tests.

$$t = \frac{M - \mu}{SEM_s} = \frac{52.4 - 50}{1.74} = 1.38$$

The *t* value associated with the sample mean of 52.4 (i.e., 1.38) was not in either critical region. This means that there is more than a 5% chance that the mean difference is due to sampling error. Therefore, we fail to reject the null hypothesis concluding that the program did not significantly impact children's self-esteem. Figure 8.3 may help you visualize the outcome of this two-tailed hypothesis test.

Figure 8.3	Visual representation of the relationship between the obtained t value and the two critical regions.

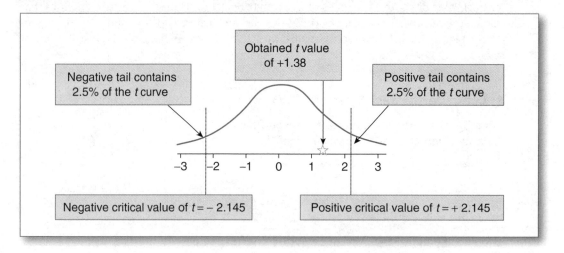

Step 4: Compute an Effect Size, and Describe It

The computation of the effect size is identical for one- and two-tailed tests.

$$\text{Cohen's } d = \frac{\text{Observed deviation between the means}}{\text{Standard deviation}} = \frac{M - \mu}{SD} = \frac{52.4 - 50}{6.74} = 0.36.$$

The effect size computation indicates that the size of the difference between the self-esteem of children who experience the new physical fitness program and those who do not is .36 standard deviations, a small-medium sized effect.

Step 5: Interpret the Results of the Hypothesis Test

The only difference in writing the summaries of one- and two-tailed hypothesis tests is that you need to let the reader know if the test you ran was one- or two-tailed. It is good practice to always do this, but we have not done so previously because you did not yet know about both types of tests. The following sentences summarizes the analysis from this example.

The average self-esteem score for the students in the new physical education program ($M = 52.40$, $SD = 6.74$) is not significantly different from the population mean ($\mu = 50$), $t(14) = 1.38$, $p > .05$ (two-tailed), $d = .36$. However, the small-medium effect size suggests that the study should be replicated with a larger sample size.

Reading Question

21. For which of the following hypothesis testing steps is there a difference between one-tailed and two-tailed tests? (You should choose 3 of the following 5 steps.)

a. Step 1: stating null and research hypotheses

b. Step 2: defining the critical region

c. Step 3: computing the test statistic

d. Step 4: computing the effect size

e. Step 5: writing the results

OTHER ALPHA LEVELS

In both of the examples above we chose to use an alpha of .05 because this is the most commonly used alpha level. However, in some cases, researchers choose to use the more stringent alpha level of .01. If you were to use $\alpha = .01$ with a two-tailed test with $df = 14$ your critical regions would be $t > 2.977$ and $t < -2.977$. If you were to use $\alpha = .01$ with a one-tailed test with $df = 14$ your critical regions would be $t > 2.624$.

When the null hypothesis is true, the probability of a Type I error is equal to the alpha value you choose. Therefore, if you choose the more stringent alpha value of .01, you are making it harder to reject the null hypothesis. This means that you are *less likely to make a Type I* error, but you also have less statistical power and are *more likely to make a Type II error* when you use an alpha value of .01 rather than .05.

Reading Question

22. Which of the following alpha values creates a greater probability of a Type I error?

a. .01

b. .05

Reading Question

23. Which of the following alpha values creates a greater probability of a Type II error?

a. .01

b. .05

Reading Question

24. Which of the following alpha values results in more statistical power?

a. .01

b. .05

SPSS

Data File

Enter the scores for the first problem (the physical fitness scores) as described in Chapter 1. When you are done, your data file should look like the one in Figure 8.4.

Figure 8.4   SPSS screenshot of data entry screen.

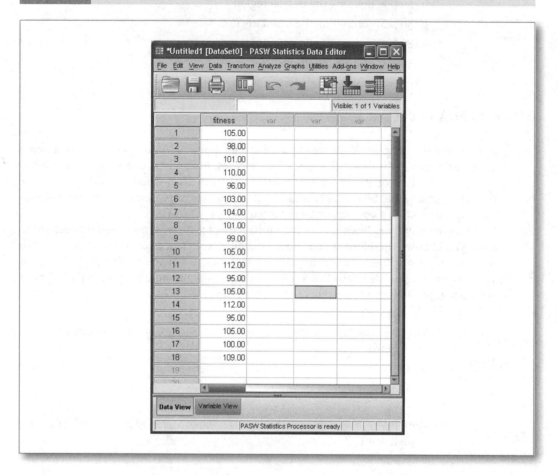

Obtaining a Single Sample *t*

- Click on the Analyze menu. Choose Compare Means and then One Sample *t* Test.
- Move the variable of interest into the variables box.
- Change the Test Value if necessary.

  ○ The Test Value is the number you are comparing the sample mean to.
  ○ If your *t* is wrong, it is most likely because you left the Test Value as 0.

- Click on the OK button.

Annotated Output

Your output will have the two boxes in Figure 8.5.

Figure 8.5 Annotated SPSS output for a one sample *t* test.

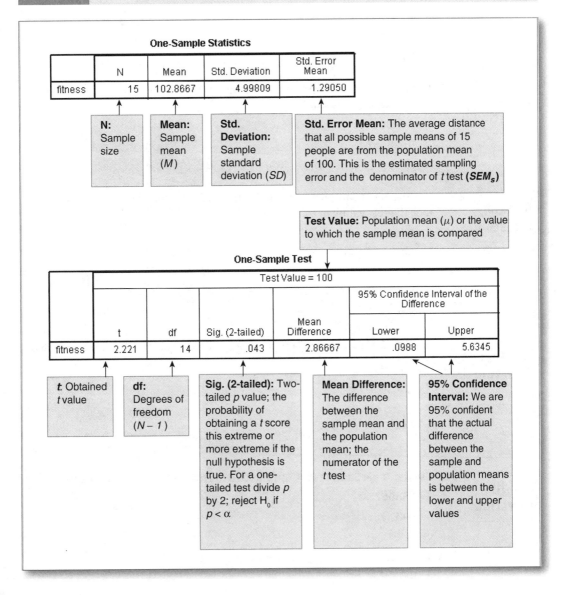

One-Sample Statistics

	N	Mean	Std. Deviation	Std. Error Mean
fitness	15	102.8667	4.99809	1.29050

N: Sample size

Mean: Sample mean (*M*)

Std. Deviation: Sample standard deviation (*SD*)

Std. Error Mean: The average distance that all possible sample means of 15 people are from the population mean of 100. This is the estimated sampling error and the denominator of *t* test (**SEM_s**)

Test Value: Population mean (μ) or the value to which the sample mean is compared

One-Sample Test

	Test Value = 100					
					95% Confidence Interval of the Difference	
	t	df	Sig. (2-tailed)	Mean Difference	Lower	Upper
fitness	2.221	14	.043	2.86667	.0988	5.6345

t: Obtained *t* value

df: Degrees of freedom (*N* – 1)

Sig. (2-tailed): Two-tailed *p* value; the probability of obtaining a *t* score this extreme or more extreme if the null hypothesis is true. For a one-tailed test divide *p* by 2; reject H₀ if $p < \alpha$

Mean Difference: The difference between the sample mean and the population mean; the numerator of the *t* test

95% Confidence Interval: We are 95% confident that the actual difference between the sample and population means is between the lower and upper values

Interpreting the SPSS Output

Reading Question

25. When you enter data into SPSS, each person's data (i.e., score) goes in its own
   a. row.
   b. column.

Reading Question

26. Use the "One-Sample Statistics" output to determine how many people were in this study (i.e., the size of the sample).

   a. 4.99809

   b. 102.8667

   c. 15

Reading Question

27. Use the "One-Sample Statistics" output to determine what the mean of the sample was in this study.

   a. 4.99809

   b. 102.8667

   c. 15

Reading Question

28. Use the "One Sample t test" output to determine the population mean (i.e., the test value) in this study.

   a. 2.86667

   b. .043

   c. 14

   d. 2.221

   e. 100

Reading Question

29. Use the "One Sample Test" output to determine the obtained t value in this study.

   a. 2.86667

   b. .043

   c. 14

   d. 2.221

   e. 100

Reading Question

30. Use the "One Sample Test" output to determine the p value in this study.

   a. 2.86667

   b. .043

   c. 14

   d. 2.221

   e. 100

Reading Question

31. Use the "One Sample Test" output to determine if the null hypothesis of this study should be rejected.

   a. The null hypothesis should be rejected because the p value (Sig.) is less than .05.

   b. The null hypothesis should NOT be rejected because the p value (Sig.) is less than .05.

Activity 8-1:   Single Sample *t*

Learning Objectives

After completing this activity, you should be able to do the following:

- Write a null hypothesis and research hypothesis using symbols and words
- Compute the degrees of freedom and define a critical region
- Compute a single sample *t* using a calculator and SPSS
- Determine if you should reject or fail to reject the null hypothesis
- Compute and interpret an effect size (*d*)
- Summarize the results of the analysis using APA style
- Interpret the SPSS output for a single sample *t*
- Explain how you decide to reject the null hypothesis based on the Sig. (*p*) value provided by SPSS for both one- and two-tailed tests

ONE- AND TWO-TAILED TESTS

1. Renner and Mackin (1998) gave a survey assessing levels of stress to 239 students at a university in the Eastern United States. The mean stress score for this group was 1,247. A student wonders if those attending a women's college have different stress levels than those attending coed colleges. She gave the same scale used by Renner and Mackin (1998) to a sample of 12 students from a women's college to determine if their stress levels were *significantly different* from the students in the original Renner and Mackin (1998) study (in which $\mu = 1247$). Given below are the data from the 12 students.

200	900	740
850	500	400
2300	650	700
1300	950	1000

2. Why can't you use a *z* test to analyze these data?

3. Analyze the data by hand. *Use a two-tailed test with an alpha of .05* to determine if the mean score for this sample is significantly different from a score of 1247 (the mean score produced by the normative sample).

a. State the null and research hypotheses in symbols and in words.

b. Compute the degrees of freedom and define the critical region.

c. Compute the test statistic. (*Note:* You will need to compute the sample M and SD.)

d. Compute an effect size, and describe the effect as small, small-medium, and so on.

e. Interpret d in terms of the standard deviation.

f. Choose one of the following APA-style summaries for the analysis you just completed. Fill in the three blanks with the (df), obtained t value, and the effect size (i.e., d) *only for the correct summary*.

    a. The students' scores ($M = 874.17$, $SD = 535.56$) were significantly lower than the population ($\mu = 1247$), t (_____) = _____, $p < .05$ (two-tailed), $d =$ _____.

    b. The students' scores ($M = 874.17$, $SD = 535.56$) were significantly higher than the population ($\mu = 1247$), t (_____) = _____, $p < .05$ (two-tailed), $d =$ _____.

    c. The students' scores ($\mu = 874.17$, $SD = 535.56$) were not significantly different from the population ($M = 1247$), t (_____) = _____, $p < .05$ (two-tailed), $d =$ _____.

4. You may have made an error when you decided to reject or fail to reject the null. Which error do you think you might have made (Type I or Type II)? Explain your choice.

5. Use SPSS to reanalyze the data you just analyzed by hand.
   - Enter the data into one column in the SPSS data editor
   - Click on the Analyze menu. Choose Compare Means and then One Sample t Test.
   - Move the Stress Scores variable into the variables box
   - Change the Test Value to the μ of the comparison group (i.e., 1247)
   - Click on the OK button

Locate each number that you computed by hand in the SPSS output. What information did you need when you computed this problem by hand that you do NOT need when you use SPSS? The obtained *t* value provided by SPSS should be the same as the value you computed by hand.

6. Explain how you decide if you should reject the null hypothesis when doing hand computations versus SPSS. Be clear about how the decision-making criteria are different for one-tailed and two-tailed tests.

7. The Women's College Coalition argues that students at women's colleges are more satisfied with their college experience than students at coed colleges. A student wonders if this is related to stress. Specifically, she wants to determine if students at a women's college experience *less* stress than the general population. To test this hypothesis, the student gives the survey to $N = 1150$ students at a women's college and obtains a mean score of 1198 with a standard deviation of 654. Is the sample mean significantly less than the normative mean of 1247? State the research and null hypotheses for this test with words and population parameters.

8. Explain why you should use a one-tailed significance test for this research scenario.

9. Define the critical region for a one-tailed test with an alpha of .05.

10. What effect does increasing the sample size have on the critical value?

11. Compute the test statistic.

12. Compute an effect size and describe the effect as small, small-medium, and so on.

13. Interpret d in terms of the standard deviation.

14. Write a summary of the results. Do more than say reject or fail to reject the null hypothesis. Explain what this means in terms of the independent variable (IV) and the dependent variable (DV). Use the options provided in Question 3f as a guide.

15. Explain why this analysis does not provide strong evidence that students at women's colleges experience less stress than the general population. Be sure to talk about the size of the effect and whether the effect was statistically significant.

16. In general, a larger sample size results in a _____ denominator of the t statistic, which will _____the value of the obtained t.
    a. smaller, increase
    b. smaller, decrease
    c. larger, increase
    d. larger, decrease

17. In the problems above, the sample sizes varied widely, and this change in sample size changed the critical values. Explain why increasing the sample size changes the critical value for a t test but not a z test.

18. True or False: The critical value for a t test changes with sample size but the size of the critical region does NOT change; it is still equal to the alpha level.

19. When computing the single sample t, we use the sample standard deviation rather than the population standard deviation to compute the test statistic. Explain why it would be better to use the population standard deviation if possible.

CHOOSE THE CORRECT STATISTIC

From this point until Chapter 16, each chapter of this book introduces a new statistic that can be used to answer research questions. In each chapter, it is obvious which statistic should be used because we work with only one statistic in each chapter. However, when you collect your own data you must determine which statistic should be used to answer your research question. Right now you know three different statistics that can be used to answer research questions: (1) the *z* for a single score, (2) the *z* for a sample mean, and (3) the single sample *t*. Determine which statistic should be used in each of the following research scenarios: *z* for a single score, *z* for sample mean, or single sample *t*.

20. A researcher wants to compare a sample mean to a population mean but the population standard deviation is unknown.

21. A researcher wants to compare a sample mean to a population mean and the population standard deviation is known.

22. A researcher wants to compare a sample mean to a value of theoretical interest.

23. A researcher wants to locate a score within a distribution of scores.

24. In order to join the U.S. Army, male and female recruits must be at least 58 inches tall. In the United States, female heights are normally distributed with a mean of $\mu = 64$ inches and a standard deviation of $\sigma = 4$ inches. What percentage of women would be unable to join the army because of the height requirement?

25. New army recruits are also required to take a test called the Armed Services Vocational Aptitude Battery (ASVAB). This test is standardized so that it is normally distributed with a mean of $\mu = 50$ and a standard deviation of $\sigma = 10$. A recruiter wonders if soldiers who are nurses have higher than average ASVAB scores. To test this, the recruiter records the ASVAB scores of a sample of 37 nurses and finds that their mean score was 58. Is this significantly higher than 50?

26. An industrial/organizational psychologist wonders if nurses in the Army are more or less satisfied with their career as nurses than nurses in the civilian sector. Previous research conducted by the psychologist revealed that civilian nurses rated their overall job satisfaction as a 7.3 on a 10-point scale. To determine if Army nurses have different levels of job satisfaction, the psychologist recruited a sample of 58 nurses in the Army and asked them to indicate their overall level of job satisfaction on a 10-point scale with 1 = *not at all satisfied* and 10 = *very satisfied*. The mean for the sample was 7.9 with a standard deviation of 1.64.

REFERENCE

Renner, M. J., & Mackin, R. (1998). A life stress instrument for classroom use. *Teaching of Psychology, 25,* 46–48.

Activity 8-2:   Practice Problems

SCENARIO 1: ONE-TAILED SINGLE SAMPLE t TEST

A health psychologist developed a program to improve the eating habits of elementary school children. In this program, students learned about the value of eating fruits and vegetables. Students played games and read stories about the importance of fruits and vegetables for a healthy diet. They also learned how to make some simple recipes. At the end of the course, the researcher asked the parents to record the number of servings of fruits and vegetables the children ate in 1 week. The researcher was interested in determining if they ate more than 5 servings a day (the minimum recommended). Data were collected over 7 days, so the researcher tested if the students reported eating more than 35 servings of fruits and vegetables that week. The servings reported for each of the 10 students were 33, 43, 44, 35, 28, 30, 31, 38, 41, 38. Do a one-tailed test with an alpha of .05.

Do this problem by hand.

1. Which of the following is the correct null hypothesis for this study?

   a. $\mu_{program} < 35$

   b. $\mu_{program} \leq 35$

   c. $\mu_{program} > 35$

   d. $\mu_{program} \geq 35$

2. Which of the following is the correct null hypothesis for this study?

   a. The children in the program will consume more than 35 servings of fruits and vegetables.

   b. The children in the program will consume significantly less than 35 servings of fruits and vegetables.

   c. The children in the program will not consume more than 35 servings of fruits and vegetables.

3. Which of the following is the correct research hypothesis for this study?

   a. $\mu_{program} < 35$

   b. $\mu_{program} \leq 35$

   c. $\mu_{program} > 35$

   d. $\mu_{program} \geq 35$

4. Which of the following is correct research hypothesis for this study?

   a. The children in the program will consume more than 35 servings of fruits and vegetables.

b. The children in the program will consume less than 35 servings of fruits and vegetables.

c. The children in the program will not consume more than 35 servings of fruits and vegetables.

5. What is the *df* for this single sample *t*-test study when $N = 10$?

6. Which of the following is the correct critical region for this one-tailed *t*-test study using an alpha value of .05?

a. Reject H_0 if $t \geq 1.833$

b. Reject H_0 if $t \leq 1.833$

c. Reject H_0 if $t \geq 2.262$

d. Reject H_0 if $t \leq 2.262$

7. What is the deviation between the sample mean and the population mean (i.e., $M - \mu$)?

8. What is the average sampling error expected in this study $\left(\text{i.e.}, SEM_S = \dfrac{SD}{\sqrt{N}} \right)$?

9. What is the obtained *t* value for this study $\left(\text{i.e.}, t = \dfrac{M - \mu}{SEM_S} \right)$?

10. Should the null hypothesis of this study be rejected?

11. What is the effect size for this study $\left(\text{i.e., Cohen's } d = \dfrac{M - \mu}{SD} \right)$?

12. Is the effect size for this study small, small-medium, medium, medium-large, or large?

13. Which of the following is the best summary of this study's results?

a. The average servings of fruits and vegetables that participants going through the nutrition program reported eating ($M = 36.1$, $SD = 5.59$) is not significantly higher than 35, $t (9) = 0.62$, $p > .05$ (one-tailed), $d = .19$.

b. The average number of servings of fruits and vegetables that participants going through the nutrition program reported eating ($M = 36.1$, $SD = 5.59$) is significantly higher than 35, $t (9) = 0.62$, $p < .05$ (one-tailed), $d = .19$.

c. The average number of servings of fruits and vegetables that participants going through the nutrition program reported eating (35) is not significantly higher than the population mean ($M = 36.1$, $SD = 5.59$), $t (9) = 0.55$, $p > .05$ (one-tailed), $d = .19$.

d. The average number of servings of fruits and vegetables that participants going through the nutrition program reported eating (35) is significantly higher than the population mean ($M = 36.1$, $SD = 5.59$), $t (9) = 0.55$, $p < .05$ (one-tailed), $d = .19$.

SCENARIO 2: ONE-TAILED SINGLE SAMPLE t TEST

A company that sells herbal supplements claims that the herb gingko biloba helps reduce memory loss in elderly people. The company describes an experimental study on its website that it says proves gingko biloba reduces memory loss. The study used a sample of 9 elderly people between 70 and 75 years of age and gave all of them gingko biloba for 6 months. After 6 months, all 9 elderly people took a standardized memory test that is often used to measure memory performance in elderly people. The company then compared their sample's mean with the mean of a comparison group of 1,004 elderly people between the ages of 70 and 75 years that was reported in a research article written by a prominent memory researcher. The mean of the comparison group was $\mu = 9$. The company claimed that the fact that their sample's score was higher than the comparison groups score proved that gingko biloba improves memory. The memory scores for the 9 participants in the sample were 10, 9, 8, 12, 12, 13, 8, 7, 11.

14. Why is the fact that the sample mean was higher than the comparison group mean NOT sufficient evidence to claim that gingko biloba reduces memory loss. (*Hint*: What might have caused the difference between the sample mean and the comparison group mean in this study?)

15. You decide to "crunch the numbers" to determine if the observed difference between the memory scores is likely or unlikely to be due to sampling error. Start the hypothesis testing process by stating the null and research hypotheses for this study. Use a one-tailed test with $\alpha = .05$.

    a. Null hypothesis (H_0):

    b. Research hypothesis (H_1):

16. Compute the *df* and define the critical region. Draw the t curve to help you locate the critical value.

17. Compute the single sample t test.

18. Determine if you should reject or fail to reject the null hypothesis.

    a. Reject

    b. Fail to reject

19. Compute the effect size for this study and interpret it as small, small-medium, and so on.

20. Summarize the results of your single sample *t* test by *choosing one of the following paragraphs.* Fill in the blanks in the paragraph you choose with the appropriate statistical information. Both are good examples but one demonstrates how to write the summary when you reject the null and the other demonstrates how to write the summary when you do not reject the null.

    a. The mean memory score for those who took gingko biloba ($M =$_____, $SD =$ _____) was significantly higher than the mean memory score for the comparison group ($\mu =$_____), t (_____) = _____, $p < .05$ (one-tailed), $d =$ _____. These results do support the claim that gingko biloba improves memory performance of elderly people.

    b. The mean memory score for those who took gingko biloba ($M =$_____, $SD =$ _____) was not significantly higher than the mean memory score for the comparison group ($\mu =$_____), t (_____) = _____, $p > .05$ (one-tailed), $d =$ _____. These results do not support the claim that gingko biloba improves memory performance of elderly people. However, the fact that the null was not rejected even though the observed effect size was medium suggests that the sample size in this study ($n = 9$) was too small. Further research is needed to clarify the impact of gingko biloba on memory.

    While the research described by the company did not support their claim that gingko biloba improves memory performance, the fact that their observed effect size was medium in size suggests that their study may have had insufficient _____ and, therefore, their failure to reject the null may have been due to their committing a _____.

21. Fill in the blanks above with the appropriate terms from the following list.

    a. Type II error

    b. Type I error

    c. statistical power

SCENARIO 3: TWO-TAILED SINGLE SAMPLE *t* TEST

Memory researchers have consistently found that there is a decline in cognitive performance as people age. However, memory researchers have also found that elderly people who perform many challenging mental tasks as part of their daily routine maintain very high levels of cognitive performance. In fact, some evidence suggests that elderly people who are highly mentally active throughout adulthood score higher on some cognitive tasks than younger people who are less mentally active. Given these findings, it is not easy to predict how a group of elderly people will compare with younger people. In situations like this, researchers typically use a two-tailed significance test.

For example, the next study examined the working memory ability of 20 older people between the ages of 60 and 65 years who all currently work in professions that are "highly cognitively demanding." The research question is how working memory scores of these mentally active older adults would compare with the mean working memory score of senior high school students, which is known to be $\mu = 9$. The researcher did a two-tailed test with an alpha of .05. The 20 working memory scores for the older participants were 10, 9, 11, 8, 7, 12, 10, 13, 9, 11, 9, 8, 12, 13, 9, 10, 12, 11, 10, 9.

22. State the null and research hypotheses.

23. Compute the *df* and define the critical region. Draw the *t* curve to help you locate the two critical regions.

24. Compute the single sample *t* test.

25. Determine if you should reject or fail to reject the null hypothesis.
   a. Reject
   b. Fail to reject

26. Compute the effect size for this study and interpret it as small, small-medium, and so on.

27. Summarize the results of your single sample *t* test. Use one of the examples provided above as a guide.

SCENARIO 4: ONE-TAILED SINGLE SAMPLE *t* TEST

Elite disc golfers are very good "putters." In other words, they have practiced to the point that they can "putt" the disc into the basket very consistently from considerable distances. In fact, at a distance of 30 feet from the basket, elite disc golfers will make 9 of 10 putts. A statistician who is curious about his disc golf skills wants to know if the number of putts he makes from 30 feet is significantly less than 9 out of 10. For 7 days in a row, the statistician attempted 10 putts from 30 feet. Each day he recorded the number of putts he made out of 10 attempts. Use the data he collected below to determine if the average number of putts he made is significantly less than the elite standard of 9 out of 10.

28. State the null and research hypotheses for this study.

29. What is the critical value for this one-tailed test?

30. Compute the test statistic for these data.

Number of putts made from 30 feet
7
6
5
8
5
4
6

31. Compute the effect size for this study and interpret it as small, small-medium, and so on.

32. Write an APA-style summary of this analysis.

33. Enter these data into SPSS and run a one sample *t* test. Confirm that the obtained *t* value you computed by hand is the same as that produced by SPSS.

SCENARIO 5: TWO-TAILED SINGLE SAMPLE *t* TEST

On a particular disc golf course, a score of 72 is considered par. A statistician who plays disc golf wants to know if his average score on the course is significantly different than par, or 72 throws. For the next 17 times he plays the course, he records his final score and determines that his average score is 75.5 with a standard deviation of 2.1.

34. State the null and research hypotheses for this study.

35. What is the critical value for this two-tailed test?

36. Compute the test statistic for these data.

37. Compute the effect size for this study and interpret it as small, small-medium, and so on.

38. Write an APA-style summary of this analysis.

39. Enter these data into SPSS and run a one sample *t* test. Confirm that the obtained *t* value you computed by hand is the same as that produced by SPSS.

CHAPTER 9

Related Samples *t* Test

LEARNING OBJECTIVES

After reading this chapter, you should be able to do the following:

- Identify when a related samples *t* test should be used
- Explain the advantages of using a related samples design over an independent samples design
- Explain the logic of the related samples *t* test
- Explain what the mean difference should be if the null hypothesis is true
- Explain what the denominator of the related samples *t* test is measuring
- Write null and research hypotheses using symbols and words for both one- and two-tailed tests
- Compute the degrees of freedom and define the critical region for one- and two-tailed tests
- Compute a related samples *t* test by hand (using a calculator) and using SPSS
- Determine if you should reject or fail to reject the null hypothesis
- Compute an effect size (*d*) and interpret it
- Summarize the results of the analysis using APA style
- Interpret the SPSS output for a related samples *t* test

OTHER NAMES

The related samples *t* test is also referred to as a paired samples *t*, repeated measures *t*, and dependent measures *t*.

When to Use the Related Samples *t* Test

Previously, you learned that researchers use the single sample *t* test when they need to compare the mean of a sample with the mean of a population. For example, to test the effects of a new physical fitness program on the fitness of elementary school children, researchers could allow a sample of children to experience the new program and then compare their fitness levels after the program with the mean fitness level of the population of children who did not experience the program. The single sample t test can also be used to compare a sample mean with a value of "theoretical interest." For example, to test the effectiveness of a weight loss program, researchers could have a sample of people use the program and compare the sample's mean weight loss with the value of 0. If the sample's mean weight loss is significantly greater than 0, it would be evidence of the program's effectiveness. Clearly, the single sample t test can be very useful to researchers. However, in many situations, researchers do not know the population's mean, or they do not have a value of theoretical interest that can be tested. In these situations, researchers cannot use the single sample t test.

Reading Question

1. For researchers to use the single sample t test, they must know either the
    _____ or have a value of theoretical interest that enables them to
    compute the deviation of their sample mean from that predicted by the null
    hypothesis.
    a. population mean
    b. population standard deviation

RELATED SAMPLES t TEST

In this chapter, you will learn the related samples t test. It is similar to the single sample t test in that it compares the deviation between two means to determine if it is likely to have been created by sampling error. However, the related samples t test is different in that the two means it compares both come from the *same sample,* which is measured twice under different conditions. For example, if researchers wanted to test the effectiveness of a new drug intended to lower anxiety, they might take a sample of people, measure their anxiety first, then give them the new drug, and finally measure their anxiety after the drug had time to work. You might recognize this as a "pre–post" test. If the drug did not work at all, one would expect the mean anxiety level to be the same before and after taking the drug. However, if the drug worked, one would expect the mean anxiety level to be significantly lower after taking the drug than before taking it. In this situation, researchers use the same group of people to represent two different populations. The predrug sample mean represents what the population's anxiety level would be if they *did not* take the drug. The post-drug sample mean represents what the population's anxiety level would be if they *did* take the drug. Thus, the researchers are using one sample to produce two different sample means, and each sample mean estimates a different population parameter. If the deviation between the two sample means is unlikely to be created by sampling error, then the drug is assumed to have changed the anxiety level of the sample.

There is another situation in which researchers use the related samples t test. In some situations, researchers form pairs of people who are similar on some variable they are interested in "controlling." For example, researchers might create pairs of people who have the same anxiety scores (i.e., two people with anxiety scores of 180, two people with scores of 210, etc.). Then the researchers would randomly give one person from each "matched" pair the drug and the other a placebo. When using this "matching approach," the researchers analyze the data as if each matched pair was really a single person. The hypotheses, critical regions, and calculations are exactly the same as those used in the previous pre–post example. The hand calculation example below illustrates how this type of matching procedure is done.

2. Researchers use the related samples *t* test to determine if _____ differ more than would be expected by sampling error.

   a. two sample means

   b. a sample mean and a population mean

3. The related samples *t* test can be used for a study that is using

   a. a matching approach.

   b. a pre–post approach.

   c. both approaches.

LOGIC OF THE SINGLE SAMPLE AND RELATED SAMPLES *t* TESTS

The logic of the related samples *t* test is similar to that of the single sample *t* test. To help illustrate the similarities and differences between these two statistical tests, both formulas are given below (*SEM* = standard error of the mean):

$$\text{Single sample } t = \frac{M - \mu}{SEM_s}$$

$$\text{Related samples } t = \frac{M_D - \mu_D}{SEM_r}$$

The denominators of both the single sample *t* test and the related samples *t* test represent the typical amount of sampling error expected. The numerator of the single sample *t* test compares a sample mean (i.e., *M*) with an expected value if the null hypothesis were true (i.e., μ). The numerator of the related samples *t* test is slightly more complicated in that rather than comparing a single sample mean (i.e., *M*) with an expected value if the null hypothesis were true (i.e., μ), it actually compares the mean difference between two sample means (i.e., M_D; the D stands for difference) with the mean difference expected if the null is true (i.e., μ_D). For example, the researchers would compare the difference between the predrug anxiety mean and the postdrug anxiety mean with the mean difference expected if the drug did not work at all (i.e., μ_D, a mean difference of 0). In fact, researchers are almost always testing to see if the observed difference is significantly different from 0. In this book, we will always use $\mu_D = 0$ because it is exceedingly rare for researchers to use a value other than 0 (SPSS does not even allow the use of other values). If you use $\mu_D = 0$, it can be eliminated from the numerator, and the *t* formula can be simplified to

$$\text{Related samples } t = \frac{M_D}{SEM_r}.$$

Another important similarity between these t tests is that if the null hypothesis for either test were true you would expect to get an obtained t value close to 0. If the obtained t value were farther from 0 than a critical value, the null hypothesis would be rejected.

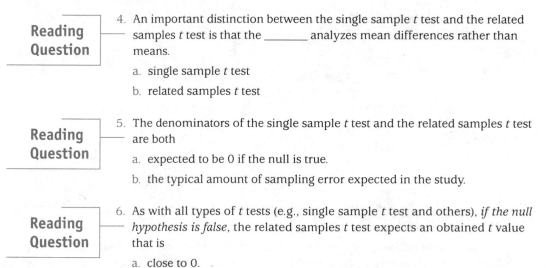

Reading Question

4. An important distinction between the single sample t test and the related samples t test is that the _____ analyzes mean differences rather than means.

    a. single sample t test

    b. related samples t test

Reading Question

5. The denominators of the single sample t test and the related samples t test are both

    a. expected to be 0 if the null is true.

    b. the typical amount of sampling error expected in the study.

Reading Question

6. As with all types of t tests (e.g., single sample t test and others), *if the null hypothesis is false*, the related samples t test expects an obtained t value that is

    a. close to 0.

    b. far from 0.

TWO-TAILED RELATED SAMPLES t TEST EXAMPLE

A medical researcher wants to determine if a new drug for treating anxiety has a side effect of *changing* cholesterol levels. Six pairs of people are matched on their preexisting cholesterol levels. Then, one person in the pair is given the new anxiety drug, while the other person is given a placebo. Eighteen weeks later, the researcher measures their cholesterol levels. Do a two-tailed hypothesis test with $\alpha = .05$ to determine if the drug *changes* cholesterol scores.

Step 1: State the Null and Research Hypotheses Symbolically and Verbally

In this case, the researcher is not sure what effect the anti-anxiety drug has on cholesterol, so she correctly chooses to do a two-tailed hypothesis test. The research hypothesis states that the drug does affect cholesterol levels. It is a nondirectional hypothesis in that it does not specify if the drug has a positive or negative effect. The null hypothesis is the opposite of the research hypothesis, stating that the drug does not affect cholesterol levels.

In this example, the researcher is using pairs of people who are matched on their pre-existing cholesterol levels. The researcher treats each matched pair of people as if they were a single participant. One person in each matched pair will get the drug, while the other will get a placebo. Those who get the drug help create a mean that represents people's cholesterol levels when taking the drug. Those who get the placebo help create a mean representing people's cholesterol levels when taking the placebo. The related samples *t* test does NOT directly compare these means. Instead, the related samples *t* test requires researchers to compute difference scores for each pair of people by subtracting each pair's placebo cholesterol score from their drug cholesterol score. The related samples *t* test determines if the mean of these difference scores is significantly different from 0. The symbolic notation for the mean of the difference scores is μ_D. Thus, the null hypothesis is that the mean of the difference scores is equal to 0 ($\mu_D = 0$), and the research hypothesis is that the mean of the difference scores is not equal to zero ($\mu_D \neq 0$). The null and research hypotheses are shown in Table 9.1.

Reading Question

7. In most research situations in which a related samples *t* test is used, the μ_D expected if the null is true is

   a. 0.

   b. 1.

   c. M_D.

Table 9.1	Symbolic and verbal representations for two-tailed research and null hypotheses for a repeated samples *t* test.

	Symbolic	Verbal
Research hypothesis (H_1)	$H_1: \mu_D \neq 0$	The anti-anxiety drug does affect cholesterol levels.
Null hypothesis (H_0)	$H_0: \mu_D = 0$	The anti-anxiety drug does not affect cholesterol levels.

Reading Question

8. Which of the following best represents the null hypothesis for a two-tailed related samples *t* test?

   a. $\mu_D \neq 0$

   b. $\mu_D = 0$

   c. $\mu_1 = \mu_2$

Reading Question

9. μ_D is the symbolic notation for

   a. the null hypothesis.

   b. the mean of the difference scores if the null hypothesis is true.

Step 2: Define the Critical Region

This research scenario uses a matched design. This means that the researcher is using a pair of people who are matched on their cholesterol levels as if they were just one person.

Therefore, when computing the degrees of freedom (*df*) for a matched design, *N* is the number of paired scores. In this case, *N* would be 6, and the *df* would be

$$df = (N-1) = (6-1) = 5.$$

To determine the critical value, you use the same table of critical *t* values we have used for all other *t* tests (Appendix B) and find it to be 2.571 when $\alpha = .05$. This means that the two-tailed critical regions are $t < -2.571$ and $t > +2.571$.

Step 3: Compute the Test Statistic

Step 3a: Compute *D* for Each Participant/Matched Pair

The first step in computing the related samples *t* statistic is computing the difference score (i.e., *D*) for each pair of scores. It is very important that you compute the difference in the same way for each pair of scores. In this case, the difference score was computed as Drug Score minus Placebo Score. The *D* for each pair of scores is computed in Table 9.2. *D* is the difference between the two scores for each participant pair.

Reading Question

10. Difference scores should always be positive.

   a. True

   b. False

Reading Question

11. The first step in computing a related samples *t* is to compute difference scores (*D*s) by

   a. subtracting the mean for Group 1 from the mean for Group 2.

   b. computing the *D* for each set of paired scores.

| Table 9.2 | Computation of *D* in a repeated samples *t* test. |

Pair	Placebo	Drug	D (Drug – Placebo)
A	180	188	8
B	200	201	1
C	190	197	7
D	170	174	4
E	210	215	5
F	195	194	−1

Step 3b: Compute the Observed Mean Difference (M_D)

The next step is to compute the numerator of the *t* (i.e., the mean of the difference scores) by adding the *D*s and dividing by the number of *D*s (*N*):

$$M_D = \frac{\Sigma D}{N} = \frac{24}{6} = 4.$$

Step 3c: Compute the Typical Mean Difference Expected Due to Sampling Error

The next step is computing the typical mean difference expected due to sampling error. At first glance, the sum of squares (*SS*) formula shown below appears different from the *SS* formula we used in previous chapters. The difference is only minor, however. The previous *SS* formula used the ΣX and ΣX^2. The following *SS* formula uses ΣD and ΣD^2 because the related samples *t* test is analyzing the change in scores (i.e., the difference scores, *D*s), not the scores themselves. The computational process is identical to that used for the single sample *t* test, except that difference scores (i.e., *D*s) are used instead of scores (*X*s) (*SD* = standard deviation):

$$SS_D = \Sigma D^2 - \frac{(\Sigma D)^2}{N} = 156 - \frac{(24)^2}{6} = 60.$$

$$SD_D = \sqrt{\frac{SS_D}{N-1}} = \sqrt{\frac{60}{5}} = \sqrt{12} = 3.46.$$

$$SEM_r = \frac{SD_D}{\sqrt{N}} = \frac{3.46}{\sqrt{6}} = 1.414.$$

This value of 1.41 is the typical sampling error for this study. It is the size of the expected difference between these sample means due to sampling error.

Reading Question

12. The related samples *t* test analyzes _____ rather than _____.

   a. deviations scores; difference scores

   b. raw scores; difference scores

   c. difference scores; raw scores

Reading Question

13. Which of the following values is a measure of sampling error?

   a. *SS*

   b. *SD*

   c. SEM_r

Step 3d: Compute the Test Statistic (Related Samples *t* Test)

The obtained *t* value for the related samples *t* test is computed below:

$$t = \frac{M_D}{SEM_r} = \frac{4}{1.414} = 2.83$$

The obtained *t* value of 2.83 is farther from 0 than the critical value of 2.571; therefore, it is in the positive critical region. Thus, you should reject the null hypothesis and conclude that people who took the anti-anxiety drug had higher cholesterol levels than people who took the placebo. This value of 2.83 indicates that the difference between the sample means was 2.83 times greater than would be expected by chance. Clearly, this large difference is very unlikely to be due to sampling error.

Reading Question

14. If the obtained *t* value (i.e., in this case 2.83) is farther from 0 than the critical value, the difference between the two means is

a. likely to be due to sampling error.

b. not likely to be due to sampling error.

Step 4: Compute an Effect Size, and Describe It

Computing the effect size (*d*) is done in a similar way as the effect size for the single sample *t* test. Specifically,

$$d = \frac{\text{Observed deviation between the means}}{\text{Standard deviation}} = \frac{M_D}{SD_D} = \frac{4}{3.46} = 1.15.$$

When computing a *d* for a related samples *t* test, the denominator is the standard deviation of the *D* scores (*SD_D*).

The same effect size cutoffs are used as with the one sample *t* test. Specifically, the effect size is small if *d* is close to .2, medium if it is close to .5, and large if it is close to .8. You should always use the absolute value when determining the size of the effect. In this case, the *d* of 1.15 is a large effect size. The difference in cholesterol levels between the placebo and drug conditions is 1.15 times larger than the standard deviation of *D* scores. This suggests that the new anti-anxiety drug has a large detrimental effect on cholesterol levels.

Reading Question

15. To compute the effect size, you divide the observed deviation between the means by

a. the standard error.

b. the standard deviation of the difference scores.

c. the mean standard deviation of the scores.

Step 5: Interpret the Results of the Hypothesis Test

The following sentences summarize the results of this related samples *t* test. You will need to compute the means for the drug and placebo groups by hand or using SPSS.

People who took the anti-anxiety drug had substantially higher cholesterol levels ($M = 194.83$, $SD = 13.64$) than people who took the placebo ($M = 190.83$, $SD = 14.29$), $t(5) = 2.83$, $p < .05$, $d = 1.15$. The drug raised cholesterol by more than 1 standard deviation. Clearly, the drug had a negative side effect on cholesterol.

Reading Question

16. The *effect size* in this study indicates that the anti-anxiety drug raised the cholesterol scores of the participants

    a. 1.15 times more than would be expected by chance.

    b. by 1.15 standard deviations, which is a very large effect.

ONE-TAILED RELATED SAMPLES *t*-TEST EXAMPLE

A new drug for treating anxiety has been developed. Obviously, it is expected to lower the anxiety scores of people with anxiety disorders. A psychiatrist recruits six people with high anxiety scores to volunteer for an evaluation study of the new drug. All six volunteers complete an anxiety inventory before taking the drug and then again after taking the drug for 1 month. Their pre- and postanxiety scores are displayed in Table 9.4. Use a one-tailed related samples *t* test with an alpha of .05 to determine if this new drug lowers anxiety scores.

Step 1: State the Null and Research Hypotheses Symbolically and Verbally

The null and research hypotheses are given in Table 9.3. Your hypotheses depend on how you compute the difference scores. In this case, the difference scores were computed as Before Drug minus After Drug. The research hypothesis predicts that anxiety scores will be lower after taking the drug. Therefore, if the difference scores are computed as Before Drug − After Drug and the research hypothesis is correct, the difference scores should be mostly negative.

Table 9.3	Symbolic and verbal representations for one-tailed research and null hypotheses for a related samples *t* test.

	Symbolic	Verbal
Research hypothesis (H_1)	$H_1: \mu_D < 0$	The drug *does* lower anxiety scores.
Null hypothesis (H_0)	$H_0: \mu_D \geq 0$	The drug *does not* lower anxiety scores.

17. Which of the following *could* represent the null hypothesis for a one-tailed related samples *t* test?

 a. $\mu_D > 0$

 b. $\mu_D < 0$

 c. $\mu_1 = \mu_2$

 d. $\mu_D \geq 0$

Step 2: Define the Critical Region

The *df* is computed identically for one- and two-tailed tests:

$$df = (N - 1) = (6 - 1) = 5$$

In this case, the critical region is $t < -2.015$.

18. When computing the *df* for a related samples *t* test, the *N* in the formula is the

 a. number of scores.

 b. number of pairs of scores.

Step 3: Compute the Test Statistic

Step 3a: Compute *D* for Each Participant/Matched Pair

As mentioned above, the related samples *t* test analyzes difference scores rather than raw scores. The difference score for each participant is computed in Table 9.4. All difference scores were computed by subtracting After Drug scores from Before Drug scores.

Table 9.4   Computing *D* for a repeated *t* test.

Volunteer	Before	After	D (Before – After)
A	22	19	−3
B	22	19	−3
C	23	18	−5
D	26	25	−1
E	23	20	−3
F	25	21	−4

19. When computing a related samples *t* test, you must remember that all of the analyses are done on

  a. the difference between the paired scores for each participant (i.e., *D*).

  b. the raw scores of each participant.

Step 3b: Compute the Observed Mean Difference (M_D)

The mean difference score (i.e., the numerator of the related samples *t* test) is computed below:

$$M_D = \frac{\Sigma D}{N} = \frac{-19}{6} = -3.17$$

Step 3c: Compute the Typical Mean Difference Expected Due to Sampling Error

The three computational steps for computing the expected sampling error are given below:

$$SS_D = \Sigma D^2 - \frac{(\Sigma D)^2}{N} = 69 - \frac{(-19)^2}{6} = 8.83$$

$$SD_D = \sqrt{\frac{SS_D}{N-1}} = \sqrt{\frac{8.83}{5}} = 1.33$$

$$SEM_r = \frac{SD_D}{\sqrt{N}} = \frac{1.33}{\sqrt{6}} = .54$$

This value of .54 is the typical expected sampling error. It is the size of the anxiety difference between the Before Drug and After Drug means that is expected due to sampling error.

Step 3d: Compute the Test Statistic (Related Samples *t* Test)

The obtained *t* value for the related samples *t* is computed below:

$$t = \frac{M_D}{SEM_r} = \frac{-3.17}{.54} = -5.87$$

The obtained *t* value of −5.87 is farther from 0 than the critical value of −2.015; therefore, it is in the negative critical region. Thus, you should reject the null hypothesis and conclude that the anxiety scores were lower after taking the drug than before taking the drug.

20. The obtained *t* value in this study indicates that

  a. the deviation between the sample means was 5.87 times larger than was expected due to sampling error.

  b. the null hypothesis should be rejected.

  c. Both a and b are correct.

Step 4: Compute an Effect Size, and Describe It

The effect size for this study is computed below:

$$\text{Cohen's } d = \frac{\text{Observed deviation between the means}}{\text{Standard deviation}} = \frac{M_D}{SD_D} = \frac{-3.17}{1.33} = -2.38.$$

A d of -2.38 is a large effect size. This means that the difference in anxiety levels between the Before Drug and After Drug treatment conditions is 2.38 times larger than the standard deviation of difference scores. This suggests that the new anti-anxiety drug is very effective at lowering anxiety levels.

Reading Question

21. The *effect size* in this study indicates that the drug lowered the anxiety of the participants

   a. 2.38 times more than would be expected by chance.

   b. by 2.38 standard deviations, which is a very large effect.

Step 5: Interpret the Results of the Hypothesis Test

The following sentences summarize the results of this study:

People had lower anxiety levels ($M = 20.33$, $SD = 2.50$) after taking the drug than they had prior to taking the drug ($M = 23.50$, $SD = 1.64$), $t(5) = -5.87$, $p < .05$ (one-tailed), $d = -2.38$. The reduction in anxiety scores was quite large, more than 2 standard deviations.

Reading Question

22. When writing the reporting statement of the results, the p value is written as less than .05 (i.e., $p < .05$) because

   a. the obtained t value was in the critical region.

   b. the null hypothesis was NOT rejected.

STATISTICAL RESULTS, EXPERIMENTAL DESIGNS, AND SCIENTIFIC CONCLUSIONS

The result of the above significance test seems to imply that the anti-anxiety drug works, and the effect size seems to imply that it is very effective. However, all statistical results must be interpreted cautiously, particularly paying close attention to the study's experimental design. In this study, the significance test indicates that something other than sampling error probably created the observed reduction in anxiety. Therefore, it may be tempting to conclude that the drug caused the reduction; but there is at least one other potential cause. In this pre–post design, participants' anxiety scores were measured before and after taking the drug; these measurements were separated by 1 month. One possible explanation is that people naturally get better with the passage of time. Participants might have gotten better without any treatment. Therefore, the passage of time is a *confound* in this study. It is also correct to say that the passage of time and the drug treatment are *confounded* in this study because it is impossible to know whether the passage of time, the drug, or some combination of both caused the reduction in anxiety. The lesson here is that you must consider potential confounding variables carefully before you interpret *any* statistical result. Ideally, researchers should use experimental designs that control for potential confounding variables. For example, researchers could control for improvement with time by using a control group of participants who received a placebo drug. If the placebo treatment did not reduce anxiety while the drug treatment did, the researchers could be pretty confident that the drug caused the anxiety reduction and not the passage of time. The key point is that a statistical result (i.e., rejecting a null or a large effect size) is only one portion of a convincing scientific argument. If a study has a confound, the statistical results are not very informative. Statistical results and experimental design are equally important to the scientific process. You will learn how to use experimental designs to control potential confounding variables in a research methods course.

Reading Question

23. When interpreting the statistical results of any study,

   a. you should consider if a confounding variable might have affected the results.

   b. you should recognize that the experimental design is just as important to the scientific conclusion as the statistical results.

   c. Both of the above are correct.

OTHER ALPHA LEVELS

When the null hypothesis is true, the probability of a Type I error is equal to the alpha value you choose. Therefore, if you choose the more stringent alpha value of .01, you are making it harder to reject the null hypothesis. This means that you are making a Type I error *less* likely but you are also making a Type II error *more* likely.

For a *two-tailed* test with $\alpha = .01$, the critical region would be

$$\text{Reject } H_0 \text{ if } t > 4.032 \text{ or } t < -4.032.$$

With a computed *t* of −5.87, you would reject the null hypothesis.

For a *one-tailed* test with $\alpha = .01$, the critical region would be

$$\text{Reject } H_0 \text{ if } t < -3.365.$$

With a computed *t* of −5.87, you would reject the null hypothesis.

Reading Question

24. How does the alpha value (i.e., α) and whether a hypothesis test is one-tailed or two-tailed influence its outcome?

   a. They both help determine the critical value, which determines the location of the "cut line" or "cut lines" between values that lead to rejecting versus not rejecting the null hypothesis.

   b. They both help determine the size of the obtained *t* value.

SPSS

Data File

To demonstrate how to run a related samples *t* test, we used the data from the first example (i.e., the effect of an anti-anxiety drug vs. placebo on cholesterol levels). To analyze repeated samples data, you need to create two columns in the data file. One column should have the placebo cholesterol levels, and the other column should have the drug cholesterol levels. When entering matched data, you must enter the data for each matched pair of participants on the same row in the data file. Likewise, when entering related samples data, in which the same people have been measured twice, you must enter the data for each participant on the same row in the data file. After you have entered them, the data from the first example problem should look like what is shown in Figure 9.1.

Obtaining a Related Samples *t* Test

- Click on the Analyze menu. Choose Compare Means and then Paired Samples *t* Test.
- Move both independent variable conditions (in this case Drug and Placebo) into the Paired Variables box. In some versions of SPSS, you have to move them into the box at the same time.
- Click on the OK button.

Figure 9.1   SPSS screenshot of the data entry screen.

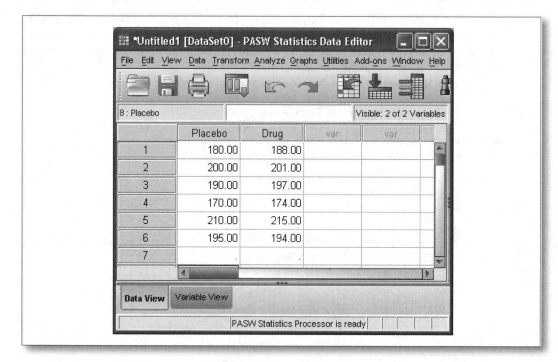

Annotated Output

Figure 9.2   Annotated SPSS output for a repeated *t* test.

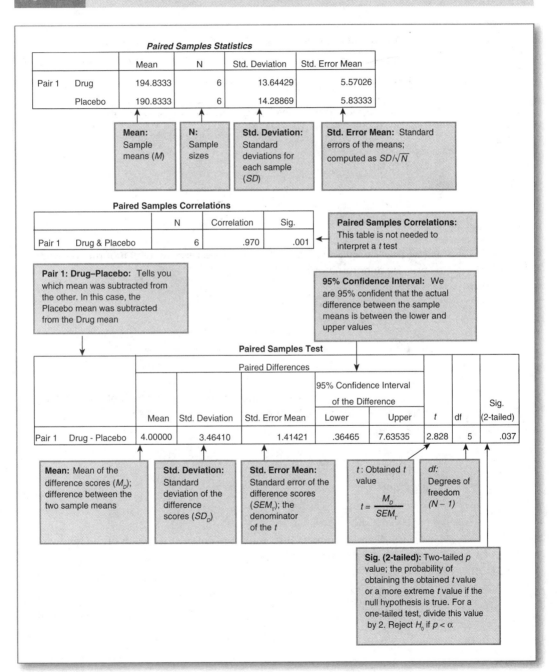

25. Use the "Paired Samples Statistics" output to determine the mean and standard deviation for the drug condition. The mean and standard deviation for the drug condition were

    a. 194.83 and 13.64, respectively.

    b. 190.83 and 14.29, respectively.

26. When you enter data for a related samples t test, you should

    a. have the paired scores on the same row of the spreadsheet.

    b. have as many columns as you have scores.

27. Use the "Paired Samples Test" output to determine which of the following was the numerator of the t test.

    a. 4.0000

    b. 3.46410

    c. 1.41421

    d. 2.828

    e. .037

28. Use the "Paired Samples Test" output to determine which of the following was the denominator of the t test.

    a. 4.0000

    b. 3.46410

    c. 1.41421

    d. 2.828

    e. .037

29. Use the "Paired Samples Test" output to determine which of the following was the obtained value for the t test.

    a. 4.0000

    b. 3.46410

    c. 1.41421

    d. 2.828

    e. .037

30. Use the "Paired Samples Test" output to determine which of the following values is the p value for this t test.

    a. 4.0000

    b. 3.46410

    c. 1.41421

    d. 2.828

    e. .037

Activity 9-1:   Hypothesis Testing With the Related Samples *t* Test

Learning Objectives

After reading the chapter and completing this activity, you should be able to do the following:

- Explain how the direction in which one computes the difference scores affects the sign of the obtained *t* value of a related samples *t* test
- Determine whether a one- or a two-tailed significance test is appropriate
- State the null and research hypotheses for a dependent *t* test in words and symbols
- Compute a dependent *t* test by hand and using SPSS
- Interpret and summarize the results of a dependent *t* test

SCENARIO 1: ONE-TAILED RELATED SAMPLES *t* TEST

In this scenario, researchers want to determine if viewing a documentary on the dangers of using a cell phone while driving would *decrease* the frequency of cell phone use while driving. To test this hypothesis, they asked 15 teenage drivers to watch a video on the dangers of driving while using a cell phone. Prior to watching the video, they were asked to indicate the extent to which they agreed with the statement "I am likely to use my cell phone while driving," using a Likert scale where 1 = *strongly disagree* and 7 = *strongly agree*. The teenage drivers then responded to the same statement again after watching the video. The data are listed below:

1. If you assume that the video has the desired effect on cell phone use while driving and you compute the difference scores as $M_{before} - M_{after}$, would you expect negative or positive difference scores?

2. If you assume that the video has the desired effect on cell phone use while driving and you compute the difference scores as $M_{after} - M_{before}$, would you expect negative or positive difference scores?

Before	After
5	5
6	5
4	4
4	4
6	5
6	5
5	6
7	6
7	7
7	6
5	4
6	6
3	3
2	2
5	5

3. Do you think the researchers should use a one-tailed test or a two-tailed test? Explain your reasoning.

4. Do you think the researchers should use $\alpha = .05$ (which has a higher Type I error rate) or $\alpha = .01$ (which has a higher Type II error rate)? Explain your reasoning; be sure to weigh the relative consequences of a Type I error versus a Type II error in this research situation.

5. State the null and research hypotheses. Regardless of what you wrote above, do a one-tailed test. A one-tailed test is probably the best choice because the researchers expect their intervention to reduce cell phone use while driving. Remember, these hypotheses make predictions about the "mean difference" expected between the responses provided before the video and after the video. We will compute the difference scores as $M_{before} - M_{after}$.

Null hypothesis (H_0):

Research hypothesis (H_1):

6. Compute the df, and locate the critical region. Use an alpha of .05. Draw an estimated t distribution, and locate the critical region on that curve.

7. Explain how you will decide if you should reject the null based on the critical region you defined above.

8. Compute the mean of the difference scores (i.e., M_D or $M_{before} - M_{after}$).

9. Compute the standard error of the difference scores $\left(\text{i.e., } SEM_r = \dfrac{SD_D}{\sqrt{N}} \right)$.

10. You should have found the standard error of the mean difference to be .15936. Which of the following is the best interpretation of the value? There are TWO correct answers provided. Find them both.

    a. The sample mean is .15936 away from the population mean with this sample size.

    b. The pretest mean is .15936 away from the posttest mean due to sampling error.

    c. The typical mean difference between sample means of this size will be .15936 simply due to sampling error.

    d. All possible sample mean differences are within .15936 of the actual population mean differences.

    e. The typical difference of all possible sample mean differences is expected to be .15936.

11. Compute the obtained *t* value for this study $\left(\text{i.e., } t = \dfrac{M_D}{SEM_r} \right)$.

12. Determine if you should reject or fail to reject the null hypothesis.

13. Compute the effect size estimate of this study $\left(\text{i.e., } d = \dfrac{M_D}{SD_D} \right)$, and interpret it as small, small-medium, and so on.

14. Summarize the results of this study using APA style by filling in the blanks below. You have not yet computed the means and standard deviations for before and after the video. You will need to do this to complete the summary statement.

People indicated that they were significantly less likely to use a cell phone while driving after watching the video ($M =$ _____, $SD =$ _____) than they were before watching the video ($M =$ _____, $SD =$_____), $t($_____$) =$ _____, $p < .05$ (one-tailed), $d =$ _____.

(Note that we wrote $p < .05$ because we rejected the null.)

SCENARIO 2: TWO-TAILED RELATED SAMPLES *t* TEST

After reading the results of the previous study, a different researcher wonders what effect watching a video on the dangers of cell phone use while driving might have on the use of hands-free cell phones while driving. She conducts a study similar to the one described above. Ten drivers rated their agreement with the statement "I am likely to use a hands-free cell phone while driving," using a Likert scale where 1 = *strongly disagree* and 7 = *strongly agree*. Ratings were made before and after watching a video on the dangers of cell phone use. The data are presented below:

Before	After
6	5
5	5
4	6
5	6
6	5
7	5
5	7
7	6
7	7
5	7

15. The researcher is not sure what effect the video might have on the use of hands-free cell phones. It is possible that the video will lead to an overall decrease in all cell phone use, but it is also possible that people will respond to the video by choosing to use their cell phones with hands-free devices. Thus, a two-tailed test is more appropriate than a one-tailed test. Which of the following best represents the *null* hypothesis?

   a. $\mu_D = 0$

   b. $\mu_1 = \mu_2$

   c. $\mu_D \neq 0$

   d. $\mu_1 \neq \mu_2$

16. Which of the following best represents the research hypothesis?

   a. $\mu_D = 0$

   b. $\mu_1 = \mu_2$

   c. $\mu_D \neq 0$

   d. $\mu_1 \neq \mu_2$

17. State the two-tailed null and research hypotheses in words.

18. Compute the *df*, and locate the critical region. Use an alpha of .05, two-tailed. If it helps, draw the *t* distribution, and locate the critical region on that curve.

19. The *t* values in the critical regions are best described as

   a. values that are very unlikely if the null hypothesis is true.

   b. values that are very likely if the null hypothesis is true.

   c. values that are very unlikely if the research hypothesis is true.

20. Compute the mean of the difference scores ($M_{before} - M_{after}$).

21. What do you expect the mean of the difference scores to equal if the null hypothesis is true?

22. Compute the standard error of the difference scores.

23. Compute the obtained t value for this study.

24. Determine whether you should reject or fail to reject the null hypothesis.

25. Compute the effect size estimate of this study, and interpret it as small, small-medium, and so on.

26. *Choose either Option a or Option b as the correct,* APA-style summary. Then fill in the blanks. You have not yet computed the means and standard deviations for before and after the video. You will need to do this to complete the summary statement.

    a. The hands-free cell phone use ratings after watching the video ($M =$ _____, $SD =$ _____) were significantly less than they were before watching the video ($M =$ _____, $SD =$_____), $t($_____$) =$ _____, $p < .05$ (one-tailed), $d =$ _____.

    b. The hands-free cell phone use ratings after watching the video ($M =$ _____, $SD =$ _____) were not significantly different from the ratings before watching the video ($M =$ _____, $SD =$_____), $t($_____$) =$ _____, $p > .05$ (one-tailed), $d =$ _____.

SPSS FOR RELATED SAMPLES t TESTS

Enter the data for the first research scenario in this activity into SPSS. You should have two columns of data: one for the scores before the video and another column for the scores after watching the video. After the data are entered, compute a related samples t by clicking on the Analyze menu. Choose "Compare Means" and then "Paired Samples *t* test." Move the before and after scores into the Variable 1 and Variable 2 boxes, respectively.

27. Record the means and standard deviations for the responses before and after watching the videos.

$$M_{before} = \text{_____}, \quad SD_{before} = \text{_____}.$$

$$M_{after} = \text{_____}, \quad SD_{after} = \text{_____}.$$

28. Find and record the value of the numerator of the *t* statistic. Verify that it is the same as what you computed by hand.

29. Find and record the value of the denominator of the *t* statistic. Verify that it is the same as what you computed by hand.

30. Find and record the value of the *t* statistic. Verify that it is the same as what you computed by hand.

31. What is the *p* value for this statistic, and what does it mean?

32. Explain how you will decide if you should reject or fail to reject H_0 based on the *p* value.

33. Enter the data for the second research scenario into SPSS, and run a paired samples *t* test. Verify that the *t* value is the same as what you computed by hand.

34. Fill in the following blanks. The *p* value for this significance test was _____. The *p* value is the probability of obtaining a *t* value of _____ or more extreme if the _____ hypothesis is true.

35. For the second research scenario, you used a two-tailed test. Explain how you will decide whether to reject the null hypothesis when given a two-tailed *p* value from SPSS.

36. For all of the examples today, we analyzed people's *self-reported* responses regarding how likely they are to use a cell phone. Suppose that the researcher replicated these studies using larger samples. Even if the researcher rejected the null hypotheses and obtained large effect sizes, we still should not conclude that the video will lead to less cell phone use. Explain why.

CHOOSE THE CORRECT STATISTIC

Determine which st*atistic* should be used in each of the following research scenarios: *z* for a single score, *z* for sample mean, single sample *t*, or related samples *t*.

37. A recent nationwide study revealed that people eat an average of just 2.9 servings of fruits and vegetables per day. A nutritionist wonders if people who live in areas where fresh fruits and vegetables are easy to grow year-round (e.g., California) eat more fruits and vegetables than the national average. To test this hypothesis, the nutritionist asks 100 residents of California to record the average number of servings of fruits and vegetables they consumed in 1 week. The mean number of servings consumed by 100 residents in California was 3.3, with a standard deviation of 1.7.

38. The same nutritionist wonders if gardening may encourage people to eat more vegetables. He recruits 23 people who have yards but do not currently have a garden to enable them participate in the study. For 1 week prior to starting the garden, the participants record the number of servings of vegetables they consumed. After that week, the nutritionist works with a master gardener to teach the participants how to grow vegetables in their yards. Near the end of the growing season, the nutritionist again asks the participants to record the average number of servings of vegetables they consumed in 1 week.

39. Suppose that the numbers of servings of fruits and vegetables consumed daily by Americans are normally distributed, with a mean of 2.90 and a standard deviation of 1.91. What percentage of Americans eat 7 or more servings a day?

40. Intelligence tests scores are influenced by a number of factors, including nutrition. A health psychologist wonders if consumption of fruits and vegetables is

associated with greater intelligence. Scores on a particular intelligence test are normally distributed, with a mean of $\mu = 100$ and a standard deviation of $\sigma = 15$. To determine if fruit and vegetable consumption is associated with greater intelligence, the psychologist recruits a sample of 43 people who eat at least 7 servings of fruits and vegetables a day and then measures their intelligence. The average intelligence test score for the sample was 104.32.

41. A social psychologist investigating the effects of mood on risky decision making needs to manipulate mood and is looking for a way to put participants in a negative mood. Rather than develop a new method, she turns to the literature to find ways that other researchers have used to induce a negative mood.

   In one study, researchers had participants fill out the Positive and Negative Affect Scale (PANAS), a questionnaire designed to assess their mood, where higher numbers indicate more negative mood. The same participants then watched a 10-minute clip of a sad movie in which a young boy watches his father die as the result of a boxing match. After the movie, they filled out the PANAS again. The mean PANAS score prior to watching the movie was $M = 1.85$, while the mean score after watching the movie was $M = 3.16$, $t(54) = 6.22$, $p < .01$ (two-tailed), $\alpha = .05$, $d = .83$.

   In another study, researchers had participants fill out the PANAS before and after a mood induction procedure. In this study, negative mood was induced by giving participants negative feedback. Specifically, participants took a challenging 30-item math test and were then told that they did very poorly on the test compared with their peers. The mean PANAS score prior to the false feedback was $M = 1.99$, while the mean score after getting the negative feedback was $M = 3.89$, $t(18) = 4.32$, $p < .01$ (two-tailed), $\alpha = .05$, $d = .99$.

   Which mood induction procedure do you think the researcher should use? Explain your answer, being sure to talk about sample size, effect size, the results of the significance, and practical considerations.

Activity 9-2: Practice Problems

SCENARIO 1: TWO-TAILED RELATED SAMPLES t TEST

After finding that an anti-anxiety drug effectively reduced anxiety, a researcher did a study to determine if the drug had any negative side effects. Specifically, she was interested in the effect of the drug on the weight of the participants. She weighed seven people, had them take the drug for 6 months, and then weighed them again. Do a two-tailed test using an alpha of .05.

Participant	Time 1 Weight	Time 2 Weight
A	150	155
B	182	183
C	124	125
D	243	239
E	115	118
F	199	201
G	164	169

1. Which of the following is the correct null hypothesis for this study?

    a. $H_0: \mu_D = 0$

    b. $H_0: \mu_D \neq 0$

    c. $H_0: \mu_D \leq 0$

    d. $H_0: \mu_D > 0$

2. Which of the following is the correct null hypothesis for this study?

    a. People will weigh more after taking the drug than before taking the drug.

    b. People will weigh less after taking the drug than before taking the drug.

    c. The drug will have no effect on the weight of the participants.

    d. The drug will have an effect on the weight of the participants.

3. Which of the following is the correct research hypothesis for this study?

    a. $H_1: \mu_D = 0$

    b. $H_1: \mu_D \neq 0$

c. $H_1: \mu_D \leq 0$

d. $H_1: \mu_D > 0$

4. Which of the following is the correct research hypothesis for this study?

   a. People will weigh more after taking the drug than before taking the drug.

   b. People will weigh less after taking the drug than before taking the drug.

   c. The drug will have no effect on the weight of the participants.

   d. The drug will have an effect on the weight of the participants.

5. What is the *df* for this related samples *t* test with seven participants?

6. What is the critical region for this study?

   a. Reject H_0 if $t \geq 2.44$ or $t \leq -2.4469$.

   b. Reject H_0 if $t \leq 2.44$ or $t \geq -2.4469$.

   c. Reject H_0 if $t \geq 2.36$ or $t \leq -2.3646$.

   d. Reject H_0 if $t \leq 2.36$ or $t \geq -2.3646$.

7. Compute the difference score (*D*) for each participant.

8. What is the observed mean difference (i.e., M_D or the mean of all the *D*s)?

9. What is the observed difference minus the difference expected if the null hypothesis is true for this study, that is $(M_D - \mu_D)$. (*Hint:* What does μ_D always equal?)

10. What is the sum of squares (*SS*) for the *D*s?

11. What is the standard deviation of the *D*s?

12. What is the expected amount of sampling error in this study?

13. What is the obtained *t* value for this study?

14. What is the effect size for this study?

15. Is the effect size small, small-medium, medium, medium-large, or large?

16. Which of the following statements best summarizes the results of this study?

    a. The weight of the participants was not significantly different before ($M =$ 168.14, $SD = 44.47$) and after ($M = 170.00$, $SD = 42.52$) taking the drug, $t(6) =$ 1.60, $p > .05$ (two-tailed), $d = .60$. However, the medium-large effect size suggests that the sample size was too small.

    b. The weight of the participants was significantly lower before ($M = 168.14$, $SD =$ 44.47) than after ($M = 170.00$, $SD = 42.52$) taking the drug, $t(6) = 1.60$, $p < .05$ (two-tailed), $d = .60$.

    c. The weight of the participants was not significantly different before and after taking the drug, $t(6) = 1.60$, $p > .05$ (two-tailed), $d = .60$.

    d. The weight of the participants was significantly lower before taking the drug than after taking the drug, $t(6) = 1.60$, $p < .05$ (two-tailed), $d = .60$.

SCENARIO 2: ONE-TAILED RELATED SAMPLES t TEST

Molecular neurobiology and gene therapy may offer an effective new treatment for manic depression. Manic depression is a mood disorder characterized by periods of euphoria as well as periods of severe depression. A research team in the United States suspects that abnormally high and abnormally low levels of a brain protein called p11 in the area of the brain that processes pleasurable experiences (the nucleus accumbens) play a critical role in manic depression. Their prediction is that when p11 levels are too low it leads to depression and when p11 levels are too high it leads to mania (i.e. euphoric periods). To test this prediction, the researchers used a sample of 12 people with manic depression. The researchers measured the p11 levels of each person when he or she was in a depressed state and again when the person was in a manic state. They expected that the p11 levels would be lower when people were depressed and higher when they were manic. The data from this study are given below. Use $\alpha = .05$, one-tailed. Compute D as p11_depressed minus p11_manic.

17. State the null and research hypotheses for this research situation

Null hypothesis (H_0):

Research hypothesis (H_1):

The p11 levels of the 12 manic depressive people when they were in a depressed state and in a manic state are given below. Higher values represent higher p11 levels. Compute D as *p11_depressed minus p11_manic.*

Participant	Depressed State	Manic State	D
1	100	111	
2	103	106	
3	99	105	
4	105	110	
5	105	112	
6	99	114	
7	110	119	
8	111	118	
9	97	106	
10	100	103	
11	104	108	
12	108	110	

18. Compute the *df*, and define the critical region. Draw the *t* curve if it helps you identify the critical region.

19. Compute the repeated *t* test using the data.

20. Determine if you should reject or fail to reject the null hypothesis.
    a. Reject
    b. Fail to reject

21. Compute the effect size, and interpret the size of the effect as small, small-medium, and so on.

22. *Choose one of the following paragraphs* to summarize the results of the repeated *t* test you just computed. After you choose one, fill in the blanks of that summary with the appropriate statistical information.
    a. When the patients were in a manic state ($M =$ _____, $SD =$ _____), their p11 levels in the nucleus accumbens were significantly higher than when they were in a depressed state ($M =$ _____, $SD =$ _____), $t($____$) =$ _____, $p < .05$ (one-tailed), $d =$ _____. The results support the conclusion that p11 levels in the nucleus accumbens play a role in manic depression.

b. When the patients were in a manic state ($M =$ _____, $SD =$ _____), their p11 levels in the nucleus accumbens were not significantly higher than when they were in a depressed state ($M =$ _____, $SD =$ _____), $t($ _____$) =$ _____, $p < .05$ (one-tailed), $d =$ _____. The results do not support the conclusion that p11 levels in the nucleus accumbens play a role in manic depression.

SCENARIO 3: TWO-TAILED RELATED SAMPLES *t* TEST

A previous study suggests that p11 levels in the area of the brain that processes pleasure do play a critical role in manic depression. Researchers may be able to develop future treatments for manic depression that work by regulating p11 levels in the brains of manic depressive people. However, this kind of treatment may have other undesired side effects. For example, increasing p11 levels could potentially cause people to overeat, or it could cause them to eat too little. To determine if this regulation of p11 levels influences caloric intake in any way, researchers performed an experiment on 14 rats. The amount of food each rat ate was measured for 1 week, and the average amount of food consumed daily was recorded. Then the researchers increased the p11 levels in every rat and kept the p11 levels high for an entire week, during which time the average amount of food consumed daily by each rat was again recorded. The researchers were interested in any change in food consumption, so they used a two-tailed test with a = .05. The average daily food consumption for each rat both before and after the p11 levels were increased is given below. Higher values represent higher consumption. Perform the statistical test on the data, and determine if increasing the p11 levels influences food consumption in any way. Compute the D as *normal − elevated*.

Rat	Normal p11 Level	Elevated p11 Level	D
1	21	23	
2	25	26	
3	23	25	
4	20	21	
5	25	26	
6	19	20	
7	23	24	
8	24	26	
9	18	21	
10	24	25	
11	23	25	
12	20	22	
13	17	19	
14	20	23	

23. State the null and research hypotheses for this research situation

    Null hypothesis (H_0):

    Research hypothesis (H_1):

24. Compute the *df*, and define the critical region. Draw the *t* curve if it helps you identify the critical region.

25. Compute the repeated *t* test using the data.

26. Determine if you should reject or fail to reject the null hypothesis.
    a. Reject
    b. Fail to reject

27. Compute the effect size, and describe it as small, small-medium, and so on.

28. Summarize the results of the repeated *t* test you just computed. Use one of the paragraphs provided above as a guide.

NOTES

Independent Samples *t* Test

After reading this chapter, you should be able to do the following:

- Explain when an independent samples *t* test should be used
- Write null and research hypotheses using symbols and words for both one- and two-tailed tests
- Compute degrees of freedom and define a critical region for both one- and two-tailed tests
- Compute an independent samples *t* by hand (using a calculator) and with SPSS
- Determine if you should reject or fail to reject the null hypothesis
- Compute an effect size, (*d*) and interpret it
- Summarize the results of the analysis using APA style
- Interpret the SPSS output for an independent samples *t*
- Explain the logic of the independent samples *t* test
- Explain what the mean difference should be if the null hypothesis is true
- Explain what the denominator of the *t* test is measuring

INDEPENDENT SAMPLES *t*

Thus far, you have learned about two different types of *t* tests: the single sample *t* and the related samples *t*. The single sample *t* is used whenever you have one sample mean that you want to compare with a population mean or a value of some theoretical interest. The related samples *t* is used to determine if two related sample means are significantly different from each other. These related samples can be either the same individuals measured at two times or pairs of matched people in different groups. When you have two sample means that come from unrelated samples, you must use a different type of test: an independent (samples) *t* test.

An example may help illustrate the difference between these different types of t tests. Suppose that a researcher was interested in the effect of a drug on weight loss. To test the efficacy of this drug, he could give the drug to a sample of people and after they are 1 month on the drug compare the mean pounds lost by the sample with zero pounds. In this case, the researcher would use a single sample t. However, the researcher could also measure the sample's mean weight before taking the drug and then again after taking the drug, then the researcher could use a related samples t to determine if the pre- and postsample means were significantly different. Finally, the researcher could also give one sample of people the drug and another sample of people a placebo. After both samples had taken their respective "drugs" for 1 month, the researcher could compare the mean weight loss of the drug sample with the mean weight loss of the placebo sample. In this final option, an independent samples t test would be used because the two samples contain different people who are not matched in any way.

The independent t test uses two samples from the population to represent two different conditions. As in the example above, it is often the case that one sample is intended to represent what the population would be like if nothing were done to it (i.e., a control condition) and another sample is intended to represent what the population would be like if it were given some treatment (i.e., experimental condition). The objective of the independent samples t test is to determine if the difference between the two sample means is likely or unlikely to be due to sampling error.

The logic of the independent t test is similar to that of the z for the sample mean, the single sample t test, and the related samples t test. All four tests compute a ratio, specifically, the observed deviation between two means over the deviation that is expected due to sampling error:

$$\text{Obtained } t \text{ or } z = \frac{\text{Observed deviation between the means}}{\text{Mean deviation expected due to sampling error}}$$

For all of these tests, the numerator is the observed deviation, or difference, between two means. If the null hypothesis is true, this difference should be zero and the test statistic should be zero. However, if the null hypothesis is false, this difference should be far from zero and the test statistic should also be far from zero.

Reading Question

1. Which of the following significance tests is used to determine if two *sample* means are significantly different from each other?

   a. z for a sample mean

   b. single sample t test

   c. independent t test

Reading Question

2. If the null hypothesis is true, the z for a sample mean, single sample t test, related samples t test, and the independent t test all expect an obtained value of

a. +1.65

b. +1.96

c. +1.00

d. 0

Although the *z* for a sample mean, single sample *t* test, related samples *t* test, and independent *t* test share a common logic, they are each used in different research situations. The *z* for a sample mean and the single sample *t* test both compare a sample mean with a population mean. The repeated *t* test compares two sample means from the same or related people. The independent *t* test compares two sample means from two unrelated or independent samples/groups.

For example, suppose that a researcher wants to investigate potential side effects of an anti-anxiety drug. Specifically, she wants to know what effect the drug may have on cholesterol levels. It may raise cholesterol levels, but it is also possible that it may lower cholesterol levels. To determine if the antianxiety drug influences cholesterol, you would need to compare the cholesterol levels of people who took the drug (i.e., an experimental group) with those who did not take the drug (i.e., a control group). In this situation, you could create two samples of people and give one sample no treatment (or a placebo treatment) and the other sample the antianxiety drug treatment (i.e., an experimental treatment). After a sufficient time, you could then measure the cholesterol levels of both the groups and compute a sample mean for each group. The sample mean from the control group would represent what the population's mean cholesterol level would be if the population received no treatment (or the placebo treatment). In contrast, the sample mean from the experimental group would represent what the population's mean cholesterol level would be if everyone received the new drug treatment. An independent samples *t* test can help you determine if the difference between these two sample means was likely or unlikely to have occurred due to sampling error. If the mean difference in cholesterol was unlikely to be due to sampling error, a researcher would reject the null hypothesis and conclude that the difference was probably created by the new antianxiety drug treatment. If the experimental group had a lower mean cholesterol, a researcher could conclude that the new drug lowers cholesterol. If, however, the experimental group had a higher mean, a researcher could conclude that the new drug raises cholesterol. Figure 10.1 illustrates the new drug scenario.

In this study, a researcher took one sample from a single population and then divided that sample to create two different groups, one received the placebo treatment and the other received the new drug treatment. The researcher essentially took people who were similar and then made them different by giving them different treatments (i.e., she gave them different levels of an IV [independent variable]). She then used the independent *t* test to determine if the different treatments influenced cholesterol differently.

In the next example, there are two distinct populations of people, namely, vegetarians and omnivores, who are already different with respect to their diets. The researcher is interested in determining if the mean cholesterol level in the vegetarians is significantly lower than that in the omnivores. To test the hypothesis, she takes a sample of

Figure 10.1   Research approach of creating two different samples to infer what the population would be like under two different situations.

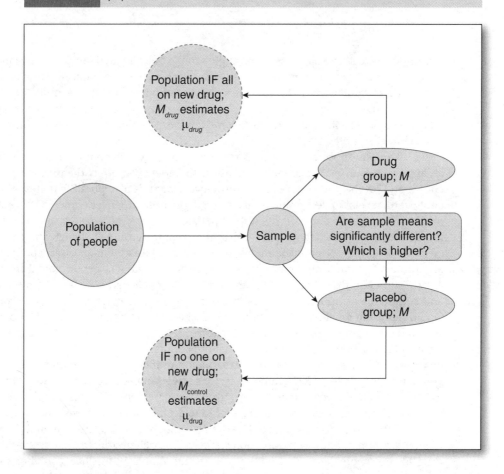

vegetarians and a sample of omnivores and measures the cholesterol levels of each group. She then uses the independent *t* test to determine if the two samples' mean cholesterol levels are significantly different. Figure 10.2 illustrates the vegetarian versus omnivore scenario.

Reading Question

3. An independent *t* test can be used to compare differences between people that

    a. are created by the researcher by providing different IV levels.

    b. already exist in different populations of people.

    c. Both of the above.

Figure 10.2	Research approach of obtaining two different samples to infer difference between two different populations.

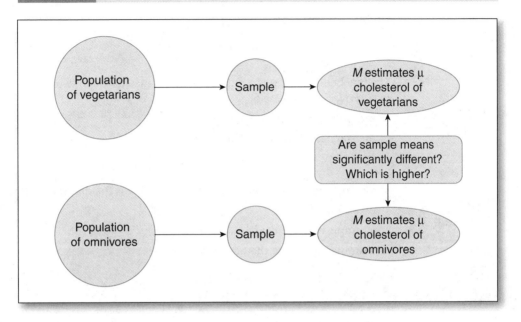

CONCEPTUAL FORMULA FOR THE INDEPENDENT SAMPLES *t*

Regardless of whether you have means from two groups with a preexisting difference or from two groups in which the researcher created a difference, the same independent *t*-test formula is used. Logically, the independent *t* test is structured as the ratio of the observed mean difference over the difference expected due to sampling error:

$$t = \frac{\text{Samples' mean difference} - \text{Populations' mean difference expected if } H_0 \text{ is true}}{\text{Mean difference expected due to sampling error}}$$

As is indicated in the above "logical formula," there are three terms in this *t* test. The two samples' mean difference is determined exclusively by the data. In the vegetarian versus omnivore scenario, this term is determined by the actual difference between the cholesterol levels of vegetarians and omnivores. The other term in the numerator is determined by the *null* hypothesis. For example, if diet (veggie vs. omnivore) has *no* impact on cholesterol, we would expect the population mean cholesterol of vegetarians and omnivores to be the same and their mean difference to be zero. In most research situations (all situations in this book), the population's mean difference that is expected if the null is true is zero. In other words, the numerator is simply the difference between the two sample means. The term in the denominator represents the amount of sampling error expected, given the size of each sample. The formula is written below:

$$t = \frac{(M_1 - M_2)}{SEM_i}$$

Reading Question

4. The independent t test is a ratio of the difference between two sample means over an estimate of

   a. sampling error.

   b. the standard deviation of the scores.

   c. variability.

Reading Question

5. The numerator of the independent samples t test is the difference between

   a. two sample means.

   b. a sample mean and a population mean.

   c. a sample mean and the null hypothesis.

TWO-TAILED INDEPENDENT t TEST EXAMPLE

Drugs often have unintended side effects. A researcher thinks that this might be the case with a new antianxiety drug. Specifically, she wants to know if a new antianxiety drug affects cholesterol levels. Twelve graduate students volunteer to participate in a clinical study of this question. Half of them are given the new antianxiety drug for 2 months, and the other half are given a placebo treatment for 2 months. The cholesterol levels of each group are then measured. Use a two-tailed t test with alpha of .05 to test this research question.

Group 1: Drug Group: 210, 215, 196, 198, 185, 201

Group 2: Placebo Group: 185, 195, 190, 184, 164, 199

Step 1: State the Null and Research Hypotheses Symbolically and Verbally

When researchers do not have a specific prediction about which of the two means will be higher, they use a two-tailed test (Table 10.1). For two-tailed tests, the research hypothesis states that the two means are different (i.e., are not equal). The null hypothesis is the exact opposite of the research hypothesis stating that the two means are not different (i.e., are equal).

Table 10.1	Symbolic and verbal representations of two-tailed research and null hypotheses for an independent *t* test.	

	Symbolic	Verbal
Research hypothesis (H_1)	$H_1: \mu_1 \neq \mu_2$ OR $H_1: \mu_1 - \mu_2 \neq 0$	Those in the drug group and those in the placebo group DO have significantly different cholesterol levels.
Null hypothesis (H_0)	$H_0: \mu_1 = \mu_2$ OR $H_0: \mu_1 - \mu_2 = 0$	Those in the drug group and those in the placebo group DO NOT have significantly different cholesterol levels.

Reading Question

6. Which of the following represents the null hypothesis when doing a two-tailed independent test?

   a. $\mu_1 = \mu_2$

   b. $\mu_1 \neq \mu_2$

Reading Question

7. Which of the following is the best summary of the two-tailed research hypothesis?

   a. People in the drug group have lower cholesterol levels than people in the placebo group.

   b. The people in the drug group will have different cholesterol levels than people in the placebo group.

Step 2: Define the Critical Region

When you computed the degrees of freedom (*df*) for the single sample *t* test, the *df* formula was $df = (N - 1)$. The *df* formula for an independent *t* test is different because the independent *t* test uses two samples rather than just one sample. Therefore, you have to compute the *df* for each sample and then combine the two *df* values to get the *df* for the independent *t* test. The independent *t*-test *df* formula is $df = (n_1 - 1) + (n_2 - 1)$; where n_1 and n_2 represent the sample sizes of the two samples, respectively.

In this case, the formula for *df* is as follows:

$$df = (n_1 - 1) + (n_2 - 1) = (6 - 1) + (6 - 1) = 10$$

You then use the correct t table of critical values (Appendix B) to find the critical value of t for this two-tailed independent t test. In this case, the critical value is 2.228. This means that the two critical regions are $t > +2.228$ and $t < -2.228$.

Step 3: Compute the Test Statistic

Step 3a: Compute the Deviation Between the Two Sample Means

As mentioned above, there are two terms in the numerator of the t statistic. The first $(M_1 - M_2)$ is the difference between the two means. The second $(\mu_1 - \mu_2)$ is the difference between the two population means, assuming the null hypothesis is true. Although it is possible to test null hypotheses that predict a specific difference other than zero (e.g., $\mu_1 - \mu_2 = 10$), these types of tests are very rare and will not be covered in this text. For our purposes, $\mu_1 - \mu_2$ will always equal 0. Thus, the numerator is simply the difference observed between the two sample means:

$$(M_1 - M_2) = (200.83 - 186.17) = 14.66$$

Reading Question	8. When computing the numerator of the independent samples t test, the population mean difference (i.e., $\mu_1 - \mu_2$) will always be
	a. 0.
	b. the same as the sample mean difference.

Step 3b: Compute the Typical Sample Error That Is Expected

Computing the denominator, or expected sampling error, requires several steps. First, compute the standard deviation for Group 1 (SD_1), and then compute the standard deviation for Group 2 (SD_2). In this problem, the standard deviation for *each group of scores* is not given to you, so you must compute each of them. In other problems, this information may be provided. As you may recall, the computational formula for sum of squares is $SS = \Sigma X^2 - \frac{(\Sigma X)^2}{n}$. Sum all of the scores from one of the groups to find ΣX for *that group of scores*. Then square every score and sum all of the squared scores to find ΣX^2 for *that group of scores*. In this example ΣX for Group 1 (i.e., ΣX_1) = 1205, and the ΣX^2 for Group 1 = 242571. There were 6 scores in Group 1 so $n_1 = 6$. Therefore, the SS_1 is as follows:

$$SS_1 = \Sigma X^2 - \frac{(\Sigma X)^2}{n} = 242571 - \frac{(1205)^2}{6} = 242571 - 242004.167 = 566.83$$

$$SD_1 = \sqrt{\frac{SS_1}{n-1}} = \sqrt{\frac{566.83}{5}} = 10.65$$

The ΣX for Group 2 = 1117, and the ΣX^2 for Group 2 = 208703. There were 6 scores in Group 2 so $n_2 = 6$. Therefore, the SS_2 is as follows:

$$SS_2 = \Sigma X^2 - \frac{(\Sigma X)^2}{n} = 208703 - \frac{(1117)^2}{6} = 208703 - 207948.167 = 754.833$$

$$SD_2 = \sqrt{\frac{SS_2}{n-1}} = \sqrt{\frac{754.833}{5}} = 12.29$$

Once you have computed the standard deviation for each group, compute the pooled variance using the following formula:

$$SD_p^2 = \frac{(n_1 - 1)SD_1^2 + (n_2 - 1)SD_2^2}{(n_1 - 1) + (n_2 - 1)} = \frac{(6-1)(10.65)^2 + (6-1)(12.29)^2}{(6-1) + (6-1)} = 132.23$$

You need the pooled variance to compute the estimated standard error of the mean difference (*SEM$_i$*) as is illustrated by the following equation. Be sure to use *n* and not *df* in the denominator and note that the pooled variance (SD_p^2) is already squared.

$$SEM_i = \sqrt{\frac{SD_p^2}{n_1} + \frac{SD_p^2}{n_2}} = \sqrt{\frac{132.23}{6} + \frac{132.23}{6}} = 6.64$$

This is the estimated standard error of the mean difference, which is a measure of expected sampling error. A standard error of 6.64 means that the difference between the two means that is expected due to sampling error is 6.64.

Reading Question

9. The estimated standard error of the mean difference is
   a. used to find the critical value for the *t* test.
   b. an estimate of how different the two sample means are expected to be due to sampling error.
   c. Both (a) and (b) are correct.

Step 3c: Compute the Test Statistic (Independent *t* Test)

The independent *t* test is the ratio of the observed deviation between the sample means divided by the estimated standard error of the mean difference:

$$t = \frac{(M_1 - M_2)}{SEM_i} = \frac{(200.83 - 186.17)}{6.64} = 2.21$$

The difference between the two means (i.e., 200.83 − 186.17 = 14.67) was 2.21 times larger than the deviation expected due to sampling error (i.e., 6.64). The critical regions of t were $t > 2.228$ and $t < -2.228$, and so the obtained t value did not fall in the critical region. The obtained t value is not sufficiently large to reject the null hypothesis.

Reading Question

10. When the obtained t value is NOT further from zero than the critical value the null hypothesis should
    a. be rejected.
    b. not be rejected.

Step 4: Compute an Effect Size, and Describe It

The formula for computing the effect size of an independent t test is similar to that of other t tests in that we divide the observed mean difference by the SD. When computing the d by hand, remember that the pooled variance (i.e., SD_p^2) can be converted to the pooled standard deviation (i.e., SD_p) by taking its square root. You computed the pooled variance in Step 3b above.

$$d = \frac{\text{Observed difference between the means}}{\text{Standard deviation}} = \frac{M_1 - M_2}{\sqrt{SD_p^2}} = \frac{200.83 - 186.17}{\sqrt{132.23}} = 1.28$$

The same effect size cutoffs are used for an independent t test. If d is close to .2, the effect size is small; if it is close to .5, the effect size is medium; and if it is close to .8, the effect size is large. An effect size of 1.28 is considered a large effect.

The results from Steps 4 and 5 may be a bit confusing. In Step 4, you failed to reject the null hypothesis, which meant that the drug did not perform differently than the placebo. However, the effect size of 1.28 indicates that the difference between the drug mean and placebo mean is large. Whenever the null is not rejected, and yet there was a medium or large effect size, the sample size used in the study was too small for the statistical test or the effect size to be trusted. In situations like this, the researcher should obtain a larger sample size and then rerun the study.

Reading Question

11. Whenever you failed to reject the null hypothesis and yet the effect size is medium or large, you should conclude
    a. that the treatment really does work.
    b. that the treatment really does not work.
    c. that your sample size was too small and you should rerun the study with a larger sample size.

Step 5: Interpret the Results of the Hypothesis Test

The following paragraph summarizes these test results.

There was no significant difference between the cholesterol scores of those who got the drug ($M = 200.83$, $SD = 10.65$) and those who got the placebo ($M = 186.17$,

$SD = 12.29$), $t(10) = 2.21$, $p > .05$, $d = 1.28$. However, the fact that the null hypothesis was not rejected while there was a large effect size suggests that the sample in the current study was too small. More research into the potential impact of this drug on cholesterol is warranted.

Reading Question

12. When writing your results if you failed to reject the null hypothesis and yet the effect size was medium or large, you should

    a. point this out to the reader so that your report does not mislead them.

    b. not include this information in your report.

ONE-TAILED INDEPENDENT *t* TEST EXAMPLE

Do vegetarians have significantly *lower* cholesterol levels than omnivores? Seven vegetarians and eight omnivores volunteered to participate in a study investigating this question. The cholesterol levels of each group were measured and are listed below. Use a one-tailed independent *t* test with an alpha level of .05 to test this research question.

Group 1: Veggie Group:

148, 130, 156, 139, 157, 132, 144 $M_1 = 143.71$; $SD_1 = 10.75$

Group 2: Omnivore Group:

208, 178, 189, 214, 226, 237, 198, 201 $M_2 = 206.38$; $SD_2 = 19.23$

Step 1: State the Null and Research Hypotheses Symbolically and **Verbally**

The research hypothesis for a one-tailed test specifies which of the two sample means will be higher if the "treatment" works. For this example, Group 1 was vegetarians and Group 2 was omnivores. The researcher expected the vegetarians to have lower cholesterol levels than the omnivores, and this prediction is represented symbolically by the research hypothesis: $\mu_1 < \mu_2$ or $\mu_1 - \mu_2 < 0$. The null hypothesis is the opposite of the research hypothesis, including all other possible outcomes. Thus, the null hypothesis states that $\mu_1 \geq \mu_2$ or $\mu_1 - \mu_2 \geq 0$. In other words, the null hypothesis is that vegetarians do not have lower cholesterol levels than omnivores. The research and null hypotheses for this one-tailed independent *t* test are shown in Table 10.2.

Reading Question

13. Which of the following *could* represent a null hypothesis when doing a one-tailed independent test?

    a. $\mu_1 \geq \mu_2$

    b. $\mu_1 < \mu_2$

    c. $\mu_1 > \mu_2$

    d. $\mu_1 = \mu_2$

Table 10.2	Symbolic and verbal representations of one-tailed research and null hypotheses for an independent t test.	

	Symbolic	Verbal
Research hypothesis (H_1)	$H_1: \mu_1 < \mu_2$ OR $H_1: \mu_1 - \mu_2 < 0$	Vegetarians DO have lower cholesterol levels than omnivores.
Null hypothesis (H_0)	$H_0: \mu_1 \geq \mu_2$ OR $H_0: \mu_1 - \mu_2 \geq 0$	Vegetarians DO NOT have lower cholesterol levels than omnivores.

Step 2: Define the Critical Region

Computing the df for one-tailed tests is done in exactly the same manner as with a two-tailed test. In this case,

$$df = (n_1 - 1) + (n_2 - 1) = (7 - 1) + (8 - 1) = 13.$$

The one-tailed t table indicates that a study with a $df = 13$ has a critical value of 1.711. The research hypothesis predicts that μ_1 will be less than μ_2, so it is predicting a negative obtained t value. Thus, the critical region is in the negative side of the distribution. The null should be rejected if $t < -1.771$. If vegetarians were labeled as Group 2 and omnivores as Group 1, we would have expected a positive t, and the critical region would have been in the positive side of the distribution.

Reading Question

14. When you are doing a one-tailed t test, the critical region is always on the side of the t distribution that is predicted by the
   a. null hypothesis.
   b. research hypothesis.

Step 3: Compute the Test Statistic

Step 3a: Compute the Deviation Between the Two Sample Means

Again, the numerator of the test is essentially the difference between the two sample means because the difference expected between the population means if the null is true is zero.

$$(M_1 - M_2) = (143.71 - 206.38) = -62.66$$

Step 3b: Compute the Sample Error That Is Expected

As in the previous example, in this problem you must first compute the standard deviation for *each group of scores*. This is done in the same manner as was done in the previous example. Review the previous example if you are unsure how this is done. Once the standard deviation for Group 1 (i.e., SD_1) and the standard deviation for Group 2 (i.e., SD_2) have been computed, they are used to compute the pooled variance (i.e., SD_p^2). This process is illustrated below:

$$SD_p^2 = \frac{(n_1 - 1)SD_1^2 + (n_2 - 1)SD_2^2}{(n_1 - 1) + (n_2 - 1)} = \frac{(7-1)(10.75)^2 + (8-1)(19.23)^2}{(7-1) + (8-1)} = 252.46$$

You will need the pooled variance to compute the estimated standard error of the mean difference and the effect size.

$$SEM_i = \sqrt{\frac{SD_p^2}{n_1} + \frac{SD_p^2}{n_2}} = \sqrt{\frac{252.46}{7} + \frac{252.46}{8}} = 8.22$$

Be sure to use *n* from each group and not *df* in the denominator when computing the estimated standard error of the mean difference. Also, note that the pooled variance (SD_p^2) is already squared, and so you should not square it again.

Reading Question

15. When computing the standard error of the mean difference, the equation calls for using
    a. the degrees of freedom for each group.
    b. the sample sizes from each group.

Step 3c: Compute the Test Statistic (Independent *t* Test)

Again, the *t*-test computation is identical to a two-tailed test:

$$t = \frac{(M_1 - M_2)}{SEM_i} = \frac{(143.71 - 206.38)}{8.22} = \frac{-62.66}{8.22} = -7.62$$

The obtained *t* value of −7.62 is further from zero than the critical value of −1.771. Therefore, the null hypothesis should be rejected.

Reading Question

16. Which of the following values can NEVER be negative?
    a. The numerator of a *t* test
    b. The obtained *t* value
    c. The standard error of the mean difference

Step 4: Compute an Effect Size, and Describe It

Again, computing the effect size for one- and two-tailed tests is identical.

$$d = \frac{\text{Observed difference between the means}}{\text{Standard deviation}} = \frac{M_1 - M_2}{\sqrt{SD_p^2}} = \frac{143.71 - 206.38}{\sqrt{252.56}} = -3.94$$

An effect size of −3.94 is very large. It means that the mean cholesterol level of the vegetarians is nearly 4 *SD*s lower than that of the omnivores.

Reading Question

17. When determining if an effect size is small, medium, or large, you should
    a. ignore the sign of the computed effect size (i.e., use its absolute value).
    b. recognize that negative effect sizes are always small effect sizes.

Step 5: Interpret the Results of the Hypothesis Test

These results might be summarized as follows:

The vegetarians ($M = 143.71$, $SD = 10.75$) had significantly lower cholesterol than the omnivores ($M = 206.38$, $SD = 19.23$), $t(13) = -7.62$, $p < .05$ (one-tailed), $d = -3.94$.

OTHER ALPHA LEVELS

If you were to use an alpha of .01, rather than .05, it would be harder to reject the null hypothesis. This means that you would have less statistical power but a lower risk of making a Type I error.

Reading Question

18. Which alpha value has a lower risk of making a Type I error?
    a. .05
    b. .01

Reading Question

19. Which alpha value has a lower risk of making a Type II error?
    a. .05
    b. .01

SPSS

Data File

To enter data for an independent samples *t* test, you will need two columns. The first is the IV (i.e., grouping variable). In this case, we need to enter a number to indicate the group that each person was in (i.e., vegetarian or omnivore). You can use any numbers, but below we used a "1" to indicate vegetarian and a "2" to indicate omnivore. The second column is the DV (the dependent variable, i.e., the variable on which the two groups are being compared). In this case, the DV is the cholesterol score of each person. When you are done, the data file should look like Figure 10.3.

Figure 10.3	SPSS screenshot of data entry screen for an independent *t* test.

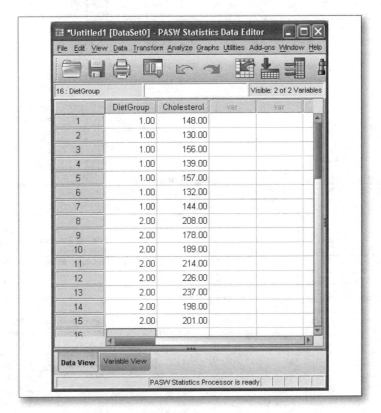

Obtaining an Independent Samples *t* Test

- Click on the Analyze menu. Choose Compare Means and then Independent Samples *t* Test.
- Move the Independent Variable (the one that indicates which group someone is in) into the Grouping Variable box, and click on "define." Enter the values you used to designate Group 1 and Group 2 in the appropriate boxes (in the above screen shot you would enter the values 1 and 2, respectively).
- Move the Dependent Variable (the one that indicates the actual scores of the participants) into the Test Variables box.
- Click on the OK button.

Annotated Output

The SPSS output for this analyses is given in Figure 10.4.

Figure 10.4   Annotated SPSS output for an independent *t* test.

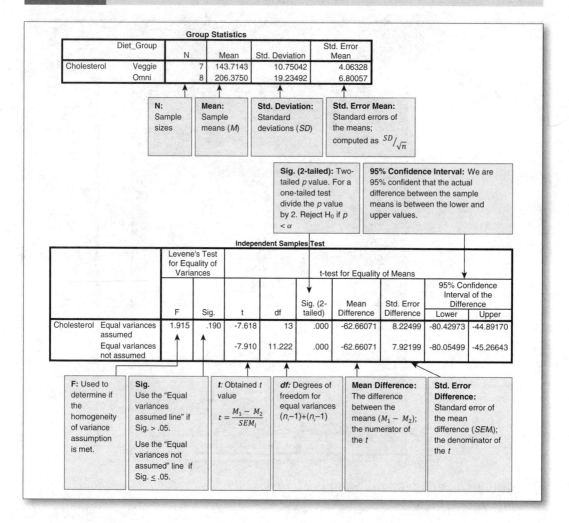

Levene's Test (Test for Homogeneity of Variance)

One of the assumptions of the independent samples *t* is homogeneity of variance. This assumption states that the variances in the two populations (e.g., vegetarians and omnivores) are the same. This assumption is important because if the variances are equal, you should compute the amount of expected sampling error using the method you have learned. However, if this assumption is violated, a different method for computing sampling error is needed. Levene's test will indicate which method for computing sampling error is most appropriate. Just as we do a *t* test to determine if two means are significantly different, we can do a test to determine if the two variances are significantly different. The standard deviation for the vegetarians was 10.75 and that for the omnivores was 19.23. Thus, the variance for the vegetarians was 10.75^2 or 115.56 and that for the omnivores was 19.23^2 or 369.79. SPSS automatically runs Levene's test for homogeneity of variance to determine if 115.56 is significantly different from 369.79.

Reading Question

20. Levene's test is automatically run by SPSS to determine if the _____ of the two groups are significantly different.

   a. means

   b. variances

If the variances of the two groups are NOT significantly different, the proper way to compute the estimate of sampling error is to use the "Equal variances assumed" method. If the variances are significantly different, the proper way to compute the estimate of sampling error is to use the "Equal variances not assumed" method. You can determine if the variances are equal or not by looking at the "Sig." value under the "Levene's Test for Equality of Variances" label in the "Independent Samples Test" output. If the Sig. value is less than or equal to .05, the variances are NOT similar and we have violated the assumption of equal variance. If the Sig. value is greater than .05, the variances are similar and we have met the assumption of equal variance.

Reading Question

21. Use the "Independent Samples Test" output to find the Sig. value for Levene's test and then determine if the variances are similar or NOT similar. The Sig. (*p*) value for Levene's test is _____ and therefore the variances for the veggie and omnivore groups _____ .

   a. .19; are similar (i.e., equal)

   b. 13; are NOT similar (i.e., not equal)

Levene's test indicated that the variances in the two groups were not significantly different. Therefore, the best way to compute the estimate of sampling error is to use the "Equal variances assumed" method. If you look in the left most cell of the "Independent Samples Test" output, you will see two labels. The one on the top is "Equal variances assumed" and the one at the bottom is "Equal variances not assumed." Levene's test indicated that we should use the "Equal variances assumed" method. SPSS automatically computes two different *t* tests—one using the "equal variances" method and the other using the "not equal variances" method. The results of both the *t* tests are shown in the output. In this case, we should choose the obtained *t* value that is across from the "Equal variances assumed" heading (i.e., −7.618).

Reading Question
22. If the Sig. for Levene's test was less than .05, the correct obtained t value would have been
   a. −7.618.
   b. −7.910.

Reading Question
23. When entering the data for an independent t test, you should have
   a. a column for each person.
   b. a column for the IV and a column for the DV.

Reading Question
24. Use the "Group Statistics" output to determine the mean and standard deviation of the veggie group. The mean and standard deviation of the veggie group were
   a. 143.7143 and 10.75042, respectively.
   b. 206.3750 and 19.23492, respectively.

Reading Question
25. The p value for this t test was
   a. .000.
   b. .19.

Reading Question
26. To get a one-tailed p value, you must
   a. divide the two-tailed p value in half.
   b. multiply the two-tailed p value by 2.

Statistical Assumptions

All statistical tests are computed based on specific assumptions. The homogeneity of variance assumption is one assumption. If one or more of the assumptions are violated, the resulting test statistic can be misleading. However, in many instances, even if an assumption is violated, test statistics produce accurate statistical conclusions. This point was illustrated here by the fact that both the equal variances assumed and the equal variances not assumed t values were similar (i.e., −7.618 and −7.910, respectively). Chapter 16 of this text describes how to determine if statistical assumptions are violated and what to do if they are violated.

Activity 10-1:   Hypothesis Testing With the Independent t Test

Learning Objectives

After reading the chapter and completing this activity, you should be able to do the following:

- State null and research hypotheses for an independent t test
- Compute and interpret the results of an independent t test

- Explain how sampling error influences an independent *t* test
- Compute and interpret the effect size estimate for an independent *t* test
- Use the distributions of sample means to locate the probabilities of Type I error, Type II error, statistical power, and the probability of rejecting a false null hypothesis
- Use hypothesis testing language correctly in a given research context

INDEPENDENT *t*-TEST EXAMPLE

It is well known that acetaminophen lessens peoples' physical pain. A recent study suggests that acetaminophen can lower people's psychological pain as well (DeWall et al., 2010). Surprised by these findings, a group of researchers decided to see if acetaminophen works for different types of psychological pain than those assessed in the original research. The researchers obtained a sample of volunteers and gave half of them acetaminophen and the other half a placebo pill. Both groups of participants read socially painful stories and rated how painful the experience would be for them. Specifically, the researchers wanted to know if the mean social pain rating of the acetaminophen group is statistically lower than the mean social pain rating of the control group. Stated differently, the researchers wanted to know if the mean difference in social pain rating between these two samples is likely or unlikely to be due to sampling error. The researchers are predicting that the acetaminophen will *reduce* social pain ratings; therefore, they used a one-tailed hypothesis test. They used a .05 alpha value (i.e., $\alpha = .05$).

$$n_{drug} = 31, \qquad M_{drug} = 213, \qquad SD_{drug} = 18.$$

$$n_{control} = 31, \qquad M_{control} = 222, \qquad SD_{control} = 20.$$

Understanding the Null and Research Hypotheses

1. State the null and research hypotheses. (*Note:* These hypotheses make predictions about the "mean difference" expected between the two samples if the null hypothesis is true or if the research hypothesis is true.)

Null hypothesis (H_0):

Research hypothesis (H_1):

2. Assuming that the null hypothesis is true (i.e., that acetaminophen does NOT affect social pain at all), what precise value would you expect for the *mean difference* between the mean ratings of social pain for the acetaminophen sample and the placebo sample?

   Precise expected value for the *mean difference* between the two sample means if the null is true = _____

3. In this situation, the researchers obtained two samples of people from the population. One sample was assigned to take acetaminophen and the other sample was assigned to take a placebo. Even if you assume that the acetaminophen does NOT impact social pain at all, given that two independent samples were obtained from the population, would you be surprised if the samples' *mean difference* was not *exactly* the value you indicated above?

   a. No, I would not be surprised. The two sample means are likely to be different because the population parameters are different.

   b. No, I would not be surprised. The two sample means are likely to be different because of sampling error even if the drug has no effect.

   c. Yes, I would be surprised. The two sample means should be exactly the same if the drug does not impact social pain.

   d. Yes, I would be surprised. The two sample means should be exactly the same because the sizes of the two samples are the same.

4. Just as was the case with the z for a sample mean, the single sample *t* test, and the related samples *t* test, researchers must compute the amount of sampling error that is "expected by chance" before they can determine if the null hypothesis is likely or unlikely to be true. The acetaminophen and control groups each had 31 people with social pain *SD*s of 18 and 20, respectively. Use the two equations provided below to compute the value for standard error of the mean difference.

$$SD_p^2 = \frac{(n_1 - 1)SD_1^2 + (n_2 - 1)SD_2^2}{(n_1 - 1) + (n_2 - 1)}$$

$$SEM_i = \sqrt{\frac{SD_p^2}{n_1} + \frac{SD_p^2}{n_2}}$$

5. Interpret this value of the standard error of the mean difference in this context.

6. Assuming that acetaminophen does NOT impact social pain at all (i.e., assuming the null hypothesis is true), create a distribution of sample *mean differences* based on the two sample sizes of $n_{drug} = 31$ and $n_{control} = 31$. This distribution represents the frequency of ALL POSSIBLE sample *mean differences* when both sample sizes are 31. You should label the frequency histogram so that it is centered on the sample *mean difference* you expect if the null is true and so it has at least 3 "standard error of the *mean difference* steps" to the right and the left of center. (*Hints:* What value do you expect for the sample *mean difference* if the null hypothesis is true? The sampling error expected [i.e., standard error of the mean difference] tells you how large to make the "steps" to the right and left of center).

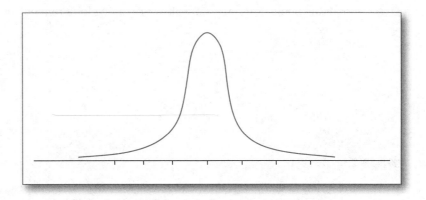

Defining the Critical Region

7. Use the independent *t* formula to "relabel" the distribution of sample mean differences. Convert each raw mean difference score on the distribution into a *t* value. Then draw a vertical line at the critical value of *t* and shade in the critical region of *t*. You will need to consult a critical *t* value table to locate the critical value of *t*.

Evaluating the Likelihood of the Null Hypothesis

8. Now that the critical region of *t* is determined, researchers can find the *t* value associated with the *mean difference* between the samples and determine if it is in the critical region of the *t* distribution (also known as the region of rejection). The sample means were $M_{drug} = 213$ and $M_{control} = 222$. Locate the mean difference on the distribution of sample mean differences above.

9. What should the researchers conclude about the null hypothesis and why?

Effect Size

The process of significance testing you just completed in the previous question tells us whether or not the null hypothesis is likely to be true. It does NOT indicate how effective the IV was in affecting the DV. In the above scenario, the null hypothesis was rejected, but the researchers only know that acetaminophen will probably decrease social pain in the population. They do not know how effective it would actually be at lowering social pain in the population. To get this information, they must compute an estimate of the study's effect size.

10. Compute the estimate of effect size (d) for acetaminophen on social pain and then interpret it as small, medium, or large. (*Note:* When computing the d for an independent t test, you need to use the "pooled standard deviation" or the square root of the pooled variance. Consult your reading for a reminder.)

Summarize the Results

11. Finally, based on the significance test and the effect size compose an APA-style summary of the results (include the needed statistical information in the proper format). Does acetaminophen help reduce social pain? If so, is it very effective or only slightly effective?

Type I Errors, Type II Errors, and Statistical Power

12. *BEFORE* collecting data from the sample that took acetaminophen, researchers can't locate the center of the distribution of sample mean differences if the research hypothesis is true. However, *AFTER* they have the data from the sample, they do have *an idea* of where the research hypothesis distribution of sample

mean differences is located. What could they use to estimate the location of this distribution? Provide a specific value. (*Hint:* What value might represent the *mean difference* between the social pain scores of ALL those who took acetaminophen and ALL those who took the placebo if the research hypothesis is true.

Specific value for the center of the research hypothesis distribution of sample *mean differences* = _____

A major benefit of locating the center of the research hypothesis distribution of sample mean differences, even if it is an *estimated* center that is inferred from sample statistics, is that it allows researchers to quantify several very important statistical concepts. This quantification process can be illustrated by "building a distribution." You have already built one of the distributions that are necessary in (6) above. As you know from (6) above, the null hypothesis distribution of sample mean differences is centered at a *t* value of 0. The null *t* distribution is re-created for you below.

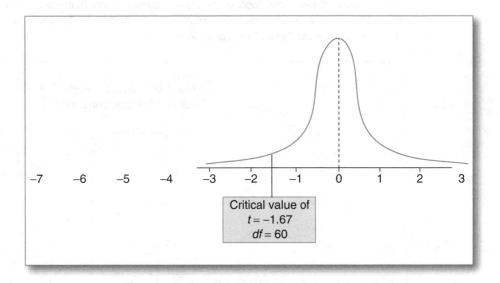

13. The second distribution we need to build is the distribution of the sample mean differences if the research hypothesis is true. As mentioned above, the center of this distribution is determined by the actual mean difference of the samples. In this case, the actual sample mean difference was −9, meaning that the center of this distribution of sample means is at −9 on the raw score number line (and at the *t* value associated with a sample mean difference of −9, or *t* = −1.86). Draw a vertical line on the above figure at −1.86 to represent the center of the distribution of sample means if the research hypothesis is true. Remember that the only reason we can locate this curve's center is because we know the actual mean difference of the samples. We can't know this *before* we collect data.

14. In Activity 6-1, you created the research hypothesis distribution of sample means by sketching a normally shaped distribution. In that situation, the research curve was normally shaped because the population standard deviation (σ) was known. In this situation, σ is unknown. One of the consequences of this uncertainty is that the research hypothesis distribution will be skewed; a negative effect creates a negative skew. The severity of the research curve's skew depends on the effect size and the sample size, but *as sample size increases, the research curve approaches a normal shape.* Here, we are less concerned with the research curve's precise shape than we are with using it to locate the Type II and statistical power regions in the research curve. Therefore, sketch in the distribution of sample mean differences if the research hypothesis is true, assuming it has a normal shape. (Just try to duplicate the null curve's shape and spread, but have it centered at -1.86 on the t score number line rather than at 0 where the null curve is centered.)

After you have completed sketching in the research hypothesis distribution of sample mean differences, look at the figure below and confirm that your figure looks like it. If it doesn't, determine what is wrong and fix it. Be sure you understand why the figure looks as it does.

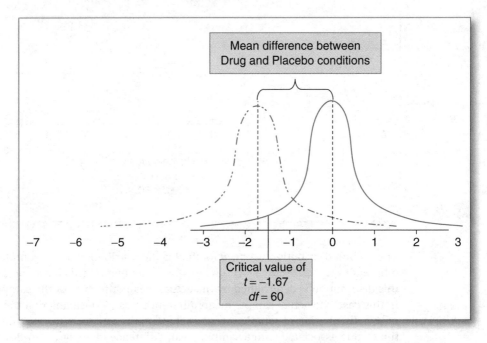

Just as can be done with the z for the sample mean, single sample t test, and the related samples t test, we can use these curves to quantify the probability of important statistical concepts. The null distribution of sample mean differences represents all possible outcomes if the null hypothesis is true. The research distribution of sample mean differences represents all possible outcomes if the research hypothesis is true. By "cutting" these curves into different sections at the critical value of t, we can estimate the probability of (1) rejecting a false null (i.e., statistical power), (2) failing to reject a false null (i.e., Type II error), (3) rejecting a true null (i.e., Type I error), and (4) failing to reject a true null. In the figure below, there is a distribution of sample mean differences for the null hypothesis and a distribution of sample mean differences for the research hypothesis. The two curves have been "separated" so that it is easier to see the distinct sections of each curve. The areas under each of these respective curves represent statistical power, Type II errors, Type I errors, and failing to reject a true null. Try to determine which areas under each curve below represent what.

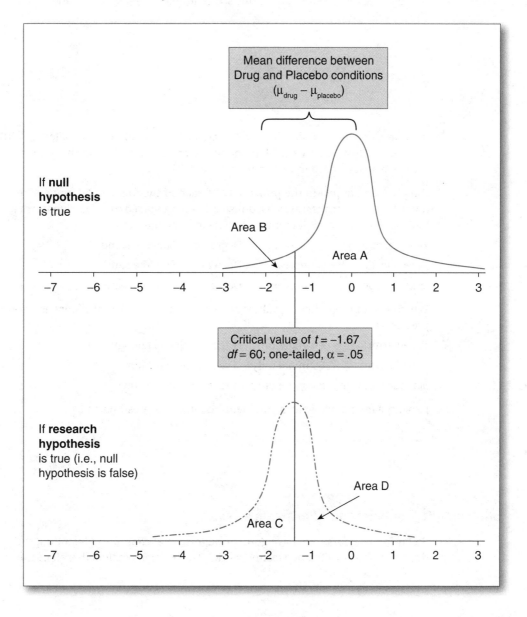

15. Match the area to the statistical outcome

    Type I error [rejecting a true null]:   Area _____

    Type II error [failing to a false null]:   Area _____

    Statistical Power [rejecting a false null]:   Area _____

    Failing to reject a true null: Area _____

16. Go back to Activity 6-1. Make note of the fact that the areas under the curve that correspond to each of the above concepts are NOT the same as in the previous activity. What is different about this scenario that changed the locations of the above concepts?

17. If a one-tailed, $\alpha = .01$ significance test was used instead of a one-tailed, $\alpha = .05$ significance test, what would happen to the critical value line in the graphs above? Would it move to the right or to the left?

18. What would happen to the probability of each of the following if a one-tailed, $\alpha = .01$ significance test was used instead of a one-tailed, $\alpha = .05$ significance test? Indicate if each would increase, decrease, or stay the same.

Type I error:	Increase	Decrease	Stay the same
Type II error:	Increase	Decrease	Stay the same
Statistical power:	Increase	Decrease	Stay the same

19. Which two of the following values are estimates and which one value is known precisely?

Type I error:	Estimate only	Precise value is known
Type II error:	Estimate only	Precise value is known
Statistical power:	Estimate only	Precise value is known

20. Explain why the two values you identified in (19) are estimates.

Summary of Key Points in Significance Testing

21. So far in this course, we have gone through several examples illustrating the details of how significance testing works. These details included each of the

following key points. Read through these key points and try to fill in the key terms that are missing. You may use some of the terms at the bottom of this page more than once.

- The _____ allows us to predict the center, shape, and spread of the distribution of sample means (or the distribution of sample *mean differences*) if the null is true. State the theorem below.

- The _____ hypothesis precisely locates the center of the null distribution of sample means (or the null distribution of sample mean differences). This location is at a *z* value of _____ or at *t* value of _____.

- The center of the _____ hypothesis distribution of sample means (or mean differences) is estimated from the sample mean (or sample mean difference) and cannot be known before data are collected.

- The probability of a _____ is set by researchers when they set the α value.

- By building the null and research hypotheses distributions of sample means (or sample mean differences), we can quantify the probability of failing to reject a false null (i.e., _____) as well as the likelihood of rejecting a false null (i.e., _____).

- The _____ of *t* or *z* "cuts" likely values if the null is true from unlikely values if the null is true; if a statistic (e.g., *z* value, *t* value) is more extreme than this value, the null hypothesis is unlikely to be true.

- If the null is rejected, the _____ hypothesis is considered likely to be true.

- After a _____ is performed, researchers know whether or not the null is likely to be true. They do not know how effective the IV was at impacting the DV. To quantify the impact of the IV on the DV, researchers must compute a/an _____.

Type I error	0	Statistical power
Type II error	Power	Central limit theorem
Null	Effect size	Significance test
Critical value	Research	

Putting It All Together

22. A researcher obtained the scores for all 1.5 million students who took the SAT (Scholastic Aptitude Test) this year and found that males scored significantly higher than females ($p < .001$). Given the sample size, what additional

information would you want before you decide if this statistically significant difference is an important difference? Explain why.

23. Suppose that you have a friend who suffers from debilitating migraines that have not been helped by treatments that are currently on the market. Your friend's doctor asks if he would like to participate in a clinical trial. There are two clinical trials available (Drug A or Drug B), and your friend asks you for help in deciding which drug seems more promising based on the available data.

Although the drugs are not yet approved by the FDA (Food & Drug Administration), one human trial has been conducted using each drug. The side effects for both drugs were minor, and all costs would be paid by an NIH (National Institutes of Health) research grant. The results from the trials are described below.

Drug A information: Two hundred and fifty participants took Drug A for 3 months, while another 250 participants took a placebo for 3 months in a double blind study. While taking the "drug," the participants recorded the number of migraines they experienced. The mean number of migraines in the Drug A group was $M = 5.12$, $SD = 4.21$, $n = 250$, while the mean number of migraines in the Placebo group was $M = 6.87$, $SD = 4.62$, $n = 250$, $t(498) = 4.43$, $p < .001$, $d = .39$. To participate in this trial, your friend would need to go to a local hospital once a week for a 1-hour visit.

Drug B information: One hundred and fifty participants took Drug B for 3 months, while another 150 participants took a placebo for 3 months in a double blind study. While taking the "drug," the participants recorded the number of migraines they experienced. The mean number of migraines in the Drug B group was $M = 5.47$, $SD = 2.89$, $n = 150$, while the mean number of migraines in the Placebo group was $M = 8.11$, $SD = 2.94$, $n = 150$, $t(298) = 7.84$, $p < .001$, $d = .70$. To participate in this trial, your friend would need to go to a hospital that is approximately 45 minutes away once a week for 1.5 hour visits.

a. Compare the sample sizes for the two studies.

b. Compare the effect sizes for the two studies.

   c. Compare the results of the significance test for the two studies.

   d. Compare the relative cost in terms of time commitment (e.g., travel time as well as treatment time).

   e. Which Drug trial would you suggest to your friend? (You must choose one.) Explain your rationale; explain the relative importance of the respective sample sizes, the results of the hypothesis tests, the effect sizes, and the relative cost in terms of time commitment (e.g., travel time as well as treatment time).

REFERENCE

DeWall, C. C., MacDonald, G., Webster, G. D., Masten, C. L., Baumeister, R. F., Powell, C., & Eisenberger, N. I. (2010). Acetaminophen reduces social pain: Behavioral and neural evidence. *Psychological Science, 21*(7), 931–937.

Activity 10-2:   Independent *t* Test

Learning Objectives

After reading the chapter and completing this activity, you should be able to do the following:

- Compute and interpret an independent samples *t* test by hand and using SPSS
- Draw a distribution of *t* scores assuming the null hypothesis is true
- Explain the assumption of homogeneity of variance and how it is tested
- Explain what the numerator and the denominator of the *t* test each measure
- Explain the effect of using a one-tailed versus a two-tailed test when hypothesis testing
- Explain how the independent samples *t* and the single sample *t* answer different questions yet can both be appropriate for a given set of data
- Explain how it is possible to fail to reject the null even if the research hypothesis is true

TWO-TAILED INDEPENDENT *t* TEST

Does the way a question is asked influence the answer people give? To investigate this question, researchers asked people to estimate the length of the Nile River using two different questions. Some people were asked if they think the Nile is longer than 800 miles (1 mile = 1.61 kilometers) and were then asked to estimate the Nile's length. Others were asked if they think the Nile is longer than 3,000 miles and were then asked to estimate the Nile's length. The actual length of the Nile is about 4,184 miles. The researchers are not interested in whether the estimates were accurate. Rather, they are interested in whether the way the question is asked influences people's estimates. Specifically, the researchers are interested in whether people who were given 800 as an "anchor" gave estimates that were *significantly different* from people who were given 3,000 as an "anchor." Use $\alpha = .05$, two-tailed. The data were as follows:

Group 1 800 Anchor	Group 2 3,000 Anchor
650	600
850	1,000
900	1,999
1,000	2,000
1,000	2,700
1,100	3,000
1,273	4,000
1,320	4,000
2,000	4,300
2,000	5,000
2,000	6,600

1. State the null and research hypotheses in words and symbols. *Do a two-tailed test.*

2. Enter the data above into SPSS. You will need two columns. One column should indicate if they were in the low anchor (800) group or the high anchor (3,000) group. The second column should indicate each participant's estimate of the length of the Nile; see the chapter for an example. To run the *t* test:

- Click on the Analyze menu. Choose Compare Means and then Independent Samples *t* Test.
- Move the Independent Variable (the one that indicates which group someone is in) into the Grouping Variable box and click on "define." Enter the values you used to designate Group 1 and Group 2 in the appropriate boxes.
- Move the Dependent Variable (the one that indicates the actual scores of the participants) into the Test Variables box. Click on the OK button.

3. What is the standard error of the mean difference? _____

4. Which of the following statements accurately describes what the standard error is measuring in this study? (*Note:* The standard error is the denominator of the *t* statistic if you calculate it by hand.)

   a. The standard error is the difference between the means of the two groups or conditions.

   b. The standard error is a measure of sampling error; we would expect a mean difference of this size to occur due to sampling error.

   c. The standard error is a measure of sampling error; *with these sample sizes*, we would expect a mean difference of this size to occur due to sampling error.

5. What two values are used to generate the mean difference? (*Note:* The mean difference is the numerator of the *t* statistic if you calculate it by hand.)

6. Give the exact mean difference value for this study. Mean difference = _____.

7. The mean difference (or numerator of the *t* statistic) is the actual difference between the mean of those who were given the 800 anchor and the mean of those who were given the 3,000 anchor. The standard error of the mean difference (or the denominator of the *t* statistic) is the size of the mean difference we would expect by sampling error. Given these two facts, which of the following is true?

   a. If the mean difference is about the same size as the standard error, the null hypothesis is likely to be false.

   b. If the mean difference is about the same size as the standard error, the null hypothesis is likely to be true.

8. Summarize the assumption of homogeneity of variance in your own words. Refer to the paragraphs about Levene's test in Chapter 10.

9. Was this assumption violated in this study?

    a. Yes, it was violated. The Sig. level for Levene's test was greater than .05.

    b. Yes, it was violated. The Sig. level for Levene's test was less than .05.

    c. No, it was not violated. The Sig. level for Levene's test was greater than .05.

    d. No, it was not violated. The Sig. level for Levene's test was less than .05.

10. What do you do if this assumption is violated?

    a. You cannot do an independent samples *t* if this assumption is violated.

    b. Use the *t*, *df*, and Sig. information from the "Equal variances assumed" row.

    c. Use the *t*, *df*, and Sig. information from the "Equal variances not assumed" row.

11. How do you use the information in the Sig. column to determine if you should reject or fail to reject the null when doing a two-tailed test?

    a. You divide the Sig. by 2 and then reject the null hypothesis if that number is less than alpha.

    b. You divide the Sig. by 2 and then reject the null hypothesis if that number is greater than alpha.

    c. You reject the null hypothesis if the Sig. is less than alpha.

    d. You reject the null hypothesis if the Sig. is greater than alpha.

    e. You divide the alpha by 2 and then reject the null hypothesis if that number is less than Sig.

    f. You divide the alpha by 2 and then reject the null hypothesis if that number is greater than Sig.

12. SPSS does not compute *d* and so you need to compute it by hand. To do so, you will need to compute the pooled variance using the *SD* values in the SPSS output.

13. Summarize the results of this study using APA style.

Those given the 800 anchor gave estimates of the length of the Nile that were significantly lower (*M* = _____, *SD* = _____) than those given the 3,000 anchor (*M* = _____, *SD* = _____), *t* (_____) = _____, *p* = _____ (two-tailed), *d* = _____.

(*Note:* The *df*, *t*, and Sig. value should all come from the "Equal variances not assumed" row.)

14. If we had predicted that the people given 3,000 as an anchor would give *higher* estimates than those given 800 as an anchor, it would have been reasonable to do a one-tailed test. What would the null and research hypotheses be if we had predicted higher estimates from the 3,000 group?

15. Would the *obtained t value* change if we did a one-tailed test?   Yes   No

16. How do you use the Sig. column of the SPSS output to determine if we should reject or fail to reject the null hypothesis when using a *one-tailed* test?

    a. You divide the Sig. by 2 and then reject the null hypothesis if that number is less than alpha.

    b. You divide the Sig. by 2 and then reject the null hypothesis if that number is greater than alpha.

    c. You reject the null hypothesis if the Sig. is less than alpha.

    d. You reject the null hypothesis if the Sig. is greater than alpha.

    e. You divide the alpha by 2 and then reject the null hypothesis if that number is less than Sig.

    f. You divide the alpha by 2 and then reject the null hypothesis if that number is greater than Sig.

17. In this case, would we reject or fail to reject the null when doing a one-tailed test with an alpha of .01?

COMPARING INDEPENDENT *t* TO SINGLE SAMPLE *t*

The actual length of the Nile is 4,184 miles. We could have analyzed people's estimates of the Nile's length by doing two single sample *t* tests. We could do one single sample *t* to determine if the 800 anchor group gave estimates that were significantly different from 4,184 and *another* single sample *t* to determine if the 3,000 anchor group gave estimates that were significantly different from 4184.

18. Perform these two tests and record the results of the *two* single sample *t* tests below. To perform these two tests, you will have to first separate the data file so that you compare the mean estimate of each group of participants with the actual length of the Nile. You can do this by doing the following:

    • Click on the Data menu. Choose Split File and then Compare Groups.
    • Move the group variable to the Groups Based on box.
    • Click OK.
    • Run a one sample *t* test by clicking on the Analyze menu. Choose Compare Means and then select the One-Sample *t* test.

- Move length of the Nile to the test variable box and change the Test Value to 4184.
- Click OK.
- The result of all of this will be two different one sample t tests, one for the high anchor group and the other for the low anchor group. Record the statistical info below. Use alpha values of .05 and a two-tailed test for both tests.

Low anchor, t (____) = _____, p = _____.
High anchor, t (____) = _____, p = _____.

19. Which TWO of the following statements best summarizes results of the two single sample t tests? (Choose two statements, one to summarize the results of each single sample t test.)

a. The estimates given by the low anchor group were not significantly different from 4184.

b. The estimates given by the low anchor group were significantly lower than 4184.

c. The estimates given by the low anchor group were significantly higher than 4184.

d. The estimates given by the high anchor group were not significantly different from 4184.

e. The estimates given by the high anchor group were significantly lower than 4184.

f. The estimates given by the high anchor group were significantly higher than 4184.

20. The results of the independent t test and the results of the two single t tests answer different research questions. What are you testing with the independent t test? What are you testing with each single sample t tests? (*Hint:* What are the null hypotheses for each test?)

21. Previous research has repeatedly demonstrated an anchoring and adjustment bias. That is, we tend to anchor on an initial number given in the question (i.e., either 3,000 or 800) and then adjust from that initial number when making estimates. Although we do adjust, we usually do not adjust enough. A student wonders if this bias can influence how people rate movies. The student goes to a movie theater and immediately after a movie asks 20 people to rate the movie. Half of the movie goers are asked if they think that it was a 2-star movie and are then asked to indicate how many stars they would give the movie. The other half of the movie goers are asked if they think that it was a 4-star movie and are asked to indicate

how many stars they would give the movie. On average, the people in the 2-star group gave the movie 2.6 stars, while the people in the 4-star group gave the movie 3.5 stars. The student conducts a *t* test and finds that the difference was not statistically significant. Based on the previous research, the student was convinced that his study would "work," and so he wants to conduct another study to retest his hypothesis. What would you recommend he change in the next study?

Activity 10-3:   How to Choose the Correct Statistic

Learning Objectives

After reading the chapter and completing the homework and this activity, you should be able to do the following:

- Read a research scenario and determine which statistic should be used

BASIC PROBLEMS

Determine which statistic should be used in each of the following situations. When you are assessing a given situation, you need to recognize that if a problem does not give you the sample mean (*M*) or the sample standard deviation (*SD*) you can always compute these values from the data. However, if a problem does not give you the population mean (μ) or the population standard deviation (σ), you should assume that these values are not known.

1. Is gender related to income? Specifically, do male teachers make more money than female teachers? Which test statistic would you use?

2. Do people have less body fat after running for 6 weeks than before they started running? Which test statistic would you use?

3. What percentage of 5-year-olds are taller than 45 inches ($\sigma = 2.6$)? Which statistic should you use?

4. Intelligence Quotient (IQ) scores have a population mean of 100 and a standard deviation of 15. Does the college football team have a mean IQ that is significantly greater than 100? Which statistic should you use?

5. Is the mean height of a sample of female volleyball players taller than 68 inches? Which statistic should you use?

DETAILED PROBLEMS

Determine which statistic should be used in each of the following research scenarios: z for a single score, z for sample mean, single sample t, related samples t, or independent samples t.

6. Previous studies have shown that exposure to thin models is associated with lower body image among women. A researcher designs a study to determine if very young girls are similarly affected by thin images. Forty kindergartners are randomly assigned to one of two groups. The first group plays with Barbie dolls for 30 minutes. The second group plays with a doll with proportions similar to the average American woman. After the 30-minute play period, the researcher measures each girl's body image using a graphic rating scale that is similar to a Likert scale. Which statistic should this researcher use to determine if girls who played with Barbie dolls reported lower body image than girls who played with dolls with proportions similar to the average American woman?

7. A teacher of an art appreciation course wants to know if his course actually results in greater appreciation for the arts. On the first day of class, the teacher asks students to complete an art appreciation survey that assesses attitudes toward a variety of forms of art (e.g., painting, theater, sculpture). Responses on the survey range between 1 = *strongly disagree* to 5 = *strongly agree*. The same survey was given on the last day of class. The teacher analyzes the survey data and finds that scores were significantly higher on the last day of class than on the first day of class. Which statistic should this researcher use to determine if students' art appreciation scores were higher after the class than before the class?

8. An insurance company keeps careful records of how long all patients stay in the hospital. Analysis of these data reveals that the average length of stay in the maternity ward for women who have had a caesarean section is $\mu = 3.9$ days with a standard deviation of $\sigma = 1.2$. A new program has been instituted that provides new parents with at-home care from a midwife for 2 days after the surgery. To determine if this program has any effect on the number of days women stay in the hospital, the insurance company computes the length of stay of a sample of 100 women who participate in the new program and find that their mean length of stay is 3.4 with a standard deviation of 1.4. Which statistic would help determine if the new program is effective at lowering the average length of mothers' hospital stay?

9. The scores on an organic chemistry test were rather low ($\mu = 53.2$, $\sigma = 8.1$). The teacher decides to give everyone who scored 2 *SD*s above the mean an A and everyone who scored 2 *SD*s below the mean an F. What statistic should the teacher use to determine which scores on the exam would result in an A and an F?

10. Abel and Kruger (2010) recently analyzed the smiles of professional baseball players listed in the Baseball Register. The photos of players were classified as

either big smiles or no smiles. The age of death for all players was also recorded. The results revealed that players with big smiles lived longer than those with no smiles. Which statistic could be used to determine if there was a significant difference in life span between those with big versus no smiles?

11. A questionnaire that assesses the degree to which people believe the world is a fair and just place has a mean of $\mu = 50$. A researcher wonders if this belief is affected by exposure to information, suggesting that the world is not a fair and just place. To answer this research question, he conducts a study with 73 students and has them watch a series of videos where bad things happen to good people. After watching these videos, he gives them the questionnaire and finds that the average score after watching the videos was 48.1 with a standard deviation of 16.2. Which statistic should the researcher use to determine if watching the video significantly reduced endorsement of the view that the world is fair and just?

12. It is well known that acetaminophen reduces physical pain. DeWall et al. (2010) found that the drug can also reduce psychological pain. Another researcher wonders if the same is true of aspirin. To test the efficacy of aspirin in treating psychological pain, they measured participants' psychological pain, gave them the drug, and then again measured their psychological pain. Psychological pain was measured using an interval scale of measurement. Which statistic should be used to determine if aspirin reduced psychological pain?

13. A new over-the-counter drug is developed to treat migraines, and the company needs to decide what dosage should be listed on the package. Clinical trials suggest that 10 mg of the drug is effective as long as the patient weighs less than 200 pounds. Suppose the average weight of women is 160 pounds with a standard deviation of 20. Which statistic could be used to determine what percentage of women will be too heavy for the recommended dosage to be effective?

14. A recent study revealed that the brains of new mothers grow bigger after giving birth. The researchers performed MRIs (magnetic resonance imagings) on the brains of 19 women and found that the volume of the hypothalamus was greater after giving birth than prior to giving birth. Which statistic would researchers use to determine if the volume of the hypothalamus was greater after giving birth than before?

15. A student takes the Graduate Record Exam (GRE) and obtains a score of 600 on the quantitative portion of the test and a 550 on the verbal portion of the test. The mean for the quantitative test is $\mu = 597$ ($\sigma = 148$), while the mean for the verbal test is $\mu = 469$ ($\sigma = 120$). What statistic could be used to determine which test the student did better on relative to other students who took the GRE?

16. If the verbal portion of the GRE has a mean of is $\mu = 469$, with a standard deviation of $\sigma = 120$. What statistic could be used to determine the percentage of test takers who obtained scores of 750 or higher (assume scores are normally distributed)?

17. A plastic surgeon notices that most of his patients think that plastic surgery will increase their satisfaction with their appearance and as a result, make them happier. To see if this is actually the case, he asks 52 of his patients to complete a survey 1 week prior to and then again 1 year after the surgery. The survey consisted of 10 questions such as "I am happy" and "Life is good." Responses to each item were scored with 1 = *strongly agree* and 5 = *strongly disagree*. Scores on all survey items were summed into one index of happiness. Which statistic should the surgeon use to determine if patients are happier after having plastic surgery than before?

REFERENCES

Abel, E. L., & Kruger, M. L. (2010). Smile intensity in photographs predicts longevity. *Psychological Science, 21*(4), 542–544.

DeWall, C. C., MacDonald, G., Webster, G. D., Masten, C. L., Baumeister, R. F., Powell, C., & Eisenberger, N. I. (2010). Acetaminophen reduces social pain: Behavioral and neural evidence. *Psychological Science, 21*(7), 931–937.

Activity 10-4: Comparing Independent, Matched, and Repeated Research Designs

Learning Objectives

After reading the chapter and completing this activity, you should be able to do the following:

- Compute and interpret independent and repeated samples *t* tests using SPSS
- Explain how the numerator of a *t* could be increased and why you would want to do this
- Explain how the denominator of a *t* could be decreased and why you would want to do this
- Describe the differences between independent samples and repeated samples designs
- Explain why repeated samples designs are generally preferable to independent samples designs

In this activity we are going to investigate the effect of an IV on a DV using an independent, matched, and repeated samples design. Specifically, we are going to measure your heart rate while sitting and standing. As a reminder, the following table displays the *t*-test formulas used for all three research designs.

Independent t Test	Matched t Test	Repeated t Test
$t = \dfrac{(M_1 - M_2)}{SEM_i}$	$t = \dfrac{M_D}{SEM_r}$	$t = \dfrac{M_D}{SEM_r}$

1. Even though the formulas for matched designs and repeated designs are the same, the data are collected differently. Describe the difference.

2. Describe what the numerator represents in all three *t*-test designs.

3. Describe what the denominator represents in all three *t*-test designs.

4. Given your descriptions above, describe what the *t* test is measuring. What does an obtained *t* tell you with regard to the numerator and the denominator?

5. Today we are going to measure your heart rate under two conditions: sitting and standing. In which of these conditions would you expect people's heart rate to be higher?

6. Identify something specific that we could do methodologically to increase the size of the numerator in this study.

7. What impact would the methodological changes you proposed in Question 6 have on statistical power?

8. Identify two things we could do to *decrease* the size of the denominator of a *t* test. (*Hint:* What two things influence the size of sampling error?)

9. What impact would the changes you proposed in Question 8 have on statistical power?

10. With which type of design would you expect to have the largest observed mean difference (i.e., numerator)?

   a. Independent design

   b. Matched design

   c. Repeated design

   d. All designs would be expected to have similar observed mean differences

11. With which type of design would you expect to have the largest estimate of sampling error (i.e., denominator)?

   a. Independent design

   b. Matched design

   c. Repeated design

   d. All designs would be expected to have similar estimates of sampling error

12. With which type of design would you expect to have the largest obtained t value?

   a. Independent design

   b. Matched design

   c. Repeated design

   d. All designs would be expected to have similar obtained t values?

13. Next, we are going to do the same basic study using three different designs: (1) an independent design, (2) a matched design, and (3) a repeated design. Our IV for each design will be whether you are sitting or standing and the DV will be your heart rate. Once these data are collected, we will analyze the data and compare the statistical estimates generated by each research design.

After we run each t test, use the results to complete the following table.

	Independent	Matched	Repeated
Number of people in the study (and number of data points)			
df	$(n_1 - 1) + (n_2 - 1)$	$(N - 1)$	$(N - 1)$
Critical value			
Observed mean difference			
Estimate of sampling error			
Obtained t value			
Sig. (p value)			
Reject or fail to reject (use $\alpha = .05$)			
Effect size			

14. Compare the critical values for each type of design, *based on the critical values,* which design should have the greatest likelihood of rejecting the null hypothesis? Explain.

15. Compare the estimates of sampling error for each type of design, *based on the sampling error*, which design should have the easiest time rejecting the null hypothesis? Explain.

16. Compare the obtained *t* values for each type of design, which design produced the largest obtained *t* value? Explain why this happened?

17. Which type of design is probably the best choice for your study and why?

18. Write an APA-style summary for all of the *t* tests we performed above.

Activity 10-5:   Practice Problems

SCENARIO 1: ONE-TAILED INDEPENDENT *t* TEST

A nutritionist is interested in the effect of eating a vegetarian diet on blood pressure. Specifically, he is interested in determining if vegetarians have lower systolic blood pressure readings than omnivores. Seven vegetarians and eight omnivores volunteered to participate in a study investigating this question. The systolic blood pressure levels of each group were measured and are listed below. Use a one-tailed independent t test with an alpha level of .05 to test this research question.

Vegetarians (Group 1): 110, 112, 125, 100, 132, 107, 111

Omnivores (Group 2): 127, 109, 105, 134, 114, 126, 114, 104

Do this problem by hand and in SPSS. Be sure you understand how to read and interpret the SPSS output file.

1. Which of the following is the correct null hypothesis for this study?
   a. $H_0: \mu_1 \leq \mu_2$
   b. $H_1: \mu_1 \geq \mu_2$
   c. $H_0: \mu_1 \geq \mu_2$
   d. $H_1: \mu_1 \leq \mu_2$

2. Which of the following is the correct research hypothesis for study?
   a. $H_0: \mu_1 \leq \mu_2$
   b. $H_1: \mu_1 \geq \mu_2$
   c. $H_0: \mu_1 \geq \mu_2$
   d. $H_1: \mu_1 \leq \mu_2$

3. Which of the following is the correct null hypothesis for this study?
   a. Vegetarians have similar (or higher blood) pressure scores than omnivores.
   b. Vegetarians and omnivores have different blood pressure scores.
   c. Vegetarians have lower blood pressure scores than omnivores.
   d. Vegetarians and omnivores have similar blood pressure.

4. Which of the following is the correct research hypothesis for this study?
   a. Vegetarians have similar (or higher blood) pressure scores than omnivores.
   b. Vegetarians and omnivores have different blood pressure scores.
   c. Vegetarians have lower blood pressure scores than omnivores.
   d. Vegetarians and omnivores have similar blood pressure.

5. What is the df for this independent t-test study with seven people in Group 1 and eight people in Group 2?

6. What is the critical region for this one-tailed, independent t-test study with $\alpha = .05$?

7. What is the deviation between the two sample means in this study (i.e., $M_1 - M_2$)?

8. What is the pooled variance for this study?

9. What is the expected sampling error in this study?

10. What is the obtained *t* value for this study?

11. Should the null hypothesis of this study be rejected?

12. What is the effect size for this study?

13. Is the computed effect size small, small-medium, medium, medium-large, or large?

14. Which of the following is the best summary of this study's results?

    a. The blood pressure scores for vegetarians ($M = 113.86$, $SD = 10.95$) and omnivores ($M = 116.63$, $SD = 11.11$) were not significantly different from each other, $t(13) = -.485$, $p = .32$ (one-tailed), $d = .251$.

    b. The blood pressure scores for vegetarians ($M = 113.86$, $SD = 10.95$) and omnivores ($M = 116.63$, $SD = 11.11$) were significantly different from each other, $t(13) = .64$, $p < .05$ (one-tailed), $d = .06$.

    c. The blood pressure scores for vegetarians ($M = 113.86$, $SD = 10.95$) were significantly lower than those for omnivores ($M = 116.63$, $SD = 11.11$), $t(13) = 5.71$, $p < .05$ (one-tailed), $d = .04$.

    d. The blood pressure scores for vegetarians ($M = 113.86$, $SD = 10.95$) were significantly higher than those for omnivores ($M = 116.63$, $SD = 11.11$), $t(13) = -.485$, $p = .32$ (one-tailed), $d = .52$.

SCENARIO 2: ONE-TAILED INDEPENDENT *t* TEST

A cognitive psychologist who studies the effects of aging on memory decides to conduct a study investigating the impact of gingko biloba on the memory performance of elderly people. She decides to take a sample of 40 elderly people between 70 and 75 years of age and to give half of them gingko biloba and give the other half a sugar pill. After 6 months of taking the herb or sugar pill, each participant's memory performance was evaluated using the same standardized memory test. Neither the participants nor the researchers evaluating the participants' memory performance knew who had taken the gingko biloba or sugar pills. The researcher decided to use a one-tailed test with $\alpha = .05$ because other researchers claimed that gingko biloba would *increase* memory performance.

15. State the null and research hypotheses.

The data from the study are shown below.

Gingko biloba: 11, 9, 7, 12, 13, 7, 14, 9, 10, 12, 8, 8, 10, 11, 9, 12, 8, 10, 9, 9

Sugar pill: 8, 9, 12, 7, 11, 8, 10, 9, 13, 8, 9, 12, 11, 9, 8, 10, 13, 6, 9, 10

16. Compute the *df* and define the critical region. Draw the *t* curve to help you locate the critical value.

17. Compute the independent samples test statistic.

18. Determine if you should reject or fail to reject the null hypothesis.
    a. Reject
    b. Fail to reject

19. Compute the effect size for this study and interpret it as small, small-medium, and so on.

20. Summarize the results of your independent *t* test by choosing one of the following paragraphs. Fill in the blanks in the paragraph you choose with the appropriate statistical information.

   a. The mean memory score for those who took gingko biloba ($M =$_____, $SD =$ _____) was significantly higher than the mean memory score for those who took the sugar pill ($M =$_____, $SD =$ _____), t (_____) = _____, $p < .05$ (one-tailed), $d =$ _____. These results support the claim that gingko biloba improves memory performance of elderly people.

   b. The mean memory score for those who took gingko biloba ($M =$_____, $SD =$ _____) was not significantly higher than the mean memory score for those who took the sugar pill ($M =$_____, $SD =$ _____), t (_____) = _____, $p > .05$ (one-tailed), $d =$ _____. These results do not support the claim that gingko biloba improves memory performance of elderly people.

SCENARIO 3: TWO-TAILED INDEPENDENT *t* TEST

Many software companies have developed computer programs that they claim will help senior citizens remain mentally active. A consumer advocacy organization conducted a study designed to evaluate two competing software applications both of which claimed to "train the brain" of senior citizens. Thirty senior citizens were recruited to participate in the study. Half were given software application A and the other half were given software application B. Both groups were taught how to use the software they were given and instructed to use it for at least 30 minutes every day for 2 months. After 2 months of using the applications, both groups' working memory performance was tested. The researchers used a two-tailed test with $\alpha = .05$.

The data from those who used application A and application B were as follows:

App A: 10, 12, 10, 9, 10, 11, 8, 10, 8, 11, 13, 13, 9, 10, 8

App B: 10, 11, 14, 10, 11, 12, 13, 12, 9, 10, 11, 15, 13, 10, 11

21. State the null and research hypotheses.

22. Compute the *df* and define the critical region. Draw the *t* curve to help you locate the two critical regions.

23. Compute the independent samples *t* test.

24. Determine if you should reject or fail to reject the null hypothesis.

    a. Reject

    b. Fail to reject

25. Compute the effect size for this study and interpret it as small, small-medium, medium, and so on.

26. Summarize the results of your independent *t* test. Use one of the examples provided above as a guide.

27. Explain why even if a researcher runs a carefully designed study free of methodological flaws and rejects the null hypothesis, she or he still cannot *prove* that a treatment worked.

28. Use the following terms to complete the paragraph on significance testing. Use each term only once. Terms: sampling error, low, null hypothesis, confounds, independent variable

    As you know, researchers use the process of significance testing to evaluate a _____. More specifically, significance testing helps determine if _____ is the likely cause of the variation in the study. If it is *unlikely* to be the cause (i.e., if the test's *p* value is _____), then the _____ is assumed to have created the variation. This conclusion is sound, as long as the specific study is free of _____.

29. For all of the significance tests in the following table, the numerator is the observed variation and the denominator is the variation expected due to sampling error. Complete the first column of the table by writing in either "a sample mean and a population mean" or "two sample means."

Significance Test	Numerator Is Observed Variation Between . . .	Denominator Is Expected Sampling Error
Single sample *t* test		
Repeated *t* test		
Independent *t* test		

30. For each significance test in the table, if the observed variation (i.e., the numerator) is substantially greater than the variation expected due to sampling error (i.e., the denominator), the null hypothesis is rejected. However, the expected amount of sampling error is computed differently for each test. Insert the sampling error equations listed below into the table.

$$SEM_r = \frac{SD_D}{\sqrt{N}} \qquad SEM_i = \sqrt{\frac{SD_p^2}{n_1} + \frac{SD_p^2}{n_2}} \qquad SEM_s = \frac{SD}{\sqrt{N}}$$

NOTES

CHAPTER 11

Estimation With Confidence Intervals

LEARNING OBJECTIVES

After reading this chapter, you should be able to do the following:

- Describe the distinct purposes of significance testing, effect sizes, and confidence intervals
- Explain the logic of all confidence intervals
- Compute a confidence interval for a population mean
- Compute a confidence interval for the difference between two population means
- Report confidence intervals in APA format
- Identify correct and incorrect interpretations of confidence intervals

THREE STATISTICAL PROCEDURES WITH THREE DISTINCT PURPOSES

In Chapters 8 through 10, you learned three statistical tests (i.e., single sample *t* test, related samples *t* test, and the independent samples *t* test) that are all designed to determine whether an observed mean difference is likely to be created by sampling error or by an independent variable (IV; i.e., the grouping variable). Each of these tests compares the mean difference observed in the data to the mean difference expected due to sampling error (i.e., SEM_p, SEM_s, SEM_r, or SEM_i). If the observed mean difference is significantly greater than the mean difference expected due to sampling error, the null hypothesis is rejected and researchers conclude that the mean difference was created by the IV. This conclusion is sound if the study does not have confounding variables.

Reading Question

1. Significance tests (e.g., *t* tests) were designed to help researchers determine if the observed difference was likely to be created by
   a. sampling error.
   b. confounds.

297

After researchers use significance tests, they compute an effect size (e.g., Cohen's *d*) to describe the magnitude of the IV's impact in the study. Computing an effect size is just as important to researchers as significance testing. For example, a researcher may reject the null hypothesis but find that the effect size is very small. This would indicate that although the results are statistically significant, they may be too small to be practically significant. Effect sizes can also be helpful when planning additional studies. For example, if a significance test is not significant but an effect size is medium or large, the significance test results should not be trusted and the study should be repeated with a larger sample size.

Reading Question	2. If a statistical test is statistically significant, it is always practically significant.

   a. True

   b. False

In this chapter, you will learn about a third type of statistical procedure that has a different purpose from either significance testing or effect size. This third type of statistical procedure, called confidence intervals, helps researchers achieve their ultimate goal—that is, to generalize the results of their studies and effect size computations to an entire population. These three statistical procedures should be used together routinely. When the results of all three procedures are interpreted correctly, the combination constitutes a wealth of information that greatly facilitates the scientific process.

For example, suppose that a health psychologist wants to determine if self-monitoring increases levels of physical activity. Sixty college students were recruited with one half assigned to an experimental group and the other half to a control group. The experimental group was told about the value of exercising at least 30 minutes a day and taught to record the time they spend exercising each day. The control group was also told about the value of exercising at least 30 minutes each day but was NOT taught to record the time they spend exercising. Therefore, the IV was self-monitoring of exercise with the experimental group doing self-monitoring and the control group not doing self-monitoring. Participants wore a heart rate monitor for the duration of the study. The average number of minutes each participant exercised each day was obtained from the heart rate monitors. An independent *t* test revealed that students who self-monitored exercised more ($M = 39.90$, $SD = 21.50$) than students who did not ($M = 25.00$, $SD = 19.50$), $t(58) = 2.81$, $p = .007$, $d = .90$.

The significance test indicates that the observed mean difference in minutes of exercise is unlikely to be due to sampling error ($p = .007$) and, therefore, that self-monitoring one's exercise may help increase physical activity. The effect size indicates that the impact of self-monitoring was large in size ($d = .90$). Now the psychologist is ready to generalize these results to the entire population of college students. In other words, he wants to estimate the mean exercise time of a population of college students who engage in self-monitoring and the mean exercise time of those who do NOT self-monitor. The best estimate of exercise time for a self-monitoring population is the mean number of minutes exercised by the self-monitoring sample. However, due to sampling error, the sample mean is not likely to be exactly the same as the actual population parameter. A confidence interval is a statistical procedure that uses the same expected sampling error formulas (i.e., SEM_p, SEM_s, SEM_r, or

*SEM*ᵢ) as hypothesis test do, but in a different way, to create a range of plausible values for the population parameter. For example, in this situation, the researcher could use a confidence interval to conclude with 95% confidence that the mean number of minutes of exercise in the population of self-monitoring college students is between 31.87 and 47.93. He could also conclude with 95% confidence that the mean number of minutes of exercise in the population of college students who do not self-monitor is between 17.72 and 32.28. Both of these confidence intervals estimate a single population's mean, that of people who do and do not self-monitor their exercise, respectively. Confidence intervals are extremely useful to researchers because they help apply their results to populations. In many situations, describing populations is the ultimate goal of research. Table 11.1 lists the three types of statistical procedures and their respective main purposes.

Table 11.1   Statistical procedures and their main purposes.

Statistical Procedure	Main Purpose
Significance/hypothesis testing	To assess the probability of a difference being created by sampling error; if the null is rejected, it is probably NOT sampling error
Effect size	If null was rejected: To quantify a treatment's effectiveness
	If null was not rejected: To help determine if significance test should be trusted
Confidence intervals	To estimate a population parameter with a specific level of confidence and precision

Reading Question

3. The purpose of a confidence interval is to
   a. test for significant differences.
   b. quantify the effectiveness of a treatment.
   c. help researchers estimate a population parameter with a specific level of confidence and precision.

LOGIC OF CONFIDENCE INTERVALS

As stated above, the purpose of confidence intervals is to provide researchers with a range of plausible values for a population parameter. This range of plausible values is defined by the upper and lower boundary values of the confidence interval. The upper boundary *is the largest plausible parameter value* and the lower boundary *is the smallest plausible parameter value*. Confidence intervals use statistics from samples to determine these boundary values. All values between these boundary values, including the boundary values themselves, are considered plausible parameter values for the population.

While there are many different kinds of confidence intervals, all of them have a similar logic. Every confidence interval uses a point estimate and a margin of error around that point estimate to find upper and lower boundary values. A point estimate *is the sample mean, which is the single most plausible value for* μ *and a* margin of error *determines the range of additional plausible values for that parameter*. In the above example, the sample mean for self-monitoring people (*M* = 39.90) is the most plausible value for the population of self-monitoring people. But, because of sampling error, this point estimate of 39.90 is probably not exactly correct. Therefore, a margin of error is added to the point estimate to obtain the upper boundary of a confidence interval. Similarly, a margin of error is subtracted from the point estimate to obtain the lower boundary. The conceptual formulas for the upper and lower boundaries of confidence intervals are given below:

$$\text{Upper boundary} = \text{Point estimate} + \text{Margin of error.}$$

$$\text{Lower boundary} = \text{Point estimate} - \text{Margin of error.}$$

Reading Question

4. Which of the following might be used as a point estimate in a confidence interval?

 a. Upper bound

 b. Lower bound

 c. Sample mean

 d. Margin of error

Reading Question

5. The size of the range of plausible parameter values provided by a confidence interval is determined by the

 a. sample mean.

 b. margin of error.

The size of the margin of error is determined by two factors: (1) the expected amount of sampling error and (2) the specific level of confidence a researcher wants to achieve (usually either 95% or 99% confidence). It probably makes sense to you that studies with larger amounts of sampling error have larger margins of error. After all, with more sampling error, a wider range of values are plausible for the population mean. It might be less obvious that if researchers want more confidence, their margin of error will be larger. By way of analogy, suppose your parents ask you to estimate your score on your upcoming statistics final. You could say, "I'm going to get a score between 84% and 86%," or you could say, "I'm going to get a score between 80% and 90%." The first estimate is more precise, but you should have less confidence in that estimate because it seems too precise. The precise estimate doesn't seem to consider all of the things that could happen before or during the final exam; its margin of error seems too small. The second estimate is considerably less precise, but you should be considerably more confident in its accuracy because it has a wider margin of error for estimating your score. There is an inverse relationship between the precision of an estimate and one's confidence in that estimate. We are more confident in wider estimates. Therefore, when all other things are equal, 99% confidence intervals are wider (i.e., less precise) than 95% confidence intervals.

Reading Question

6. Which of the following contribute to the size of the margin of error? (Choose two)
   a. Sample mean
   b. Confidence level
   c. Expected sampling error

Reading Question

7. In general, 99% confidence intervals are _____ than 95% confidence intervals.
   a. wider
   b. narrower
   c. more precise

COMPUTING A CONFIDENCE INTERVAL FOR A POPULATION MEAN

The formulas in the previous section are "conceptual" formulas in that they help explain the general logic of confidence intervals. The formulas described in this section will be the ones you actually use when estimating a population's mean. As mentioned above, a sample mean serves as the point estimate, and a margin of error is added to or subtracted from the sample mean to find a confidence interval's upper and lower boundaries, respectively. In this section, you will learn to compute the margin of error. Also, as mentioned above, the margin of error is derived from the expected sampling error and a specific level of confidence (usually 95% or 99%).

When using a sample mean to estimate a population's mean, the expected amount of sampling error is defined by the SEM_s $\left(\text{i.e., } \dfrac{SD}{\sqrt{N}}\right)$. The specific level of confidence (95% or 99%) is defined by a specific t value from a critical t table (Appendix B). As always, the specific critical t value depends on the degrees of freedom (df) associated with the sampling error formula, in this case, $df = n - 1$. When computing a 95% CI, use the df to look up the critical t value in the two-tailed .05 critical t table. When computing a 99% CI, use the df to look up the critical t value in the two-tailed .01 critical t table. The first activity in this section will help explain why these specific tables are used for 95% and 99% CIs, respectively. At this point, it is enough that you know when to use which t table.

In the example at the beginning of this chapter, a researcher compared the mean number of minutes exercised by college students who self-monitored their exercise with college students who did not self-monitor their exercise. He found that self-monitoring students exercised more ($M = 39.90$, $SD = 21.50$) than nonmonitoring students ($M = 25.00$, $SD = 19.50$), $t(58) = 2.81$, $p = .007$, $d = 90$. Now the researcher needs to compute a 95% CI for each of the sample means. We'll start by using the following formulas to estimate the population parameter for self-monitoring students.

$$\text{Upper boundary} = M + (t_{CI})(SEM_s)$$

$$\text{Lower boundary} = M - (t_{CI})(SEM_s)$$

For both equations, we need the same three values: (1) the point estimate, (2) the correct critical t value, and (3) the expected sampling error. The point estimate comes from the self-monitoring sample mean ($M = 39.90$). The critical t score is found in the two-tailed .05 critical t table because we are computing a 95% CI. The df is 29 ($df = n - 1 = 30 - 1 = 29$), so the critical t is 2.045. And the SEM_s is $\dfrac{SD}{\sqrt{N}}$ or $\dfrac{21.50}{\sqrt{30}} = 3.93$. Therefore, the upper boundary of the 95% CI is as follows:

$$\text{Upper boundary} = M + (t_{CI})(SEM_s)$$

$$\text{Upper boundary} = 39.90 + (2.045)(3.93)$$

$$\text{Upper boundary} = 39.90 + (8.04) = 47.94$$

You should notice that the final line of the above calculation is identical to the conceptual formula discussed in the previous section, the point estimate of 39.90 plus the margin of error of 8.04. The lower boundary is as follows:

$$\text{Lower boundary} = M - (t_{CI})(SEM_s)$$

$$\text{Lower boundary} = 39.90 - (2.045)(3.93)$$

$$\text{Lower boundary} = 39.90 - (8.04) = 31.86$$

Again, it is worth noticing that the lower boundary is the point estimate of 39.90 minus the margin of error of 8.04. Based on these computations, we can be 95% confident that the actual mean number of minutes exercised by a population of self-monitoring college students is between 31.86 and 47.94 minutes per day.

If you follow the same procedure for the nonmonitoring sample mean, its lower and upper boundaries are:

$$\text{Upper boundary} = M + (t_{CI})(SEM_s)$$

$$\text{Upper boundary} = 25 + (2.045)\left(\frac{19.50}{\sqrt{30}}\right)$$

$$\text{Upper boundary} = 25 + (7.28) = 32.28$$

$$\text{Lower boundary} = M - (t_{CI})(SEM_s)$$

$$\text{Lower boundary} = 25 - (2.045)\left(\frac{19.50}{\sqrt{30}}\right)$$

$$\text{Lower boundary} = 25 - (7.28) = 17.72$$

Based on these computations, we can be 95% confident that the actual mean number of minutes exercised for a nonmonitoring population of college students is between 17.72 and 32.28 minutes per day.

Reading Question

8. Which of the following determine the correct *t* score for a given confidence interval? (Choose two)

   a. Confidence level (e.g., 95% or 99%)
   b. The *df*
   c. Expected sampling error

Reading Question

9. When computing a 95% CI, you should look up the correct *t* score in the two-tailed _____ critical *t* table.

   a. .05
   b. .01

COMPUTING CONFIDENCE INTERVALS FOR A DIFFERENCE BETWEEN POPULATIONS

In the previous section, we computed confidence intervals that provided plausible values for a specific population mean. Specifically, we computed the plausible values for the mean number of minutes exercised by self-monitoring and nonmonitoring people. In this section, we will compute a different kind of confidence interval that estimates the *mean difference* in exercise between the self-monitoring population and the nonmonitoring population. Like all other confidence intervals, this one is computed with a point estimate, an expected sampling error, and a critical *t* score. The point estimate is the mean difference between the sample mean for self-monitoring students ($M = 39.90$) and the sample mean for nonmonitoring students ($M = 25.00$), in this case it is $39.90 - 25.00 = 14.90$. The expected sampling error is the SEM_i from an independent *t* test where

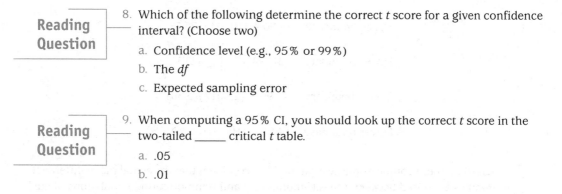

$$SD_p^2 = \frac{(n_1 - 1)SD_1^2 + (n_2 - 1)SD_2^2}{(n_1 - 1) + (n_2 - 1)} = \frac{29(21.50)^2 + 29(19.50)^2}{29 + 29} = 421.25$$

$$SEM_i = \sqrt{\frac{SD_p^2}{n_1} + \frac{SD_p^2}{n_2}} = \sqrt{\frac{421.25}{30} + \frac{421.25}{30}} = 5.30$$

The critical t score is found using the df associated with SEM_i, or $df = (n_1 - 1) + (n_2 - 1)$ where n_1 is the number of people in Sample 1 and n_2 is the number of people is Sample 2. In this case, $df = (30 - 1) + (30 - 1) = 58$. Therefore, using the two-tailed .05 critical t table for the 95% CI, the correct critical t value is 2.0017. The upper and lower boundaries of the 95% confidence interval are computed below.

$$\text{Upper boundary} = (M_1 - M_2) + (t_{CI})(SEM_i)$$

$$\text{Upper boundary} = 14.90 + (2.0017)(5.30)$$

$$\text{Upper boundary} = 14.90 + (10.61) = 25.51$$

$$\text{Lower boundary} = (M_1 - M_2) - (t_{CI})(SEM_i)$$

$$\text{Lower boundary} = 14.90 - (2.0017)(5.30)$$

$$\text{Lower boundary} = 14.90 - (10.61) = 4.29$$

Based on these computations, we can be 95% confident that the actual mean difference in minutes exercised between the self-monitoring and nonmonitoring populations of students is between 4.29 and 25.51 minutes per day. You should note that the mean difference of zero is NOT a plausible value. If a mean difference of zero is NOT a plausible value, then it is logical to conclude that the two populations are significantly different from each other. This conclusion is completely consistent with the results of the significance test that was described at the beginning of the chapter. This will ALWAYS be the case. If you conduct a two-tailed significance test with an alpha value of .05 and you reject the null and then compute a 95% confidence interval for a mean difference, it will always be the case that zero is NOT a plausible value (i.e., zero will NOT be between the upper and lower boundaries). Furthermore, if the null was not rejected by the significance test, then zero will ALWAYS be one of the plausible values (i.e., zero will be between the upper and lower boundaries).

Reading Question

10. When computing a confidence interval for a mean difference if zero is between the upper and lower boundaries, the two sample means are

   a. NOT significantly different.

   b. significantly different.

Why should you conduct a confidence interval for a mean difference after conducting a significance test? The answer harkens back to the beginning of the chapter. The two statistical procedures have distinct purposes. The significance test indicates whether or not a given effect was likely created by sampling error. Then, the effect size describes the effect's magnitude. And finally, the confidence intervals help you generalize your results to the respective populations by identifying plausible values for the populations as well as the mean difference between the populations. Each statistic has its own purpose even though the results of each are not completely independent (e.g., the relationship between significance testing and confidence intervals for differences will always be consistent).

Reading Question

11. Which of the following determines plausible values for population parameters?
   a. Significance testing
   b. Effect sizes
   c. Confidence intervals

This chapter illustrated how to compute two different types of confidence intervals. There is a third confidence interval for computing the mean difference between related samples (e.g., when estimating the change that an IV had on a sample in a pretest–posttest design). This third confidence interval follows the same logic as the others. Table 11.2 displays the three types of confidence intervals, the appropriate *df* formula, and the specific confidence interval formula.

Table 11.2 Confidence interval types, their degrees of freedom, and specific formulas.

CI Type	df Formula	Specific CI Formula
Estimating μ	$df = N - 1$	$UB = M + (t_{CI})\left(\dfrac{SD}{\sqrt{N}}\right)$ $LB = M - (t_{CI})\left(\dfrac{SD}{\sqrt{N}}\right)$
Estimating $\mu_1 - \mu_2$ for independent samples	$df = (n_1 - 1) + (n_2 - 1)$	$UB = M + (t_{CI})\left(\sqrt{\dfrac{SD_p^2}{n_1} + \dfrac{SD_p^2}{n_2}}\right)$ $LB = M - (t_{CI})\left(\sqrt{\dfrac{SD_p^2}{n_1} + \dfrac{SD_p^2}{n_2}}\right)$
Estimating μ_D for related samples (i.e., repeated or matched designs)	$df = N - 1$	$UB = M + (t_{CI})\left(\dfrac{SD_D}{\sqrt{N}}\right)$ $LB = M - (t_{CI})\left(\dfrac{SD_D}{\sqrt{N}}\right)$

Note: CI = confidence interval; *df* = degrees of freedom; UB = upper boundary; LB = lower boundary.

REPORTING CONFIDENCE INTERVALS IN AMERICAN PSYCHOLOGICAL ASSOCIATION FORMAT

While the confidence interval procedure is not new, its prominence within the behavioral sciences has been increasing. Evidence for the increasing importance of confidence intervals is found in the most recent version of the *Publication Manual of the American Psychological Association*. The manual strongly recommends that researchers compute and interpret confidence intervals in conjunction with significance tests and effect sizes when reporting results (American Psychological Association [APA], 2010, p. 34). Specifically, the APA *Publication Manual* recommends that authors use a confidence interval approach when discussing the implications of their research findings.

The following format is consistent with the latest APA manual recommendations for reporting significance tests, effect sizes, and confidence intervals. Note how the confidence interval information we computed in this chapter is integrated into the report. The first time you report a confidence interval for a set of analyses, you report the level of confidence (e.g., 95%). After that, you do not need to indicate the level of confidence because the reader can infer that you used the same level of confidence for all analyses.

An independent t test revealed that students who self-monitored their exercise time exercised more ($M = 39.90$, $SD = 21.50$; 95% CI [31.86, 47.94]) than students who did not ($M = 25.00$, $SD = 19.50$; CI [17.72, 32.28]), $t(58) = 2.81$, $p = .007$, $d = .90$, CI [4.29, 25.51].

Reading Question

12. The APA recommends that researchers use
    a. confidence intervals rather than significance testing.
    b. confidence intervals in conjunction with significance testing and effect sizes.

CONFIDENCE INTERVALS FOR EFFECT SIZES

The APA also recommends that confidence intervals be reported for each reported effect size. Unfortunately, these computations are complex and, therefore, beyond the scope of this book. Cumming (2012) provides detailed, yet extremely readable, discussions of confidence intervals for effect sizes. He also provides a free Microsoft Excel spreadsheet for computing and graphing many types of confidence intervals, including those for effect sizes. We highly recommend Cumming's book to readers wanting a greater understanding of the confidence interval statistical approach.

INTERPRETATIONS OF CONFIDENCE INTERVALS

The main purpose of confidence intervals is to help researchers generalize their study's results to populations. Cumming (2012) identifies six ways this could be done. We will present four ways to interpret confidence intervals.

First, a 95% CI suggests that you can be 95% confident that the true population mean falls between the lower and upper boundaries, including the boundary values themselves. In other words, a confidence interval can be interpreted as *a set of plausible values for the population parameter* (i.e., a population mean or a population mean difference, depending on the confidence interval). The point estimate is considered the most plausible value for μ, and the respective plausibility of each value decreases as you move away from the point estimate. Values *outside* of the upper and lower boundaries are interpreted as *implausible*.

Second, the width of confidence intervals helps researchers interpret the precision of a given study's point estimate. *Narrower confidence intervals (i.e., those with smaller margins of error) provide more precise estimates.*

Third, *a 95% CI has a .83 replication recapture rate*. This interpretation requires some more explanation. If a given study produces a 95% CI of [10, 20], the first confidence interval interpretation described above indicates that researchers should be 95% confident that μ is between 10 and 20, inclusively. However, this does NOT mean that if the researchers repeated the study a second time, the mean of the second study would be between 10 and 20, 95% of the time. In fact, assuming that the second study was done exactly as the first, the mean of the second study is expected to be between 10 and 20 only 83% of the time. This is referred to as the replication recapture rate, *the probability that the point estimate of a replicated study will fall between the upper and lower boundaries of a previous study*. So the third interpretation is that if a given study is replicated, 83% of the time the point estimate will fall between the boundaries of the original study's 95% CI.

Finally, we'll mention an additional way to use confidence interval logic that is limited to confidence intervals for *mean differences*. It is a logical extension of the first interpretation we discussed above, namely, that values *outside* the confidence interval boundaries are *implausible*. When computing a 95% CI for a *mean difference,* if zero is a plausible value (i.e., if it is between the 95% CI boundaries), then the two sample means would NOT be significantly different when using a significance test with an alpha value of .05. On the other hand, if zero is outside of the 95% CI boundaries, the two means would be significantly different when using an alpha value of .05. Again, this last interpretation could reasonably be thought of as a specific application of the first interpretation described above.

Reading Question

13. Which of the following is NOT a correct interpretation of a 95% CI?

   a. A range of plausible parameter values

   b. A wider CI is less precise than a narrow CI

   c. A 95% CI of [15, 30] means that 95% of the time a replicated study will produce a mean between 15 and 30

A COMMON MISCONCEPTION OF CONFIDENCE INTERVALS

Many people mistakenly believe that if two confidence intervals share values (i.e., overlap), then their respective sample means are NOT significantly different. This is not true. In the self-monitoring example, the 95% CI for self-monitoring students was [31.86, 47.94] and the 95% CI for nonmonitoring students was [17.72, 32.28]. You should notice that the lower bound for self-monitoring overlaps slightly with the upper bound for nonmonitoring and yet the p value for the difference between the means was $p = .007$, indicating that the two means are significantly different. Furthermore, clearly substantially greater overlap of the two intervals is possible and the two means would still be significantly different.

Cumming (2012) suggests some general "rules of eye" for *estimating p* values from the overlap of two confidence intervals. However, these rules only work with independent samples designs. As a general rule, if you want to know if two means are significantly different, do a significance test.

Reading Question

14. If two confidence intervals share plausible values, the two sample means are NEVER significantly different.
   a. True
   b. False

REFERENCES

American Psychological Association (APA). (2010). *Publication manual of the American Psychological Association* (6th ed.). Washington, DC: Author.

Cumming, G. (2012). *Understanding the new statistics: Effect sizes, confidence intervals, and meta-analysis*. New York, NY: Routledge Academic.

SPSS

SPSS computes 95% confidence intervals for *mean differences* automatically for all t tests. Refer back to the respective t test chapters for the instructions. If you want to compute the 99% confidence interval around the mean difference, click Options and change the confidence interval to 99%. When computing any t test, SPSS does not automatically compute the confidence intervals around individual sample means. You can get SPSS to compute confidence intervals around the individual means by splitting your data file based on the grouping variable and then running a series of single sample t tests, but in this book, we will simply compute them by hand.

SPSS can also create graphs of the confidence intervals around individual means. The steps for creating confidence interval graphs for each t test are given below. Note that these instructions are for the confidence intervals around individual means, not around mean differences.

Creating a Confidence Interval Graph for a Sample Mean

To create a graph for a single sample mean

- Click on the Graphs menu, select Legacy Dialogs and then Error Bar.
- Click on the Simple Graph.

- Select Summaries of Separate Variables, and then click on the Define button.
- Select the variable of interest from the list on the left and move it into the Error Bars box.
- Where it says Bars represent, make sure that Confidence Interval for Mean is selected.
- Type in the appropriate confidence interval (i.e., 95% or 99%).
- Click on the OK button.

Creating a Confidence Interval Graph for Two or More Independent Sample Means

To create a graph for two or more independent samples

- Click on the Graphs menu, select Legacy Dialogs and then Error Bar.
- Click on the Simple Graph.
- Select Summaries for Groups of Cases, and then click on the Define button.
- Move the grouping variable into the Category axis box.
- Move the dependent variable into the Variable box.
- Where it says Bars represent, make sure that Confidence Interval for Mean is selected.
- Type in the appropriate confidence interval (i.e., 95% or 99%).
- Click on the OK button.

Creating a Confidence Interval Graph for Two or More Related Sample Means

To create a graph for two or more related samples

- Click on the Graphs menu, select Legacy Dialogs and then Error Bar.
- Click on the Simple Graph.
- Select Summaries of Separate Variables, and then click on the Define button.
- Select the variables of interest (i.e., pre and post) from the list on the left and move them into the Error Bars box.
- Where it says Bars represent, make sure that Confidence Interval for Mean is selected.
- Type in the appropriate confidence interval (i.e., 95% or 99%).
- Click on the OK button.

Output

The output in Figure 11.1 is from an exercise journal study where an independent t test revealed that students who kept an exercise journal exercised more ($M = 39.90, SD = 21.50$; 95% CI [31.86, 47.94]) than students in the control group ($M = 25.00, SD = 19.50$; CI [17.72, 32.28]), $t(58) = 2.81, p = .007, d = 90$, CI [4.29, 25.51].

Reading Question	15. The output below displays which of the following?

        a. A 95% CI for a sample mean

        b. A 95% CI for two sample means

        c. A 95% CI for the mean difference of samples

Figure 11.1 Annotated SPSS output for a 95% confidence interval for a mean difference.

Group Statistics

	Group	N	Mean	Std. Deviation	Std. Error Mean
MinutesExercised	exercise journal	30	39.9000	21.50116	3.92556
	no journal control	30	25.0000	19.50243	3.56064

Independent Samples Test

		Levene's Test for Equality of Variances		t-test for Equality of Means						
									95% Confidence Interval of the Difference	
		F	Sig.	t	df	Sig. (2-tailed)	Mean Difference	Std. Error Difference	Lower	Upper
Minutes Exercised	Equal variances assumed	.011	.916	2.811	58	.007	14.90000	5.29983	4.29124	25.50876
	Equal variances not assumed			2.811	57.456	.007	14.90000	5.29983	4.28911	25.51089

Lower and upper 95% CI boundaries

The confidence interval graph in Figure 11.2 represents the point estimates for each sample mean with a dot. The "whiskers" above and below each dot represent the upper and lower margins of error, respectively. It is impossible to obtain the exact upper and lower boundaries from the graph. If you want the exact values, you would have to compute them by hand (we did this earlier in the chapter).

The margin of error for the exercise journal group mean ($M = 39.90$) is ± 8.04. If you look at the graph, you can see that the confidence interval bars extend 8.04 above and below the point estimate ($M = 39.90$). Thus, the bars' lengths are a graphical representation of the margin of error. Similarly, the margin of error for the no exercise journal control group mean ($M = 25.00$) is ± 7.28, and so the bars extend 7.28 above and below the point estimate.

It is important to note the different types of information we have available. The t test results for this analysis were $t(58) = 2.81$, $p = .007$. Thus, you can reject the null hypothesis and conclude that the mean difference is not likely to be due to sampling error; rather the difference may be due to keeping an exercise journal. The effect size was large ($d = .90$), indicating that the exercise journal group exercised substantially more than the no journal control group (by .90 SD). Finally, the confidence intervals tell you

| Figure 11.2 | Annotated SPSS output for a point and whisker plot of two different sample means (only one is annotated). |

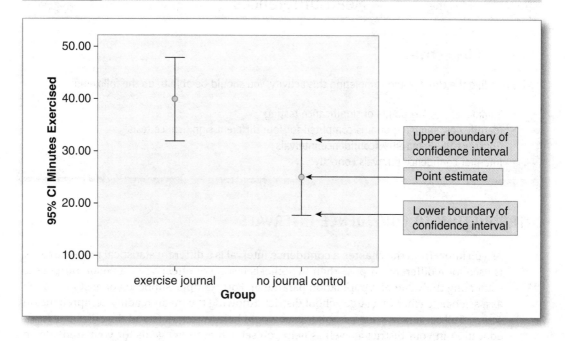

that we are 95% confident that the mean difference between the populations falls between 4.29 and 25.51 (obtained from the t test SPSS output). Furthermore, we are 95% confident that the population mean for the exercise journal group falls between 31.86 and 47.54 and that the population mean for the no journal control group falls between 17.72 and 32.28.

Other Types of Error Bars

In the above graph, "whiskers" represent the positive and negative margins of error. You should also know that "whiskers" are also used to represent standard errors of the mean or standard deviations. Given that "whiskers" are used to represent multiple statistical concepts (e.g., margins of error, *SEM*s, and *SD*s), it is absolutely critical that graphs explicitly identify what whiskers represent. So when creating your own graphs, be sure to label your "whiskers."

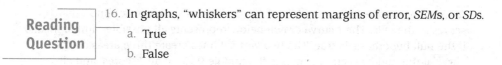

Reading Question

16. In graphs, "whiskers" can represent margins of error, *SEM*s, or *SD*s.

a. True

b. False

Activity 11-1:   Estimating Sample Means and Sample Mean Differences

Learning Objectives

After reading the chapter and completing this activity, you should be able to do the following:

- Summarize the key points of significance testing
- Identify how sampling error is computed for four different significance tests
- Construct 95% and 99% confidence intervals
- Interpret confidence intervals correctly

INTRODUCTION TO CONFIDENCE INTERVALS

As you know from the chapter, a confidence interval is a different statistical procedure that is used for a different purpose than hypothesis testing or effect sizes. Its main purpose is estimating the value of a population parameter. For example, suppose you just took a job as a science teacher in a large school district. Knowing the mean reading comprehension score of all seniors in your school district would help you understand the current state of education in your district as well as help you set achievement goals for your students. In this situation, you could use a sample of 50 seniors' standardized reading comprehension scores to estimate the mean reading comprehension score for the entire population. Of course, we have used samples to represent populations throughout this book. However, how much confidence should you have that the sample mean is a good estimate of the actual population parameter? Confidence intervals answer this question. A confidence interval is *a range of values that contain the actual population parameter with a specific degree of certainty or confidence.* For example, in this situation, you could compute a 95% confidence interval of 29 to 43. *This confidence interval would mean that you could be 95% confident that the actual reading comprehension score for the population of seniors in your district is between 29 and 43.*

This activity will teach you how to compute and interpret 95% and 99% confidence intervals. However, there is some preliminary information you must work through before you can start computing confidence intervals.

Review of *t* Distributions

1. As you know, scores in the middle of *t* distributions are more common than scores in the tails. The *t* curve drawn below represents all possible sample means if the null hypothesis is true. The two vertical lines create three areas on the curve, if the middle section contains the middle 95% of all *t* scores (and all

sample means), what percentage of all sample means is contained in the left and right tails of the distribution?

a. 5% in the left and 5% in the right

b. 2.5% in the left and 2.5 % in the right

c. 1% in the left and 1% in the right

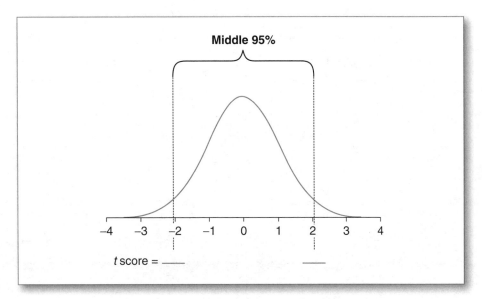

2. To compute a 95% confidence interval, you must know the two *t* scores that contain the middle 95% of all possible sample means. In the previous question, you determined that the left and right tails contained the top and bottom 2.5% of all sample means. Now we need to find the *t* scores that define the top and bottom 2.5% of *t* scores. Which table of critical *t* values could you use to find the positive and negative *t* scores that define the top and bottom 2.5% of *t* scores?

a. One-tailed $\alpha = .05$ table

b. Two-tailed $\alpha = .05$ table

c. One-tailed $\alpha = .01$ table

d. Two-tailed $\alpha = .01$ table

3. As you know, the *t* distribution changes shape as sample size changes. Therefore, if you want to know the *t* scores that define the middle 95% of all possible *t* scores (and all possible sample means), you need to know the sample size so you can compute the degrees of freedom and then find the correct *t* score. If the sample size is 50 and $df = N - 1$, what are the *t* scores that define the middle 95% of sample means? Find these values and place them on the above figure.

4. Complete the following figures and charts by first determining which critical *t* table you need to use to find the middle 95% of sample means and middle 99% of sample means. After you determine which table to use for each middle percentage, use the provided sample size to find the specific *t* values for each middle percentage.

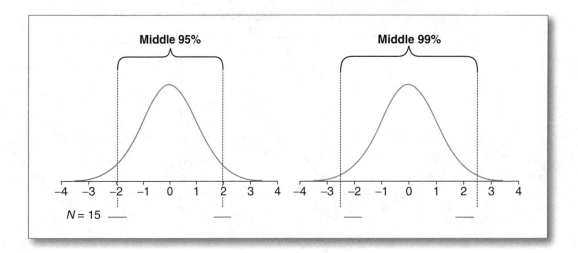

Sample Size	Middle % of t Scores/Sample Means	Critical t Table to Use	Specific t Scores Defining the Middle %
N = 15	95%	Two-tailed .05	
N = 15	99%		

5. Now complete the following table that provides a different sample size.

Sample Size	Middle % of t Scores/Sample Means	Critical t Table to Use	Specific t Scores Defining the Middle %
N = 50	95%		
N = 50	99%		

STATISTICAL ESTIMATION

As mentioned above, in some situations, the goal is estimating the value of a population parameter rather than testing a hypothesis. In the hypothetical example outlined above, you are a science teacher in a large school district and you want to know the mean reading comprehension score of all seniors in your district.

6. Let's assume that the entire population of seniors is too large for you to actually measure every senior's reading comprehension ability, what could you do to estimate the mean reading comprehension score of seniors from this district?

7. You decide to collect a random sample of 50 seniors and give them a standardized reading comprehension test. Based on the central limit theorem, the mean of this sample is expected to be equal to the _____ _____.
However, because of _____ _____ you would not expect the mean of the sample to be exactly equal to the mean of the population. In this situation, you can use the expected amount of sampling error to construct a range of values that probably contains the actual mean reading comprehension score of the population (i.e., the population parameter). Researchers call this range of values a *confidence interval*.

Confidence intervals have three components: (a) a point estimate, (b) a specific confidence level, and (c) an expected amount of sampling error. Point estimates come from samples. In this case, the sample mean estimates the population mean; the sample mean is the point estimate. Confidence levels come from the *t* scores that define the middle of the *t* distributions (i.e., like those values you found in the above tables). *If you want to be 95% confident that your interval of values contains the true population mean, you would use the* t *scores that contain the middle 95% of sample means.* If you want to be 99% confident, you would use the *t* scores that correspond to the middle 99%. Finally, the expected sampling error is computed using one of the three *SEM* formulas you have learned. In this situation, we are estimating the *value of a population mean* so you would use the *SEM* from the single sample *t* test $\left(\text{i.e., } \dfrac{SD}{\sqrt{N}} \right)$. The specific formulas for constructing the upper and lower boundaries of a confidence interval for a population mean are given below:

$$\text{Upper boundary} = M + (t_{CI})(SEM_s).$$

$$\text{Lower boundary} = M - (t_{CI})(SEM_s).$$

Therefore, if $N = 50$, $M = 36$, and $SD = 5$, the upper boundary of a 95% confidence interval would be

$$\text{Upper boundary} = 36 + (2.0096)\left(\frac{5}{\sqrt{50}} \right) = 37.42.$$

8. Compute the lower boundary.

9. The proper interpretation of this confidence interval:

    a. We are 95% confident that the actual mean reading comprehension score for the entire population of seniors in the school district is between the lower and upper boundary values of _____ and _____.

    b. We are 95% confident that the true population mean is 36.

COMPUTING CONFIDENCE INTERVALS: BASIC PROBLEMS

For the following problems, use the information provided to compute the appropriate confidence interval.

10. $M = 59$; $SD = 4$; $N = 15$; compute a 95% confidence interval; you are estimating a population mean, so use $\dfrac{SD}{\sqrt{N}}$ for sampling error.

    a. Upper boundary =

    b. Lower boundary =

    c. Using the correct option from Question 9 above as your guide, write the appropriate interpretation of this confidence interval.

11. $M = 59$; $SD = 4$; $N = 15$; compute a 99% confidence interval; you are estimating a population mean, so use $\dfrac{SD}{\sqrt{N}}$ for sampling error.

    a. Upper boundary =

    b. Lower boundary =

    c. Write the appropriate interpretation of this confidence interval.

12. $M = 59$; $SD = 2$; $N = 15$; compute a 95% confidence interval; you are estimating a population mean, so use $\dfrac{SD}{\sqrt{N}}$ for sampling error.

    a. Upper boundary =

b. Lower boundary =

c. Write the appropriate interpretation of this confidence interval.

13. When all other factors are held constant, as sampling error gets smaller what happens to the width of confidence intervals? (*Hint*: Compare Question 10 and Question 12.)

a. They get wider.

b. They get narrower.

c. It stays the same.

14. When all other factors are held constant, as confidence levels decrease (i.e., 99% to 95%) what happens to the width of confidence intervals? (*Hint:* Compare Question 10 and Question 11.)

a. It gets wider.

b. It gets narrower.

c. It stays the same.

15. Not surprisingly, there is a trade-off when constructing confidence intervals. Generally speaking, higher confidence levels are associated with less precision (i.e., wider confidence intervals). If you require a high degree of confidence in your estimate, the interval will be _____ (choose one: wider, narrower). In contrast, if you desire a high degree of precision in your estimate, your confidence level will be _____ (choose one: lower, higher).

Scenario 1: Estimating a Mean

A company designing an electric lawn mower wants to know how much weight a typical person can comfortably push over a grassy field. They hire a human factors psychologist who has a sample of 41 people go through several trials of pushing carts of varying weights across a flat grassy field. The sample comfortably pushed a mean weight of 51 pounds (*SD* = 10 pounds).

16. What is your point estimate in this scenario?

17. Which table of critical values should you use to create a 95% confidence interval?

18. What is the correct *t* score to create a 95% confidence interval for this scenario?

19. Use $\dfrac{SD}{\sqrt{N}}$ to compute the sampling error because you are estimating a population mean. Compute the upper and lower boundaries for this confidence interval below.

20. Write an interpretation of this confidence interval. Your interpretation should be specific to this scenario (i.e., describe what you are estimating; use the answer from Question 9 as your guide).

Scenario 2: Estimating a Mean

A researcher wants to estimate the mean intelligence quotient (IQ) score of advanced placement high school students in his state. He obtains a sample of 25 such students and finds their mean IQ to be 121 (SD =15). He wants to be 95 % confident in his estimate.

21. What is your point estimate in this scenario?

22. Which table of critical values should you use to create the confidence interval?

23. What is the correct t score to create the confidence interval?

24. Use $\dfrac{SD}{\sqrt{N}}$ to compute the sampling error because you are estimating a population mean. Compute the upper and lower boundaries for this confidence interval below.

25. Write an interpretation of this confidence interval. Mention by name what you are estimating.

Scenario 3: Estimating a Mean Difference

All of the confidence intervals you constructed thus far were estimating a population mean. Confidence intervals can also estimate the *mean difference* between two populations. For example, a researcher studying anxiety might estimate the *mean difference* between the anxiety scores of men and the anxiety scores of women. In this situation, the researcher could use a sample of men and a sample of women to estimate the actual mean difference in anxiety scores between the populations of men and women. The *mean difference* between the sample means is the point estimate. Here, sampling error is computed as in an independent t test, $\sqrt{\dfrac{SD_p^2}{n_1} + \dfrac{SD_p^2}{n_2}}$, because there is sampling error created by two independent sample means (i.e., one for men and one for women). Use the following information to construct a 95% confidence interval for the *mean difference* between men's and women's anxiety scores.

Sample of men: $M_1 = 30$, $SD_1 = 4$, $n_1 = 15$.

Sample of women: $M_2 = 33$, $SD_2 = 5$, $n_2 = 15$.

26. What is your point estimate in this scenario?

27. Which table of critical values should you use to create a 95% confidence interval?

28. What is the correct t score to create the confidence interval?

29. Use $SEM_i = \sqrt{\dfrac{SD_p^2}{n_1} + \dfrac{SD_p^2}{n_2}}$ to compute the expected amount of sampling error below. You will first have to compute the pooled variance, $SD_p^2 = \dfrac{(n_1 - 1)SD_1^2 + (n_2 - 1)SD_2^2}{(n_1 - 1) + (n_2 - 1)}$.

30. Compute the upper and lower boundaries for this confidence interval below.

31. Write an interpretation of this confidence interval. Mention by name what you are estimating.

Scenario 4: Estimating a Mean Difference

The previous confidence interval estimated the mean difference between two independent populations, namely, men and women. It is also possible to estimate the mean difference between two *related* populations. For example, a researcher might estimate the *mean change* in voters' attitudes by measuring a sample's attitudes before and after watching an advertisement.

32. The mean difference between pre and post advertisement scores would be the _____ for the confidence interval.

  a. *t* score

  b. confidence level

  c. point estimate

33. In this situation, the correct *SEM* to compute sampling error would be the same equation used for a/an

  a. one-sample *t* test; $SEM_s = \dfrac{SD}{\sqrt{N}}$.

  b. independent *t* test; $SEM_i = \sqrt{\dfrac{SD_p^2}{n_1} + \dfrac{SD_p^2}{n_2}}$.

  c. related samples *t* test; $SEM_r = \dfrac{SD_D}{\sqrt{N}}$.

Use the following information to compute a 95% confidence interval for the change in attitudes as a result of the advertisement.

$N = 25$; attitude before: $M_{before} = 7$; attitude after: $M_{after} = 5$; *SD* of attitude change $(SD_D) = .5$

34. What is your point estimate in this scenario?

35. Which table of critical values should you use?

36. What is the correct *t* score?

37. Use $\dfrac{SD_D}{\sqrt{N}}$ to compute the sampling error because you are estimating a mean difference between related scores. Compute the upper and lower boundaries for this confidence interval.

38. Write an interpretation of this confidence interval. Mention by name what you are estimating.

RELATIONSHIP BETWEEN CONFIDENCE INTERVALS AND HYPOTHESIS TESTING

While confidence intervals and significance tests are typically used for different purposes, these two statistical procedures are closely related. For example, the mean difference confidence interval you just computed could be used to test the null hypothesis that pre- and postadvertisement scores are not significantly different.

39. If the pre- and postscores really are NOT significantly different, what specific value would you expect to get as the difference between the pre- and postadvertisement scores?

Of course, because of sampling error, you should not be surprised if the mean difference you obtain is not exactly zero. However, if your point estimate is "close" to zero, you should conclude that the pre- and postscores are NOT significantly different. In the confidence interval context, a point estimate is considered "close" to zero if the upper and lower boundaries contain a zero.

40. Based on the above information and the confidence interval you computed in Question 37, are the pre- and postadvertisement scores significantly different? Explain your reasoning.

41. Based on the confidence interval you computed for Scenario 3, are the mean anxiety levels of men and women similar?

Activity 11-2: Practice Problems

SCENARIO 1: CONFIDENCE INTERVAL FOR A SINGLE MEAN

People often complain about the length and frequency of commercials on TV. A company is considering offering TV shows online without commercial interruptions for an additional cost. Before pursuing this plan, the marketing department wants to know how much people would be willing to pay for such a service. To get an estimate of the amount people will pay, they survey a random sample of 67 TV watchers and find that the mean amount is $38.65 with a standard deviation of $25.32.

1. Compute the margin of error for a 95% confidence interval.

2. Construct a 95% confidence interval around the point estimate of 38.5.

3. Explain why a larger sample size would be beneficial in this case.

4. Explain why a confidence interval is more useful than a single sample *t* in this case.

5. Would a 99% confidence interval be narrower or wider than the 95% confidence interval?

SCENARIO 2: RELATED SAMPLES DESIGN WITH TWO MEANS

The health psychologist who studied the effect of self-monitoring on exercise used an independent samples design. Suppose that a different psychologist conducted a study using the same IV but used a related samples design. Specifically, the researcher asked 30 people to wear a heart rate monitor for 1 month. During that period the participants were instructed to keep a daily exercise journal. A related samples *t* test revealed that students exercised more when they self-monitored ($M = 44.60$, $SD = 18.62$) than when they did not ($M = 20.50$, $SD = 16.87$), $t(29) = 6.62$, $p < .001$, $d = 1.21$. The standard deviation of the difference scores was 10.1.

6. Compute the point estimate for the confidence interval of the *mean difference*.

7. Compute the margin of error for the confidence interval of the *mean difference*.

8. Compute the 95% confidence interval for the *mean difference*.

9. Based on these data, the researcher is 95% confident that the mean difference in the number of minutes exercised is between _____ and _____.

10. What is the point estimate for the confidence interval for the students *before* they were instructed to self-monitor their exercise?

11. Compute the margin of error for the confidence interval for the students *before* they were instructed to self-monitor their exercise.

12. Compute the 95% confidence interval for the students *before* they were instructed to self-monitor their exercise.

13. Based on these data, the researcher is 95% confident that number of minutes exercised *before* self-monitoring is between _____ and _____.

14. What is the point estimate for the confidence interval for the students *after* they were instructed to self-monitor their exercise?

15. Compute the margin of error for the confidence interval for the students *after* they were instructed to self-monitor their exercise.

16. Compute the 95% confidence interval for the students *after* they were instructed to self-monitor their exercise.

17. Based on these data, the researcher is 95% confident that number of minutes exercised *after* self-monitoring is between _____ and _____.

SCENARIO 3: INDEPENDENT SAMPLES DESIGN WITH TWO MEANS

A psychiatrist conducts a study to determine if the new drug is more effective than selective serotonin reuptake inhibitors (SSRIs) for treating depression. Sixty people who have been diagnosed with depression are recruited to participate in the study. Half were assigned to the New Drug group and the other half were assigned to the SSRI group. After 3 months of treatment, depression is assessed by using the Beck Depression Inventory (BDI). Scores on this inventory range between 0 and 63 with higher scores indicating greater levels of depression.

After treatment, the average BDI score for the New Drug group was ($M = 7.20, SD = 4.92$) significantly lower than the average BDI score for the SSRI group ($M = 4.04$, $SD = 3.88$), $t(48) = 2.52, p = .03, d = .52$.

18. Compute the point estimate for the *mean difference*.

19. Compute the 95% confidence interval for the *mean difference*.

20. How much of a difference is there between the two groups relative to the overall range of depression scores (0 to 63)?

21. What is the point estimate for the *New Drug* group?

22. Compute the 95% confidence interval for the *New Drug* group.

23. What is the point estimate for the *SSRI* group?

24. Compute the 95% confidence interval for the *SSRI* group.

SCENARIO 4: USING SPSS TO GENERATE CONFIDENCE INTERVALS

25. Researchers want to determine if viewing a documentary on the dangers of using a cell phone while driving would *decrease* the frequency of cell phone use while driving. To test this hypothesis, they asked 15 teenage drivers to watch a video on the dangers of driving while using a cell phone. Prior to watching the video, they were asked to indicate the extent to which they agreed with the statement "I am likely to use my cell phone while driving" using a Likert scale, where 1 = *strongly disagree* and 7 = *strongly agree*. The teenage drivers then responded to this same statement again after watching the video. The data are listed here. Enter the data into SPSS and generate error bars around each of the means. Use SPSS to generate a 95% confidence interval around the mean difference.

For additional practice with SPSS, you can use data from any of the problems in the *t* test chapters.

Before	After
5	5
6	5
4	4
4	4
6	5
6	5
5	6
7	6
7	7
7	6
5	4
6	6
3	3
2	2
5	5

CHAPTER 12

One-Way Independent Samples ANOVA

After reading this chapter, you should be able to do the following:

- Identify when to use an independent samples ANOVA
- Explain the logic of the ANOVA F ratio
- Explain how measurement error, individual differences, and treatment effects influence the numerator and the denominator of the F ratio
- Write null and research hypotheses using symbols and words
- Complete an ANOVA summary table by computing the degrees of freedom, MSs, and F ratio
- Define a critical region and determine if you should reject or fail to reject the null hypothesis
- Compute an effect size (η_p^2) and describe it
- Explain when and why post hoc tests are necessary
- Summarize the results of an independent samples ANOVA using APA style
- Use SPSS to compute an independent samples ANOVA, including post hoc tests
- Interpret the SPSS output for an independent samples ANOVA

INDEPENDENT SAMPLES ANOVA

The independent t test and the related samples t test both compare two sample means to determine if their deviation is more than would be expected by sampling error. Both of these t tests share a major limitation in that they can only compare two sample means at a time. An ANOVA is substantially more flexible in that it can compare two *or more* sample means at the same time to determine if the deviation between any pair of sample means is greater than would be expected by sampling error. So one-way ANOVA or a single-factor ANOVA can compare two treatments (e.g., Treatment A and Treatment B) to each other as well as compare each of these treatments to a control condition (e.g., placebo).

Reading Question

1. A major advantage of the ANOVA is that it can
   a. be done without ever making a Type I error.
   b. be done without ever making a Type II error.
   c. compare the data from more than two conditions with a single analysis.

OTHER NAMES

ANOVA is an abbreviation for ANalysis Of Variance. An independent ANOVA, as with an independent *t* test, is used when there are different people in each condition of the design. For example, if there were three different treatments that you wanted to compare in an independent samples design, some people would receive Treatment A, others Treatment B, and the remaining Treatment C. This type of design is also referred to as a between-subject design or an independent measures design. A related samples ANOVA, as with a related samples *t* test, is used when the sample means are generated by the same sample or a matched sample. Independent samples ANOVAs and related samples ANOVAs that involve just one categorical variable (e.g., one independent variable, IV) are often referred to as one-way ANOVAs. In this book, we only discuss independent samples ANOVAs.

Reading Question

2. Which of the following is another name for an independent samples ANOVA?
   a. Related samples one-way ANOVA
   b. Between-subjects ANOVA

LOGIC OF THE ANOVA

All of the significance tests that you have learned thus far (i.e., *z* for a sample mean, single sample *t* test, independent *t* test, and the repeated *t* test) share a common logic. Namely, for all of them, you computed the observed difference between two means and then divided this difference by the difference that would be expected due to sampling error. The logic of the ANOVA test is different.

As is probably evident from the name, an analysis of variance analyzes the variance of scores. Specifically, an ANOVA analyzes the variance of scores both *between-* and *within-*IV conditions in an attempt to determine if the different treatment conditions affect scores differently. For example, you could use an ANOVA to determine if three different treatment conditions lead to different depression scores.

To comprehend the logic of ANOVAs, you must understand that exactly three things affect the variance of scores.

1. Measurement error: There will *always* be variance in scores *between people* because variables cannot be measured perfectly.

2. Individual differences: There will *always* be variance in scores *between people* because people are naturally different from each other.

3. Treatment effect: There *might be* variance in scores *between groups* because people experienced different IV conditions or treatments.

It is critical to recognize that the first two sources of variance in scores, measurement error and individual differences, will always be present. These two sources of variance are often referred to as "error variance" because they have nothing to do with the point of the study, which is to determine if there is a treatment effect. The third source of variance is really what researchers care about. Researchers use ANOVAs to estimate the amount of score variance created by the different IV treatment conditions. By doing the activities in this chapter you will be able to understand this better. For now you have enough information to understand the logic of the ANOVA.

Reading Question

3. Which of the following is the best example of variability due to measurement error?

a. Two people with the same level of depression produce different scores on a depression inventory.

b. People getting Treatment A have lower depression scores than those getting Treatment B because Treatment A is more effective at helping depressed people.

c. Some people are more resistant to treatment for depression than others.

Reading Question

4. Which of the following is the best example of variability due to individual differences?

a. Two people with the same level of depression produce different scores on a depression inventory.

b. People getting Treatment A have lower depression scores than those getting Treatment B because Treatment A is more effective at helping depressed people.

c. Some people are more resistant to treatment for depression than others.

Reading Question

5. Which of the following is the best example of variability due to a treatment effect?

a. Two people with the same level of depression produce different scores on a depression inventory.

b. People getting Treatment A have lower depression scores than those getting Treatment B because Treatment A is more effective at helping depressed people.

c. Some people are more resistant to treatment for depression than others.

Reading
Question

6. Of the three sources of variance that can potentially influence scores only two of them always influence scores. Which two of the following sources of variability always influence the variability of scores?

a. Measurement error

b. Individual differences

c. Treatment effect

Reading
Question

7. In research studies, researchers are most interested in evaluating which of the following sources of score variance?

a. Measurement error

b. Individual differences

c. Treatment effect

The ANOVA analyzes the *relative* amounts of these three sources of score variability, namely, (1) treatment effects, (2) individual differences, and (3) measurement error, to produce an *F* statistic. The conceptual formula of the ANOVA is a ratio of the variability *between* treatment conditions to the variability *within* treatment conditions. Two representations of the conceptual formula for an independent ANOVA are shown below.

$$F = \frac{\text{Variability between treatment conditions}}{\text{Variability within treatment conditions}}$$

$$F = \frac{\text{Treatment effect \& individual differences \& measurement error}}{\text{Individual differences \& measurement error}}$$

The numerator of the *F* ratio is the variability in scores that exists across the different treatment groups (i.e., IV conditions), which is called between-group variability. For example, if one condition had scores that were very high and another condition had scores that were very low, the between-group variability would be larger than if the scores in all conditions were very similar to each other. There are three possible sources for this between-treatment variability. One potential source is that the different treatments had different effects on the dependent variable. This is the variability that researchers are most interested in. However, some of the differences in scores between the three treatment conditions are also caused by individual differences and measurement error. Thus, for between-treatment variance, the numerator of the *F* ratio consists of variability created by *treatment effects*, *individual differences*, and *measurement error*.

Reading
Question

8. Which sources of score variance can contribute to between-treatment variance (i.e., the numerator of an F ratio)?

   a. Treatment effects

   b. Individual differences

   c. Measurement error

   d. All of the above

The denominator of the F ratio is the variability in scores that exists within the different treatment groups (i.e., IV conditions), which is called within-group variability. There are two possible sources for *within*-treatment variability: (1) individual differences and (2) measurement error. It is important to note that differences in scores *within* each treatment condition are NOT caused by differences in treatment effectiveness because all people *within a particular group* experienced the same treatment. The only sources for differences *within* a treatment condition are *individual differences* and *measurement error*. The denominator of the F ratio is often called the "error term" because it only contains variance created by sampling error.

Reading
Question

9. Two of the sources of score variance listed below always contribute to within-treatment variance (i.e., the denominator of an F ratio). Which source of score variance listed below NEVER contributes to within-treatment variance?

   a. Treatment effects

   b. Individual differences

   c. Measurement error

Reading
Question

10. The denominator of the F ratio estimates the amount of variability created by

   a. the treatment.

   b. sampling error.

If you look at the sources of variance in the numerator and denominator of the independent ANOVA, you can see that the only difference is that the numerator includes *treatment effects* and the denominator does not. This fact is critical to the logic of independent ANOVA. Imagine a situation in which the treatment effect creates zero variance (i.e., the treatment does not work at all). If you replace "treatment effect" in the conceptual formula with a "0," the equation would be as follows:

$$F = \frac{0 \ \& \ \text{individual differences} \ \& \ \text{error}}{\text{Individual differences} \ \& \ \text{error}}$$

With the treatment effect variance being zero, the F ratio would equal 1 because the numerator and denominator would be the same number. So if the treatment creates no variability in scores, the ANOVA is expected to produce an *F* statistic value close to 1. Conversely, if the treatment effect creates a lot of score variability, the *F* value is expected to be substantially greater than 1. An ANOVA *F* value *cannot* be negative because it is the ratio of two variances and variances must be positive.

Reading Question

11. If the null hypothesis is TRUE, the ANOVA *F* value is expected to be close to

   a. 0.

   b. −1.

   c. 1.

Reading Question

12. If the null hypothesis is FALSE, the ANOVA *F* value is expected to be

   a. substantially less than 1.

   b. substantially greater than 1.

ANOVA PROBLEM: EXAMPLE

The independent samples ANOVA is used when you need to compare the means of two *or more* groups/samples containing different people. For example, suppose that a psychologist is interested in determining if cognitive behavioral therapy (CBT) is more or less effective than psychodynamic therapy (PDT) in treating depression. The psychologist identifies a sample of people with major depression and randomly divides them into three different groups. One group undergoes CBT for 6 months, the second group undergoes PDT for 6 months, and the third group receives no treatment (NT). After 6 months, their levels of depression are assessed using the Beck Depression Inventory (BDI; scores range from 0 to 63), with higher scores indicating greater depression. The depression scores are listed in Table 12.1. In this study, the IV is the type of treatment and the DV (dependent variable) is each person's depression score on the BDI.

Table 12.1   Depression scores after three different types of treatment.

Group 1 Cognitive Behavioral Therapy	Group 2 Psychodynamic Therapy	Group 3 No Treatment Control
5	16	14
9	17	19
11	18	16
6	13	9
2	10	15
15	19	25
$M_1 = 8.0$	$M_2 = 15.5$	$M_3 = 16.3333$

Step 1: S

The
sta
m
re
h

Re
Q

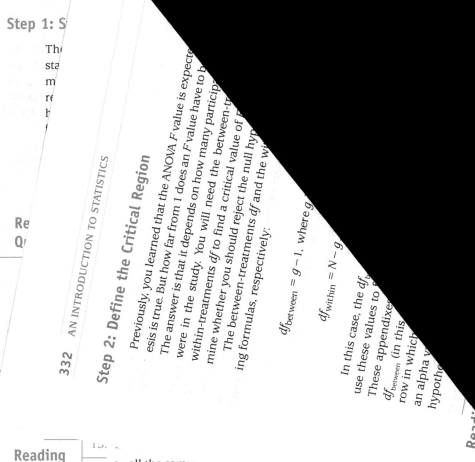

Step 2: Define the Critical Region

Previously, you learned that the ANOVA F value is expecte
esis is true. But how far from 1 does an F value have to b
The answer is that it depends on how many particip
were in the study. You will need the between-tr
within-treatments df to find the between-tr
mine whether you should reject the null hyp
The between-treatments df and the w
ing formulas, respectively:

$$df_{between} = g - 1, \text{ where } g$$

$$df_{within} = N - g$$

In this case, the df_b
use these values to
These appendixes
$df_{between}$ (in this
row in which
an alpha v
hypothe

Read
Qu

**Reading
Question**

13.

a. all the sample ...

b. all the sample means are the same.

c. at least one of the sample means is different from a
    other sample means.

Table 12.2	Symbolic and verbal representations of two-tailed research and null hypotheses for a one-way independent samples ANOVA.

	Symbolic	Verbal
Research hypothesis (H_1)		At least one of the mean depression scores is NOT equal to at least one of the other means.
Null hypothesis (H_0)	$H_0: \mu_1 = \mu_2 = \mu_3 \ldots$	The mean depression scores for each treatment condition ARE all equal.

d to be close to 1 if the null hypoth-
e in order to reject the null hypothesis?
nts and how many treatment conditions
eatments degrees of freedom (*df*) and the
. The critical value of *F* is then used to deter-
othesis.

hin-treatments *df* are computed with the follow-

s the number of groups/treatment conditions, and

where *N* is the number of scores in the entire study.

etween would be = 3 − 1 = 2, and the df_{within} would be = 18 − 3 = 15. You
find the critical value of *F* in the *F* critical values table in Appendix C.
contain critical values for alpha levels of .05 and .01, respectively. The
case, 2) indicates the column and the df_{within} (in this case, 15) indicates the
to find the *F* critical value. The critical value of *F* with 2 and 15 *df* when using
alue of .05 is 3.68. Therefore, if the obtained *F* value is greater than 3.68, the null
sis should be rejected.

16. If the computed *F* value is greater than the critical value of *F*, the null
hypothesis should

a. not be rejected.

b. be rejected.

Step 3: Compute the Test Statistic

Steps 3a Through 3d: Completing the ANOVA Summary Table

To compute the *F* ratio, you need to compute two numbers: (1) the variance between-treatment conditions and (2) the variance within-treatment conditions. Thus far you have generally computed the standard deviation to measure variability. When doing an ANOVA, you compute the variance as a measure of variability. You may remember that the sample variance is the *mean squared* deviation from the mean and that it is computed by dividing the *SS* by its *df*. In ANOVA terminology, the variance is referred to as the *mean square* (abbreviated *MS*). Although the terminology is a bit different, the logic is the same. To compute each *MS*, you divide the *SS* by its *df*. These computations are typically done using a software package (we will use SPSS), and the results are often presented in an ANOVA source table.

An ANOVA source table is a valuable summary of the ANOVA statistical analysis because it shows how the *F* is created. The source table lists the sources of variance discussed in previous sections, between and within treatments (error), in the first column. The column headings indicate steps required to compute an *F: SS, df, MS,* and finally *F.* Table 12.3 is an ANOVA source table. The formulas for *df, MS, F,* and η_p^2 are presented because the best way to understand the interrelationships among these terms is to understand how each value is generated.

Table 12.3   An ANOVA source table with formulas.

	Step 3a	Step 3b	Step 3c	Step 3d	Step 4
Source of Variance	SS	df	MS	F	η_p^2
Between treatments	252.78	$g-1$	$\dfrac{SS_{between}}{df_{between}}$	$\dfrac{MS_{between}}{MS_{within}}$	$\dfrac{SS_{between}}{SS_{between}+SS_{error}}$
Within treatments (Error)	308.83	$N-g$	$\dfrac{SS_{within}}{df_{within}}$		
Total	561.61	$N-1$			

Note: g = Number of IV conditions (*g* = 3; CBT, PDT, NT) and *N* = Number of people in the study (in this case, 18).

The values for $SS_{between}$ (252.78) and the SS_{within} (308.83) are provided in the table. The $SS_{between}$ represents the sum of the variability created by the treatment effect, individual differences, and measurement error. The $SS_{between}$ can be found by computing the SS for the means of the different groups and then multiplying this SS_{means} value by *n* (i.e., the number of people in each group). In this case, the means for the three treatment conditions were 8.0, 15.5, and 16.3333, respectively. Therefore, SS_{means} would be the SS of those three means:

Treatment Conditions	Means (M)	M^2
CBT	8	64
PDT	15.5	240.25
NT	16.3333	266.7767
	$\sum X = 39.8333$	$\sum X^2 = 571.0267$

$$SS_M = \sum M^2 - \frac{(\sum M)^2}{n} = 571.0267 - \frac{(39.8333)^2}{3} = 42.1294.$$

Therefore, the SS_{between} would be

$$SS_{\text{between}} = (SS_M)n = (42.1294)6 = 252.7766 \approx 252.78.$$

The SS_{between} is the variability among the means for each treatment condition multiplied by the number of people in each condition. In this case, the number of people in each treatment condition was 6. The above formula for SS_{between} only works when there are an equal number of people in each treatment condition. In situations where the sample sizes are not equal, a different computational formula must be used but the logic of the SS_{between} is still the same. The resulting value represents the variability created by the different treatment conditions, individual differences, and measurement error. We do not present the computational formula needed when you have unequal sample sizes here. We are more interested in your understanding the logic of ANOVA and how to interpret its results than your ability to compute an ANOVA with unequal sample sizes from raw data.

The SS_{within} is the sum of the variability created by individual differences and measurement error within each condition. The SS_{within} can be computed by computing the SS for each treatment condition separately and then summing them.

$$\text{The SS for CBT is } SS_{\text{CBT}} = \Sigma X^2 - \frac{(\Sigma X)^2}{n} = 492 - \frac{(48)^2}{6} = 108$$

$$\text{The SS for PDT is } SS_{\text{PDT}} = \Sigma X^2 - \frac{(\Sigma X)^2}{n} = 1499 - \frac{(93)^2}{6} = 57.5$$

$$\text{The SS for NT is } SS_{\text{NT}} = \Sigma X^2 - \frac{(\Sigma X)^2}{n} = 1744 - \frac{(98)^2}{6} = 143.3333$$

$$\text{Therefore, the } SS_{\text{within}} = SS_{\text{CBT}} + SS_{\text{PDT}} + SS_{\text{NT}} = 308.83333 \approx 308.83$$

The SS_{total} represents the total variability in the entire set of data, and so it is the sum of the variability between conditions (i.e., SS_{between}) and the variability within conditions (i.e., SS_{within}).

$$SS_{\text{total}} = SS_{\text{between}} + SS_{\text{within}} = 252.78 + 308.83 = 561.61$$

The F is computed as the ratio of MS_{between} and MS_{within}, and so we need to convert each SS into an MS (mean square) before we can compute the F. To compute the MS, you divide each SS value by its own df value.

$$MS_{\text{between}} = \frac{SS_{\text{between}}}{df_{\text{between}}} = \frac{252.78}{2} = 126.39$$

$$MS_{within} = \frac{SS_{within}}{df_{within}} = \frac{308.83}{15} = 20.59$$

The F is computed by dividing the $MS_{between}$ by the MS_{within}.

$$F = \frac{MS_{between}}{MS_{within}} = \frac{126.39}{20.59} = 6.14$$

Table 12.4 is an ANOVA source table for this analysis. Confirm that you understand how each of the SSs, dfs, MSs, and F values was computed.

Table 12.4	A complete ANOVA source table.				
Source of Variance	SS	df	MS	F	η_p^2
Between treatments	252.78	2	126.39	6.14	.45
Within treatments (error)	308.83	15	20.59		
Total	561.61	17			

Reading Question

17. The $MS_{between}$ is divided by the MS_{within} to produce the
    a. SS.
    b. df.
    c. obtained F value.

In this case, the obtained F value was 6.14, which is greater than the critical F value of 3.68 ($\alpha = .05$). Therefore, the null hypothesis should be rejected, meaning that at least one sample mean is significantly different from one of the other sample means.

Step 3e: If Necessary, Compute Post Hoc Tests

The null hypothesis for an ANOVA is that all of the means are equal. Rejecting the null does not indicate which pairs of means are significantly different from each other. Thus, if you reject the null hypothesis, and there are three or more IV conditions in the study, you need to perform pairwise post hoc tests to determine which pair or pairs of means are different from each other. In this case, three pairwise comparisons are needed. The CBT group needs to be compared with the PDT group and the NT group. In addition, the PDT group needs to be compared with the NT group.

Reading Question

18. Post hoc tests are needed whenever you
    a. perform an ANOVA.
    b. reject an ANOVA's null hypothesis and there were more than two IV conditions.

There are a number of different post hoc tests that can be computed. The one we use throughout this book is Tukey's Honestly Significant Difference (*HSD*) Test. The *HSD* test reveals how far apart any two means must be to be statistically significant. Therefore, any pair of means that differ by more than the *HSD* value are significantly different. The formula for computing the *HSD* is as follows:

$$HSD = q\sqrt{\frac{MS_{within}}{n}}$$

The MS_{within} is obtained from the overall ANOVA summary table. In this case, $MS_{within} = 20.59$. The number of scores within each treatment condition is n, in this case, $n = 6$. The value of q (called the studentized range statistic) changes, based on the number of treatment conditions (i.e., g), the *df* for the error term, and the alpha value. A table of q values is in Appendix D. In this case, $g = 3$, the *df* for the error term (df_{within}) $= 15$, and the alpha level (α) $= .05$. Based on these values, the q statistic is 3.67. Thus, the *HSD* value can be computed as follows:

$$HSD = q\sqrt{\frac{MS_{within}}{n}} = 3.67\sqrt{\frac{20.59}{6}} = 6.80$$

The *HSD* value is then compared with the absolute value of the observed difference between each pair of means. For example, the mean difference between the CBT and PDT means is $(8 - 15.5) = -7.5$. The absolute value of this difference is greater than the *HSD* value of 6.80. Consequently, the CBT group ($M = 8$) had significantly lower levels of depression than the PDT group ($M = 15.5$). The two remaining post hoc tests are summarized in Table 12.5.

Based on these analyses, we can conclude that the CBT group had significantly lower levels of depression than the PDT group. Similarly, the CBT group had significantly lower levels of depression than the NT group. Finally, the PDT and NT groups were not significantly different in their levels of depression.

It is important to note that the *HSD* formula presented above can only be used when the number of scores within each treatment condition is the same. When n is different within each condition, separate *HSD* values are computed for each pairwise comparison. We will use SPSS to compute the *HSD* values when this is the case.

Table 12.5 Post hoc comparisons.

Comparison	Mean Difference	Significance
CBT & PDT	$8 - 15.5 = -7.5$	Significant
CBT & NT	$8 - 16.33 = -8.33$	Significant
NT & PDT	$15.5 - 16.33 = -.83$	Not significant

Step 4: Compute the Effect Size, and Describe It

When we had just two groups we used Cohen's *d* as a measure of effect size. We cannot use *d* as a measure of effect size for an overall ANOVA because there are more than two groups and we cannot compute a single mean difference. Thus, a different measure of effect size is required. The most common effect size measure for ANOVAs is partial eta squared (η_p^2). The computations are as follows:

$$\eta_p^2 = \frac{SS_{between}}{SS_{between} + SS_{within}} = \frac{252.78}{252.78 + 308.83} = .45$$

For one-way ANOVAs, partial eta squared is typically interpreted as the percentage of variability in the DV explained by the IV. In this case, 45% of the variability in depression scores across the three treatment conditions can be explained by the type of treatment participants experienced.

To interpret the size of an effect, the guidelines in Table 12.6 are used for η_p^2 when similar research studies are not available to provide a relative comparison.

The obtained effect size of .45 is greater than .25 and so it is a large effect.

Reading Question

19. The most common effect size used for an ANOVA is η_p^2. If a study were to be done in which the effectiveness of three different treatments for social anxiety were compared and $\eta_p^2 = .22$, which of the following would be the best interpretation of η_p^2?

    a. The anxiety scores resulting from the different treatments were 22% different from each other.

    b. The type of treatment people received explained 22% of the variability in anxiety scores.

You may find that some people simply refer to this measure of effect size for one-way ANOVAs as eta squared rather than partial eta squared. For one-way ANOVAs, both eta squared and partial eta squared yield identical values. We have chosen to use the formula and terminology for the partial eta squared because it is consistent with SPSS output. This distinction becomes more important when working with more complex factorial designs.

Table 12.6   General guidelines for interpreting η_p^2

η_p^2	Estimated Size of the Effect
Close to .01	Small
Close to .09	Medium
Close to .25	Large

Step 5: Summarize the Results

When reporting an ANOVA you must report the $df_{between}$, df_{within}, the obtained F value, the p value, MSE, and η_p^2. You must also indicate which treatment conditions were significantly different from each other. The following text is an example of how this analysis could be summarized.

An ANOVA was conducted with treatment condition as the IV and depression score as the DV. The effect was significant, $F(2, 15) = 6.14, p < .05,$ $\eta_p^2 = .45, MSE = 20.59.$ Tukey's *HSD* post hoc tests revealed that the CBT group had lower BDI scores ($M = 8.00, SD = 4.65$) than the PDT group ($M = 15.50, SD = 3.39$) and the No Treatment group ($M = 16.33, SD = 5.35$). Those receiving PDT were no better off than those receiving no treatment at all.

FAMILY-WISE ERROR AND ALPHA INFLATION

You may be wondering why we bother with ANOVAs if we are just going to do pairwise post hoc tests after we do an ANOVA. Why don't we just do *t* tests to compare all pairs of means? The answer lies in the error rate for the study (often called family-wise error). When you set the alpha level of a test at .05, you are setting the Type I error rate at 5%. A Type I error is the probability of saying that a treatment worked when it really did not work. However, if you do a bunch of *t* tests, *each t* test has a 5% chance of producing a Type I error. If you perform multiple *t* tests, the exact probability that you made *at least one* Type I error is given by the family-wise error formula shown below:

Family-wise error $= 1 - (1 - \alpha)^c$, where c is the number of comparisons.

If we have just one comparison, you can see that the Type I error rate would be

$$1 - (1 - .05)^1 = .05, \text{ or } 5\%.$$

However, if we have three comparisons within the same study, the probability that you made *at least one* Type I error is quite a bit higher at .14 or 14%.

$$1 - (1 - .05)^3 = .14$$

To keep the family-wise error rate at .05, you can do a single ANOVA rather than multiple *t* tests. There are a variety of post hoc tests to choose from, but the general idea behind all of them is that they are used to keep the Type I error rate from escalating.

Reading Question

20. Why is it better to conduct an ANOVA than multiple *t* tests when you are comparing multiple conditions?

   a. An ANOVA provides an *F* value which is better than multiple *t* values.

   b. A single ANOVA helps keep the probability a Type I error lower than doing multiple *t* tests.

SPSS

Data File

When creating SPSS data files, all the data that came from a single person (or matched persons) must be on the same row in the data file. For the independent ANOVA, there is one column to indicate which treatment each person received and another column to indicate each person's depression score. In this file, a "1" indicates that the person received CBT, a "2" indicates PDT, and a "3" indicates that no therapy was given to these individuals. It will help you read the output if you enter this coding system into SPSS. From the Data View screen click on the Variable View tab at the bottom left of the screen. On the Variable View screen enter the variable names. Then, across from the treatment variable click on the cell under the Values column heading. When a "button" appears click on it. In the Value box enter "1." In the Label box, enter CBT, click the Add button. Then, enter "2" and PDT in the value and label boxes, respectively, and click Add. Finally enter "3" and NT, click Add, and then click OK.

Your data file should look like the one in Figure 12.1.

| **Figure 12.1** | SPSS screenshot of data entry screen. |

Obtaining an Independent Samples ANOVA

- Click on the Analyze menu. Choose General Linear Model and then select Univariate.
- Move the IV into the Fixed Factors box and move the DV into the Dependent Variable box.
- Click on Options then check Descriptive Statistics and Estimates of Effect Size.
- Click on Continue.
- To obtain post hoc tests, click on the Post Hoc button and then move the IV into the box labeled Post hoc tests for.
- Select the Tukey check box and then Continue.
- Click on OK to run the ANOVA.

Annotated Output

For SPSS output, see Figures 12.2 to 12.5.

Figure 12.2   SPSS screenshot of descriptive statistics.

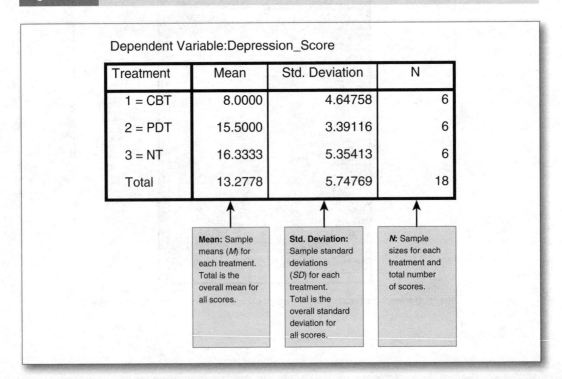

Dependent Variable:Depression_Score

Treatment	Mean	Std. Deviation	N
1 = CBT	8.0000	4.64758	6
2 = PDT	15.5000	3.39116	6
3 = NT	16.3333	5.35413	6
Total	13.2778	5.74769	18

Mean: Sample means (*M*) for each treatment. Total is the overall mean for all scores.

Std. Deviation: Sample standard deviations (*SD*) for each treatment. Total is the overall standard deviation for all scores.

N: Sample sizes for each treatment and total number of scores.

Figure 12.3 An SPSS screenshot of ANOVA source table.

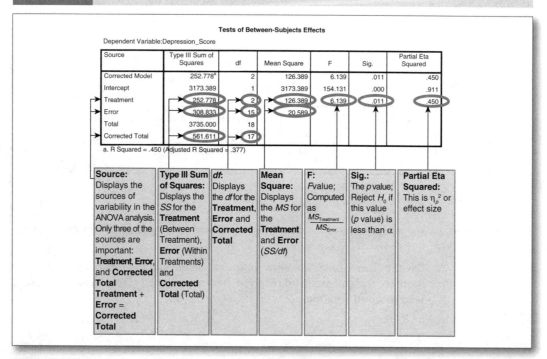

Tests of Between-Subjects Effects

Dependent Variable:Depression_Score

Source	Type III Sum of Squares	df	Mean Square	F	Sig.	Partial Eta Squared
Corrected Model	252.778[a]	2	126.389	6.139	.011	.450
Intercept	3173.389	1	3173.389	154.131	.000	.911
Treatment	252.778	2	126.389	6.139	.011	.450
Error	308.833	15	20.589			
Total	3735.000	18				
Corrected Total	561.611	17				

a. R Squared = .450 (Adjusted R Squared = .377)

Source: Displays the sources of variability in the ANOVA analysis. Only three of the sources are important: **Treatment, Error,** and **Corrected Total** Treatment + Error = **Corrected Total**	**Type III Sum of Squares:** Displays the *SS* for the **Treatment** (Between Treatment), **Error** (Within Treatments) and **Corrected Total** (Total)	*df:* Displays the *df* for the **Treatment, Error** and **Corrected Total**	**Mean Square:** Displays the *MS* for the **Treatment** and **Error** (*SS/df*)	**F:** *F*value; Computed as $\frac{MS_{Treatment}}{MS_{Error}}$	**Sig.:** The *p* value; Reject H_o if this value (*p* value) is less than α	**Partial Eta Squared:** This is η_p^2 or effect size

Figure 12.4 An SPSS screenshot of post hoc tests with pairwise comparisons.

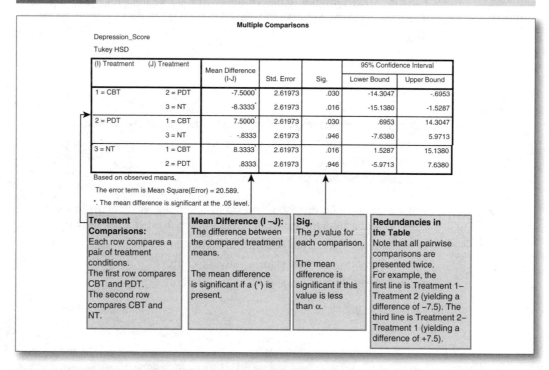

Multiple Comparisons

Depression_Score

Tukey HSD

(I) Treatment	(J) Treatment	Mean Difference (I–J)	Std. Error	Sig.	95% Confidence Interval	
					Lower Bound	Upper Bound
1 = CBT	2 = PDT	-7.5000[*]	2.61973	.030	-14.3047	-.6953
	3 = NT	-8.3333[*]	2.61973	.016	-15.1380	-1.5287
2 = PDT	1 = CBT	7.5000[*]	2.61973	.030	.6953	14.3047
	3 = NT	-.8333	2.61973	.946	-7.6380	5.9713
3 = NT	1 = CBT	8.3333[*]	2.61973	.016	1.5287	15.1380
	2 = PDT	.8333	2.61973	.946	-5.9713	7.6380

Based on observed means.

The error term is Mean Square(Error) = 20.589.

*. The mean difference is significant at the .05 level.

Treatment Comparisons: Each row compares a pair of treatment conditions. The first row compares CBT and PDT. The second row compares CBT and NT.	**Mean Difference (I –J):** The difference between the compared treatment means. The mean difference is significant if a (*) is present.	**Sig.** The *p* value for each comparison. The mean difference is significant if this value is less than α.	**Redundancies in the Table** Note that all pairwise comparisons are presented twice. For example, the first line is Treatment 1– Treatment 2 (yielding a difference of –7.5). The third line is Treatment 2– Treatment 1 (yielding a difference of +7.5).

Figure 12.5	An SPSS screenshot of post hoc tests with homogenous subsets.

Depression_Score

Tukey HSD[a]

Treatment	N	Subset for alpha = 0.05	
		1	2
1 = CBT	6	8.0000	
2 = PDT	6		15.5000
3 = NT	6		16.3333
Sig.		1.000	.946

Means for groups in homogeneous subsets are displayed.

Homogeneous Subsets:

This table displays the same information as the previous table in a less precise but more readable way; this table groups means that are NOT significantly different into the same column; conversely, means that are statistically different are placed in different columns.

21. Use the "Descriptive Statistics" output to determine the mean depression score for the patients who received Treatment 2 (PDT). The mean for those who received Treatment 2 was

  a. 8.00.

  b. 15.50.

  c. 16.33.

22. Use the "ANOVA" output to determine what the p value is for the ANOVA test. The p value for the ANOVA test was

  a. 2.

  b. 6.139.

  c. .011.

  d. .04.

23. When you enter data into SPSS to run an independent ANOVA you should have

  a. a column for the IV (i.e., type of treatment) and a column for the DV (i.e., each person's score).

  b. a column for each DV (i.e., each person's score).

24. Use the "Multiple Comparisons" output to determine which of the following pairs of means are significantly different from each other. Choose all that apply.

  a. Treatments 1 and 2 are significantly different.

  b. Treatments 1 and 3 are significantly different.

  c. Treatments 2 and 3 are significantly different.

Reading Question (×4, marginal labels for questions 21–24)

Activity 12-1:   Independent ANOVA

Learning Objectives

After reading the chapter and completing this activity, you should be able to do the following:

- Describe within-group and between-group variance within the context of an independent ANOVA
- Identify things that increase and decrease within-group variance and between-group variance
- Explain the logic of the independent ANOVA using the terms within-group variance and between-group variance
- Explain how a relatively large within-group variance affects the F ratio
- Explain how a relatively large between-group variance affects the F ratio

WITHIN AND BETWEEN GROUP VARIABILITY IN THE INDEPENDENT ANOVA

As you know from the chapter, the independent ANOVA can be used to determine if different levels of an IV affect DV scores differently. It was also mentioned in the reading that the ANOVA computes two types of variance: (1) within-group variability and (2) between-group variability. The following fictional scenario is designed to help you develop a conceptual understanding of within-group variability and between-group variability.

A Fable About Types of Variance, Sunflowers, and Types of Liquid

A few weeks ago, a statistics instructor went to a local farmers market. He started a conversation with a man who claimed to hold the world record for growing the tallest sunflower in the world. The stats instructor asked the man for advice for how to grow tall sunflowers. The man said, "The single best thing you can do to grow tall sunflowers is to use cola rather than water." The stats instructor was skeptical. He asked the man if he had any evidence that using cola rather than water actually lead to taller sunflowers. The man said, "Well, I never ran an experiment if that is what you mean." That was the beginning of a now legendary (if fictional) experiment. The stats instructor and the sunflower farmer designed and conducted the following study.

The unlikely colleagues took a sample of sunflower seeds ($N = 9$) from the farmer's population of seeds. They then found three identical pots and put identical soil in them. They then randomly assigned (planted) 1/3 of their sample in each pot. The figure to the right is a visual representation of the study they designed. The seeds in the first pot were given cola, those in the second pot were given club soda (to see if carbonation was sufficient to increase growth), and those in the third pot were given normal, uncarbonated water.

The farmer and statistician took every step possible to ensure that the three pots of seeds got the same amount of sun and the same amount of their designated liquid (i.e., cola, club soda, or water). In short, they tried to make everything identical for the three groups of seeds except for the type of liquid. Logically then, any systematic differences between the heights of the sunflowers in the different conditions would be caused by the different types of liquid the different groups of seeds received (i.e., the IV).

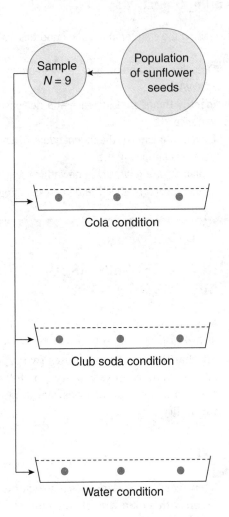

The dependent variable in this study is sunflower height. The figures to the right represent the height of each sunflower in each IV condition. Clearly, even though sunflowers within each condition were treated identically, there is still variability in sunflower height. This variability is called within group variance. Within group variance is also called error variance because it is created by individual differences in seed quality and/or methodological error (e.g., one seed getting more sun than another). You should notice that there is within group variability in every condition. These within group differences are combined to create a single value representing "within group variability" or "error variability."

Between-group variance is measured by comparing the average sunflower heights produced by each IV condition. The average height produced by each condition is represented by the "dotted sunflowers." Clearly, there is substantial between group variance in average sunflower height. This between group variability is created by the different types of liquid in each condition, as well as individual differences and error.

As is explained in the chapter, if the between group variability is "small" relative to the within group variability it is assumed that the IV did not create systematic differences across the different IV conditions. In thiscase the between group variance is relatively large compared to the within group variance. This would result in a relatively large F-value that would lead the researchers to reject the null hypothesis. As a result, the researchers concluded that type of liquid systematically impacts sunflower height.

Height difference *within group* is
Error Variance

Cola condition

Error Variance

Club soda condition

Error Variance

Water condition

The figure to the right represents the comparison of average sunflower height produced by each IV condition. The researchers have rejected the null hypothesis because the between group variance (variance created by the IV) was relatively large compared with the within group variance (variance created by individual differences and error).

Next, researchers perform post hoc tests to determine which pairs of conditions are significantly different from each other. There are three different pairs to compare:

(1) Cola versus club soda,
(2) Cola versus water, and
(3) Club soda versus water.

The results of each post hoc comparison are shown to the right. The cola is significantly better than both club soda and water, furthermore; club soda is NOT significantly different from water.

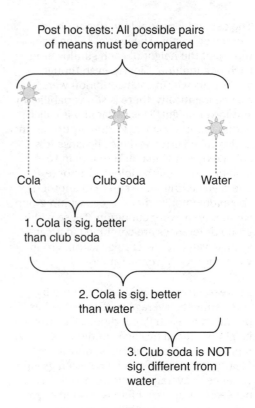

Post hoc tests: All possible pairs of means must be compared

Cola   Club soda   Water

1. Cola is sig. better than club soda

2. Cola is sig. better than water

3. Club soda is NOT sig. different from water

1. Identify two or three things that the researchers did that probably reduced the within-group variance in this study.

2. Identify the one thing that researchers want to cause the between-group variance.

3. Identify two other things that contribute to the between-group variance that the researchers do not want.

4. In the scenario above, the researchers rejected the null hypotheses. What is the null hypothesis for an ANOVA comparing three treatment conditions?

5. In the scenario above, the researchers rejected the null hypotheses. This means that the F ratio they computed (i.e., the obtained F value) was significantly greater than 1. Explain why the F ratio will be greater than 1 if the IV had an effect on the DV.

After reviewing the evidence illustrating the dramatic beneficial effect of "watering" sunflowers with cola, two different research teams attempt to replicate the same study with a different species of sunflowers. As with the previous study you read about, each research team took a sample of nine sunflower seeds from the population of seeds. The seeds were randomly assigned to treatment conditions and their heights were recorded. The data collected from each team are tabulated as follows.

Research Team 1			Research Team 2		
Group 1: Cola	Group 2: Club Soda	Group 3: Water	Group 1: Cola	Group 2: Club Soda	Group 3: Water
88	83	80	85	80	77
90	85	82	90	85	82
92	87	84	95	90	87
$M_1 = 90.0$	$M_2 = 85.0$	$M_3 = 82.0$	$M_1 = 90.0$	$M_2 = 85.0$	$M_3 = 82.0$
$SD_1 = 2.0$	$SD_2 = 2.0$	$SD_3 = 2.0$	$SD_1 = 5.0$	$SD_2 = 5.0$	$SD_3 = 5.0$
$SS_1 = 8.0$	$SS_2 = 8.0$	$SS_3 = 8.0$	$SS_1 = 50.0$	$SS_2 = 50.0$	$SS_3 = 50.0$

6. If you look at the data within each group, you should be able to see that there is variability within each treatment condition. Flowers within each group were not exactly the same height. For example, for Research Team 1, the heights within the cola condition are all different from each other (88, 90, 92). There are two possible reasons for this variability *within-treatment conditions*. List them below.

7. How can you tell which research team has more within-group variability? It may help you remember that SS_{within} is computed by summing the SS for each treatment condition.

  a. Look at the means for the treatment conditions (i.e., cola, club soda, and water). The researcher with larger differences between the means for the three treatment conditions will have more within-treatments variability.

  b. Look at the standard deviation for each treatment condition (i.e., cola, club soda, and water). The researcher with larger standard deviations will have more within-treatments variability.

8. You should remember that the standard deviation is the typical distance between each score in a condition and the condition mean. Look at the variability of raw scores within each condition for Research Team 1 and compare it with the variability within each condition for Research Team 2. Which researcher had more within-group variability in their data?

  a. Researcher 1

  b. Researcher 2

9. Speculate as to why one researcher may have more or less within-treatment variability in their data than the other researcher.

10. The SSs are provided below for each researcher. Use the SSs and the information in the problem (i.e., the number of groups and participants) to complete the ANOVA summary tables.

	Researcher 1					Researcher 2			
Source	SS	df	MS	F	Source	SS	df	MS	F
Between treatments	98.0	_____	_____	_____	Between treatments	98.0	_____	_____	_____
Within treatments	24.0	_____	_____		Within treatments	150.0	_____	_____	
Total	122.0	_____			Total	248.0	_____		

11. How do you compute $df_{between}$?

  a. Subtract one from the number of people in the study.

  b. Subtract one from the number of treatment conditions.

  c. Subtract the number of treatment conditions from the number of people in the study.

  d. Subtract the number of people in the study from the number of treatment conditions.

12. How do you compute df_{within}?

    a. Subtract one from the number of people in the study.

    b. Subtract one from the number of treatment conditions.

    c. Subtract the number of treatment conditions from the number of people in the study.

    d. Subtract the number of people in the study from the number of treatment conditions.

13. How do you compute the $MS_{between}$ when you know $SS_{between}$ and $df_{between}$?

    a. Divide the $SS_{between}$ by the $df_{between}$.

    b. Multiply the $SS_{between}$ by the $df_{between}$.

    c. Divide the $df_{between}$ by the $SS_{between}$.

14. Given your answer to the previous question, how do you compute the MS_{within} when you know SS_{within} and df_{within}?

15. After you have the $MS_{between}$ and the MS_{within}, how do you compute the obtained F value?

    a. Multiply the $MS_{between}$ times the MS_{within}.

    b. Divide the $MS_{between}$ by the MS_{within}.

    c. Divide the MS_{within} by the $MS_{between}$.

16. Use the $df_{between}$, the df_{within}, and the table of critical F values in Appendix C to find the critical value of each of these studies. Use an alpha of .05. What is the critical value for these studies?

Critical value for Research Team 1 = _____ Critical value for Research Team 2 = _____

Explain why the critical values are the same for these two studies.

17. Should Researcher 1 reject the null hypothesis?

    a. Yes, the obtained F value is less than the critical value.

    b. Yes, the obtained F value is greater than the critical value.

    c. No, the obtained F value is less than the critical value.

    d. No, the obtained F value is greater than the critical value.

18. Should Researcher 2 reject the null hypothesis?

   a. Yes, the obtained F value is less than the critical value.

   b. Yes, the obtained F value is greater than the critical value.

   c. No, the obtained F value is less than the critical value.

   d. No, the obtained F value is greater than the critical value.

19. Based on the differing results of these two studies, explain how two research teams can have identical mean differences (and identical $MS_{between}$) and one reject the null and the other fail to reject the null. What is different about these two studies that made them have different results? (*Hint*: How was the obtained F computed for each research team?)

After hearing about the success that the farmer had using cola on sunflowers, two other researchers conducted studies to determine if cola, club soda, and water differentially affected the growth of tomato plants. The data are presented as follows.

Researcher 1			Researcher 2		
Group 1: Cola	Group 2: Club Soda	Group 3: Water	Group 1: Cola	Group 2: Club Soda	Group 3: Water
49	42	40	47	44	43
52	45	43	50	47	46
55	48	46	53	50	49
$M_1 = 52.0$	$M_2 = 45.0$	$M_3 = 43.0$	$M_1 = 50.0$	$M_2 = 47.0$	$M_3 = 46.0$
$SD_1 = 3.0$	$SD_2 = 3.0$	$SD_3 = 3.0$	$SD_1 = 3.0$	$SD_2 = 3.0$	$SD_3 = 3.0$
$SS_1 = 18.0$	$SS_2 = 18.0$	$SS_3 = 18.0$	$SS_1 = 18.0$	$SS_2 = 18.0$	$SS_3 = 18.0$

Source	SS	df	MS	F	Source	SS	df	MS	F
Between treatments	134.0	____	____	____	Between treatments	26.0	____	____	____
Within treatments	54.0	____	____		Within treatments	54.0	____	____	
Total	188.0	____			Total	80.0	____		

20. Complete the ANOVA summary tables for Researcher 1 and Researcher 2.

21. Look at the standard deviations and SSs for each condition in both studies. These values all represent *within-group* variability. Given that all of these values are identical for Researcher 1 and Researcher 2 and that the number of participants is the same in both studies, the _____ for these two studies must also be identical.

    a. $MS_{between}$

    b. MS_{within}

22. You should also notice that the means are different between the treatment conditions of each study. There are three possible reasons for this between-group variability in a single experiment. List them below.

23. Identify the critical value for each study, and explain why the critical values are the same for these two studies.

24. Based on these results, explain how two studies can have identical variability within-treatment conditions (i.e., identical MS_{within}) and one study reject the null and the other study fail to reject the null.

The makers of ginger ale are dismayed to hear of the results of these studies because they are sure that their carbonated beverage is every bit as good as cola for "watering" plants. To test the effect of their product on plant growth, they do a study similar to those above, but with four different treatment conditions and with nine seeds per condition. The data are as follows.

Ginger Ale	Cola	Club Soda	Water
95	87	80	92
88	90	74	81
87	94	81	90
91	89	78	76
89	98	90	79
83	89	66	78
92	86	93	87
95	87	92	90
84	70	81	68

25. Complete the ANOVA summary table based on the data from the previous page.

Source	SS	df	MS	F	η_p^2
Between treatments	399.6	_____	_____	_____	_____
Within treatments	1757.6	_____	_____		
Total	2157.2	_____			

26. Based on the results summarized in the above ANOVA summary table, should the null hypothesis for this study be rejected or not?

   a. The null should be rejected because the obtained F value is greater than the critical value.

   b. The null should not be rejected because the obtained F value is less than the critical value.

The following questions ask you to compare the relative amount of within-treatment and/or between-treatment variability that is present in two different data sets. Within-group variability is higher when the scores within the treatment conditions are more different from each other. In other words, studies with more within-group variability have higher SDs and SSs. Between-group variability is higher when the means for each condition are more different from each other. In other words, studies with more between-group variability have greater differences among the condition means. Use the following two data sets to answer Questions 27–30.

	Researcher 1			Researcher 2	
Group 1: Cola	Group 2: Club Soda	Group 3: Water	Group 1: Cola	Group 2: Club Soda	Group 3: Water
54	59	64	59	69	79
55	60	65	60	70	80
56	61	66	61	71	81
$M_1 = 55.0$	$M_2 = 60.0$	$M_3 = 65.0$	$M_1 = 60.0$	$M_2 = 70.0$	$M_3 = 80.0$
$SD_1 = 1.0$	$SD_2 = 1.0$	$SD_3 = 1.0$	$SD_1 = 1.0$	$SD_2 = 1.0$	$SD_3 = 1.0$
$SS_1 = 2.0$	$SS_2 = 2.0$	$SS_3 = 2.0$	$SS_1 = 2.0$	$SS_2 = 2.0$	$SS_3 = 2.0$

27. Which researcher's data set has more variability within treatments (i.e., a higher MS_{within})? (*Hint*: Look at the standard deviations within the treatment conditions for Researcher 1 and Researcher 2.)

    a. Researcher 1

    b. Researcher 2

    c. They have the same amount of within-treatments variability

28. Which researcher's data set has more variability between treatments (i.e., a higher $MS_{between}$)? (*Hint*: Look at the means for Researcher 1 and Researcher 2.) Which researcher has more variability between the means?

    a. Researcher 1

    b. Researcher 2

    c. They have the same amount of between-treatments variability

29. Which researcher's data sets will result in a larger F value? (*Hint*: The F ratio is computed as $MS_{between}/MS_{within}$.) In this case, the researchers have the same denominator for their F ratio (i.e., the same MS_{within}). Which researcher has the larger numerator and hence the larger F?

    a. Researcher 1

    b. Researcher 2

    c. They have the same F value

30. Which researcher's study is more likely to lead to rejecting the null hypothesis?

    a. Researcher 1

    b. Researcher 2

Use the following two data sets to answer Questions 31–35.

	Researcher 1			Researcher 2	
Group 1: Cola	Group 2: Club Soda	Group 3: Water	Group 1: Cola	Group 2: Club Soda	Group 3: Water
36	36	26	56	54	46
40	38	30	60	58	50
44	42	34	64	62	54
$M_1 = 40$	$M_2 = 38$	$M_3 = 30$	$M_1 = 60$	$M_2 = 58$	$M_3 = 50$
$SD_1 = 4$	$SD_2 = 4$	$SD_3 = 4$	$SD_1 = 4$	$SD_2 = 4$	$SD_3 = 4$
$SS_1 = 32$	$SS_2 = 32$	$SS_3 = 32$	$SS_1 = 32$	$SS_2 = 32$	$SS_3 = 32$

31. Which researcher's data set has more variability within treatments (i.e., has a higher MS_{within})?

   a. Researcher 1

   b. Researcher 2

   c. They have the same amount of within-treatments variability

32. Which researcher's data set has more variability between treatments (i.e., has a higher $MS_{between}$)?

   a. Researcher 1

   b. Researcher 2

   c. They have the same amount of between-treatments variability

33. Which researcher's data sets will result in a larger F value? It is important to note that in this case both researchers have the same numerator for the F (i.e., $MS_{between}$)

   a. Researcher 1

   b. Researcher 2

   c. They have the same F value

34. The two studies have the same $df_{between}$, the same df_{within}, which means that they will have the same _____ . (Do you know why the dfs for the two studies are the same? If not, figure that out first.)

   a. Obtained F value

   b. Critical value

   c. MS_{within}

   d. $MS_{between}$

35. The two studies have the same MS_{within} and the same $MS_{between}$, which means that they will have the same _____ . (Do you know why the MSs for the two studies are the same, even though all of the scores are different for the two studies? If not, figure that out first.)

   a. Obtained F value

   b. Critical value

   c. MS_{within}

   d. $MS_{between}$

Use the following two data sets to answer Questions 36–40.

	Researcher 1			Researcher 2	
Group 1: Cola	Group 2: Club Soda	Group 3: Water	Group 1: Cola	Group 2: Club Soda	Group 3: Water
48	58	68	40	50	60
50	60	70	50	60	70
52	63	72	60	70	80
$M_1 = 50$	$M_2 = 60$	$M_3 = 70$	$M_1 = 50$	$M_2 = 60$	$M_3 = 70$
$SD_1 = 2$	$SD_2 = 2$	$SD_3 = 2$	$SD_1 = 10$	$SD_2 = 10$	$SD_3 = 10$
$SS_1 = 8$	$SS_2 = 8$	$SS_3 = 8$	$SS_1 = 200$	$SS_2 = 200$	$SS_3 = 200$

36. Which researcher's data set has more variability within treatments (i.e., a higher MS_{within})?
    a. Researcher 1
    b. Researcher 2
    c. They have the same amount of within-treatments variability

37. Which researcher's data set has more variability between treatments (i.e., a higher $MS_{between}$)?
    a. Researcher 1
    b. Researcher 2
    c. They have the same amount of between-treatments variability

38. Which researcher's data sets will result in a larger F value?
    a. Researcher 1
    b. Researcher 2
    c. They have the same amount of within-treatments variability

39. Which researcher's study is more likely to lead to rejecting the null hypothesis?
    a. Researcher 1
    b. Researcher 2

40. Why is the MS_{within} for Researcher 1 *smaller* than the MS_{within} for Researcher 2?

   a. The scores of Researcher 1 within each treatment condition are more variable (i.e., more different).

   b. The scores of Researcher 1 within each treatment condition are closer together (i.e., more similar).

The following questions are NOT based on any specific data sets.

41. When a data set has a lot of measurement error and the individuals being measured are very different from each other the data will tend to have

   a. a large MS_{within}.

   b. a large $MS_{between}$.

42. When the different treatments vary in their effectiveness (i.e., some treatments are better than others), the data will tend to have

   a. a large MS_{within}.

   b. a large $MS_{between}$.

43. Why do researchers want to minimize within-treatment variability? (Choose two answers)

   a. Lowering within-treatment variability generally results in higher F values.

   b. Lowering within-treatments variability increases the between-treatments variability.

   c. Lowering within-treatments variability makes rejecting the null more likely.

   d. Lowering within-treatments variability lowers the between-treatments variability.

44. Why do researchers want to maximize between-treatment variability? (Choose two answers)

   a. Increasing between-treatment variability generally results in higher F values.

   b. Increasing between-treatments variability decreases the within-treatments variability.

   c. Increasing between-treatments variability makes rejecting the null more likely.

   d. Increasing between-treatments variability increases the within-treatments variability.

45. To determine the effectiveness of a new pain killer on migraines, a medical researcher recruits 80 people with migraines. Twenty of the participants receive a placebo, 20 receive 1 mg of the pain killer, 20 receive 2 mg of the pain killer, and 20 receive 3 mg of the pain killer. Each participant recorded the severity of their migraine 1 hour after taking their respective migraine treatments. Which of the

following would be the most effective way to increase between-treatments variability in this study?

   a. Use only women in the study.

   b. Use fewer participants.

   c. Use doses of the drug that are more different (e.g., 10, 20, and 30 mg rather than 1, 2, and 3 mg).

46. Which of the following would be the most effective way to decrease within-treatments variability in this study?

   a. Use only women in the study.

   b. Use fewer participants.

   c. Give larger doses of the drugs (e.g., 10 mg rather than 1 mg, etc.).

47. This activity focused on explaining within-group and between-group variability of an ANOVA and how each of these types of variability affects the size of the obtained F value. The activity further emphasized that the larger the obtained F value, the more likely the null hypothesis will be rejected. If an ANOVA is comparing three or more groups, what additional analysis must be performed?

   a. Post hoc tests must be performed to determine which of the groups are significantly different from each other.

   b. Another ANOVA must be performed.

   c. A bunch of t tests must be performed.

48. Finally, try to explain to someone who has never taken a statistics course how an ANOVA compares within-group and between-group variability to determine if three or more treatment options are equally effective.

Activity 12-2:   Independent ANOVA With SPSS

Learning Objectives

After reading the chapter and completing this activity, you should be able to do the following:

- Use SPSS to conduct an independent ANOVA
- Interpret the SPSS output
- Compose an APA-style summary of the ANOVA results
- Describe the relationship between an independent t test and an independent ANOVA with two conditions
- Read a research scenario and determine what statistical test is appropriate

COLLEGE STUDENTS' CYNICISM

In this activity, you will work with the data file titled "Cynicism.sav." This file contains data about cynicism toward college from 76 hypothetical students. Each student answered four questions about three different types of cynicism, specifically their cynicism toward the academic, social, and institutional aspects of their college. All questions used the same Likert scale, where 1 = *strongly disagree*, 2 = *disagree*, 3 = *neither agree or disagree*, 4 = *agree* and 5 = *strongly agree*. Their responses yielded one average score for each type of cynicism. Example questions for each type of cynicism are listed below.

Academic: "For many of my courses, going to class is a waste of time."

Social: "It takes a great deal of effort to find fun things to do here."

Institutional: "I would not recommend this place to anyone."

ACADEMIC CYNICISM

For the first analysis, we are going to conduct an ANOVA to determine if year in school (i.e., freshman, sophomore, junior, senior) is associated with academic cynicism.

1. The null hypothesis is:
   a. The mean level of academic cynicism will not be the same across all 4 years in school.
   b. The mean level of academic cynicism will be the same across all 4 years in school.

2. The research hypothesis is:
   a. The mean level of academic cynicism will not be the same across all 4 years in school.
   b. The mean level of academic cynicism will be the same across all 4 years in school.

Running the SPSS ANOVA

Compute a single-factor, independent samples ANOVA using YearInSchool as the IV (factor) and AcademicCynicism as the DV.

- Click on the Analyze menu. Choose General Linear Model and then select Univariate.
- Move YearInSchool into the Fixed Factor box and Academic into the Dependent Variable box.
- Click on Options, check Descriptives and estimates of effect size, and then click continue.

- Click on post hoc, move YearInSchool into the post hoc tests for box.
- Check Tukey and then click Continue.
- Finally, click OK.

3. Record the mean level of academic cynicism for each year in school below. As always, also include the standard deviation for each group.

Freshmen	$M = $ _____	, $SD = $ _____
Sophomores	$M = $ _____	, $SD = $ _____
Juniors	$M = $ _____	, $SD = $ _____
Seniors	$M = $ _____	, $SD = $ _____

4. Complete the ANOVA summary table.

Source	SS	df	MS	F	p (sig)	η^2_p
Between treatments	___	___	___	___	___	___
Within treatments	___	___	___			
Total	___	___				

5. Whenever you obtain a significant F value and there are more than two means, post hoc tests are required. In this case, we need to compare the freshmen mean, sophomore mean, junior mean, and senior mean for academic cynicism. More specifically, we need to compare all possible pairs of two means. All of the possible pairwise comparisons are listed below. For example, the first line represents the comparison between freshmen and sophomores. Likewise, the second line represents the comparison between freshmen and juniors. The Tukey post hoc tests computed by SPSS indicate which of these comparisons are significantly different from each other. Circle "Yes" if the pairwise comparison is statistically significant and "No" if the comparison is not statistically significant.

Comparison	Is It Significant?
Freshmen ($M = $ _____) and sophomores ($M = $ _____)	Yes/No
Freshmen ($M = $ _____) and juniors ($M = $ _____)	Yes/No
Freshmen ($M = $ _____) and seniors ($M = $ _____)	Yes/No
Sophomores ($M = $ _____) and juniors ($M = $ _____)	Yes/No
Sophomores ($M = $ _____) and seniors ($M = $ _____)	Yes/No
Juniors ($M = $ _____) and seniors ($M = $ _____)	Yes/No

Once you have determined which of the pairwise comparisons are significant, you need to determine which group had higher levels of academic cynicism. Look at the means for each group and circle the group in each pair with the highest mean cynicism score. Note that you only need to do this for significant pairwise comparisons.

6. *Choose ONE of the following summary statements based on whether you rejected or failed to reject the null.* Fill in the blanks only for that summary statement. After you fill in the blanks, this paragraph should serve as an example for writing future one-way ANOVAs. The ANOVA results are reported using the following format:

$F\ (df_{between}, df_{within}) = F$ value, $p < \alpha$, MSE = mean square error, η_p^2 = partial eta squared.

a. To determine if Class Standing was associated with Academic Cynicism, a one-way, independent samples ANOVA was computed with Class Standing as the IV and Academic Cynicism as the DV. This analysis revealed a significant effect, $F\ (\underline{\hspace{1cm}}, \underline{\hspace{1cm}}) = \underline{\hspace{1cm}}, p < \underline{\hspace{1cm}}$, $MSE = \underline{\hspace{1cm}}$, $\eta_p^2 = \underline{\hspace{1cm}}$. Tukey's *HSD* post hoc test indicated that freshmen had lower levels of cynicism $(M = \underline{\hspace{1cm}}, SD = \underline{\hspace{1cm}})$ than sophomores $(M = \underline{\hspace{1cm}}, SD = \underline{\hspace{1cm}})$. No other differences were significant (juniors, $M = \underline{\hspace{1cm}}, SD = \underline{\hspace{1cm}}$; seniors, $M = \underline{\hspace{1cm}}, SD = \underline{\hspace{1cm}}$).

(The last sentence is included because means and standard deviations for all groups are to be reported, and juniors and seniors were not discussed previously.)

b. To determine if class standing was associated with academic cynicism, a one-way, independent samples ANOVA was computed with class standing as the IV and academic cynicism as the DV. Year in school was not associated with academic cynicism, $F\ (\underline{\hspace{1cm}}, \underline{\hspace{1cm}}) = \underline{\hspace{1cm}}, p = \underline{\hspace{1cm}}$, $MSE = \underline{\hspace{1cm}}$, $\eta_p^2 = \underline{\hspace{1cm}}$. The mean levels of cynicism were as follows: Freshmen $(M = \underline{\hspace{1cm}}, SD = \underline{\hspace{1cm}})$, sophomores $(M = \underline{\hspace{1cm}}, SD = \underline{\hspace{1cm}})$, juniors $(M = \underline{\hspace{1cm}}, SD = \underline{\hspace{1cm}})$, and seniors $(M = \underline{\hspace{1cm}}, SD = \underline{\hspace{1cm}})$.

General format for reporting an ANOVA:

- Tell what kind of ANOVA you ran.
- Tell whether the null hypothesis was rejected or not, include the statistical information. (*Note*: If you have a significant effect, the null hypothesis was rejected.)
- If the result was statistically significant, report which group means were significantly different, include the mean and standard deviations for each group.

INSTITUTIONAL CYNICISM

Repeat the same steps that you used to generate the previous ANOVA, except replace "AcademicCynicism" with "InstitutionalCynicism" in the Dependent list.

7. What is the null hypothesis for this analysis?

8. What is the research hypothesis for this analysis?

9. Record the mean level of institutional cynicism for each class standing below. Include the standard deviation for each group.

   Freshmen $M = $ _____ , $SD = $ _____.

   Sophomores $M = $ _____ , $SD = $ _____.

   Juniors $M = $ _____ , $SD = $ _____.

   Seniors $M = $ _____ , $SD = $ _____.

10. Complete the ANOVA summary table.

Source	SS	df	MS	F	p (sig.)	η^2_p
Between treatments	____	____	____	____	____	____
Within treatments	____	____	____			
Total	____	____				

11. All pairwise comparisons are listed below. First determine if each pairwise comparison is statistically significant. Circle "Yes" if the pairwise comparison is statistically significant and "No" if the comparison is not statistically significant. Next, for all significant pairwise comparisons, determine which group had the higher mean institutional cynicism score.

Comparison	Is It Significant?
Freshmen and sophomores	Yes/No
Freshmen and juniors	Yes/No
Freshmen and seniors	Yes/No
Sophomores and juniors	Yes/No
Sophomores and seniors	Yes/No
Juniors and seniors	Yes/No

12. Report the results in an APA-style summary. Do not skip the questions that require you to write an APA-style summary. During exams students often find writing an APA-style summary difficult, and the only way to ensure that you can do this is to practice and check your work.

SOCIAL CYNICISM

Finally, you are going to look at differences in social cynicism among freshmen, sophomores, juniors, and seniors.

13. What is the null hypothesis for this analysis?

14. What is the research hypothesis for this analysis?

15. Record the mean level of social cynicism for each year in school below. As always, include the standard deviation for each group.

   Freshmen $M =$ _____, $SD =$ _____.

   Sophomores $M =$ _____, $SD =$ _____.

   Juniors $M =$ _____, $SD =$ _____.

   Seniors $M =$ _____, $SD =$ _____.

16. Complete the ANOVA summary table.

Source	SS	df	MS	F	p (sig)	η_p^2
Between treatments	____	____	____	____	____	____
Within treatments	____	____	____			
Total	____	____				

17. Explain why post hoc analyses are not necessary for this ANOVA.

18. Report the results in an APA-style summary. Write the entire summary as if this is an exam question.

19. Overall, does it look like levels of cynicism are very high in this data set? Remember that 1 indicates strong disagreement with the statements (i.e., low cynicism), 3 indicates neither agreement nor disagreement, and 5 indicates strong agreement with the statements (i.e., high cynicism).

ANOVAs AND t TESTS

Although we typically use ANOVAs when we have three or more groups, ANOVAs can also be used instead of a t test when you have two groups. Compute an independent samples t test to determine if gender is associated with social cynicism.

You can run the t test by doing the following:

- Click on the Analyze menu. Choose Compare Means and then select Independent Samples t Test.
- Move "Gender" to the Grouping Variable box and "SocialCynicism" to the Test Variables box.
- Click on Define Groups. Enter a 1 in the group 1 box (1 = male in the data file) and enter a 2 in the group 2 box (2 = female in the data file).

20. Record the results of the t test here:

   Male $M =$ _____, $SD =$ _____.

   Female $M =$ _____, $SD =$ _____.

   $t =$ _____ p (sig.) two-tailed = _____.

   Was the null hypothesis rejected?   Yes   No

21. Compute a one-way ANOVA using "Gender" as the Factor and "SocialCynicism" as the DV. Record the results of the ANOVA below:

   Male $M =$ _____, $SD =$ _____.

   Female $M =$ _____, $SD =$ _____.

$F =$ _____ p (sig.) = _____.

Was the null hypothesis rejected?   Yes   No

You should have found that the means, standard deviations, and the significance levels (i.e., p values) for the t test and the two-group ANOVA were all *identical*. Additionally, both of these tests lead to the same decision about the null hypothesis. However, the t and F values were different. Although the t and F values are different, the relationship between the t and the F is always: $t^2 = F$ when there are only two groups in the analysis. Verify that this is true for the statistics you reported above.

22. A researcher ran an independent t test and got an obtained t value of 4.7. A second researcher in the same lab analyzed the same data with an ANOVA. What would be the F value obtained by the second researcher? $F =$ _____.

23. Suppose that you chose to do an ANOVA rather than a t test for a study with two groups. Explain why you would not have to do post hoc tests even if you rejected the null.

WHY INCLUDE ALL THAT STATISTICAL INFORMATION?

24. Students sometimes wonder why they have to report all of the statistical information. Why would anyone care about all of these numbers? The reason researchers should report all of this information is that readers who know what they are doing can recreate the entire ANOVA source table when the statistical information is reported properly. For example, suppose that a researcher reported the following results: $F (3, 56) = 6.40$, $p < .05$, $MSE = 6.25$. You should be able to use this information to "work backward" and complete the source table below.

    a. How many treatment conditions (groups) were in this study? _____.

Source	SS	df	MS	F	p (sig.)	η_p^2
Between treatments	_____	_____	_____	_____	_____	_____
Within treatments	_____	_____	_____			
Total	_____	_____				

    b. How many people participated in this study? _____.

    c. What is the critical value for the F (using an alpha of .05)? _____.

    d. Should you reject or fail to reject the null hypothesis? _____.

    e. Explain why post hoc tests needed to be done:

The next questions you should have are, "Ok, so we can re-create the source table. Why is that worth doing? Why would a researcher want to do that?" Well, there are many potential reasons way a researcher might be interested in the details of the source table. One of the most compelling is that if researchers are reading many different experiments on the same topic, they can compare or combine the results across different experiments using a statistical procedure called "meta-analysis." To do this procedure, the researchers need the details that are in the ANOVA source table.

25. For the preceding problems, the data were already entered into SPSS for you. However, you should also be able to enter the data into SPSS. Indicate how you would enter the data from the following independent measures design with three groups into SPSS:

Group 1: 36, 40, 44

Group 2: 37, 38, 41

Group 3: 44, 43, 42

Activity 12-3: Choose the Correct Statistic

Learning Objectives

After reading the chapter, completing the homework and this activity, you should be able to do the following:

- Read a research scenario and determine which statistic should be used

Determine which statistic should be used in each of the following research scenarios: z for a single score, z for sample mean, single sample t, related samples t, independent samples t, or one-way independent samples ANOVA.

1. A psychologist examined the effect of physical exercise on a standardized memory test. Scores on this test for the general population form a normal distribution with a mean of 50 and a standard deviation of 8. A sample of 62 people who exercise at least 3 hours per week has a mean score of 57. Is there evidence for improved memory for those who exercise?

2. A psychologist is interested in the effects of social pressure on conformity behaviors. To investigate the phenomena, she has a subject first sit in a room alone and judge the length of a line. Then, she has the subject sit with confederates who state that the line is much longer than it really is. After the confederates have made their estimates, the subject makes his or hers. The mean length given when they are alone is 5, with a standard deviation of 1.1. The mean length given when they are in a room with confederates is 7, with a standard deviation of 1.9. Which statistic would you use to determine if the length estimates that were provided while the subject was alone were significantly different from those given while the subject was with the confederates?

3. A researcher would like to determine whether the students with anxiety disorders sleep more or less than most students. Suppose it is known that the number of hours college students sleep is normally distributed with a mean of 8. The researcher takes a sample of 32 students with anxiety disorders and records the amount of sleep they get each night. It is found that they average 7.8 hours, with a standard deviation of 1. Which statistic would help determine if students with anxiety disorders sleep more or less than students without anxiety disorders?

4. Farmer Brown was curious which of three types of food, Wonder Food, Miracle Grow, or Sorghum, would make cows gain the most weight. He could maximize his profit if he used the feed that was the most effective. But he also had to consider the cost of the food. He would be willing to buy the most expensive feed as long as there was evidence that it was "worth the cost." He purchased a few bags of each type of feed. He randomly selected 30 cows from his herd. He then randomly assigned the cows to be fed Wonder Food, Miracle Grow, or Sorghum. Three months later, he weighed the 30 cows and compared the mean weights of those fed with the different foods. Which statistic would allow you to determine if one of the foods is significantly better than the two?

5. A research scientist for the Air Force was asked to determine which of two landing gear systems should be installed on a new aircraft that would soon go into production. He had two identical prototypes of the new aircraft and had one of the landing gear systems installed on each aircraft. He obtained the services of 10 highly skilled Air Force pilots and by drawing names from a hat assigned 5 to fly each aircraft. Immediately after each pilot landed, he or she was instructed to rate how well the landing gear performed on a 10-point scale (e.g., 1 = *poorly*

and 10 = *very well*). Which statistic would help you determine if one prototype received significantly higher ratings than the other?

6. For a project in their undergraduate stats class, a group of students showed participants a video clip of a car accident. After watching, the video participants had to estimate how fast one of the two cars was going when the accident occurred. A third of the participants were asked, "How fast was the car going when it *bumped* the other car?" A third were asked, "How fast was the car going when it *hit* the other car?" And the final third were asked, "How fast was the car going when it *smashed* the other car?" Which statistic would enable you to determine whether the three different ways of asking the question lead to different estimates of the car's speed.

7. Executives at a large corporation hired a psychologist to evaluate two physical fitness programs with the intent of adopting one for their employees. The two fitness programs were creatively labeled Plan A and Plan B. Three different work teams (employees who work together) volunteered to participate in some kind of fitness program. These three work teams were randomly assigned to one of the two different fitness plans. After 6 months, the psychologist used corporation records to determine the rate of absenteeism (number of work days missed) for employees in each plan. Which statistic would help you determine if Plan A or Plan B leads to less absenteeism?

8. A researcher studies the effect of a drug on the number of nightmares occurring in veterans with posttraumatic stress disorder (PTSD). A sample of clients with PTSD kept records of each incident of a nightmare for 1 month before treatment. Subjects were then given the medication for 1 month, and they continued to record each nightmare. Which statistic would help you determine if the medication significantly reduced nightmares?

9. A college professor has noted that this year's freshman class appears to be smarter than classes from previous years. The professor obtains a sample of $N = 36$ freshmen and computes an average IQ ($M = 114.5$) and the variance in IQ ($SD^2 = 324$) for the sample. College records indicate that the mean IQ for entering freshman from previous years was 110.3. Is the incoming class significantly smarter (as measured by IQ) than the mean for previous years?

10. A group of participants had to press the brake on a driving simulator whenever they saw a ball roll into the road ahead of them. Every driver performed the task while talking on a cell phone and while not talking on a cell phone. The DV was how long in milliseconds it took to press the brake pedal. The researchers compared the mean reaction time in the cell phone condition with the mean reaction time in the control condition. Which statistic would help determine if talking on a cell phone leads to slower response times?

11. A neurologist had two groups of patients with different kinds of aphasia (i.e., brain disorders). One group had a damage to Broca's area and the other had damage to Wernicke's area. The researcher also used a third group of people who had no

brain abnormalities. People in each group were shown line drawings of common household objects (i.e., a lamp, a chair, etc.) and were asked to name the object. Which statistic would determine if the number of objects correctly identified differed across the three groups?

12. Henry was in a motorcycle accident and suffered a head injury. A clinical psychologist uses a standardized object-naming task to determine if Henry's head trauma has caused a significant object-naming deficit. Henry named five items correctly. The mean performance on the task was $M = 10$, $\sigma = 2$. What is the percentile rank of Henry's performance?

Activity 12-4: Practice Problems

INDEPENDENT ANOVA AND SPSS

A psychologist would like to determine which of three therapies is most effective in treating agoraphobia: (1) CBT, (2) systematic desensitization, or (3) hypnosis. Fifteen individuals diagnosed with agoraphobia were randomly assigned to each of the three therapies. After 3 months of therapy, the psychologist asks the participants to record the number of times they leave their house/apartment building during a 2-week period.

Cognitive Behavioral Therapy	Systematic Desensitization	Hypnosis
7	12	2
8	7	3
6	8	1
9	9	4
10	6	2

1. Which of the following best represents the null hypothesis for this study?
   a. $H_0: \mu_1 = \mu_2 \neq \mu_3$
   b. $H_0: \mu_1 \neq \mu_2 = \mu_3$
   c. $H_0: \mu_1 \neq \mu_2 \neq \mu_3$
   d. $H_0: \mu_1 = \mu_2 = \mu_3$

2. Which of the following best represents the *research hypothesis* for this study?
   a. The mean number of times patients with agoraphobia leave their homes after treatment are the same for CBT, systematic desensitization, and hypnosis.
   b. The mean number of times patients with agoraphobia leave their homes after treatment are NOT the same for CBT, systematic desensitization, and hypnosis.

3. The following ANOVA source table came from the above study, but it is only partly complete. Complete the entire table and use it to answer Questions 4 through 11. (Complete the table by hand *before* you analyze the data using SPSS.)

Source of Variance	SS	df	MS	F
Between treatments	112.53			
Within treatments	36.40			
Total	148.93			

4. What is the between treatments *df* for this study with three groups (i.e., three conditions)?

5. What is the within treatments *df* for this study with five people in each of the three groups?

6. What is the critical value of *F* for this study that is using an alpha value of .05?

7. What is the error term (i.e., MS_{within})?

8. What is the obtained *F* value for this study?

9. Should the null hypothesis of this study be rejected?

10. Which of the following accurately describes the results of the Tukey post hoc tests?

   a. Systematic desensitization was significantly better than CBT and hypnosis. CBT and hypnosis were the same.

   b. Systematic desensitization and CBT were equally effective. Hypnosis was worse than both of them.

   c. Hypnosis was the best, CBT was the second best, and systematic desensitization was the worst.

11. What is the effect size for this study?

12. Is the effect size small, small-medium, medium, medium-large, or large?

13. Which of the following is the best summary of the results of this study?

   a. The three treatments for agoraphobia were all equally effective, $F(2, 12) = 18.55, p > .05, \eta_p^2 = .76$.

   b. The three treatments for agoraphobia were not all equally effective, $F(2, 12) = 18.55, p < .05, \eta_p^2 = .76$. Post hoc tests revealed that the CBT group ($M = 8.0, SD = 1.58$) and the systematic desensitization group ($M = 8.4, SD = 2.30$) both left their homes more often than the hypnosis group ($M = 2.4, SD = 1.14$).

   c. The three treatments for agoraphobia were not all equally effective, $F(2, 14) = 56.27, p < .05, \eta_p^2 = .76$. Post hoc tests revealed that the CBT group ($M = 8.0, SD = 1.58$) and the systematic desensitization group ($M = 8.4, SD = 2.30$) both were less effective than the hypnosis group ($M = 2.4, SD = 1.14$).

d. The three treatments for agoraphobia were not all equally effective, $F(2, 14) = 56.27$, $p < .05$, $\eta_p^2 = .76$. Post hoc tests revealed that the systematic desensitization group ($M = 8.4$, $SD = 2.30$) did the best, the CBT group ($M = 8.0$, $SD = 1.58$) did the second best, and the hypnosis group ($M = 2.4$, $SD = 1.14$) did the worst.

BETWEEN AND WITHIN TREATMENT VARIABILITY

Researcher 1			Researcher 2		
Group 1: Cola	Group 2: Club Soda	Group 3: Water	Group 1: Cola	Group 2: Club Soda	Group 3: Water
48	56	64	40	40	40
50	60	70	50	60	70
52	64	76	60	80	100
$M_1 = 50$	$M_2 = 60$	$M_3 = 70$	$M_1 = 50$	$M_2 = 60$	$M_3 = 70$
$SD_1 = 2$	$SD_2 = 4$	$SD_3 = 6$	$SD_1 = 10$	$SD_2 = 20$	$SD_3 = 30$
$SS_1 = 8$	$SS_2 = 32$	$SS_3 = 72$	$SS_1 = 200$	$SS_2 = 800$	$SS_3 = 1800$

Use the following two data sets to answer Questions 14–18.

14. Which researcher's data set has more variability within treatments (i.e., a higher MS_{within})?

   a. Researcher 1

   b. Researcher 2

   c. They have the same amount of within treatments variability

15. Which researcher's data set has more variability between treatments (i.e., a higher $MS_{between}$)?

   a. Researcher 1

   b. Researcher 2

   c. They have the same amount of between-treatments variability

16. Which researcher's data sets will result in a larger F value?

   a. Researcher 1

   b. Researcher 2

   c. They have the same F value

17. Which researcher's study is more likely to lead to rejecting the null hypothesis?

   a. Researcher 1

   b. Researcher 2

18. Which data set probably has more measurement error?
    a. The data set of Researcher 1
    b. The data set of Researcher 2

Use the following two data sets to answer Questions 19–22.

Researcher 1			Researcher 2		
Group 1	Group 2	Group 3	Group 1	Group 2	Group 3
5	3	1	1	2	3
6	5	4	2	3	4
7	7	7	3	4	5

19. Which researcher's data set has more variability within treatments (i.e., a higher MS_{within})?
    a. Researcher 1
    b. Researcher 2
    c. They have the same amount of within-treatments variability

20. Which researcher's data set has more variability between treatments (i.e., a higher $MS_{between}$)?
    a. Researcher 1
    b. Researcher 2
    c. They have the same amount of between-treatments variability

21. Which researcher's data sets will result in a larger F value?
    a. Researcher 1
    b. Researcher 2
    c. They have the same F value

22. Which researcher's study is more likely to lead to rejecting the null hypothesis?
    a. Researcher 1
    b. Researcher 2

Use the following two data sets to answer Questions 23–26.

Researcher 1			Researcher 2		
Group 1	Group 2	Group 3	Group 1	Group 2	Group 3
3	2	1	3	2	6
5	5	6	4	3	7
8	7	7	5	4	6

23. Which researcher's data set has more variability within treatments (i.e., has a higher MS_{within})?

    a. Researcher 1

    b. Researcher 2

    c. They have the same amount of within-treatments variability

24. Which researcher's data set has more variability between treatments (i.e., has a higher $MS_{between}$)?

    a. Researcher 1

    b. Researcher 2

    c. They have the same amount of between-treatments variability

25. Which researcher's data sets will result in a larger F value?

    a. Researcher 1

    b. Researcher 2

    c. They have the same F value

26. Which researcher's study is more likely to lead to rejecting the null hypothesis?

    a. Researcher 1

    b. Researcher 2

UNDERSTANDING THE ANOVA SOURCE TABLE

27. A researcher reported the following results: $F(2, 72) = 4.00$, $p < .05$, $MSE = 6$. Use this information to "work backward" and complete the source table below.

Source	SS	df	MS	F	η_p^2
Between treatments	_____	_____	_____	_____	_____
Within treatments	_____	_____	_____		
Total	_____	_____			

    a. How many treatment conditions (groups) were in this study? _____.

    b. How many people participated in this study? _____.

    c. What is the critical value for the F (using an alpha of .05)? _____.

    d. Should you reject or fail to reject the null hypothesis? _____.

    e. Explain why post hoc tests needed to be done:

Two-Factor Independent Measures ANOVA

PURPOSE OF THE TWO-FACTOR ANOVA

In the previous chapter, you learned about the ANOVA (also called the single-factor independent ANOVA). Researchers use this statistic to determine if a single independent variable (IV) has a significant effect on a dependent variable (DV). When conducting ANOVAs, IVs are often referred to as factors; therefore, an ANOVA used to evaluate a single IV is called a single-factor ANOVA or a one-way ANOVA.

This chapter introduces the two-factor ANOVA, or the two-way ANOVA. The two-way ANOVA is used frequently by researchers in the behavioral sciences because it can test for the effect of two IVs/factors at the same time. In fact, the two-way ANOVA allows researchers to determine if the two IVs *interact*. In many situations, a given treatment (i.e., IV) works only when it is presented in conjunction with a second treatment. In these situations, if researchers used one or more one-way ANOVAs to test each IV separately, their results could be quite misleading. The example used in this chapter will illustrate how two different IVs interact to influence how frequently one is bitten by mosquitoes. In fact, the two-way ANOVA allows researchers to test for three effects: (1) the effect of the first IV on the DV, (2) the effect of the second IV on the DV, and (3) the effect of the interaction between the two IVs on the DV. It is easiest to understand these three effects in the context of a study, so we will illustrate each effect by describing an actual study investigating how alcohol consumption (Factor 1) and one's body temperature (Factor 2) influence the number of times people are bitten by mosquitoes.

Reading Question

1. A two-way ANOVA (also called a two-factor ANOVA) has two
   a. IVs.
   b. DVs.

Reading Question

2. How many effects are tested by a two-factor ANOVA?
   a. 1
   b. 2
   c. 3

TWO-FACTOR INDEPENDENT MEASURES ANOVA: EXAMPLE

Did you know that mosquitoes prefer biting some people more than others? The variables influencing this preference are of interest to researchers because mosquitoes carry a variety of diseases (e.g., malaria, West Nile virus), and therefore, those who are more frequently bitten are at a higher risk of contracting these diseases. Two variables that seem to influence how frequently people are bitten by mosquitoes are one's body temperature and alcohol consumption. In the following scenario, researchers use a two-way ANOVA to determine how body temperature and alcohol consumption independently influence the number of mosquito bites one receives and how these variables *interact* to determine how frequently people are bitten by mosquitoes.

The researchers recruited two groups of participants. Half of the participants had an average basal body temperature below 98.2°F, and half had an average basal body temperature above 99.0°F. When the participants arrived for the study, the researchers randomly assigned half of those from each body temperature group to drink either 24 ounces of beer or 24 ounces of a placebo (alcohol-free beer). After consuming their assigned beverage, the participants placed their arm in a chamber filled with mosquitoes for five minutes. The number of mosquito bites each person received during that period was recorded. The data for each of the four experimental conditions are reported in Table 13.1.

Table 13.1	Number of mosquito bites based on body temperature and alcohol consumption.

Low Body Temperature		High Body Temperature	
Beer	Placebo	Beer	Placebo
10	5	14	11
8	8	17	8
7	6	12	9
8	7	19	13
9	4	18	8
7	10	15	12
12	7	12	10
11	9	21	9
M = 9	M = 7	M = 16	M = 10

The design has two separate IVs: body temperature and alcohol consumption. Each of these variables has two levels. The two levels for body temperature are low (i.e., a basal body temperature below 98.2°F) or high (i.e., a basal body temperature above 99.0°F). The two levels for alcohol consumption are drinking 24 ounces of beer or drinking 24 ounces of nonalcoholic beer (i.e., placebo). There are two factors, and each has two levels, so this study is a 2 × 2 design. Typically, these types of designs are represented by 2 × 2 tables (see Table 13.2). The entries inside each cell of the table indicate the mean number of bites suffered by those in each condition of the study. These means in the cells of the table are often called *cell means*.

Table 13.2	Cell means for the body temperature × alcohol consumption interaction.

	Beer	Placebo
Low temperature	9	7
High temperature	16	10

Reading Question

3. If participants in this study drank beer, wine, or placebo, how many levels would the IV of alcohol consumption have?

a. 1

b. 2

c. 3

Reading Question

4. If participants in this study with high or low body temperatures drank beer, wine, or placebo, how many cell means would the study produce?

   a. 3

   b. 4

   c. 6

Step 1: Set Up the Null and Research Hypotheses

The two-factor ANOVA tests for three different effects. Specifically, it determines (1) if body temperature has an effect on the number of mosquito bites suffered, (2) if alcohol consumption has an effect on the number of mosquito bites suffered, and (3) if body temperature and alcohol consumption interact to have an effect on the number of mosquito bites suffered. If the two variables interact, it means that the effect alcohol consumption has on the number of mosquito bites is different for people with high body temperatures compared with people with low body temperatures.

The ANOVA tests for three different effects, so there are three different sets of null and research hypotheses.

Step 1a: Interaction Null and Research Hypotheses

The primary advantage in using a two-factor design is that it allows the researchers to determine if body temperature and alcohol consumption interact to affect the number of mosquito bites people suffer. An interaction between body temperature and alcohol consumption exists if the effect alcohol consumption has on the number of mosquito bites is different for people with high versus low body temperature. Thus, the interaction research hypothesis is that the effect of alcohol consumption is different for people with high versus low body temperature. The interaction null hypothesis is that the effect of alcohol consumption is the same for people with high and low body temperatures. The interaction hypotheses are summarized in Table 13.3. You will notice that there is no symbolic notation associated with these hypotheses.

Table 13.3   Verbal representations of the research and null hypotheses for the body temperature × alcohol interaction.

	Symbolic	*Verbal*
Research hypothesis (H_1)		The effect of alcohol consumption on the number of mosquito bites one receives is different for people with high versus low body temperatures (i.e., there is an interaction between the two IVs).
Null hypothesis (H_0)		The effect of alcohol consumption on the number of mosquito bites one receives is the same for people with high and low body temperatures (i.e., there is NO interaction between the two IVs).

Reading Question

5. The null hypothesis for the interaction states that the effect of alcohol consumption on the number of mosquito bites

    a. is the same for people with high and low body temperatures.

    b. is different for people with high and low body temperatures.

Reading Question

6. The research hypothesis for the interaction states that the effect of alcohol consumption on the number of mosquito bites

    a. is the same for people with high and low body temperatures.

    b. is different for people with high and low body temperatures.

To determine if there might be an interaction, you begin by looking at the cell means. The cell means indicate that participants with a *low* body temperature were bitten more often when they drank beer ($M = 9$) than when they drank the placebo ($M = 7$). The participants with *high* body temperature were also bitten more often when they drank beer ($M = 16$) than when they drank the placebo ($M = 10$). Although both body temperature groups received more bites when drinking beer, the effect of alcohol consumption was more pronounced for the high body temperature group than for the low body temperature group. The participants with a low body temperature were bitten an average of 7 times when they drank the placebo and 9 times when they drank beer, an increase of 2 bites. Participants with a high body temperature were bitten an average of 10 times when they drank the placebo and 16 times when they drank beer, an increase of 6 bites. It appears that drinking beer created a larger increase in bites for participants with high body temperatures, 6 more bites instead of 2 more bites.

Reading Question

7. Participants with a low body temperature received ____ more bites when they drank alcohol rather than the placebo. Participants with a high body temperature received ____ more bites when they drank alcohol rather than the placebo.

    a. 2; 9

    b. 2; 6

    c. 6; 9

The fact that the increase in mosquito bites associated with drinking alcohol was 2 for low body temperature participants and 6 for high body temperature participants suggests that there might be an interaction between alcohol consumption and body temperature; however, to determine if the interaction is statistically significant, the researchers must show that the different patterns of results for participants with low and high body temperatures were not likely to be due to sampling error. Later, you will compute an F test to determine if this interaction is *statistically significant*. In other words, you will determine if the difference between 2 more bites and 6 more bites is due to an interaction between alcohol and body temperature or due to sampling error.

8. To determine if an interaction is *statistically significant*, you will have to
   a. interpret the cell means.
   b. compute an *F* test.

In this case, we chose to interpret the interaction by determining if the effect of alcohol consumption is different for participants with high versus low body temperature. We could have chosen to interpret the interaction by determining if the effect of body temperature is different for participants who consume beer versus the placebo. Either way will work. Researchers typically choose the one that makes the most sense in terms of their theory or the research literature. You can choose the one that makes the most sense to you.

Step 1b: Main Effect Null and Research Hypotheses for Body Temperature

The second effect is the impact of body temperature on the number of mosquito bites. When you are analyzing the effect of just one IV, it is referred to as a main effect. The null hypothesis for the main effect of body temperature is that participants with high and low body temperatures receive an equal number of mosquito bites. The research hypothesis is that participants with high and low body temperatures receive different numbers of mosquito bites. The symbolic notations as well as their verbal equivalents are provided in Table 13.4.

Table 13.4	Symbolic and verbal representations of the research and null hypotheses for the main effect of body temperature.

	Symbolic	Verbal
Research hypothesis (H_1)	H_1: $\mu_1 \neq \mu_2$	The number of mosquito bites is not equal for the groups with low and high body temperatures.
Null hypothesis (H_0)	H_0: $\mu_1 = \mu_2$	The number of mosquito bites is equal for the groups with low and high body temperatures.

Reading Question

9. When you are investigating the effect of one IV on the DV, the effect is called
   a. a main effect.
   b. an interaction effect.

Reading Question

10. The null hypothesis for the main effect of body temperature states that
    a. the mean number of mosquito bites for the low body temperature group will be equal to the mean number of mosquito bites for the high body temperature group.
    b. the mean number of mosquito bites for the low body temperature group will be different from the mean number of mosquito bites for the high body temperature group.

Reading Question

11. The research hypothesis for the main effect of body temperature states that
    a. the mean number of mosquito bites for the low body temperature group will be equal to the mean number of mosquito bites for the high body temperature group.
    b. the mean number of mosquito bites for the low body temperature group will be different from the mean number of mosquito bites for the high body temperature group.

It is important to understand which two means are being compared by the main effect of body temperature. This main effect is comparing the mean for all participants in the study with a low body temperature with the mean for all participants with a high body temperature. These two means are not in the table and need to be computed. When there are the same number of participants in each cell of the design, the mean number of bites for participants with a low body temperature is the mean of the beer ($M = 9$) and placebo ($M = 7$) cell means for those with low body temperatures. The mean of 7 and 9 is 8, and so the mean number of mosquito bites for all participants in the low body temperature group is 8. This mean of the low-temperature cell means is typically written on the margin of the table, so it is referred to as a marginal mean (see Table 13.5).

Similarly, the mean number of bites for all participants with a high body temperature is the mean of the beer ($M = 16$) and placebo ($M = 10$) cell means for those with high body temperatures. In this case, the marginal mean is 13, and so the mean number of mosquito bites for all those with high body temperatures is 13.

Later, you will compute an F value to determine if the main effect of body temperature is statistically significant. In other words, you will determine if the difference between the marginal means of 8 bites and 13 bites is likely created by sampling error or not. If the difference is not likely to be created by sampling error, the mean difference was probably created by differences in body temperature.

Reading Question

12. To test for the main effect of body temperature, you will compute an _____ to determine if the marginal means of _____ and _____ are significantly different.
    a. F test; 9; 7
    b. F test; 8; 13

Table 13.5   Marginal means for the main effect of body temperature.

	Beer	Placebo	Marginal Means
Low temperature	9	7	8
High temperature	16	10	13

Step 1c: The Other Main Effect Null and Research Hypotheses for Alcohol Consumption

The last test is for the main effect of alcohol consumption on the number of mosquito bites. The null hypothesis for the main effect of alcohol consumption is that participants who drank beer and the placebo suffered the same number of mosquito bites. The research hypothesis is that participants who drank beer and the placebo received different numbers of mosquito bites. The symbolic and verbal representations of the hypotheses are given in Table 13.6.

Table 13.6	Symbolic and verbal representations of the research and null hypotheses for the main effect of alcohol consumption.	

	Symbolic	Verbal
Research hypothesis (H_1)	$H_1: \mu_1 \neq \mu_2$	The number of mosquito bites is not equal for the beer and the placebo groups.
Null hypothesis (H_0)	$H_0: \mu_1 = \mu_2$	The number of mosquito bites is equal for the beer and the placebo groups.

Reading Question

13. The null hypothesis for the main effect of alcohol consumption predicts that
   a. the mean number of mosquito bites for the beer group will be equal to the mean number of mosquito bites for the placebo group.
   b. the mean number of mosquito bites for the beer group will be different from the mean number of mosquito bites for the placebo group.

Reading Question

14. The research hypothesis for the main effect of alcohol consumption predicts that
   a. the mean number of mosquito bites for the beer group will be equal to the mean number of mosquito bites for the placebo group.
   b. the mean number of mosquito bites for the beer group will be different from the mean number of mosquito bites for the placebo group.

This main effect is comparing the mean for all participants in the study who drank beer with the mean for all participants who drank the placebo. As can be seen in Table 13.7, the marginal mean for all participants who drank beer is 12.5, the mean of 9 and 16, which were the cell means for the participants who drank beer. Similarly, the marginal mean for the participants who drank the placebo is 8.5, the mean of 7 and 10, which were the cell means for the participants who drank the placebo. Later, you will compute an F value to determine if the difference between 12.5 bites and 8.5 bites is statistically significant (i.e., if the difference is not likely to be caused by sampling error).

**Reading
Question**

15. Which two means are
    being compared when you
    compute the F test for the
    main effect of alcohol
    consumption?

    a. 9 and 7

    b. 12.5 and 8.5

Table 13.7	Marginal means for the main effect of alcohol consumption.	
	Beer	*Placebo*
Low temperature	9	7
High temperature	16	10
Marginal Means	**12.5**	**8.5**

Step 2: Define the Critical Regions

As you learned in the previous section,
the two-way ANOVA produces three F tests. Each test has its own critical region. To determine the critical regions for each test, you will need to compute the degrees of freedom
separately for each test. For this problem, we are going to use an alpha of .05. The F table
for an alpha of .05 is located in Appendix C.

Step 2a: Define the Critical Region for the Interaction Test

The df of the numerator and the df of the denominator of the F value determine the
critical value of every F test. It is easier to discuss dfs if we introduce a bit of notation.
Specifically, we will use a to indicate the number of levels of Factor A (body temperature),
b to indicate the number of levels of Factor B (alcohol consumption), and N to indicate the
number of people in the study.

The numerator df for the interaction is computed as $df_{A \times B} = (a - 1)(b - 1)$. In this case,
both factors have two levels, and so $df_{A \times B} = (2 - 1)(2 - 1) = 1$. The denominator df is
computed as $df_{error} = N - ab$. Thus, $df_{within} = 32 - (2)(2) = 28$. If you look in the table of
critical F values, you will find that the critical value of F with 1 and 28 degrees of
freedom is 4.20.

**Reading
Question**

16. If alcohol consumption had three levels (e.g., beer, wine, and placebo), the
    degrees of freedom for the numerator of the interaction would be

    a. 1.

    b. 2.

    c. 3.

Step 2b: Define the Critical Region for the First Main Effect Test
(Factor A, Body Temperature)

The numerator df for the main effect of body temperature is computed as $df_A = (a - 1)$.
Body temperature has two levels, so $df_A = 2 - 1 = 1$. The df for the denominator is the same
as it is for the interaction: $df_{within} = N - ab = 32 - (2)(2) = 28$. As before, the critical value of
F with 1 and 28 degrees of freedom is 4.20.

Reading
Question

17. If 40 people had participated in the study, the degrees of freedom for the denominator of the main effect of body temperature would be

 a. 40.

 b. 36.

 c. 42.

Step 2c: Define the Critical Region for the Second Main Effect Test (Factor B, Alcohol Consumption)

The numerator df for the main effect of alcohol consumption is computed as $df_B = (b - 1)$. Alcohol consumption has two levels, so $df_B = 2 - 1 = 1$. The df for the denominator is the same as it is for the interaction: $df_{within} = N - ab = 32 - (2)(2) = 28$. As before, the critical value of F with 1 and 28 degrees of freedom is 4.20.

Reading
Question

18. If alcohol consumption had three levels (e.g., beer, wine, and placebo), the degrees of freedom for the numerator of the main effect would be

 a. 1.

 b. 2.

 c. 3.

In this case, all three sets of dfs were identical. While it will always be the case that the denominator dfs are the same for all three tests, the numerator dfs will not always be the same. When Factor A and Factor B have a different number of levels, the numerator dfs will be different for the two main effect tests. Consequentially, when the factors have a different number of levels, the two main effect tests will have different critical values.

Step 3: Compute the Test Statistics (Three F Tests)

To determine if the three effects (i.e., the interaction and the two main effects) are statistically significant, you need to compute three F values. Although you could do these computations by hand, we will be doing these computations using SPSS. When you analyze the data in SPSS, you obtain an ANOVA summary table similar to the one displayed in Table 13.8. Table 13.9 includes the formulas used to obtain the df, MS (mean squares), and Fs. In future activities, we will work with the complete ANOVA summary table. For now, we will focus on interpreting the F values.

Step 3a: F Test for the Interaction

There are three F values in Table 13.8. The F value testing the interaction between body temperature and alcohol consumption is 5.90. Previously, we determined that the critical F value for the interaction is 4.20. The obtained F value of 5.90 is larger than the

Table 13.8   ANOVA source table for a two-way independent samples ANOVA.

Source	SS	df	MS	F
Between	360	3		
Temperature	200	1	200	36.84
Alcohol	128	1	128	23.58
Temperature × Alcohol	32	1	32	5.90
Within (Error)	152	28	5.43	
Total	512	31		

Table 13.9   Formulas for *df*, *MS*, and *F* for a two-way independent samples ANOVA.

Source	SS	df	MS	F
Between	360			
Temperature (A)	200	$a - 1$	$\dfrac{SS_A}{df_A}$	$\dfrac{MS_A}{MS_{within}}$
Alcohol (B)	128	$b - 1$	$\dfrac{SS_B}{df_B}$	$\dfrac{MS_B}{MS_{within}}$
Temperature × Alcohol (A × B)	32	$(a - 1)(b - 1)$	$\dfrac{SS_{A \times B}}{df_{A \times B}}$	$\dfrac{MS_{A \times B}}{MS_{within}}$
Within (Error)	152	$N - (a)(b)$	$\dfrac{SS_{within}}{df_{within}}$	
Total	512	$N - 1$		

critical *F* value, so we reject the interaction null hypothesis. This means that the different patterns of results we described for low and high body temperature participants are not likely to be due to sampling error. We will interpret this interaction in more detail when we summarize the results below. Appendix H describes hand calculations.

Step 3b: F Test for the First Main Effect (Body Temperature)

The F value for the main effect of body temperature is 36.84. The critical value of F for this main effect is 4.20. The obtained F is greater than the critical value, so we reject the body temperature null hypothesis and conclude that participants with a high body temperature ($M = 13$) received significantly more mosquito bites than participants with a low body temperature ($M = 8$).

Step 3c: F Test for the Second Main Effect (Alcohol Consumption)

The F value for the main effect of alcohol consumption is 23.58, and the critical value of F for this main effect is 4.20. The obtained F is greater than the critical value, so we reject the alcohol consumption null hypothesis and conclude that participants who drank alcohol ($M = 12.5$) received more bites than participants who drank the placebo ($M = 8.5$).

Reading Question

19. Which of the three effects were significant? Choose all that apply.
    a. Main effect of body temperature
    b. Main effect of alcohol consumption
    c. Interaction between body temperature and alcohol consumption

Step 4: Compute the Effect Sizes and Describe Them

Step 4a: Effect Size for the Interaction (Body Temperature by Alcohol Consumption)

Table 13.10	General guidelines for interpreting η_p^2.
η_p^2	*Estimated Size of the Effect*
Close to .01	Small
Close to .09	Medium
Close to .25	Large

After determining if each null hypothesis is rejected, the next step is computing an effect size for each test and describing each as small, medium, or large. Partial eta squared (η_p^2) measures the effect size of F values (Table 13.10).

We will start by computing the effect size for the interaction effect. The formula for computing the effect size of an interaction is given below:

$$\eta_p^2 = \frac{SS_{A \times B}}{SS_{A \times B} + SS_{within}} = \frac{32}{32 + 152} = .17$$

The SS_{within} is the SS from the denominator of the F ratio. The effect size for the interaction between body temperature and alcohol consumption is .17, which is a medium-large effect. It is important to note that partial eta squared is different from eta squared. The distinction between eta squared and partial eta squared is beyond the scope of this book. For now, you should know that partial eta squared is what is computed by SPSS. Using partial eta squared rather than the "classic" eta squared means that the eta-squared values from all three F tests can sometimes sum to more than 1.

20. When interpreting η_p^2, values close to _____ are considered large effect sizes.

    a. .01

    b. .25

    c. .09

Step 4b: Effect Size for the First Main Effect (Body Temperature)

The formula for computing the effect size for the main effect of body temperature is similar to the formula for computing the effect size for the interaction:

$$\eta_p^2 = \frac{SS_{body\ temp}}{SS_{body\ temp} + SS_{within}} = \frac{200}{200 + 152} = .57$$

The effect size is .57, which is a large effect.

Step 4c: Effect Size for the Second Main Effect (Alcohol Consumption)

The formula for computing the effect size for the main effect of alcohol consumption is given below:

$$\eta_p^2 = \frac{SS_{alcohol}}{SS_{alcohol} + SS_{within}} = \frac{128}{128 + 152} = .46$$

The effect size is .46, which is a large effect.

21. When computing the effect size for a two-way ANOVA,

    a. you will only need to compute one η_p^2 because the effect size will always be the same for all three F tests in a two-way ANOVA.

    b. you will have to compute a separate η_p^2 for each F test.

Step 5: Writing Up the Results of a Two-Way ANOVA

Students can find summarizing a two-way ANOVA daunting because there are three different significance tests and lots of statistical information that must be presented in a very specific format. However, there is a general format you can follow that should make writing the results easier.

General Format

1. Tell if the interaction was significant, and report the statistical information in the correct format.

2. If the interaction is significant, describe the interaction, using one sentence to describe the pattern of cell means for each level of the IV.

3. Tell if the first main effect was significant, and report the statistical information in the correct format.

4. If the first main effect was significant, describe which marginal mean(s) was (were) significantly higher.

5. Tell if the second main effect was significant, and report the statistical information in the correct format.

6. If the second main effect was significant, describe which marginal mean(s) was (were) significantly higher.

Specific Example

There was a significant interaction between body temperature and alcohol consumption: $F(1, 28) = 5.90$, $p = .02$, $MSE = 5.43$, $\eta_p^2 = .17$. The results indicate that participants with a low body temperature were bitten an average of 9 times ($M = 9.00$, $SD = 1.85$) after having beer and 7 times ($M = 7.00$, $SD = 2.00$) after having the placebo. Participants with a high body temperature were bitten an average of 16 times ($M = 16.00$, $SD = 3.30$) after having beer and 10 times ($M = 10.00$, $SD = 1.85$) after having the placebo. Although both groups were bitten more after drinking beer, the difference was larger for the high body temperature group than for the low body temperature group. There was also a significant main effect of body temperature: $F(1, 28) = 36.84$, $p < .001$, $\eta_p^2 = .57$. Overall, participants with a high body temperature ($M = 13.00$, $SD = 4.03$) were bitten more often than participants with a low body temperature ($M = 8.00$, $SD = 2.13$). Finally, there was a significant main effect of alcohol consumption: $F(1, 28) = 23.58$, $p < .001$, $\eta_p^2 = .46$. Participants were bitten more often after drinking beer ($M = 12.50$, $SD = 4.06$) than after drinking the placebo ($M = 8.50$, $SD = 2.42$).

SPSS

The following pages illustrate how to use SPSS to analyze the same "mosquito study" discussed throughout this chapter.

Data File

The SPSS data file should have three columns: one for the first IV (body temperature), one for the second IV (alcohol consumption), and one for the DV (number of mosquito bites). The body temperature and alcohol consumption variables are used to indicate which group each participant was in. In this file, we used a "1" to indicate that the person has a low body temperature and a "2" to indicate that the person has a high body temperature, but any two numbers can be used to label the two groups. For the alcohol consumption variable, we used a "0" to indicate that the person drank the placebo and a "1" to indicate that the person drank the beer. Your file should have 32 rows, one row for each person. The first eight people in our data file have a "1" and a "0" followed by their DV score. The next eight people have a "2" and a "0" followed by their DV score. The third group of eight people have a "1" and a "1" followed by their DV score. The final group of eight people have a "2" and a "1" followed by their DV score. The first 15 lines can be seen in Figure 13.1.

Reading Question

22. When entering the data for a two-way ANOVA, you will need two columns to indicate

a. which combination of IV conditions each participant was in.

b. each person's DV score.

Figure 13.1	SPSS screenshot of data entry screen.

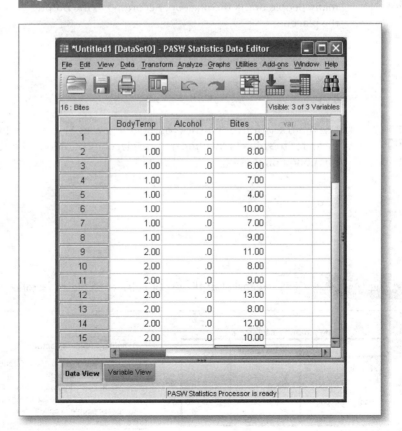

Obtaining a Two-Factor ANOVA

- Click on the Analyze menu. Choose General Linear Model, and then select Univariate.
- Move the DV into the Dependent Variable box.
- Move both IVs to the Fixed Factors box.
- Click on Options, and then click on Descriptive Statistics and Estimates of Effect Size.
- Click on Continue.
- You can also create graphs by clicking on the Plots button.

  To graph the interaction, choose one IV (i.e., grouping variable) to put on the horizontal axis and one IV to make separate lines for. Click Add and then Continue. In this case, we put body temperature on the horizontal axis and made separate lines for alcohol consumption.

- Click the OK button.

Annotated Output

Figures 13.2 to 13.5 show the output in SPSS.

Reading Question

23. Use the "Between-Subjects Factors" output (Figure 13.2) to determine how many people drank the placebo. According to the output, _____ people drank the placebo.

    a. 0

    b. 1

    c. 8

    d. 16

Reading Question

24. Use the "Descriptive Statistics" output (Figure 13.3) to determine the cell mean for the high body temperature, placebo condition. The cell mean for this condition was _____.

    a. 7

    b. 9

    c. 10

    d. 16

| Figure 13.2 | SPSS screenshot of the list of between-subjects factors. |

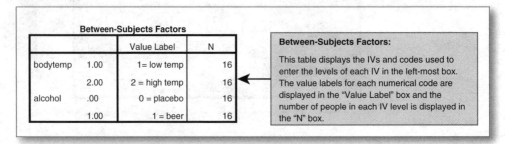

Between-Subjects Factors

		Value Label	N
bodytemp	1.00	1= low temp	16
	2.00	2 = high temp	16
alcohol	.00	0 = placebo	16
	1.00	1 = beer	16

Between-Subjects Factors:

This table displays the IVs and codes used to enter the levels of each IV in the left-most box. The value labels for each numerical code are displayed in the "Value Label" box and the number of people in each IV level is displayed in the "N" box.

Figure 13.3   SPSS screenshot of the list of descriptive statistics.

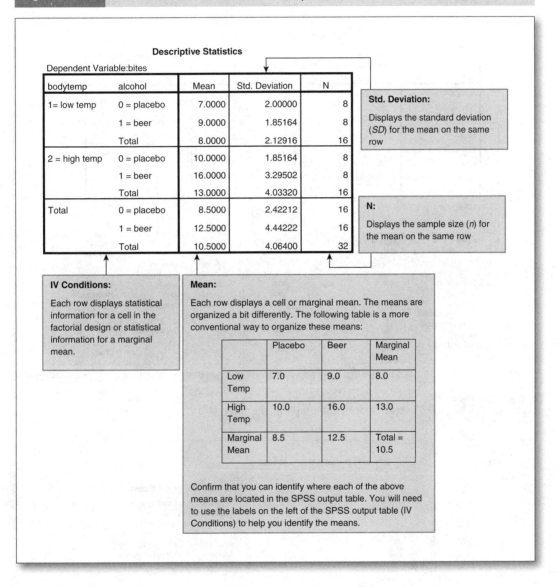

Descriptive Statistics

Dependent Variable:bites

bodytemp	alcohol	Mean	Std. Deviation	N
1= low temp	0 = placebo	7.0000	2.00000	8
	1 = beer	9.0000	1.85164	8
	Total	8.0000	2.12916	16
2 = high temp	0 = placebo	10.0000	1.85164	8
	1 = beer	16.0000	3.29502	8
	Total	13.0000	4.03320	16
Total	0 = placebo	8.5000	2.42212	16
	1 = beer	12.5000	4.44222	16
	Total	10.5000	4.06400	32

Std. Deviation:

Displays the standard deviation (*SD*) for the mean on the same row

N:

Displays the sample size (*n*) for the mean on the same row

IV Conditions:

Each row displays statistical information for a cell in the factorial design or statistical information for a marginal mean.

Mean:

Each row displays a cell or marginal mean. The means are organized a bit differently. The following table is a more conventional way to organize these means:

	Placebo	Beer	Marginal Mean
Low Temp	7.0	9.0	8.0
High Temp	10.0	16.0	13.0
Marginal Mean	8.5	12.5	Total = 10.5

Confirm that you can identify where each of the above means are located in the SPSS output table. You will need to use the labels on the left of the SPSS output table (IV Conditions) to help you identify the means.

Reading Question

25. Use the "Tests of Between-Subjects Effects" output (Figure 13.4) to determine the p value for the interaction. The p value for the interaction between body temperature and alcohol consumption was _____.

a. .174

b. .022

c. .000

Figure 13.4 SPSS screenshot of the list of ANOVA source tables.

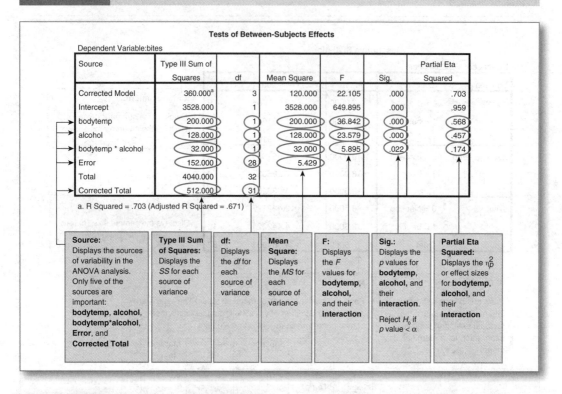

Tests of Between-Subjects Effects

Dependent Variable:bites

Source	Type III Sum of Squares	df	Mean Square	F	Sig.	Partial Eta Squared
Corrected Model	360.000[a]	3	120.000	22.105	.000	.703
Intercept	3528.000	1	3528.000	649.895	.000	.959
bodytemp	200.000	1	200.000	36.842	.000	.568
alcohol	128.000	1	128.000	23.579	.000	.457
bodytemp * alcohol	32.000	1	32.000	5.895	.022	.174
Error	152.000	28	5.429			
Total	4040.000	32				
Corrected Total	512.000	31				

a. R Squared = .703 (Adjusted R Squared = .671)

Source: Displays the sources of variability in the ANOVA analysis. Only five of the sources are important: **bodytemp, alcohol, bodytemp*alcohol, Error,** and **Corrected Total**	**Type III Sum of Squares:** Displays the *SS* for each source of variance	**df:** Displays the *df* for each source of variance	**Mean Square:** Displays the *MS* for each source of variance	**F:** Displays the *F* values for **bodytemp, alcohol,** and their **interaction**	**Sig.:** Displays the *p* values for **bodytemp, alcohol,** and their **interaction**. Reject H_0 if *p* value $< \alpha$	**Partial Eta Squared:** Displays the η_p^2 or effect sizes for **bodytemp, alcohol,** and their **interaction**

Figure 13.5 SPSS screenshot of the graph of the interaction.

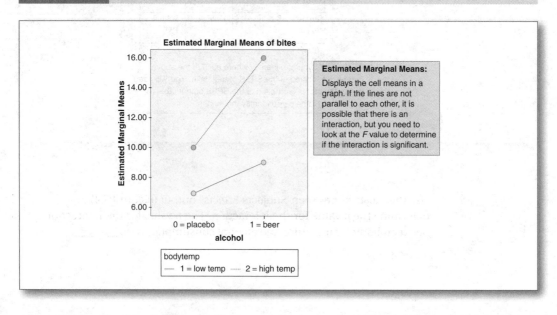

Estimated Marginal Means of bites

(y-axis: Estimated Marginal Means — 6.00, 8.00, 10.00, 12.00, 14.00, 16.00)
(x-axis: alcohol — 0 = placebo, 1 = beer)

bodytemp
— 1 = low temp
---- 2 = high temp

Estimated Marginal Means: Displays the cell means in a graph. If the lines are not parallel to each other, it is possible that there is an interaction, but you need to look at the *F* value to determine if the interaction is significant.

When reporting the statistical information in APA format, you will need to extract the needed numbers from the "Tests of Between-Subjects Effects" output (Figure 13.4). The correct format for a main effect is $F(df_{body\ temp}, df_{within})$ = obtained F value, p value, η_p^2 value. Therefore, the correct way to write the statistical information for the main effect of body temperature is as follows: $F(1, 28) = 36.84, p < .001, MSE = 5.43, \eta_p^2 = .57$.

Reading
Question

26. Use the "Tests of Between-Subjects Effects" output (Figure 13.4) to determine which of the following is the correct statistical information for the interaction between body temperature and alcohol consumption:

    a. $F(1, 28) = 23.58, p < .001, MSE = 5.43, \eta_p^2 = .46$
    b. $F(1, 28) = 5.90, p = .02, MSE = 5.43, \eta_p^2 = .17$

Activity 13-1:   Using SPSS to Conduct Two-Factor ANOVAs

Learning Objectives

After reading the chapter and completing this activity, you should be able to do the following:

- Identify the main effects and the interaction effect produced by a two-way ANOVA
- Identify the null hypotheses for both main effects and the interaction effect
- Use SPSS to compute and then interpret a two-way independent ANOVA
- Create graphs representing the main effects and the interaction of a two-way ANOVA
- Clearly summarize the results of a two-factor ANOVA for a lay audience

GENDER AND EXERCISE EXAMPLE

A sports psychologist is interested in the effects of different types of exercise on muscle gain for males and females. Male and female college students are randomly assigned to participate in weight training classes three times a week or yoga classes three times a week. After 6 months, the amount of muscle (in pounds) each participant gained was recorded. Thus, there are two IVs, each having two levels: gender (male or female) and type of exercise program (weight training or yoga). The DV is the amount of muscle gained in pounds. The 2×2 table below may help you visualize the four conditions of this 2×2 factorial design:

		Gender	
		Male	Female
Type of exercise	Weight training		
	Yoga		

Three Significance Tests Generated by Factorial ANOVA

1. The 2 × 2 factorial design described above will yield three significance tests. In the list below, circle the three significance tests that the above design will produce.

   a. The main effect of weight training

   b. The main effect of yoga

   c. The main effect of exercise

   d. The main effect of male

   e. The main effect of female

   f. The main effect of gender

   g. The interaction between weight training and gender

   h. The interaction between yoga and female

   i. The interaction between exercise and gender

Three Null Hypotheses Tested by Factorial ANOVA

2. Each of the three significance tests produced by two-factor designs has its own null hypothesis. For each of the significance tests produced by this 2 × 2 design, identify the correct null hypothesis. Write the letter of the correct null from the list below for each test in the blank provided.

   Test 1. Main effect of gender: _____.

   Test 2. Main effect of exercise: _____.

   Test 3. Interaction between gender and exercise: _____.

   a. Yoga and weight training will produce equal amounts of muscle gain.

   b. Males lifting weights will gain the same amount of muscle as females lifting weights.

   c. Males and females will gain equal amounts of muscle.

   d. The type of exercise that produces the most muscle gain will not differ for males and females.

   e. Females practicing yoga will gain equal amounts of muscle as males lifting weights.

Data Entry

The number of pounds of muscle gained by each person who participated in each condition of this experiment is listed below:

Males assigned to weight training:	9, 6, 7, 6, 3, 8, 7, 8, 4, 11
Females assigned to weight training:	3, 5, 4, 6, 2, 1, 4, 3, 2, 5
Males assigned to yoga:	3, 6, 4, 4, 5, 3, 1, 4, 5, 5
Females assigned to yoga:	2, 3, 4, 3, 1, 6, 7, 2, 1, 2

Enter these data into SPSS. Be sure that you create three columns: one for each IV (gender and exercise type) and one for the DV (muscle gained). You will have to use a coding system for each IV. For example, for exercise type, you might enter a "1" for weight training and a "2" for yoga. For gender, you might enter "1" for male and "2" for female.

Value Labels

It would also be a good idea to create value labels, using the following steps:

- Click on the Variable View tab at the bottom of your screen.
- Click on the cell across from the Exercise Program variable in the Values column.
- Enter a "1" in the Value box, and type a label, such as "Weight Training," in the Label box. Click the Add button.
- Enter a "2" in the Value box, and type a label, such as Yoga, in the Label box. Click "Add" and then "OK."
- Repeat this procedure for the gender variable.

Running a Two-Way ANOVA

Run a two-way ANOVA by doing the following:

- Click on the Analyze menu. Choose General Linear Model, and then select Univariate.
- Move the DV into the Dependent box, and move the IV into the Fixed Factors box.
- Click on Options, and then click on Descriptives and Estimates of Effect Size.
- Click Continue.
- Click on Plot, and move one IV onto the horizontal axis and the other into the Separate Lines box.
- Click Add, click Continue, and then click OK.

Interpreting a Two-Way ANOVA

3. Find the cell and marginal means in the SPSS output, and record them below:

		Gender	
		Male	Female
Exercise program	Weight training		
	Yoga		

4. Graph the main effect of gender using a bar graph. (*Hint:* You need to graph the marginal means for males and females.)

5. First choose one of the following sentences as the correct APA-style reporting statement, and then fill in the blanks for the main effect of gender.

   a. The main effect of gender was significant, indicating that males gained more muscle ($M =$ _____, $SD =$ _____) than females ($M =$_____, $SD =$ _____), $F($___, ___$) =$ _____, $p =$ _____, $MSE =$ _____, $\eta_p^2 =$ _____.

   b. The main effect of gender was not significant, indicating that males ($M =$ _____, $SD =$ _____) and females ($M =$_____, $SD =$ _____) gained similar amounts of muscle, $F($___, ___$) =$ _____, $p =$ _____, $MSE =$ _____, $\eta_p^2 =$ _____.

6. Graph the main effect of exercise. (*Hint:* You need to use the marginal means for yoga and weight training.)

7. *First choose* one of the following sentences as the correct APA-style reporting statement, and then fill in the blanks for the main effect of exercise:

   a. The main effect of exercise was significant, revealing that those who lifted weights ($M =$ _____, $SD =$ _____) gained more muscle than those who did yoga ($M =$ _____, $SD =$ _____), $F($___, ___$) =$ _____, $p =$ _____, $MSE =$ _____, $\eta_p^2 =$ _____.

   b. The main effect of exercise was not significant, revealing that those who lifted weights ($M =$ _____, $SD =$ _____) and those who did yoga ($M =$ _____, $SD =$ _____) gained similar amounts of muscle, $F ($___, ___$) =$ _____, $p =$ _____, $MSE =$ _____, $\eta_p^2 =$ _____.

8. Create a line graph of the gender × exercise program interaction below. (*Hint:* You need to use the four cell means. Put one variable on the x-axis, and use separate lines to represent the different levels of the other IV.)

9. To interpret an interaction, you need to look at the *simple effects*. For example, in this study the interaction was significant, indicating that there was a different pattern of results for men and for women. To describe the differing results for men and women, we compute the simple effects. The simple effect for women is computed for you below. Compute the simple effect for men.

   Women: $M_{\text{weight training}} - M_{\text{wyoga}} = 3.5 - 3.1 = .4$

   Men: $M_{\text{weight training}} - M_{\text{wyoga}} =$ ___ $-$ ___ $=$ ___

There are ways to test whether each simple effect is statistically significant. Unfortunately, simple effects cannot be computed via the point-and-click menus in SPSS. To compute simple effects, you must either do them by hand or use the syntax method in SPSS. The syntax method is described in Appendix I.

10. *First choose* one of the following sentences as the correct reporting statement, and then fill in the blanks for the interaction between gender and exercise type.

   a. There was a significant interaction between gender and type of exercise, $F(\_\_\_, \_\_\_) = _____$, $p = _____$, $MSE = \_\_\_\_\_$, $\eta_p^2 = _____$. The results indicated that females who weight trained ($M = _____$, $SD = _____$) gained 0.4 more pounds of muscle than women who practiced yoga ($M = _____$, $SD = _____$). Men who weight trained ($M = _____$, $SD = _____$) gained 2.9 more pounds of muscle than men who practiced yoga ($M = _____$, $SD = _____$). These results indicate that weight training produced only slightly more muscle gain than yoga for women. However, weight training produced significantly more muscle gain than yoga for men.

   b. The interaction between gender and type of exercise was not significant, $F(\_\_\_, \_\_\_\_) = _____$, $p = _____$, $MSE = \_\_\_\_\_$, $\eta_p^2 = _____$.

Reporting an Interaction

Note how when describing a significant interaction the researcher pointed out the different patterns of results for males and females. This difference between males and females is the key point that *must* be described.

Goal of Statistics

The point here is that statistics are intended to help discover or explain relationships. It is not enough to "get the numbers and report them." Your goal should be to get the numbers and then communicate *what the numbers mean* to your reader.

11. What is the point of statistics?

   a. To get the numbers

   b. To get the numbers and then communicate what they mean to the reader

DATING WEBSITE EXAMPLE

Below is the output from a completely different two-way ANOVA. This experiment looked at the type of ads people place on dating websites. Specifically, the study looked at the number of times people refer to their potential partner's income in the personal ads as the DV. The first IV was gender (levels were male and female). The second IV was sexual orientation (levels were homosexual and heterosexual). Use the output to answer the following questions.

Between–Subjects Factors

		Value Label	N
Gender	1.00	male	12
	2.00	female	12
SexualOrientation	1.00	homosexual	12
	2.00	heterosexual	12

Descriptive Statistics

Dependent Variable: Income

Gender	SexualOrientation	Mean	Std. Deviation	N
male	homosexual	1.0000	.63246	6
	heterosexual	1.1667	.75277	6
	Total	1.0833	.66856	12
female	homosexual	2.1667	.75277	6
	heterosexual	4.5000	1.04881	6
	Total	3.3333	1.49747	12
Total	homosexual	1.5833	.90034	12
	heterosexual	2.8333	1.94625	12
	Total	2.2083	1.61458	24

Tests of Between–Subjects Effects

Dependent Variable: Status

Source	Type III Sum of Squares	df	Mean Square	F	Sig.	Partial Eta Squared
Corrected Model	46.792[a]	3	15.597	23.692	.000	.780
Intercept	117.042	1	117.042	177.785	.000	.899
Gender	30.375	1	30.375	46.139	.000	.698
SexualOrientation	9.375	1	9.375	14.241	.001	.416
Gender * SexualOrientation	7.042	1	7.042	10.696	.004	.348
Error	13.167	20	.658			
Total	177.000	24				
Corrected Total	59.958	23				

a. R Squared = .780 (Adjusted R Squared = .747)

12. Identify the three significance tests produced by this 2 × 2 factorial design. Then write the null hypothesis for each of these tests.

    Test 1: Main effect of _____;
    Null

Test 2: Main effect of _____;
Null

Test 3: Interaction effect of _____ and _____;
Null

13. Graph both main effects (you will need to make two different graphs).

14. Graph the gender × sexual orientation interaction below.

15. Compute the simple effects for men and women.

16. Summarize the results of this study using APA style. For each effect that is significant, you need to provide details.

    A two-factor ANOVA was conducted with _____ as one factor, _____ as the other factor, and the number of times income was mentioned in personal ads as the DV. There was a significant interaction between gender and sexual orientation, $F(\underline{\hspace{1cm}}, \underline{\hspace{1cm}}) = \underline{\hspace{1cm}}, p = \underline{\hspace{1cm}}$, $MSE = \underline{\hspace{1cm}}, \eta_p^2 = \underline{\hspace{1cm}}$.

    Describe the pattern of results here. Be sure to give means and standard deviations for all four cells and discuss the simple effects. Specifically, talk about the difference between heterosexual and homosexual ads for men, and then talk about this same difference for women. Finally, be clear how the effect of sexual orientation was different for men and women.

There was also a significant main effect of gender, $F($ _____, _____$) = $ _____, $p = $ _____, $MSE = $ _____, $\eta_p^2 = $ _____.

Describe the pattern of results here. Be sure to give the means and standard deviations for men and women and indicate which gender mentioned income more often.

Finally, there was a significant main effect of sexual orientation, $F($ _____, _____$) = $ _____, $p = $ _____, $MSE = $ _____, $\eta_p^2 = $ _____.

Describe the pattern of results here. Be sure to give the means and standard deviations for heterosexuals and homosexuals and indicate if heterosexuals or homosexuals mentioned income more often.

Activity 13-2:   Writing Results for Two-Factor ANOVAs

SCENARIO 1: GUIDED WRITING RESULTS EXAMPLE

A researcher wants to determine if Drug A or Drug B is more effective for improving memory in men and women. A sample of 32 people (16 males and 16 females) were given either Drug A or Drug B, followed by a memory test. The SPSS output is given below:

Descriptive Statistics

Dependent Variable:MemoryScore

Gender	Drug	Mean	Std. Deviation	N
male	A	19.6250	2.32609	8
	B	16.7500	1.98206	8
	Total	18.1875	2.56174	16
female	A	17.1250	2.23207	8
	B	19.8750	2.23207	8
	Total	18.5000	2.58199	16
Total	A	18.3750	2.55278	16
	B	18.3125	2.60048	16
	Total	18.3438	2.53504	32

Tests of Between Subjects Effects

Dependent Variable:MemoryScore

Source	Type III Sum of Squares	df	Mean Square	F	Sig.	Partial Eta Squared
Corrected Model	64.094[a]	3	21.365	4.427	.011	.322
Intercept	10767.781	1	10767.781	2231.252	.000	.988
Gender	.781	1	.781	.162	.690	.006
Drug	.031	1	.031	.006	.936	.000
Gender * Drug	63.281	1	63.281	13.113	.001	.319
Error	135.125	28	4.826			
Total	10967.000	32				
Corrected Total	199.219	31				

a. R Squared = .322 (Adjusted R Squared = .249)

1. Insert the means and standard deviations into the following table:

	Male M (SD)	Female M (SD)
Drug A	_____ (_____)	_____ (_____)
Drug B	_____ (_____)	_____ (_____)

2. Record the statistics for the gender × drug interaction using APA style:

$F(\underline{\hspace{1cm}}, \underline{\hspace{1cm}}) = \underline{\hspace{1cm}}, p = \underline{\hspace{1cm}}, \eta_p^2 = \underline{\hspace{1cm}}, MSE = \underline{\hspace{1cm}}.$

3. Compute the simple effect for males across Drug A and Drug B. Then compute the simple effect for females across Drug A and Drug B.

4. Which of the following is the *best* description of this interaction?

   a. Women had higher scores on the memory test than men. In addition, Drug A was more effective than Drug B.

   b. Women who took Drug B had higher scores on the memory test than women who took Drug A. The pattern of results was the opposite for men. Men who took Drug B had lower scores on the memory test than men who took Drug A.

5. Record the statistics for the gender main effect using APA style:

$F(\underline{\hspace{1cm}}, \underline{\hspace{1cm}}) = \underline{\hspace{1cm}}, p = \underline{\hspace{1cm}}, \eta_p^2 = \underline{\hspace{1cm}}, MSE = \underline{\hspace{1cm}}.$

6. Record the means and standard deviations for the two means being compared by the *F* value above:

   Females (*M* = _____, *SD* = _____); Males (*M* = _____, *SD* = _____).

7. Summarize the results of this main effect.

8. Record the statistics for the drug main effect using APA style:

   F(_____, _____) = _____, *p* = _____, η_p^2 = _____, *MSE* = _____.

9. Record the means and standard deviations for the two means being compared by the *F* value above:

   Drug A (*M* = _____, *SD* = _____); Drug B (*M* = _____, *SD* = _____).

10. Summarize the results of this main effect.

11. Questions 1 to 9 include all of the information necessary for constructing an APA-style write-up of these analyses. An example of a write-up is included below so that you can see how each part relates to the overall summary. In the boxes to the left, indicate which questions each section came from.

This information came from questions _____ through _____.	There was a significant interaction between gender and drug treatment, *F*(1, 28) = 13.11, *p* = .001, η_p^2 = .32, *MSE* = 4.83. Women who took Drug B (*M* = 19.88, *SD* = 2.23) had scores on the memory test that were 2.75 higher than the scores for women who took Drug A (*M* = 17.13, *SD* = 2.23). The pattern of results was the opposite for men. Men who took Drug B (*M* = 16.75, *SD* = 1.98) had scores on the memory test that were 2.88 lower than those for men who took Drug A (*M* = 19.63, *SD* = 2.32).
This information came from questions _____ through _____.	The main effect of gender was not statistically significant, *F*(1, 28) = 0.16, *p* = .69, η_p^2 = .01, *MSE* = 4.83. Memory test scores for males (*M* = 18.19, *SD* = 2.56) were not significantly different from scores for females (*M* = 18.50, *SD* = 2.58).
This information came from questions _____ through _____.	Finally, the main effect of drug was not statistically significant, *F*(1, 28) = 0.01, *p* = .94, η_p^2 = .00, *MSE* = 4.83. Memory test scores for people taking Drug A (*M* = 18.38, *SD* = 2.55) were not significantly different from scores for people taking Drug B (*M* = 18.31, *SD* = 2.60).

SCENARIO 2: GUIDED WRITING RESULTS EXAMPLE

A researcher wants to determine if Drug A or Drug B is more effective for improving memory in men and women. A sample of 32 people (16 males and 16 females) were given either Drug A or Drug B, followed by a memory test. The SPSS output is given below:

Descriptive Statistics

Dependent Variable:MemoryScore

Gender	Drug	Mean	Std. Deviation	N
male	A	19.6250	2.32609	8
	B	15.7500	1.98206	8
	Total	17.6875	2.89180	16
female	A	20.3750	1.92261	8
	B	19.8750	2.23207	8
	Total	20.1250	2.02896	16
Total	A	20.0000	2.09762	16
	B	17.8125	2.94887	16
	Total	18.9063	2.75165	32

Tests of Between–Subjects Effects

Dependent Variable:MemoryScore

Source	Type III Sum of Squares	df	Mean Square	F	Sig.	Partial Eta Squared
Corrected Model	108.594[a]	3	36.198	8.036	.001	.463
Intercept	11438.281	1	11438.281	2539.321	.000	.989
Gender	47.531	1	47.531	10.552	.003	.274
Drug	38.281	1	38.281	8.499	.007	.233
Gender * Drug	22.781	1	22.781	5.057	.033	.153
Error	126.125	28	4.504			
Total	11673.000	32				
Corrected Total	234.719	31				

a. R Squared = .463 (Adjusted R Squared = .405)

12. Insert the means and standard deviations into the following table:

	Male M (SD)	Female M (SD)
Drug A	_____ (_____)	_____ (_____)
Drug B	_____ (_____)	_____ (_____)

13. Record the statistics for the gender × drug interaction using APA style:

$F($_____, _____$) = $_____, $p = $_____, $\eta_p^2 = $_____, $MSE = $_____.

14. Compute the simple effect for males across Drug A and Drug B. Then compute the simple effect for females across Drug A and Drug B.

15. Which of the following is the *best* description of this interaction?

    a. Both men and women who took Drug A had higher scores on the memory test than those who took Drug B.

    b. Women who took Drug A had higher scores on the memory test than women who took Drug B. Men who took Drug A had higher scores on the memory test than men who took Drug B.

    c. Women who took Drug A had scores on the memory test that were 0.5 higher than the scores for women who took Drug B. Men who took Drug A had scores on the memory test that were 3.88 higher than those for men who took Drug B.

16. Record the statistics for the gender main effect using APA style:

    $F(\underline{\hspace{1cm}}, \underline{\hspace{1cm}}) = \underline{\hspace{1cm}}, p = \underline{\hspace{1cm}}, \eta_p^2 = \underline{\hspace{1cm}}, MSE = \underline{\hspace{1cm}}.$

17. Record the means and standard deviations for the two means being compared by the F value above:

    Females ($M = \underline{\hspace{1cm}}, SD = \underline{\hspace{1cm}}$); Males ($M = \underline{\hspace{1cm}}, SD = \underline{\hspace{1cm}}$).

18. Summarize the results of this main effect.

19. Record the statistics for the drug main effect using APA style:

    $F(\underline{\hspace{1cm}}, \underline{\hspace{1cm}}) = \underline{\hspace{1cm}}, p = \underline{\hspace{1cm}}, \eta_p^2 = \underline{\hspace{1cm}}, MSE = \underline{\hspace{1cm}}.$

20. Record the means and standard deviations for the two means being compared by the F value above:

    Drug A ($M = \underline{\hspace{1cm}}, SD = \underline{\hspace{1cm}}$); Drug B ($M = \underline{\hspace{1cm}}, SD = \underline{\hspace{1cm}}$).

21. Summarize the results of this main effect.

22. Complete the APA-style summary below:

The information in this section comes from Questions 11–13 above	There was a significant interaction between gender and drug treatment, $F(1, 28) = 5.06$, $p = .03$, $MSE = 4.50$, $\eta_p^2 = .15$.

The information in this section comes from Questions 14–16 above	The main effect of gender was also statistically significant, $F(1, 28) = 10.55$, $p = .003$, $MSE = 4.50$, $\eta_p^2 = .27$.

The information in this section comes from Questions 17–20 above	Finally, the main effect of drug was significant, $F(1, 28) = 8.50$, $p = .007$, $MSE = 4.50$, $\eta_p^2 = .23$.

SCENARIO 3: GUIDED WRITING RESULTS EXAMPLE

A researcher wants to determine if Drug A or Drug B is more effective for improving memory in men and women. A sample of 32 people (16 males and 16 females) were given either Drug A or Drug B, followed by a memory test. The SPSS output is given below:

Descriptive Statistics

Dependent Variable:MemoryScore

Gender	Drug	Mean	Std. Deviation	N
male	A	19.5000	2.44949	8
	B	15.3750	1.68502	8
	Total	17.4375	2.94321	16
female	A	20.3750	1.92261	8
	B	17.0000	2.00000	8
	Total	18.6875	2.57472	16
Total	A	19.9375	2.17466	16
	B	16.1875	1.97379	16
	Total	18.0625	2.79328	32

(Continued)

(Continued)

Tests of Between–Subjects Effects

Dependent Variable:MemoryScore

Source	Type III Sum of Squares	df	Mean Square	F	Sig.	Partial Eta Squared
Corrected Model	126.125^a	3	42.042	10.170	.000	.521
Intercept	10440.125	1	10440.125	2525.473	.000	.989
Gender	12.500	1	12.500	3.024	.093	.097
Drug	112.500	1	112.500	27.214	.000	.493
Gender * Drug	1.125	1	1.125	.272	.606	.010
Error	115.750	28	4.134			
Total	10682.000	32				
Corrected Total	241.875	31				

a. R Squared = .521 (Adjusted R Squared = .470)

23. Insert the means and standard deviations into the following table:

	Male M (SD)	Female M (SD)
Drug A	_____ (_____)	_____ (_____)
Drug B	_____ (_____)	_____ (_____)

24. Record the statistics for the gender × drug interaction using APA style:

$F(\underline{\hspace{1cm}}, \underline{\hspace{1cm}}) = \underline{\hspace{1cm}}, p = \underline{\hspace{1cm}}, \eta_p^2 = \underline{\hspace{1cm}}, MSE = \underline{\hspace{1cm}}.$

25. Compute the simple effects for males across Drug A and Drug B. Then compute the simple effects for females across Drug A and Drug B.

26. Which of the following is the *best* description of this interaction?

   a. Women had higher scores on the memory test than men. In addition, Drug A was more effective than Drug B.

   b. Women who took Drug B had higher scores on the memory test than women who took Drug A. The pattern of results was the opposite for men. Men who took Drug B had lower scores on the memory test than men who took Drug A.

   c. Drug A and Drug B affected the memory scores of males and females in similar ways (i.e., there was no interaction between drug type and gender).

27. Record the statistics for the gender main effect using APA style:

$F(\underline{\hspace{1cm}}, \underline{\hspace{1cm}}) = \underline{\hspace{1cm}}, p = \underline{\hspace{1cm}}, MSE = \underline{\hspace{1cm}}, \eta_p^2 = \underline{\hspace{1cm}}.$

28. Record the means and standard deviations for the two means being compared by the F value above:
   Females ($M =$ _____, $SD =$ _____); Males ($M =$ _____, $SD =$ _____).

29. Summarize the results of this main effect.

30. Record the statistics for the drug main effect using APA style:
   $F($ _____, _____$) =$ _____, $p =$ _____, $MSE =$ _____, $\eta_p^2 =$ _____.

31. Record the means and standard deviations for the two means being compared by the F value above:
   Drug A ($M =$ _____, $SD =$ _____); Drug B ($M =$ _____, $SD =$ _____).

32. Summarize the results of this main effect.

33. Complete the APA-style summary below:

| The information in this section comes from Questions 22–24 above | The interaction between gender and drug treatment was not significant, $F(1, 28) = 0.27$, $p = .61$, $MSE = 4.13$, $\eta_p^2 = .01$. |

| The information in this section comes from Questions 25–27 above | The main effect of gender was also not significant, $F(1, 28) = 3.02$, $p = .09$, $MSE = 4.13$, $\eta_p^2 = .10$. |

The information in this section comes from Questions 28–31 above

Finally, the main effect of drug was significant, $F(1, 28) = 27.21$, $p < .001$, $MSE = 4.50$, $\eta_p^2 = .49$.

Activity 13-3: Simple Effects in Two-Factor ANOVAs

Learning Objectives

After reading the chapter and completing this activity, you should be able to do the following:

- Read a description of an experimental study and identify the IV, its levels, and the DV
- Create a 2 × 2 table that describes a specific factorial design
- Write the null hypotheses for a specific factorial design
- Determine if each null hypothesis should be rejected
- Write a summary of the results of a factorial design

The following scenarios are based on an actual study conducted by Langer, Holzner, Magnet, and Kopp (2005). In all the scenarios described below, the participants operated driving simulators under various conditions. In all the scenarios, the DV was the time it took the participants to step on the simulator's brake pedal (called reaction time). It is worth pointing out that if a driver's reaction time slows by even a fraction of a second, it could result in a deadly accident. Therefore, any driving condition that significantly slows drivers' reaction times is potentially dangerous. The data in this activity are consistent with the data presented by Langer et al. (2005).

SCENARIO 1: ALCOHOL AND DRIVING EXPERIENCE

The researchers recruited 40 drivers. Half the drivers drove a high-fidelity driving simulator after consuming a "low dose" of alcohol (i.e., 4–5 g per 100 ml blood), and half had not consumed any alcohol. *Additionally*, half the participants *in each of these conditions* had "high driving experience" (i.e., more than 50,000 km), and half had "low driving experience" (i.e., less than 50,000 km). The DV was the drivers' reaction time to a stimulus presented in their peripheral vision. Obviously, longer reaction times indicate *worse* performance.

1. What are the IVs? What are the levels of each IV?

IV 1: Alcohol consumption: Level 1 = _____, Level 2 = _____.

IV 2: _____: Level 1 = _____, Level 2 = _____.

2. Use your answers to the previous question to label all of the conditions (i.e., cells) included in the factorial design described above. In other words, use the 2 × 2 below to create a table that will display the cell and marginal means for this study.

IV 1: _____

Level 1: _____   Level 2: _____

Level 1: _____

IV 2: _____

Level 2: _____

3. How many people are there in *each cell* (i.e., condition) of this design?

You should have created a 2 (driver experience: high or low) × 2 (alcohol consumption: alcohol or no alcohol) factorial design. The following are cell mean reaction times and standard deviations from the Langer et al. (2005) study. Place them in the appropriate cells of the table you created above.

	Mean (SD)
Those drivers with high driving experience who had no alcohol	0.70 (0.19)
Those drivers with low driving experience who had no alcohol	0.82 (0.18)
Those drivers with high driving experience who had alcohol	0.89 (0.14)
Those drivers with low driving experience who had alcohol	1.17 (0.25)

4. Compute the marginal means for the main effect of driving experience and the marginal means for the main effect of alcohol, and include them in the table you created above.

Null Hypotheses

5. What was the null hypothesis for the *interaction* between driving experience and alcohol consumption?

   a. The reaction times of those with high and low driving experience will be affected by alcohol in similar ways.

b. The reaction times of those who drank alcohol and those who did not will be similar.

c. The reaction times of those with high and low driving experience will be similar.

d. All of the above are correct.

6. An interaction tests if the effect of one IV depends on the level of the other IV. For this example, an interaction would test if the effect of alcohol depends on whether the participants had low or high driving experience. Thus, the interaction is testing whether the mean differences between the alcohol and no-alcohol conditions are different for drivers with low experience and drivers with high experience.

a. What is the difference between the alcohol and no-alcohol condition for low driving experience?

_____ – _____ = _____ (This is called a *simple effect*.)

b. What is the difference between the alcohol and no-alcohol condition for high driving experience?

_____ – _____ = _____ (This is called a *simple effect*.)

The interaction is testing to see if these two simple effects are significantly different. If they are, there is a significant interaction.

7. What was the null hypothesis for the main effect of driving experience?

a. The reaction times of those with high and low driving experience will be affected by alcohol in similar ways.

b. The reaction times of those who drank alcohol and those who did not will be the same.

c. The reaction times of those with high and low driving experience will be the same.

d. All of the above are correct.

8. Which marginal means are being compared for the main effect of driving experience?

9. What was the null hypothesis for the main effect of alcohol consumption?

a. The reaction times of those with high and low driving experience will be affected by alcohol in similar ways.

b. The reaction times of those who drank alcohol and those who did not will be the same.

c. The reaction times of those with high and low driving experience will be the same.

d. All of the above are correct.

10. Which marginal means are being compared for the main effect of alcohol consumption?

Reporting Results

11. The obtained F value for the *interaction between driving experience and alcohol consumption* was $F(1, 36) = 8.90$, $p < .05$, $\eta_p^2 = .32$. Should you reject the null hypothesis and say that there is a significant interaction?

    a. Yes, because the p value was less than alpha.

    b. No, because the p value was greater than alpha.

12. The obtained F value for the *main effect of driving experience* was $F(1, 36) = 2.10$, $p > .05$, $\eta_p^2 = .09$. Should you reject the null hypothesis and say that there is a significant main effect for driving experience?

    a. Yes, because the p value was less than alpha.

    b. No, because the p value was greater than alpha.

13. The obtained F value for the *main effect of alcohol consumption* was $F(1, 36) = 5.30$, $p < .05$, $\eta_p^2 = .18$. Should you reject the null hypothesis and say that there is a significant main effect for alcohol consumption?

    a. Yes, because the p value was less than alpha.

    b. No, because the p value was greater than alpha.

Now that you know the results of all three hypothesis tests, you must communicate the results to others. While there are many correct ways to write up the results, all of them require very specific information, which is frequently presented in a very specific order. If you follow the general format provided below, your summary will be a good one.

General Format

a. Tell if the *interaction* was significant. Be sure to include all of the necessary statistical information (i.e., *dfs*, obtained F value, p value information, *MSE*, and effect size information).

b. If the interaction is significant, describe the interaction, using one sentence to describe the pattern of cell means for each level of the IV. You MUST describe the different simple effects (e.g., the mean differences between the alcohol and no-alcohol conditions for each level of driving experience; how much alcohol consumption slowed down drivers in the low-experience condition compared with the high-experience condition). Give the cell means with standard deviations in the paragraph.

c. Sometimes authors add a sentence explaining the interaction.

    d. Tell if the *first main effect* was significant. Be sure to include all of the necessary statistical information (i.e., *dfs,* obtained *F* value, *p* value information, *MSE,* and effect size information).

    e. If the first main effect was significant, describe which marginal mean(s) was (were) significantly higher.

    f. Tell if the *second main effect* was significant. Be sure to include all of the necessary statistical information (i.e., *dfs,* obtained *F* value, *p* value information, *MSE,* and effect size information).

    g. If the second main effect was significant, describe which marginal mean(s) was (were) significantly higher.

14. Use the general format provided above to summarize the results of this study.

SCENARIO 2: DRIVING EXPERIENCE AND CELL PHONE USE

The researchers recruited 40 new drivers. Each driver drove a high-fidelity driving simulator while having a conversation on a cell phone with a friend or having no conversation. Additionally, half the participants *in each of these conditions* had "high driving experience" (i.e., more than 50,000 km), and half had "low driving experience" (i.e., less than 50,000 km). The DV was the drivers' reaction time to a stimulus presented in their peripheral vision. Obviously, slower reaction times indicate *worse* performance.

15. Label the following table, insert the cell means and standard deviations, and compute the marginal means:

	Mean (SD)
High experience/no conversation	0.70 (0.19)
Low experience/no conversation	0.82 (0.18)
High experience/conversation	1.03 (0.23)
Low experience/conversation	1.18 (0.35)

16. Look at the table you created above. Which of the three effects tested by this factorial ANOVA looks like it *might be* significant (i.e., end up rejecting its null hypothesis)? Explain your reasoning.

17. How would you actually determine if each null should be rejected? Why can't you just look at the numbers in the above table?

SCENARIO 3: DRIVING EXPERIENCE AND DISTRACTED DRIVING

Another set of researchers is interested in directly comparing the driving performance of people who had previously consumed alcohol with that of people talking on cell phones while driving. They recruited 40 new drivers. Half the drivers had a low dose of alcohol before driving the simulator, and the other half had conversations with a friend while driving the simulator. As was done in the previous study, half of the participants in each condition had "high driving experience," and the other half had "low driving experience." The DV was the reaction time to a stimulus presented in the drivers' peripheral vision, as in the previous studies. The data listed below came from 8 of the 40 participants in this study.

18. Enter the following data into the spreadsheet below as if it was an SPSS spreadsheet and you wanted to analyze the data from the study described in the previous paragraph. Use the following coding system: driving experience, 1 = *low experience*, 2 = *high experience*; driving condition, 1 = *consumed alcohol*, 2 = *talking on cell phone*. The first row should have the variable names. You will NOT need to fill every cell of the provided spreadsheet.

	Response Times for Two Individuals in Each Condition
These two drank and had high experience	0.89, 0.91
These two talked and had high experience	1.03, 1.05
These two drank and had low experience	1.17, 1.19
These two talked and had low experience	1.18, 1.17

The SPSS output on the next page came from the study described above. The first IV was driving experience (low or high). The second IV was driving condition (driving after drinking alcohol or driving while talking on a cell phone).

19. Determine which of the three null hypotheses should be rejected and then write a complete summary of these data. Be sure to include a reporting statement for the interaction as well as for both main effects. Also be sure to include all of the necessary statistical information in the correct format.

Descriptive Statistics

Dependent Variable:Reaction_Time

Driving_Experience	Driving_Condition	Mean	Std. Deviation	N
Low	Alcohol	1.2680	.08053	10
	Cell Phone	1.1900	.08287	10
	Total	1.2290	.08902	20
High	Alcohol	1.0860	.09336	10
	Cell Phone	1.2080	.09355	10
	Total	1.1470	.11041	20
Total	Alcohol	1.1770	.12616	20
	Cell Phone	1.1990	.08651	20
	Total	1.1880	.10735	40

Tests of Between–Subjects Effects

Dependent Variable:Reaction_Time

Source	Type III Sum of Squares	df	Mean Square	F	Sig.	Partial Eta Squared
Corrected Model	.172[a]	3	.057	7.445	.001	.383
Intercept	56.454	1	56.454	7327.428	.000	.995
Driving_Experience	.067	1	.067	8.727	.005	.195
Driving_Condition	.005	1	.005	.628	.433	.017
Driving_Experience * Driving_Condition	.100	1	.100	12.980	.001	.265
Error	.277	36	.008			
Total	56.903	40				
Corrected Total	.449	39				

a. R Squared = .383 (Adjusted R Squared = .331)

REFERENCE

Langer, P., Holzner, B., Magnet, W., & Kopp, M. (2005). Hands-free mobile phone conversation impairs the peripheral visual system to an extent comparable to an alcohol level of 4–5g 100 ml. *Human Psychopharmacology: Clinical and Experimental, 20*(1), 65–66.

Activity 13-4: Choose the Correct Statistic

Learning Objectives

After reading the chapter and completing the homework and this activity, you should be able to do the following:

- Read a research scenario and determine which statistic should be used

Determine which of the following statistics should be used in each of the following research scenarios: z for a single score, z for sample mean, single sample t, related samples t, independent samples t, one-way independent samples ANOVA, or two-way independent samples ANOVA.

1. Mark Haub, a professor at Kansas State University, reported that he lost 27 pounds in 2 months by consuming 1,800 calories a day of primarily junk food (e.g., Twinkies). Given the low caloric intake, the weight loss was not surprising, but he reported that his cholesterol levels also improved. A nutritionist wonders what the long-term effects of a junk food diet are and so designs an experiment using rats. The cholesterol levels of a group of 50 rats are measured, and then the rats are fed a diet of Twinkies and Doritos for 1 year. At the end of that year, the rat's cholesterol levels are measured again. Which statistic should be used to determine if the diet had a significant effect on cholesterol levels?

2. Professor Haub reported that his Body Mass Index (BMI) was 24.9 at the end of the 2 months. If BMIs in the general population of males are normally distributed with a mean of 25 and a standard deviation of 5, what would the percentile rank be for his new BMI?

3. Another researcher reads of Professor Haub's experience and learns that he consumed one serving of vegetables a day while on this diet and wonders if this small amount of vegetables was an important factor in lowering his cholesterol levels. To test the effects of this diet plus vegetables on cholesterol levels, she obtains a random sample of 75 people and randomly assigns them to eat 1,800 calories a day of only junk food, 1,800 calories a day of junk food and one serving of vegetables, or 1,800 calories a day of only vegetables. Cholesterol levels were measured after 2 months on the diet. Which statistic should be used to determine if there is a significant difference in cholesterol levels among the three different diets?

4. A number of web reports indicate that Professor Haub's experience suggests that the quality of food is not as important as the amount of food people consume. A

nutritionist decides to test this by randomly assigning 100 people with 25% body fat to eat either 1,800 calories a day or 2,500 calories a day. He also manipulates the quality of the food. Half of the participants eat only junk food, and the other half eat a healthy diet consisting of fruits, vegetables, whole grains, and lean protein. After 2 months on this diet, the percentage of body fat was recorded for each participant. Which statistic should the nutritionist use to determine that the effect of caloric intake on body fat percentage is different for junk food and for healthy food diets?

5. A statistics teacher thinks that doing homework improves scores on statistics exams. To test this hypothesis, she randomly assigns students to two groups. One group is required to work on the homework until all problems are correct. Homework is optional for the second group. At the end of the semester, final grades are compared between the two groups, and the results reveal that the required-homework group had higher final grades than the optional-homework group. Which statistic should be used to compare the final grades of those in each homework group?

6. Encouraged by the results of the first study, the statistics teacher wonders if it is necessary to complete the entire homework assignment until it is correct. Perhaps just working on the homework is sufficient to improve grades. Thus, the following semester she randomly assigns students to three groups: (1) homework is optional, (2) must get all homework questions correct, and (3) need to answer each homework question, but they do not have to be correct. At the end of the semester, final grades are compared between the three groups. What statistic could be used to compare the final grades of the three groups?

7. A recent study revealed that students from the University of Washington who studied abroad reported that they drank more alcohol while studying abroad than they used to before they studied abroad. Which statistic should be used to make this comparison?

8. A college counselor does a survey of students and finds that students on her campus are feeling consistently tired. In an attempt to get the students to sleep more, the counseling center sends an e-mail to all students on campus. This e-mail discusses the benefits of sleep as well as the dangers of sleep deprivation. In addition to the e-mail, the counseling center gives presentations about the value of sleep to all incoming freshmen. Later in the semester, a random sample of 78 students is asked to report the number of hours of sleep they get on an average weekday. They report an average of 7.1 hours of sleep, with a standard deviation of 0.9. After the intervention, did students report sleeping more than the national average for college students of 6.5 hours per night?

9. A school counselor wants to identify students who are struggling with reading comprehension so that they can receive extra help. To identify these students, the

counselor gives a reading comprehension test to all students in sixth grade. This test is standardized, with a mean of $\mu = 75$ and $\sigma = 10$. Any student who scores 2 or more standard deviations below the mean will be identified as needing additional help with reading comprehension. What statistics should the counselor use to determine the percentage of students who are likely to score at or below 2 standard deviations below the mean?

10. Twenty-six students were identified as needing additional help with reading comprehension. These students took an extra class during summer that specifically focused on understanding what they were reading in short stories, novels, and newspaper articles. After the summer course, the students' average score was 70. What statistic should be used to determine if the mean for this sample of students is significantly different from the mean for the population ($\mu = 75$ and $\sigma = 10$)?

11. A person with schizophrenia is more likely to suffer a relapse if family members are highly critical, hostile, and overinvolved in that person's life. Some psychologists wondered if training the family members of schizophrenic patients to be less critical and less hostile would reduce the patients' symptoms. The psychologists divided a sample of people with schizophrenia into two groups. The family members of the first group were trained to reduce their critical and hostile interaction patterns. The family members of the second group of patients received no training. Six months later, patients in both groups were evaluated and given scores that reflected the severity of their schizophrenic symptoms. Which statistic should be used to determine if there is a significant difference between the severity of the schizophrenic symptoms across the trained and not trained groups?

12. In a related study, researchers divided a sample of family members of schizophrenic patients into two groups. One group of family members was trained to be less critical. The other group of family members was not trained at all. Additionally, half of the people in each group of family members were male, and half were female. Is the training program equally effective at reducing critical verbal comments made by males and by females?

13. Based on a previous research study, it is known that the mean number of critical comments made by family members of schizophrenic patients in a day is $\mu = 28.2$. A researcher wanted to know if family members of schizophrenic patients make more critical comments than people who do not have a family member who is diagnosed with schizophrenia. The researcher obtained a sample of people who do not have a family member diagnosed with schizophrenia and found that the number of critical comments made in a day by these people was $\mu = 25.3$, with a standard deviation of 2.5. Which statistic should be used to determine if the number of critical comments was significantly different in schizophrenic and nonschizophrenic families?

Activity 13-5:   Practice Problems

After reading about the study investigating how the effects of body temperature and alcohol consumption influence the number of mosquito bites people suffer, a researcher decides to do a similar study to determine if different types of insect repellant are more or less effective based on a person's body temperature. Specifically, she investigates the relative effectiveness of an insect repellant containing DEET versus an insect repellant containing natural ingredients (e.g., lemon, eucalyptus, and citronella). The researcher uses the same procedures described in the previous study. Analyze the data reported below using SPSS.

Low Body Temperature		High Body Temperature	
Natural	*DEET*	*Natural*	*DEET*
5	6	12	10
6	5	11	9
7	7	13	11
8	8	14	12
6	7	15	13
4	6	17	15
7	7	18	11

1. Which of the following is the best verbal summary of the null hypothesis for the interaction?

   a. The effect of type of insect repellant is the same for people with high and low body temperatures.

   b. The effect of type of insect repellant is different for people with high and low body temperatures.

2. Which of the following is the best verbal summary of the research hypothesis for the interaction?

   a. The effect of type of insect repellant is the same for people with high and low body temperatures.

   b. The effect of type of insect repellant is different for people with high and low body temperatures.

3. How many degrees of freedom are there in the numerator for the interaction test (i.e., $df = (a - 1)(b - 1)$)?

4. How many degrees of freedom are there in the denominator for the interaction test (i.e., $df = N - (a)(b)$)?

5. What is the critical value for the interaction test if alpha is .05?

6. On average, how many times were people with a lower body temperature bitten while wearing the natural insect repellant (i.e., what is the cell mean for these people)?

7. On average, how many times were people with a higher body temperature bitten while wearing the natural insect repellant (i.e., what is the cell mean for these people)?

8. On average, how many times were people with a lower body temperature bitten while wearing the insect repellant containing DEET (i.e., what is the cell mean for these people)?

9. On average, how many times were people with a higher body temperature bitten while wearing the insect repellant containing DEET (i.e., what is the cell mean for these people)?

10. What is the F statistic for the interaction?

11. You should reject the null hypothesis if (choose all that apply)
    a. the p value is less than alpha.
    b. the p value is greater than alpha.
    c. the obtained F statistic is greater than the critical value.
    d. the obtained F statistic is less than the critical value.

12. What is the p value for the interaction reported by SPSS?
    a. .000
    b. .110
    c. .032

13. Should the null hypothesis for the interaction be rejected?
    a. Yes, reject the null for the interaction.
    b. No, fail to reject the null for the interaction.

14. What is the effect size for the interaction?

15. Is the effect size for the interaction small, small-medium, medium, medium-large, or large?

16. Which of the following best summarizes the results of the interaction?

    a. People with a higher body temperature ($M = 12.93$, $SD = 2.62$) were more likely to be bitten than people with a lower body temperature ($M = 6.36$, $SD = 1.15$), and people were more likely to be bitten when they used the natural insect repellant ($M = 10.21$, $SD = 4.66$) than when they used the repellant containing DEET ($M = 9.07$, $SD = 3.00$), $F(1, 24) = 5.20$, $p = .03$, $MSE = 3.32$, $\eta_p^2 = .18$.

    b. People with a higher body temperature were much less likely to be bitten when they used the insect repellant containing DEET ($M = 11.57$, $SD = 1.99$) than when they used the natural insect repellant ($M = 14.29$, $SD = 2.56$), whereas people with lower body temperatures were somewhat less likely to be bitten when they used the natural insect repellant ($M = 6.14$, $SD = 1.35$) as compared with the repellant containing DEET ($M = 6.57$, $SD = .98$), $F(1, 24) = 5.20$, $p = .03$, $MSE = 3.32$, $\eta_p^2 = .18$.

    c. The interaction between body temperature and type of insect repellant was not statistically significant, $F(1, 24) = 5.20$, $p = .03$, $MSE = 3.32$, $\eta_p^2 = .18$.

17. Which of the following is the best verbal summary of the null hypothesis for the main effect of body temperature?

    a. People with a higher body temperature will be bitten more often than people with a lower body temperature.

    b. People with a higher body temperature will be bitten less often than people with a lower body temperature.

    c. The mean number of mosquito bites for the higher body temperature group will not be different from the mean number of mosquito bites for the lower body temperature group.

    d. The mean number of mosquito bites for the higher body temperature group will be different from the mean number of mosquito bites for the lower body temperature group.

18. Which of the following is the best verbal summary of the research hypothesis for the main effect of body temperature?

    a. People with a higher body temperature will be bitten more often than people with a lower body temperature.

    b. The mean number of mosquito bites for the higher body temperature group will not be different from the mean number of mosquito bites for the lower body temperature group.

19. How many degrees of freedom are there in the numerator for the main effect of body temperature (i.e., $df = a - 1$)?

20. How many degrees of freedom are there in the denominator for the main effect of body temperature (i.e., $df = N - (a)(b)$)?

21. What is the critical value for the main effect of body temperature?

22. On average, how many times were people with a lower body temperature bitten (i.e., what is the marginal mean for these people)?

23. On average, how many times were people with a higher body temperature bitten (i.e., what is the marginal mean for these people)?

24. What is the F statistic for the main effect of body temperature?

25. What is the p value for the main effect of body temperature reported by SPSS?

26. Should the null hypothesis for the main effect of body temperature be rejected?

27. What is the effect size for the main effect of body temperature?

28. Is the effect size for the main effect of body temperature small, small-medium, medium, medium-large, or large?

29. Which of the following best summarizes the results for the main effect of body temperature?
    a. People with a higher body temperature ($M = 12.93$, $SD = 2.62$) were more likely to be bitten than people with a lower body temperature ($M = 6.36$, $SD = 1.15$), $F(1, 24) = 91.01$, $p < .001$, $MSE = 3.32$, $\eta_p^2 = .79$.
    b. People with a higher body temperature ($M = 12.93$, $SD = 2.62$) were more likely to be bitten than people with a lower body temperature ($M = 6.36$, $SD = 1.15$), and people were more likely to be bitten when they used the natural insect repellant ($M = 10.21$, $SD = 4.66$) than when they used the repellant containing DEET ($M = 9.07$, $SD = 3.00$), $F(1, 24) = 91.01$, $p < .001$, $MSE = 3.32$, $\eta_p^2 = .79$.
    c. The main effect of body temperature was not statistically significant, $F(1, 24) = 91.01$, $p < .001$, $MSE = 3.32$, $\eta_p^2 = .79$.

30. Which of the following is the best verbal summary of the null hypothesis for the main effect of type of insect repellant?

    a. The mean number of mosquito bites for people using the insect repellant containing DEET will not be different from the mean number of mosquito bites for people using the natural insect repellant.

    b. The mean number of mosquito bites for people using the insect repellant containing DEET will be different from the mean number of mosquito bites for people using the natural insect repellant.

31. Which of the following is the best verbal summary of the research hypothesis for the main effect of type of insect repellant?

    a. The mean number of mosquito bites for people using the insect repellant containing DEET will not be different from the mean number of mosquito bites for people using the natural insect repellant.

    b. The mean number of mosquito bites for people using the insect repellant containing DEET will be different from the mean number of mosquito bites for people using the natural insect repellant.

32. How many degrees of freedom are there in the numerator for the main effect of type of insect repellant (i.e., $df = b - 1$)?

33. How many degrees of freedom are there in the denominator for the main effect of type of insect repellant (i.e., $df = N - (a)(b)$)?

34. What is the critical value for the main effect of insect repellant?

35. On average, how many times were the people who used the insect repellant containing DEET bitten (i.e., what is the marginal mean for these people)?

36. On average, how many times were the people who used the natural insect repellant bitten (i.e., what is the marginal mean for these people)?

37. What is the F statistic for the main effect of type of insect repellant?

38. What is the p value for the main effect of type of insect repellant reported by SPSS?

39. Should the null hypothesis for the main effect of type of insect repellant be rejected?

40. What is the effect size for the main effect of type of insect repellant (i.e., $\eta_p^2 = SS_{body\ temp} / (SS_{body\ temp} + SS_{within})$)?

41. Is the effect size for the main effect of type of insect repellant small, small-medium, medium, medium-large, or large?

42. Which of the following best summarizes the results for the main effect of type of insect repellant?

    a. People were more likely to be bitten when they used the natural insect repellant ($M = 10.21$, $SD = 4.66$) than when they used the insect repellant containing DEET ($M = 9.07$, $SD = 3.00$), $F(1, 24) = 2.75$, $p = .11$, $MSE = 3.32$, $\eta_p^2 = .10$.

    b. The main effect of type of insect repellant was not statistically significant, $F(1, 24) = 2.75$, $p = .11$, $MSE = 3.32$, $\eta_p^2 = .10$. The medium effect size suggests that a larger sample size is needed to test this hypothesis.

C H A P T E R   1 4

Correlation and Regression

LEARNING OBJECTIVES

After reading this chapter, you should be able to do the following:

- Identify when to use Pearson's and Spearman's correlations
- Interpret the sign and value of a correlation coefficient
- Draw and interpret a scatterplot
- Write null and research hypotheses using words and symbols
- Compute the degrees of freedom (*df*) and determine the critical region
- Compute a Pearson's correlation coefficient by hand (using a calculator)
- Determine if you should reject or fail to reject the null hypothesis
- Compute an effect size (r^2) and describe it
- Summarize the results of the analysis using APA style
- Compute Pearson's and Spearman's correlations and draw scatterplots using SPSS
- Interpret the SPSS correlation output

INTRODUCTION TO CORRELATION AND REGRESSION

All of the test statistics you have learned so far compare means. For example, when doing an independent *t* test, you have one grouping variable (e.g., male vs. female) and one variable measured on an interval/ratio scale (e.g., test scores). A mean is computed for each group (i.e., males and females), and a statistical test is done to determine if the means are significantly different. Comparing means is a very common research approach. Another type of research that is very common tries to determine if two variables are related to each other. For example, are intelligence quotient (IQ) scores related to annual income? Researchers could measure a sample of people's IQ scores and their annual income and then compute a statistic to determine if the two variables are related. Note that in this research approach the researcher is not comparing groups of people; instead, the researcher is determining if a high score on one variable (e.g., IQ) is associated with a high or low score on another variable (e.g., annual income). In these situations, researchers use a correlation coefficient. Correlation coefficients can be positive or negative. For example, if high IQ scores are associated with high annual incomes (and vice versa), the correlation coefficient between these variables would be positive. However, if high IQ scores are associated with low annual incomes, the correlation coefficient would be negative. The absolute size of the correlation coefficient (i.e., its distance from 0) describes how strongly the two variables are related. When two variables are strongly related (i.e., when there is a large absolute correlation coefficient between two variables), researchers sometimes use a closely related statistical procedure called regression. If IQ scores and annual income were strongly associated, one could use regression to predict a person's annual income if you knew his or her IQ score. First, in this chapter, you will learn how to compute and interpret correlation coefficients. Second, if the coefficient is sufficiently large, you will learn how to use regression to predict a score on one variable from someone's score on the other variable.

Reading Question

1. A correlation coefficient is used to

   a. compare the mean of one variable with the mean of another variable.

   b. determine if and how two variables might be related to each other.

   c. predict a person's score on one variable from his or her score on another variable.

Reading Question

2. Regression is used to

   a. compare the mean of one variable with the mean of another variable.

   b. determine if and how two variables might be related to each other.

   c. predict a person's score on one variable from his or her score on another variable.

REVIEW OF z SCORES

Correlation coefficients are closely related to z scores, and so we will begin with a brief review. You previously learned that a z score enables you to rank individual scores relative to other scores in the same or different distributions. For example, if three people took a statistics exam, converting their raw scores to z scores would not only reveal who scored the highest but also how each person's score compared with the test's mean and if one or more of the scores were exceptionally high or exceptionally low. For instance, if Lola had a z score of $+0.62$, Bobby had a z score of -0.84, and Aaron had a z score of $+1.8$, you should know from this information that Lola scored a little better than average, Bobby scored a little worse than average, and Aaron's score was exceptionally good.

**Reading
Question**
3. Positive z scores represent values that are

   a. below average.

   b. average.

   c. above average.

**Reading
Question**
4. The _____ of a z score indicates how much better or worse a given score is than the mean score.

   a. sign

   b. absolute value

LOGIC OF CORRELATION

The z score is called a univariate statistic because it uses data from a single variable and conclusions drawn from the statistic must be limited to that variable. In the above example, the z scores allow us to comment on the relative performance of students on the statistics exam, but nothing else. There are situations in which researchers want to know if scores on one variable are associated with scores on another variable. For example, researchers may want to know if students who scored above average on a statistics exam also tended to score above average on a history exam. Imagine that a group of students all took the same statistics exam, followed by the same history exam. If we used the univariate z score statistic to compute a z score for statistics grades and a z score for history grades and then compared individuals' z scores, we may be able to determine if people who scored above average on the statistics exam tended to score above average, average, or below average on the history exam. For example, the z scores of Lola, Bobby, and Aaron for both tests are shown in Table 14.1.

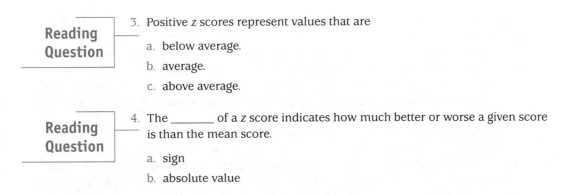

Table 14.1 z scores for three students on two exams.

Student	Statistics z Score (X)	History z Score (Y)
Lola	+0.62	+0.48
Bobby	−0.84	−0.28
Aaron	+1.80	+1.24

An astute observer with some knowledge of z scores could probably look at the above data and conclude that those who scored above average on the statistics exam also tended to score above average on the history exam. While this general observation might be true, there are at least two serious limitations to this "visual analysis." First, it would be much more difficult to discern an association between statistics exam z scores and history exam z scores if you had the scores of a group of 30, 60, or 100 students to examine. Second, the general statement that if a statistics score is high then the history score will be high (or low) is not very precise. It would be much more helpful if we (a) had a more reliable way of identifying if an association actually exists between statistics scores and history scores and (b) could quantify precisely how strong (or weak) the association is between statistics scores and history scores.

As you might have anticipated, the statistical procedure of correlation is designed to (a) determine if scores on one variable are associated with scores on a second variable and (b) quantify precisely the strength of the association. The correlation definitional formula below reveals how z scores can be used to quantify a bivariate (i.e., two variable) association between the statistics exam and the history exam. The statistical symbols for a sample correlation and a population correlation are ρ and ρ (rho), respectively. The sample and population correlation formulas are presented in Table 14.2.

Table 14.2   Formulas for computing ρ and r.

Population Correlation Formula	Sample Correlation Formula
$$\rho = \frac{\Sigma z_x z_y}{N}$$	$$r = \frac{\Sigma z_x z_y}{N-1}$$

By looking at the above formulas, you might be able to tell that the correlations are the average product of each person's pair of z scores. In the statistic and history test scores example, each person's statistics and history z scores are multiplied, and all the products are summed and then divided by the number of paired scores, or $N-1$. In this case, we will treat these three people as if they are a population, and so the correlation would be computed as

$$\rho = \frac{\Sigma z_x z_y}{N} = \frac{(.62)(.48)+(-.84)(-.28)+(1.80)(1.24)}{3} = .92.$$

When hypothesis testing, you will always be working with a sample, and therefore, you will use the formula for r. The only difference between the two formulas is that when working with a population you divide by N (the number of pairs of scores) whereas when working with a sample you divide by $N-1$.

Reading Question

5. Which of the following are correlations designed to accomplish? Choose 2.

   a. Determine if two variables are associated

   b. Determine if a score is above or below the mean score

   c. Quantify the degree or strength of the association between two variables

   d. Quantify the distance that a score is above or below the mean score

6. When, on average, both paired z scores tend to be positive or both paired z scores tend to be negative, the resulting r value is

   a. negative.

   b. positive.

Reading Question

7. When, on average, paired z scores tend to have opposite signs, the resulting r value is

   a. negative.

   b. positive.

The possible range of correlation coefficients is between -1 and $+1$. The coefficient reveals two things about the bivariate association. First, if it is negative, it means that those people who scored high on one variable tended to score low on the other variable. An example of a negative association might be the number of hours studied in a week and the number of hours worked in a week. If someone had to work a lot in a given week, he or she probably studied less during that week. Conversely, if the coefficient is positive, low scores on one variable are associated with low scores on the second variable and high scores are associated with high scores. An example of a positive association might be the number of hours spent studying for an exam and the score on that exam. Those who studied a lot tended to score high on the exam, and those who studied very little tended to score low on the exam. The second thing revealed by the coefficient is the precise strength of the bivariate association. The more extreme the r value (i.e., the farther it is from 0), the stronger the bivariate association. A coefficient of 1 or -1 is the strongest association that is possible. Thus, the correlation of .92 between statistics exam scores and history exam scores is a very strong one.

Reading Question

8. A negative correlation between two variables indicates that high scores on one variable are associated with _____ scores on the second variable.

   a. high

   b. low

   c. average

Reading Question

9. Which of the following indicates the strongest association between two variables?

   a. −.25

   b. .35

   c. −.67

   d. 1.1

PEARSON'S (*r*) AND SPEARMAN'S (*r*_S) CORRELATIONS

You will be learning about two different types of correlations, Pearson's correlation and Spearman's correlation. Pearson's r is used when both variables are measured on interval/ratio scales. In the examples described above, Pearson's correlation would be used because exam scores are ratio data. Spearman's r is used when one (or both) of the variables is ordinal data (i.e., rank-ordered data). For example, researchers would use Spearman's r if they wanted to assess the bivariate association between the order of finish in a swimming race (1st, 2nd, 3rd, etc.) and the hours of swimming practice in the previous month.

Another important difference between Pearson's and Spearman's correlations is that Pearson's correlation can only be used when the bivariate association is linear. In other words, if you created a scatterplot of the two variables, the data points would form a "linear trend" rather than a "curved trend." If after creating a scatterplot, you discover that the data points do not seem to follow a linear trend, you should not use Pearson's correlation. If the data are not linear but they are monotonic (see Figure 14.1), you can use Spearman's correlation instead. "Monotonic" simply means that the data have a trend in only one direction. If the data trend upward and then downward, they are nonmonotonic (see Figure 14.1), and neither Pearson's nor Spearman's r can be used.

Figure 14.1   Graphs representing linear, monotonic, and nonmonotonic relationships.

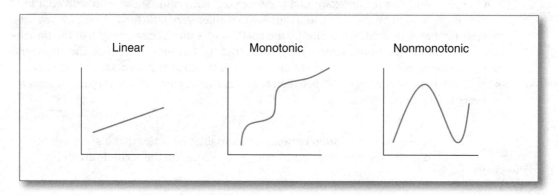

Linear   Monotonic   Nonmonotonic

Reading Question

10. If both variables being analyzed are measured on an interval or ratio scale, a _____ correlation should be used.

   a. Pearson's

   b. Spearman's

Reading Question

11. If one of the variables is measured on an ordinal scale and the other variable is measured on an ordinal, interval, or ratio scale, a _____ correlation should be used.

   a. Pearson's

   b. Spearman's

**Reading
Question**

12. If the trend revealed by a scatterplot is not linear but it is monotonic, what correlation should be used?

    a. Pearson's
    b. Spearman's

ALTERNATIVE USE FOR CORRELATION

Finally, in most situations in which a correlation is appropriate, researchers have scores from the same person for both variables. However, in some situations you can also use a correlation to assess the association between the scores obtained from different individuals. For example, if a researcher wanted to assess the relationship between spouses' marital satisfaction, they could measure the marital satisfaction of many married couples to see if their respective satisfaction scores are associated. If one person in a marriage is satisfied, does the other person tend to be satisfied as well? And if so, how strong is the association between married couples' satisfaction scores? The key is that the two variables being correlated must be "paired" in some way. The data must include paired scores that came from the same source (i.e., the same person, the same marriage, etc.).

**Reading
Question**

13. A correlation can only be used if the scores on each variable

    a. come from the same people.
    b. are paired or linked to each other in some way.

HYPOTHESIS TESTING WITH CORRELATION

As you know from your work with other statistics, researchers often collect data from a representative sample and infer that the results they find approximate the results they would have found if they had studied the entire population. The same is done with both Pearson's and Spearman's correlations. Additionally, as with the previous statistics you have worked with, researchers assume that a null hypothesis is true unless they find sufficient evidence to reject that null hypothesis. In the case of correlation, the null hypothesis is that the two variables being studied are NOT associated. If the null were true, the calculated r value would be close to 0. If the calculated r value is far from 0, the null is *not likely* to be true.

**Reading
Question**

14. If the null hypothesis is true and two variables are not associated with each other, the r value should be close to

    a. -1.
    b. 1.
    c. 0.

As with other statistics, researchers use a critical value to define "far from 0." The critical value of r changes based on the sample size used in the study (i.e., $df = N - 2$). A table of r critical values is used to find the specific critical value associated with each df value. If the obtained r value is more extreme than the critical value (i.e., farther from 0), the null hypothesis should be rejected. A complete example is provided below.

Reading Question

15. If an obtained r value is farther from 0 than the critical value, you should
   a. reject the null hypothesis.
   b. fail to reject the null hypothesis.

As with t tests, correlations can be one-tailed or two-tailed. If the research hypothesis predicts a positive association or a negative association, a one-tailed correlation is used. If however, the research hypothesis does not predict a specific direction, only that the two variables will be related somehow, a two-tailed correlation is used.

Reading Question

16. A two-tailed critical value should be used when the research hypothesis
   a. predicts a positive correlation.
   b. does not predict a specific direction for the relationship between the two variables.
   c. predicts a negative correlation.

TWO-TAILED PEARSON'S CORRELATION EXAMPLE

A psychologist wonders if body image is associated with shopping behavior. Specifically, she wants to know if body image is associated with the number of items of clothing bought in a given month. She does not understand these variables well enough to predict a positive or negative relationship; she just wants to know if they are associated at all. To investigate this relationship, she has her clients complete a questionnaire that measures body image and another that asks how many items of clothing were purchased in the past 2 weeks. A higher body image score indicates a more positive body image. The data from this study are given in Table 14.3. The z scores have already been computed using the formula for z for an individual score: $z = (X–M)/SD$.

Step 1: Draw a Scatterplot of the Data, and Determine Which Correlation Is Appropriate

A scatterplot has the possible values for one variable on the x-axis (Body Image) and the possible values for the other variable on the y-axis (Items of Clothing Purchased). It does not matter which variable goes on which axis. A dot at the paired coordinates represents each person's score on both variables. For example, Participant A's dot should be at the coordinates of Body Image 1 and Items of Clothing Purchased 3. Every person has a dot representing their combination of scores. If two or more people have the same scores for

Table 14.3   Computation of a correlation coefficient using the definitional *z* score formulas.

Participant	Body Image (X)	Body Image (z Score)	Clothing Purchased (Y)	Clothing Purchased (z Score)	$z_x z_y$
A	1	(1 − 2.6)/ 0.97 = −1.66	3	(3 − 4.4)/ 1.35 = −1.04	(−1.66)(−1.04) = 1.73
B	3	0.41	4	−0.30	−0.12
C	3	0.41	4	−0.30	−0.12
D	3	0.41	6	1.19	0.49
E	1	−1.66	4	−0.30	0.50
F	3	0.41	5	0.44	0.18
G	4	1.45	6	1.19	1.73
H	2	−0.62	2	−1.78	1.10
I	3	0.41	4	−0.30	−0.12
J	3	0.41	6	1.19	0.49
	$M_x = 2.6$ $SD_x = 0.966$		$M_y = 4.4$ $SD_y = 1.35$		$\sum z_x z_y = 5.86$

Figure 14.2   Scatterplot of body image and items of clothing purchased.

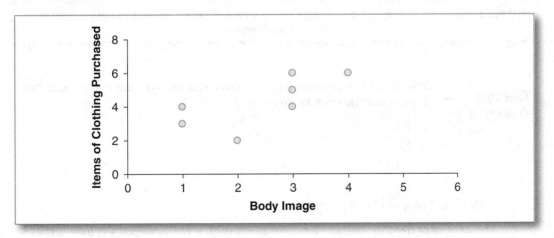

both variables, there will be two dots at the same coordinate location. The complete scatterplot for this example is plotted in Figure 14.2. The scores seem to follow a straight line sloped upward, and so the trend represented in the figure is sufficiently linear to conduct a Pearson's correlation.

If the trend was not linear but was still monotonic, you would need to use Spearman's correlation. If the trend was nonmonotonic, both the Pearson's and the Spearman's correlations would be inappropriate, and you should ask for help with your data.

17. In a scatterplot, each dot represents
    a. a set of paired X and Y scores.
    b. an X score.
    c. a Y score.

Step 2: State the Null and Research Hypotheses Symbolically and Verbally

The research hypothesis is that the two variables have a linear relationship, whereas the null hypothesis is that they do not have a linear relationship. These hypotheses are presented verbally and symbolically in Table 14.4. You will notice that the Greek letter rho (ρ) represents the population parameter for correlations. In other words, the statistic r is an estimate of the population parameter ρ.

Table 14.4	Symbolic and verbal representations of two-tailed research and null hypotheses for a Pearson's correlation.

	Symbolic	Verbal
Research hypothesis (H_1)	H_1: $\rho \neq 0$	Body image scores and number items of clothing purchased are linearly related.
Null hypothesis (H_0)	H_0: $\rho = 0$	Body image scores and number of items of clothing purchased are NOT linearly related.

18. The research hypothesis for a two-tailed Pearson's correlation predicts that the test statistic r will be far from
    a. 1.
    b. 0.
    c. −1.

Step 3: Define the Critical Regions

The degrees of freedom formula for correlations is $df = N - 2$, where N is the number of paired scores, not the number of scores. Therefore, in this case,

$$df = N - 2 = 10 - 2 = 8.$$

The two-tailed critical value associated with $df = 8$ can be found in the table of Pearson's r critical values in Appendix E. The two critical regions for this example are $+.632$ and $-.632$. If the obtained r value is more extreme than these values, the null hypothesis should be rejected. If the obtained r is in the negative tail of the r distribution, the two variables have a significant negative association, and if it is in the positive tail, they have a positive association.

Reading Question

19. A two-tailed correlation has _____ critical region(s).

   a. no

   b. one

   c. two

   d. three

Step 4: Compute the Test Statistic

Much of the computational work was completed in the above data table. For each person, we converted the raw scores into z scores (Columns 3 and 4). Next, for each person, we multiplied the two z scores ($z_x z_y$) and entered the result in the last column. The values in the last column were then added to compute the sum of the products of the z scores $(\Sigma z_x z_y)$.

$$r = \frac{\Sigma z_x z_y}{N-1} = \frac{5.83}{9} = .65$$

The obtained r value of .65 was in the positive critical region (i.e., it was farther from 0 than the critical value of $+.632$), which means that Body Image and Items of Clothing Purchased have a significant positive association. That is, those with a more positive body image also seem to purchase more items of clothing.

Reading Question

20. A correlation coefficient can be computed by

   a. multiplying the paired scores and then dividing by the number of scores.

   b. multiplying the paired z scores, summing the products and then dividing by the number of paired scores.

   c. dividing by the number of scores and then multiplying the paired z scores minus 1.

Step 5: Compute the Effect Size and Describe It

The size of a correlation is described by r^2, which is also called the "coefficient of determination."

$$r^2 = (.65)^2 = .42$$

The coefficient of determination is interpreted as a percentage. Specifically, $r^2 = .42$ indicates that 42% of the variability in items of clothing purchased is predicted by the variability in body image scores. If the r^2 between number of items of clothing purchased and body image were 1, you could perfectly predict items of clothing purchased from body image scores. The general guidelines for interpreting r^2 are presented in Table 14.5 and are the same as those for η_p^2.

Table 14.5 General guidelines for interpreting r^2.

r^2 Value	Effect Size Label
Close to .01	Small
Close to .09	Medium
Close to .25	Large

Reading Question

21. If $r^2 = .36$, it means that 36% of the variability in one variable is

    a. unpredictable.

    b. predicted by the variability in the other variable.

Step 6: Interpret the Results

This correlation analysis can be summarized by the following sentences.

There is a positive association between clients' body image score and the number of items of clothing purchased in a 2-week period, $r(8) = .65, p < .05$. That is, those clients with higher body image scores also tended to purchase more clothing.

The APA reporting format for correlations is similar to that used for other statistics; however, with other statistics, an effect size estimate is included in the summary statement. This is typically not done with correlations because the effect size estimate is so easily computed from the r value (i.e., effect size $= r^2$).

Reading Question

22. If $r(8) = .65, p < .05$, the number of paired scores in the study was _____ and $r^2 =$ _____.

    a. 10; .65

    b. 8; .4225

    c. 8; .65

    d. 10; .4225

COMPUTATIONAL FORMULAS

Formulas that help explain the logic of a statistic are called definitional formulas. The z score formula for correlation coefficients is a definitional formula. It helps us understand how correlations work because it literally defines how the two types of scores are related. However, definitional formulas can be tedious to use. For example, if working with a large data set, it would be cumbersome to convert all raw scores to z scores and then compute an r value. Computational formulas are less intuitive, but they are easier to use when working with raw scores (i.e., not z scores). The computational formulas presented below allow you to compute an r value directly from raw scores without first converting everything to z scores; this saves a lot of time. While it is difficult to see why computational formulas work by looking at them, they yield the exact same value as the definitional r formula (i.e., the one that uses z scores).

$$SS_{xy} = \Sigma XY - \frac{(\Sigma X)(\Sigma Y)}{N}, \qquad r = \frac{SS_{xy}}{\sqrt{SS_x SS_y}}$$

The computational approach requires you to use two formulas. You must first compute the shared variability of X and Y (i.e., SS_{xy}) and then use that value to compute r. Computing SS_{xy} requires ΣXY, ΣX, ΣY, and N. ΣXY is obtained by first multiplying the paired X and Y values and then summing the products. ΣX and ΣY are the sum of the X and Y values, respectively. The sum of square deviations (SS) for X and Y is then computed in the same way as in Chapter 3. All of these computations for SS_{xy} are shown below in Table 14.6.

$$SS_{xy} = \Sigma XY - \frac{(\Sigma X)(\Sigma Y)}{N} = 122 - \frac{(26)(44)}{10} = 7.6$$

$$r = \frac{SS_{xy}}{\sqrt{(SS_x)(SS_y)}} = \frac{7.6}{\sqrt{(8.4)(16.4)}} = .65$$

Table 14.6 Computation of a correlation coefficient using the computational formulas.

Participant	Body Image (X)	Items of Clothing Purchased (Y)	XY
A	1	3	3
B	3	4	12
C	3	4	12
D	3	6	18
E	1	4	4
F	3	5	15
G	4	6	24
H	2	2	4
I	3	4	12
J	3	6	18
	$\Sigma X = 26$ $SS_x = 8.4$	$\Sigma Y = 44$ $SS_y = 16.4$	$\Sigma XY = 122$

Of course, all of the steps for hypothesis testing with correlations are the same whether you are using the computational or the definitional formulas to compute the correlation coefficient.

23. When computing statistics by hand, researchers most often use _____ formulas. When trying to understand how a statistic works, students will find it easier to work with _____ formulas. However, both formulas will always produce _____ value(s).

    a. computational; definitional; the same

    b. computational; definitional; different

    c. definitional; computational; the same

    d. definitional; computational; different

ONE-TAILED PEARSON'S CORRELATION EXAMPLE

You are interested in replicating the previous psychologist's work on body image and shopping behavior at your college. She found a strong positive association, and you expect to find a similar relationship at your college. Therefore, your research hypothesis is that there will be a positive linear correlation between these variables. You collect data from 10 students attending your college. The data are presented in Table 14.7.

Table 14.7   Computation of a correlation coefficient using the computational formulas.

Participant	Body Image (X)	Clothing Purchased (Y)	XY
A	1	2	2
B	2	2	4
C	2	4	8
D	3	4	12
E	1	3	3
F	3	3	9
G	2	4	8
H	2	3	6
I	3	3	9
J	3	4	12
	$\sum X = 22$ $SS_x = 5.6$	$\sum Y = 32$ $SS_y = 5.6$	$\sum XY = 73$

Step 1: Draw a Scatterplot of the Data, and Determine Which Correlation Is Appropriate

The data for this example are plotted in Figure 14.3. The trend represented in the figure is sufficiently linear to conduct a Pearson's correlation.

Figure 14.3   Scatterplot of scores for Body Image and Items of Clothing Purchased.

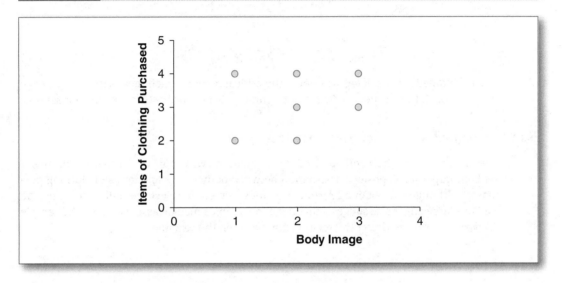

Step 2: State the Null and Research Hypotheses Symbolically and Verbally

The null and research hypotheses are presented in Table 14.8.

Table 14.8   Symbolic and verbal representations of the one-tailed research and null hypotheses for a Pearson's correlation.

	Symbolic	Verbal
Research hypothesis (H_1)	H_1: $\rho > 0$	Body image scores and number of clothing items purchased are positively related.
Null hypothesis (H_0)	H_0: $\rho \leq 0$	Body image scores and number of clothing items purchased are NOT positively related.

Step 3: Define the Critical Regions

In this case, $df = N - 2 = 10 - 2 = 8$.

The one-tailed critical value associated with a $df = 8$ is .549. You predicted a positive correlation, so the critical region for this example is $+.549$. If the obtained r value is larger than this critical r value, the null hypothesis should be rejected.

Step 4: Compute the Test Statistic

In this example, we will use the computational formula to first compute SS_{xy} and then r.

$$SS_{xy} = \sum XY - \frac{(\sum X)(\sum Y)}{N} = 73 - \frac{(22)(32)}{10} = 2.6$$

$$r = \frac{SS_{XY}}{\sqrt{(SS_X)(SS_Y)}} = \frac{2.6}{\sqrt{(5.6)(5.6)}} = .46$$

The obtained r value of .46 was not in the critical region, which means that body image and items of clothing purchased were not significantly positively correlated in your sample.

Step 5: Compute the Effect Size and Describe It

In this case, r^2, or the coefficient of determination, was .46^2, or .21. This indicates a medium-large–sized, positive association between body image and items of clothing purchased. Although the obtained r value was not sufficient to reject the null hypothesis, the medium-large effect size suggests that the two variables may be associated but the sample size was too small to detect the relationship between the variables.

Step 6: Interpret the Results

The following short paragraph summarizes the results of this analysis.

The students' body image scores and number of clothing items purchased were not significantly correlated, $r(8) = .46$, $p > .05$. However, the medium-large association between the variables suggests that the null hypothesis may not have been rejected because the sample size ($N = 10$) was too small. A larger sample size is needed to study the relationship between these variables.

Reading Question

24. If a null hypothesis in NOT rejected, the p value is frequently written as

   a. $p > .05$.

   b. $p < .05$.

WHAT IF YOU NEED TO DO A SPEARMAN'S CORRELATION?

You learned that if a scatterplot is monotonic rather than linear you must do a Spearman's correlation rather than a Pearson's correlation. The interesting fact about Spearman's correlation is that it uses the exact same formulas as Pearson's correlation. The only difference between the two correlations is in the type of data that are used. While Pearson's correlation uses the raw scores, Spearman's correlation analyzes the ranks of the scores rather than the scores themselves. Therefore, if you need to conduct a Spearman's correlation by hand, you must first convert all of the scores for Variable 1 into ranks and all of the scores for Variable 2 into ranks. Table 14.9 displays how the raw scores for each variable would be converted into ranks for a small data set of four scores for each variable. Higher scores represent better scores for both Variable 1 and Variable 2.

Table 14.9   Converting raw scores into rank scores for Spearman's correlation.

Variable 1 Raw Scores	Variable 1 Rank Scores	Variable 2 Raw Scores	Variable 2 Rank Scores
23	3	10	1
15	4	5	3
30	1	9	2
27	2	2	4

After converting the raw scores for Variables 1 and 2 into ranks, the remaining steps for computing Spearman's correlation are the same as those for Pearson's correlation. If you are using SPSS to conduct a Spearman's correlation, the program will convert the raw scores to ranked scores for you. The only thing you will have to do is indicate that you want a Spearman's rather than a Pearson's correlation.

Reading Question

25. If you need to do a Spearman's correlation because the data are monotonic but not linear, you need to convert the raw scores to _____ and then use the same steps/formulas that you would use to perform a Pearson's correlation.

   a. *z* scores

   b. ranked scores

SPSS

In this section, we reanalyze the first example in this chapter to illustrate how to use SPSS to perform a correlation.

A psychologist wonders if body image is associated with shopping behavior. Specifically she wants to know if body image is associated with the number of items of clothing bought in a given month. She does not understand these variables well enough to predict a positive or negative relationship; she just wants to know if they are associated at all. To investigate this relationship, she has her clients complete a questionnaire that measures self-esteem and another that asks how many items of clothing were purchased in the past month. Higher scores indicate higher levels of self-esteem. The data from this study are shown in Figure 14.4.

Data File

After you enter your data, it should look like the screenshot in Figure 14.4.

Figure 14.4 SPSS screenshot of data entry screen.

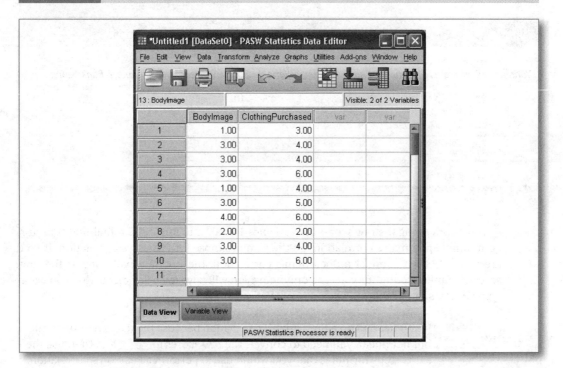

Reading Question

26. When entering data for a correlation analysis in SPSS,

    a. each variable is in its own column.

    b. each set of paired scores is in its own column.

Obtaining a Scatterplot

There are two ways to create scatterplots in SPSS:

1. Option 1 (Legacy Dialogs)
   - Go to the Graphs menu. Choose Legacy Dialogs, and then select Scatter/Dot.
   - Choose Simple Scatter, and click Define.
   - Put one variable on the x-axis and the other variable on the y-axis.

2. Option 2 (Chart Builder)
   - Go to the Graphs menu, and select Chart Builder.
   - A box may pop up that warns you to make sure that the appropriate level of measurement is specified in the data file. Close this box by clicking on OK.

- You will see two windows. One is labeled "Element Properties," and the other is labeled "Chart Builder." Close the Element Properties window.
- To create the scatterplot, click on the Gallery tab on the lower half of the screen, and then click on "Scatter/Dot."
- Once you have done that, there will be several pictures of different types of scatterplots. Double-click on the first one. If you hold your cursor over it, it will say "Simple Scatter."
- Next, you need to indicate which variable you want on the *x*-axis and which you want on the *y*-axis. Just choose one variable from the variable box and drag it onto the *x*-axis, and then drag the other variable onto the *y*-axis. Click OK to create the scatterplot.

Output

Your output file should look similar to the one in Figure 14.5. (*Note:* If you put Body Image on the horizontal axis, your dots will be in different locations.) The plot below is sufficiently linear to conduct a Pearson's correlation.

| Figure 14.5 | SPSS screenshot of scatterplot. |

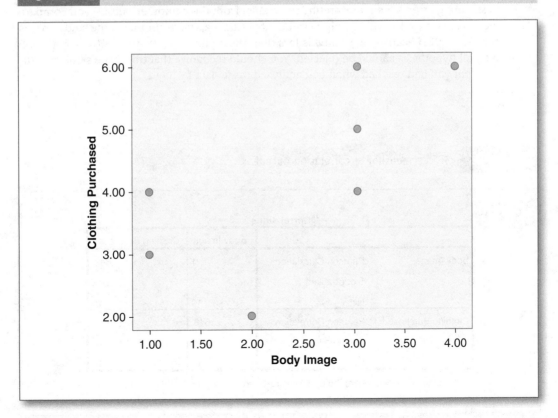

Reading Question

27. Which of the following sets of paired scores is NOT represented in the above scatterplot? The body image score is listed first, followed by the clothing purchased score.

   a. 2, 2
   b. 3, 5
   c. 4, 6
   d. 3, 3

Obtaining a Correlation

- Go to the Analyze menu. Choose Correlate, and then select Bivariate.
- Move the variables you want a correlation for into the Variables box.
- Check Pearson's or Spearman's correlation.

The output you see in Figure 14.6 is called a correlation matrix. Note that the correlation, or r value, of .648 is the same as the r value that was computed by hand at the beginning of the chapter. Also, note that SPSS always presents the correlation twice. The Sig. (2-tailed) value, or p value, for this correlation is .043. This means that when the sample size is $N = 10$, an r value of .648 would be expected to occur about 4 times out of 100 due to sampling error. When interpreting the results from the computer output, you compare the p value (i.e., .043) with the alpha value that was set at the beginning of the study; in this case, $\alpha = .05$. Because the p value is less than the alpha value, that is, p (.043) < α (.05), the null hypothesis should be rejected. You should recognize that this is the same conclusion that you had reached when you analyzed these data by hand.

Figure 14.6   SPSS screenshot of correlation output.

Correlations

		Body Image	Clothing Purchased
Body Image	Pearson Correlation	1	.648[*]
	Sig. (2-tailed)		.043
	N	10	10
Clothing Purchased	Pearson Correlation	.648[*]	1
	Sig. (2-tailed)	.043	
	N	10	10

*. Correlation is significant at the 0.05 level (2-tailed).

Reading
Question

28. What is the exact *p* value produced by the above SPSS output?

    a. 1
    b. 10
    c. .648
    d. .043

Activity 14-1:   Correlations

Learning Objectives

After reading the chapter and completing this activity, you should be able to do the following:

- Determine if it is appropriate to use a correlation by viewing a scatterplot
- Estimate the correlation coefficient by inspecting a scatterplot
- Conduct a one-tailed and a two-tailed hypothesis test using a Pearson's correlation
- Compute a Pearson's correlation by hand and using SPSS
- Compute a Spearman's correlation using SPSS
- Summarize the results of a correlation in APA format

ESTIMATING CORRELATIONS FROM SCATTERPLOTS

Before computing correlations, you should get some practice looking at scatterplots and deter-mining the strength of the relationship between two variables just based on the graph. In gen-eral, the closer the data points are to a straight line, the stronger the relationship between the variables. Go to the following website, and answer the questions until you can accurately asso-ciate a graph with the appropriate correlation coefficient: http://istics.net/stat/Correlations/ (© John I. Marden. Used with permission).

1. My longest correct answer streak was _____.

2. What characteristic of a scatterplot determines the strength of the relationship between the two variables? Describe this characteristic to someone who has not taken a statistics class.

3. What characteristic of a scatterplot determines the direction of the relationship between the two variables? Describe this characteristic to someone who has not taken a statistic class.

INTERPRETING SCATTERPLOTS

Before computing the correlation between two quantitative variables, researchers should generate a scatterplot of the data to determine if Pearson's or Spearman's correlation, or neither of them, should be used. As discussed in the reading, if the scatterplot is *linear*, a Pearson's correlation can be run. If the scatterplot is *monotonic*, or "slightly curvy but not dramatically changing its overall trend," a Spearman's correlation can be used. And if the scatterplot of data is *nonmonotonic*, or "dramatically changing directions," neither Pearson's nor Spearman's correlation should be performed. The figures exemplify possible trends and the type of correlation that should be used to analyze them.

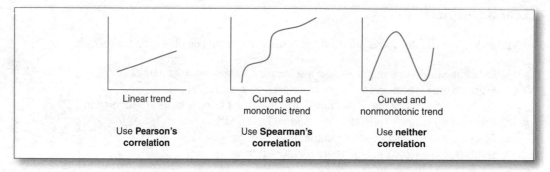

Linear trend	Curved and monotonic trend	Curved and nonmonotonic trend
Use **Pearson's** correlation	Use **Spearman's** correlation	Use **neither** correlation

For the next four questions, you should look at the scatterplot and determine if a Pearson's or Spearman's correlation should be performed or neither of the two.

4. To determine if arousal is associated with running speed, a sports psychologist obtains a sample of runners and measures their reported level of arousal on a 10-point scale, with higher numbers indicating higher levels of arousal. After measuring their arousal, each person is asked to run 400 meters, and the times are recorded.

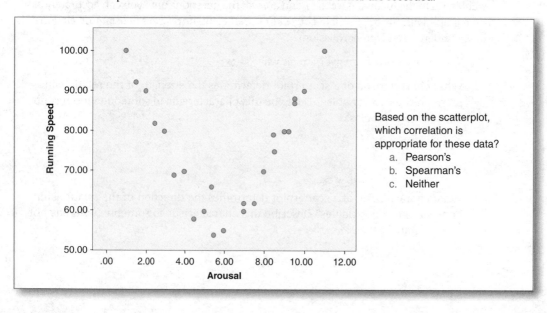

Based on the scatterplot, which correlation is appropriate for these data?
a. Pearson's
b. Spearman's
c. Neither

5. The following height and shoe size data came from a sample of 17 college students:

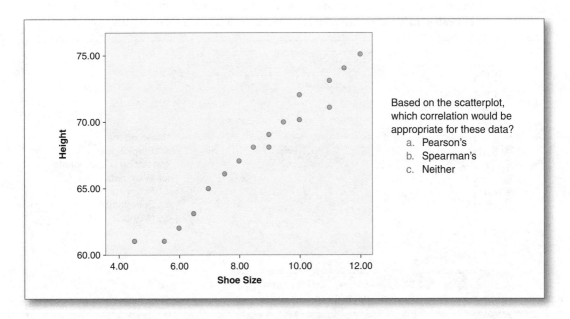

Based on the scatterplot, which correlation would be appropriate for these data?
a. Pearson's
b. Spearman's
c. Neither

6. The members of a college admissions committee want to know if the Math portion of the Scholastic Aptitude Test (SAT) is a good predictor of college performance. They obtain Math SAT scores as well as first-year college grade-point averages (GPAs) from a sample of 23 students.

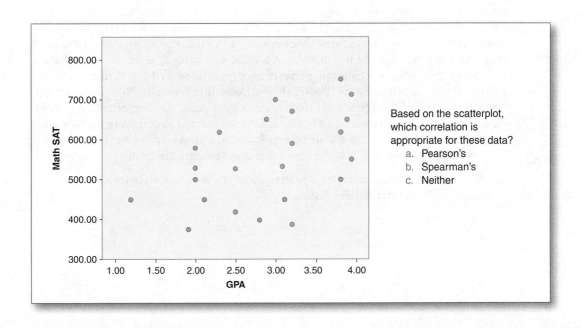

Based on the scatterplot, which correlation is appropriate for these data?
a. Pearson's
b. Spearman's
c. Neither

7. A student notices that she is usually in a bad mood when she is sleep deprived and wonders if this is true for other people. To investigate this, she asks students to report the number of hours of sleep they received the previous night and conducts a survey assessing their current mood (higher numbers indicate a more negative mood).

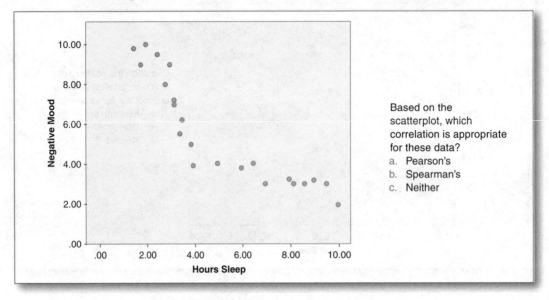

Based on the scatterplot, which correlation is appropriate for these data?
a. Pearson's
b. Spearman's
c. Neither

COMPUTING A CORRELATION BY HAND (TWO-TAILED)

Some psychologists suggest that people possess a variety of different types of intelligences, including bodily–kinesthetic intelligence, linguistic intelligence, and musical intelligence. However, some suggest that there is a general intelligence factor that underlines all of these different types of intelligence. If there is a general intelligence, then people who have high scores on one type of intelligence should also have high scores on a different type of intelligence. A school psychologist tests this by assessing the relationship between academic performance (measured by High School GPA) and athletic ability (a measure of bodily–kinesthetic intelligence). The psychologist obtained the GPA of 10 high school students in a gym class. He then obtained a rating of each student/athlete's athletic ability by asking the teacher to complete the following question for each student: On a scale of 1 to 9, rate this player's athletic ability: 1 = *far below average*, 5 = *average*, 9 = *far above average*. The data are in the table below.

8. Use the space below to create a scatterplot of the relationship between High School GPA (*X*) and Athletic Rating (*Y*).

Participant	High School GPA (X)	High School GPA (z Score)	Athletic Rating (Y)	Athletic Rating (z Score)	$z_x z_y$
A	2.6	−0.50962	6	−0.60764	0.310
B	3.0	0.07280	7	0.15191	0.011
C	2.8	−0.21841	5	−1.36720	0.299
D	3.6	0.94645	8	0.91147	0.863
E	2.1	−1.23766	5	−1.36720	1.692
F	3.3	0.50962	7	0.15191	0.077
G	3.9	1.38327	8	0.91147	1.261
H	2.4	−0.80084	6	−0.60764	0.487
I	2.0		7		
J	3.8		9		
	$M_x = 2.95$ $SD_x = 0.687$			$M_y = 6.80$ $SD_y = 1.317$	$\Sigma z_x z_y =$

9. State the two-tailed null hypothesis for this study.

10. State the two-tailed research hypothesis for this study.

11. Compute the *df*, and define the critical region for *r*.

12. Use the definitional formula to compute the correlation coefficient by hand. The first step is to compute the *z* score (i.e., $z = (X - M) / SD_X$) for each *X* and the *z* score for each *Y* (i.e., $z = (Y - M) / SD_Y$). This has been done for Participants A through H in the above table. Complete the table by doing the same thing for Participants I and J.

13. Look at the pairs of z scores. If one z score is positive, does its pair also tend to be positive, or does the other in each pair tend to be negative? What does this imply about the sign of the final correlation (r) between these variables?

   a.   The final correlation will be positive.

   b.   The final correlation will be negative.

14. Multiply each pair of z scores, and then sum all of the products to find $\Sigma z_x z_y$. Place the value in the above table.

15. Use the definitional correlational formula below to compute a correlation between High School GPA and Athletic Rating.

$$r = \frac{\Sigma z_x z_y}{N-1} =$$

16. Compute the effect size for this study, and interpret it as small, small-medium, and so on.

17. Confirm that your hand calculations are correct by entering the data into SPSS and running a Pearson's correlation. Do this by clicking on the Analyze menu. Choose Correlate, and then select Bivariate. Move the two variables you want to correlate into the Variables box. Then click OK.

WRITING AN APA-STYLE REPORTING STATEMENT

18. After confirming that the r you computed by hand is correct, choose the paragraph below that best summarizes the correlation results. Then fill in the blanks with the appropriate statistical information.

   a.   There was a significant correlation between the High School GPAs and the Ratings of Athletic Ability of high school students, $r(\_\_\_)$ = _____, $p < .05$. Those with high GPA tended to have higher ratings of athletic ability.

   b.   There was no significant correlation between the High School GPAs and the Ratings of Athletic Ability of high school students, $r(\_\_\_)$ = _____, $p > .05$.

   c.   There was a significant correlation between the High School GPAs and the Ratings of Athletic Ability of high school students, $r(\_\_\_)$ = _____, $p < .05$. Those with high GPA tended to have lower ratings of athletic ability.

19. Use the previous example as a guide to compose a correct reporting statement for the following example:

   A school psychologist wanted to determine if students' math ability (measured by students' scores on a standardized math test) was correlated with their reading ability (measured by students' scores on a standardized reading test). He collected data from 22 students, and the correlation was .65. Compose an APA-style reporting statement for this result.

COMPUTING A CORRELATION BY HAND (ONE-TAILED)

A health psychologist was interested in the relationship between stress (measured by a survey yielding a score ranging from 0 to 10, with higher numbers representing more stress) and exercise. The psychologist obtained the stress scores of nine college students and asked them to report the number of hours they exercise in a typical week. She expects that higher levels of exercise will be associated with less stress.

20. State the one-tailed null hypothesis for this study.

21. State the one-tailed research hypothesis for this study.

22. Compute the df, and define the critical region for r; use $\alpha = .05$.

23. Use the space below to create a scatterplot of the relationship between stress score and hours of exercise.

Participant	Stress Score (X)	Stress Score (z Score)	Hours of Exercise (Y)	Hours of Exercise (z Score)	$z_x z_y$
A	2	−1.708	4	1.667	−2.847
B	5	0.066	3	0.667	0.044
C	7	1.248	1	−1.333	−1.664
D	4	−0.526	1	−1.333	0.701
E	6	0.657	3	0.667	0.438
F	5	0.066	3	0.667	0.044
G	7	1.248	2	−0.333	−0.416
H	3		2		
I	5		2		
	$M_x = 4.889$ $SD_x = 1.691$		$M_y = 2.333$ $SD_y = 1.000$		$\Sigma z_x z_y =$

24. Use the definitional formula to compute the correlation coefficient. You will need to complete some parts of the above table.

$$r = \frac{\sum z_x z_y}{N - 1}$$

25. Compute the effect size for this study, and interpret it as small, small-medium, and so on.

26. Confirm that your hand calculations are correct by entering the data into SPSS and running a Pearson's correlation. Do this by clicking on the Analyze menu. Choose Correlate, and then select Bivariate. Then move the two variables you want to correlate into the Variables box. Then click OK.

27. After confirming that the r you computed by hand is correct, write an APA-style summary of the results. Use the examples from Question 18 as a guide.

SPEARMAN'S CORRELATION EXAMPLE

A sports psychologist is interested in determining if people who finish earlier in a race tend to be more flexible than people who finish later in a race. She obtained the finishing positions for 15 people in a marathon and then assessed their flexibility. Flexibility was measured by asking the runners to sit with their legs straight in front of them and then reach as far as they could. Higher numbers indicated greater flexibility.

Finishing Place	Flexibility
1	8
2	6
3	7
4	7
5	5
6	9
7	4
8	3
9	5
10	4
11	6
12	7
13	2
14	3
15	8

28. State the one-tailed null hypothesis for this study.

29. State the one-tailed research hypothesis for this study.

30. Explain why Spearman's correlation is more appropriate for these data than Pearson's correlation.

31. Enter the data into SPSS, and create a scatterplot. To do this, click on the Graphs menu. Choose Legacy Dialogs, and then select Scatter/Dot. Choose Simple Scatter, and click Define. Next, you need to indicate which variable you want on the x-axis and which variable you want on the y-axis. Click OK to create the scatterplot. Does a Spearman's correlation look appropriate for these data?

32. Run a Spearman's correlation. Do this by clicking on the Analyze menu. Choose Correlate, and then select Bivariate. Move the two variables you want to correlate into the Variables box. Check the box for Spearman's and uncheck the box for Pearson's. Then click OK.

$$r_s = \underline{\hspace{3cm}}.$$

33. Compute the effect size for this study, and interpret it as small, small-medium, and so on.

34. Write an APA-style summary of the results.

Activity 14-2: Introduction to Regression and Prediction

Learning Objectives

After reading the chapter and completing this activity, you should be able to do the following:

- Compute a regression equation by hand and using SPSS
- Summarize the results of a regression analysis in APA format
- Predict a score using a regression equation

INTRODUCTION TO REGRESSION

Correlation coefficients provide a measure of the strength and direction of the relationship between two variables. Through hypothesis testing, you can determine whether the relationship between two variables is statistically significant. If the relationship is significant, you should be able to predict one variable if you know the scores on the other variable. For example, if height and foot length are significantly correlated, you can use foot length to predict someone's height. You cannot use correlation coefficients directly to do this. Instead, you must create a regression equation. The following example illustrates how this is done.

Predicting Height From Foot Length

Anthropometry is the study of the relationships among human body measurements. Data from anthropometric studies are used to design desks, movie seats, cars, and a variety of other products. These same data can also help investigators solve crimes. For example, a police officer may know the length of a suspect's foot from a footprint left at a crime scene. Most people are not accustomed to looking at foot length, so describing the suspect as having a foot 10.5 inches long would probably not help find the suspect. It would be far more useful to tell people to look for a suspect who is of a certain height. Investigators might be able to use the suspect's foot length to predict the suspect's height. The accuracy of this prediction would depend on the size of the correlation between foot length and height. To determine if foot length is a good predictor of height, a researcher collects the following data:

Foot Length (X) (inches)	Height (Y) (inches)
8.5	64
10	67
11	71
8	61
9.5	67

1. Compute the Pearson's correlation between height and shoe size. You may use SPSS or do it by hand.

You should have found a correlation coefficient of $r = .98$. Clearly, there was a strong correlation between foot length and height. This strong correlation can help you predict the suspect's height from the suspect's foot length. You will need to use a regression equation specifically designed to predict height from foot length.

2. What is the primary purpose of a regression equation?

The regression equation you will use has this general format:

$$\hat{Y} = bX + a$$

where $\hat{Y}$ is the variable we are trying to predict (in this case height) and X is the variable we use to make the prediction (in this case foot length). Both b and a are values that change based on the specific values of X and Y, and therefore their exact values must be computed for each regression equation. Specifically, b is the slope of the regression line and is computed by dividing the standard deviation of the variable height (SD_Y) by the standard deviation of foot length (SD_X) and then multiplying the quotient by the correlation coefficient (r).

3. Compute b.

$$b = r\left(\frac{SD_Y}{SD_X}\right) =$$

You should have found that $b = 3.07$. Next, you will need to compute a, which is the y intercept of the regression line. To compute a, you multiply the mean of foot length (M_X) by b and subtract the result from the mean of height (M_Y).

4. Compute a.

$$a = M_Y - bM_X =$$

5. You should have found that $a = 37.14$. The general regression equation is displayed below. Use the specific values for b and a that you computed above to create a regression equation that predicts height from foot length. In other words, substitute the specific values of b and a into the general regression equation, and write that specific regression equation below.

$$\hat{Y} = bX + a$$

6. You can now use this equation to predict a person's height based on his or her foot length. For example, use the equation to predict the height of someone with a foot that is 7 inches long. In other words, when $X = 7$, what does $\hat{Y}$ equal?

7. Use the same equation to predict the height of someone with a foot that is 10.5 inches long. What is the predicted height of the suspect who left the footprint at the crime scene?

8. Below is a scatterplot of the foot length and height data from the first page of this activity. Plot the two predicted data points from Questions 6 and 7 on the scatterplot, and then draw a straight line through those two points.

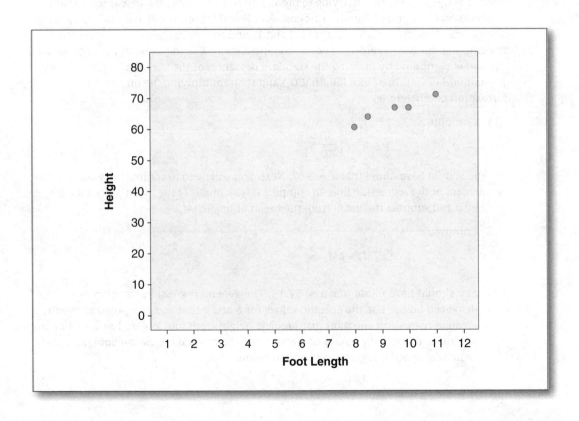

The line you just drew is called the foot length–height regression line because it was created using the foot length–height regression equation. The regression equation gives you the line that best fits the data. In this case, the line fits the data very well. Overall, the individual data points are very close to the line. This should not be too surprising given that the correlation between height and foot length was .98. In general, the greater the magnitude of the correlation (the closer it is to -1 or $+1$), the closer the data points will be to the line.

9. You can estimate how well the regression equation predicts Variable Y (foot length) by computing r^2 (the coefficient of determination). Compute r^2.

10. Which of the following correlations (i.e., r values) will result in the most accurate predictions?

   a. $-.84$

   b. $+.40$

   c. 0

Using SPSS to Do Regression

You can also compute a regression equation using SPSS. First, enter the data into SPSS by creating one column for height and another for foot length. Second, compute the regression equation with the following steps:

- Click on the Analyze menu. Choose Regression, and then select Linear.
- Move foot length into the Independent measures box and height into the Dependent Variables box.
- Click on OK to run the analysis.

The relevant portion of the output is provided below:

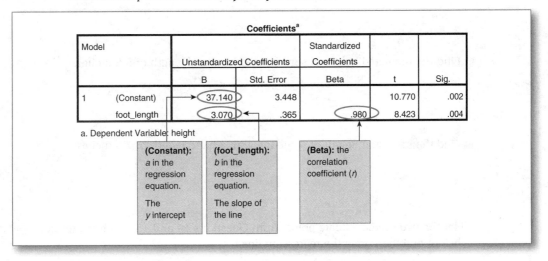

Coefficients[a]

Model		Unstandardized Coefficients		Standardized Coefficients	t	Sig.
		B	Std. Error	Beta		
1	(Constant)	37.140	3.448		10.770	.002
	foot_length	3.070	.365	.980	8.423	.004

a. Dependent Variable: height

(Constant): a in the regression equation. The y intercept	(foot_length): b in the regression equation. The slope of the line	(Beta): the correlation coefficient (r)

Using SPSS to Predict Height From Hand Length

When the partial remains of a skeleton are found, investigators often need to know the height of the person to help identify who the person was. Although foot length is a good predictor, it is not always available, and other predictors must be used. A researcher wants to know how accurately the length of the hand can predict height. She collects the following data:

Hand Length (X) (inches)	Height (Y) (inches)
5.9	65
7.8	69
6.3	68
6.5	67
6.9	70
6.2	62

11. The correlation between hand length and height was $r = .648$. Compute b.

$$b = r\left(\frac{SD_Y}{SD_X}\right) =$$

12. Compute a.

$$a = M_Y - bM_X =$$

13. Write the specific regression equation for predicting height from hand length. In other words, substitute a and b into the general regression equation, and write the specific regression equation.

14. Find the predicted height of someone with a hand length of 5.5 inches.

15. Find the predicted height of someone with a hand length of 7.5 inches.

16. Plot the two predicted data points from Questions 14 and 15 in the scatterplot below, and then draw the regression line.

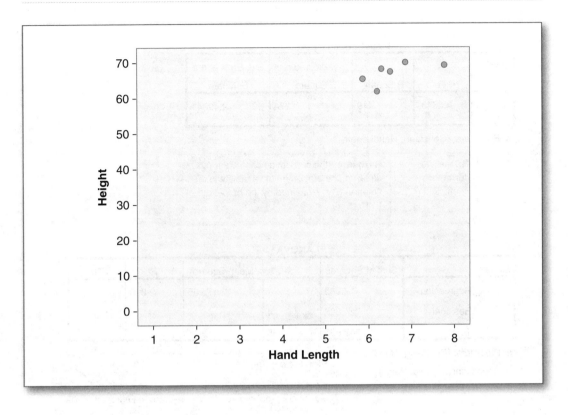

17. Compute r^2.

18. Explain how you can use the scatterplots for foot length and hand length to determine which variable (hand length or foot length) is the better predictor of height.

19. Explain how you can use r^2 to determine which variable (hand length or foot length) is the better predictor of height.

20. Enter the hand length data into SPSS, and run a regression equation to predict height from hand length. The relevant portions of the SPSS regression output are given below:

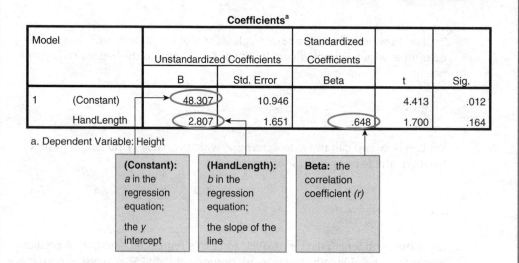

Model Summary

Model	R	R Square	Adjusted r Square	Std. Error of the Estimate
1	.648[a]	.419	.274	2.49341

a. Predictors: (Constant), HandLength

R: the correlation coefficient *(r)*

R Square: the correlation coefficient *(r)* squared; the proportion of variability in the criterion (DV) explained by the predictor (IV)

ANOVA[b]

Model		Sum of Squares	df	Mean Square	F	Sig.
1	Regression	17.965	1	17.965	2.890	.164[a]
	Residual	24.868	4	6.217		
	Total	42.833	5			

a. Predictors: (Constant), HandLength

b. Dependent Variable: Height

Sig: the *p* value;

If $p \leq \alpha$ conclude that the predictor (IV) explains a significant proportion of the variability in the criterion (DV)

If $p > \alpha$ conclude that the predictor (IV) does not explain a significant proportion of the variability in the criterion (DV)

Coefficients[a]

Model		Unstandardized Coefficients		Standardized Coefficients	t	Sig.
		B	Std. Error	Beta		
1	(Constant)	48.307	10.946		4.413	.012
	HandLength	2.807	1.651	.648	1.700	.164

a. Dependent Variable: Height

(Constant): *a* in the regression equation;

the *y* intercept

(HandLength): *b* in the regression equation;

the slope of the line

Beta: the correlation coefficient *(r)*

You can use the SPSS output to locate b and a and thus create the regression equation. The output also gives a way to determine how well the data points fit the regression line (i.e., it gives you an effect size for the correlation you are using to make your prediction). The r^2 value of .419 (in the "Model Summary" output) tells you that 41.9% of the variance in height can be explained by hand length. The value of r^2 should be interpreted using the same guidelines as for η_p^2: Namely, values close to .1 are small, values close to .09 are medium, and values close to .25 are considered large. The correlation between hand length and height is a large correlation. To determine whether 49.1% is a statistically significant amount of the variance, you look at the "ANOVA" output. The F value was 2.89, with a p value of .164 (Sig.). If the Sig. value is less than or equal to alpha (.05), you conclude that the predictor (hand length) does explain a statistically significant proportion of the variance in the criterion (height). If the Sig. value is greater than alpha (.05), you conclude that the predictor does not explain a significant proportion of the variance in the criterion.

21. Does hand length explain a statistically significant proportion of the variance in height?

22. What conclusion can you draw from the fact that the r^2 (i.e., the effect size) between hand length and height was large and yet hand length did not predict a significant portion of the variance in height (i.e., hand length was NOT a good predictor of height)?

23. Which of the following is the best summary of these results?
    a. Hand length explained a significant proportion of the variance in height, $r^2 = .42$, $F(1, 4) = 2.89$, $p < .05$.
    b. Hand length did not explain a significant proportion of the variance in height, $r^2 = .42$, $F(1, 4) = 2.89$, $p > .05$, but the sample size was probably too small to draw any conclusions from this study.

The following SPSS output is from a regression analysis using head circumference (measured in millimeters) to predict height (in millimeters).

Model Summary

Model	R	R Square	Adjusted r Square	Std. Error of the Estimate
1	.352[a]	.124	.119	62.314

a. Predictors: (Constant), Head_Cir

ANOVA[b]

Model		Sum of Squares	df	Mean Square	F	Sig.
1	Regression	94998.467	1	94998.467	24.465	.000[a]
	Residual	671757.510	173	3882.991		
	Total	766755.977	174			

a. Predictors: (Constant), Head_Cir

b. Dependent Variable: Height

Coefficients[a]

Model		Unstandardized Coefficients		Standardized Coefficients	t	Sig.
		B	Std. Error	Beta		
1	(Constant)	811.290	190.647		4.255	.000
	Head_Cir	1.660	.336	.352	4.946	.000

a. Dependent Variable: Height

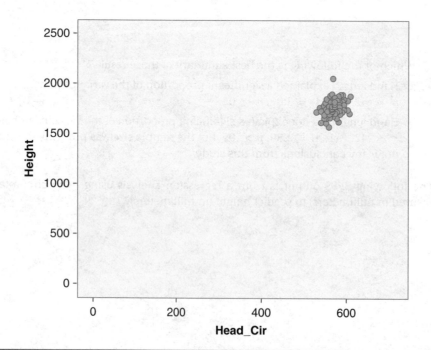

24. Write the regression equation for predicting height from head circumference below.

25. If someone had a head circumference of 570 millimeters, what would be your prediction of that person's height?

26. What was the value of r^2?

27. Does head circumference explain a significant proportion of the variance in height?

28. Summarize the results in APA style.

29. Head circumference was a significant predictor of height, but hand length was not, despite the fact that r^2 was actually higher for hand length ($r^2 = .419$) than for head circumference ($r^2 = .124$). Why was head circumference a significant predictor but hand length not a significant predictor?

Activity 14-3:   Choose the Correct Statistic

Learning Objectives

After reading the chapter and completing this activity, you should be able to do the following:

- Read a research scenario and determine which statistic should be used

Determine which of the following statistics should be used in each of the research scenarios given below: z for a single score, z for sample mean, single sample t, related samples t, independent samples t, one-way independent samples analysis of variance (ANOVA), two-way independent samples ANOVA, Pearson's correlation, or Spearman's correlation.

1. A researcher wants to know if the relative wealth of a nation is associated with literacy. To determine if these two variables are related, the researcher obtains data from two different sources. The International Monetary Fund (IMF) ranks countries by their gross domestic product (GDP), while the United Nations Development Programme ranks countries by their literacy rates. Which statistic would help the researcher determine if GDP is associated with literacy rates?

2. An English professor is troubled by the quality of his students' papers and believes that they are not putting much effort into their work. He wonders if requiring students to post their papers on the Internet may increase the effort students put into the paper and hence the quality of those papers. To test this, the professor assigns students in two different sections of the class to write a research paper. One class is told that they will turn their final paper in to the professor. The other class is told that they will turn their final paper in by posting it on the Internet. A different professor reads the papers (without knowing if they were posted on the Internet) and rates them for quality on a 10-point scale, with 1 being the worst and 10 being the best. Analysis of the results revealed that the papers that were posted online received higher scores ($M = 6.59$) than the papers that were turned in to the professor ($M = 5.12$). Which statistic could be used to determine if the online papers were significantly better than the papers that were just turned into the professor?

3. Although posting papers on the Internet was effective, it was quite a bit of work for the professor and the students. Thus, the English professor wonders if posting on the Internet is really necessary. It is possible that this increase in quality is the result of students being concerned about people other than the professor reading their papers. If this is the case, the professor reasons, having other students in class read their papers would have the same effect. For the next paper, the students were placed in one of three groups: The first group was asked to give the paper only to the professor; the second group, to give the paper to another student and the professor; and the third group, to post the paper online. Again, the quality of the papers was judged on a 10-point scale. Which statistic could be used to determine if there was a difference in quality across the three groups?

4. A number of patients tell a physical therapist (PT) that yoga seems to help improve balance. The PT wants to know if yoga may help her elderly patients, who are particularly prone to fractures following falls. To determine if yoga improves balance, the PT assesses balance in each of 29 patients. Each patient completes a series of tasks (e.g., standing on one foot) and then receives a score between 0 and 75, with higher numbers indicating better balance. All patients then participate in 1-hour-long yoga sessions twice a week for 3 months. At the end of the 3 months,

balance is assessed once again. What statistic could be used to determine if balance scores were higher after completing the yoga sessions than before?

5. Car seat laws vary by state, but one common law is that infants must be in a rear-facing car seat until they are 1 year old or weigh 20 pounds. If the average weight of 1-year-old infants is 23 pounds, with a standard deviation of 1 pound, what percentage of children will not be ready to move out of a rear-facing car seat when they are 1 year old?

6. A therapist working in a college counseling center finds that a common problem facing students is loneliness. He wonders if loneliness changes throughout their 4 years in college. He collects data from 20 freshmen, 20 sophomores, 20 juniors, and 20 seniors. Loneliness is measured using a questionnaire that results in scores ranging from 1 to 60, with higher numbers indicating greater loneliness. What statistic could be used to determine if freshmen were lonelier than sophomores, juniors, and seniors?

7. A counselor at a different college hears of these results and wonders if the same would be true of her students. More than half of her students live at home, and she thinks that these students may be less susceptible to loneliness than students who do not live at home. To test, this she collects data on loneliness through a questionnaire from freshmen, sophomores, juniors, and seniors. She also asks them whether or not they live at home. What statistic could be used to determine if the relationship between year in school and loneliness is the same for students who live at home and for students who live at school?

8. Each year, *US News & World Report* ranks U.S. colleges and universities. A number of different variables go into these rankings, including selectiveness of admissions. In general, the more selective the admission criteria, the higher the ranking. To help improve their ranking, a university admissions committee decides that students will only be admitted if their ACT scores are above 28. If ACT scores are normally distributed with a mean of 21.1 and a standard deviation of 4.7, what percentage of students would be eligible for admission to this university?

9. A researcher conducts a study to determine if sugar consumption is associated with depression. The researcher records per capita sugar consumption for 30 different countries and also records the prevalence of depression in those countries. Prevalence rates were recorded as the estimated percentage of the population with depression. What statistic should be used to determine if as sugar consumption rises, so does the prevalence of depression?

10. The study about sugar consumption and depression is picked up by the media, with many suggesting that sugar consumption is the cause of depression. Of course, the previous study did not allow the researcher to determine if one variable caused the other. To answer this question, another researcher designed a carefully controlled study with 53 participants. At the beginning of the study, the researcher measured the depression levels for all 53 participants. For 1 month

following the initial assessment, the participants were instructed to consume at least 400 grams of white sugar each day. At the end of the month, depression scores were again recorded. What statistic should be used to determine if depression scores were higher after 1 month of a high sugar diet?

11. A statistics instructor wants to know if hard work really pays off in her course, and so at the end of the semester, the instructor gives students a questionnaire assessing how much effort they have put into the course. The effort questionnaire yields one value between 0 and 100, with higher numbers indicating more effort. She also records the students' final grade in the course (A, B, C, D, or F). What statistic should be used to determine if effort is associated with course grades?

12. Research has shown that exercise leads to increased HDL cholesterol levels (HDL is the good cholesterol); however, exactly how much exercise is needed is not known. Thus, a researcher designs a study in which participants with low levels of HDL are randomly assigned to exercise for 0 minute a day, 30 minutes, 60 minutes, or 90 minutes. After 3 months of these exercise regimens, the HDL cholesterol levels are measured. Women and men often react differently to treatments, and so the researcher also investigated the impact of gender in the study. What statistic could be used to determine if the effect of exercise on cholesterol is the same for males and females?

13. To test the efficacy of new cancer treatments, patients with cancer must be recruited to participate in clinical trials. A doctor notices that some of his colleagues seem to be very likely to enroll patients in these trials while others seem to be less likely to enroll their patients in clinical trials. She wonders if this discrepancy is a function of the specialty of the physician. Specifically, she wants to know if surgeons are more likely than nonsurgeons to enroll their patients in clinical trials. To test this, she records whether each of 54 doctors are surgeons or not and then also records the percentage of each doctor's cancer patients who enrolled in clinical trials. What statistic could she use to determine if the percentage of patients in clinical trials is the same for surgeons and nonsurgeons?

14. An industrial/organizational psychologist is interested in understanding the effect of spending time on the Internet at work doing things unrelated to work. She wonders if time spent off the job is harmful to performance on the job or if it provides a needed break and actually improves performance. To assess the relationship between Internet use and performance, she sends 98 employees an anonymous survey. On the survey, they are asked to indicate how many minutes they spend each day on the Internet doing things that are not related to work. She also asks them to report their score on their annual performance review. Scores on the performance review range from 1 to 10, with higher scores indicating better performance. What statistic could be used to determine whether there is a statistically significant relationship between time on the Internet and performance scores?

15. Every year, students in a particular school district take a standardized test that is designed to assess reading and writing skills. Last year, the average score on this

test was 49 (slightly below average). The principal of this district attempts to improve these scores by trying a new program with a sample of 50 third graders. This new program rewards kids for reading throughout the school year and the summer. She hopes that this extra reading will improve the scores on the test. What statistic could she use to determine if reading scores were higher in the group that participated in the new program?

Activity 14-4:   Practice Problems

SCENARIO 1: CORRELATION AND REGRESSION

A student in a statistics class thinks that people who like to run are weird. To test this hypothesis, she gives a sample of students two questionnaires to complete. One assesses how much they like to run, with higher numbers indicating a more favorable attitude toward running. The other questionnaire assesses weirdness, with higher numbers indicating more weirdness. Here are the data she obtained. Given her expectation that those who like to run are also weird, she chooses to do a one-tailed test. She also chooses an alpha of .05.

Running Rating	Weirdness Rating
5	7
9	9
4	6
5	3
2	4
1	6
4	4
7	6
6	5
4	8
4	5

1. Create a scatterplot, and determine if a Pearson's or a Spearman's correlation is appropriate.

   a. The trend in the scatterplot is sufficiently linear, so a Pearson's correlation can be used.

   b. The trend in the scatterplot is not sufficiently linear, so a Pearson's correlation should not be used.

2. Which of the following is the correct symbolic representation of the null hypothesis for this one-tailed test?

   a. $H_0: \rho > 0$

   b. $H_0: \rho < 0$

   c. $H_0: \rho \geq 0$

   d. $H_0: \rho \leq 0$

3. Which of the following is the best verbal representation of the null hypothesis for this one-tailed test?

   a. How much people like to run is positively associated with how weird they are.

   b. How much people like to run is negatively associated with how weird they are.

   c. How much people like to run is not associated with how weird they are, or it is negatively associated with how weird they are.

4. Which of the following is the correct symbolic representation of the research hypothesis for this test?

   a. $H_1: \rho > 0$

   b. $H_1: \rho < 0$

   c. $H_1: \rho \geq 0$

   d. $H_1: \rho \leq 0$

5. Which of the following is the best verbal representation of the research hypothesis for this test?

   a. How much people like to run is positively associated with how weird they are.

   b. How much people like to run is negatively associated with how weird they are.

   c. How much people like to run is not associated with how weird they are.

6. What is the df for this correlation (i.e., $df = N - 2$)?

7. What is the critical value for this one-tailed Pearson's correlation?

8. Compute Pearson's r.

9. What is the effect size for this study (i.e., r^2)?

10. Is the effect size small, small-medium, medium, medium-large, or large?

11. The effect size of this study indicates that
    a. 18% of the variability in scores for liking to run can be explained by the variability in weirdness scores.
    b. 18% of the scores for liking to run are unexplainable.
    c. 18% of the scores for liking to run are explainable.

12. Which of the following is the best summary of this study's results?
    a. How much people like to run and their weirdness scores are significantly correlated, $r(9) = .43, p < .05$.
    b. How much people like to run and their weirdness scores are not significantly correlated, $r(9) = .43, p > .05$. However, the medium-large effect size suggests that the study's sample size was too small.
    c. How much people like to run and their weirdness scores are significantly correlated, $r(9) = .34, p > .05$.
    d. How much people like to run and their weirdness scores are not significantly correlated, $r(9) = .34, p < .05$.

13. Suppose that a track coach wants to try to identify middle school students who might be good runners by giving students the weirdness questionnaire. Because there was a positive correlation, the coach reasons that students who are weird would be good runners. Why is it not a good idea to use the weirdness ratings to predict running ability?
    a. Because the correlation coefficient was not significant
    b. Because running is a better predictor of weirdness than weirdness is of running

14. After the coach realizes that weirdness is not a good predictor of running ability, she decides to collect data to determine if grip strength is a good predictor of running speed. To assess the relationship between grip strength and running speed, she measures the grip strength of 78 students. The average grip strength for the students was $M = 60.85, SD = 17.03$, with higher numbers indicating greater grip strength. The same students then run a quarter of a mile. The average running speed was $M = 86.73$ seconds, $SD = 26.17$ seconds. The correlation between the two measures was $r(76) = -.29, p < .05$. Compute b for the regression equation.
    a. .19
    b. −.19
    c. .45
    d. −.45

15. Compute a for the regression equation.

    a. 114.11

    b. − 114.11

    c. 99.88

    d. −99.88

16. Which of the following is the correct regression equation?

    a. $\hat{Y} = -99.88X + 99.88$

    b. $\hat{Y} = -.45X + 114.11$

    c. $\hat{Y} = 114.11 + 99.88X$

17. Use the regression equation to predict the running speed of a person with a grip strength score of 50.

    a. 80.25

    b. 66.59

    c. 91.61

    d. 78.92

18. Compute r^2.

    a. .08

    b. −.08

19. Based on the r^2 value you computed above, is hand grip strength a good predictor of running speed?

    a. Yes

    b. No

SCENARIO 2: CORRELATION

As a class project, a group of students wanted to determine if there was an association between the number of Facebook friends a person added that week and that person's current satisfaction with life. The students asked a sample of 10 people to reveal how many Facebook friends they added that week. They also asked the students to complete a satisfaction with life scale. A higher score on the scale indicated higher life satisfaction. Use the data the students collected to test the null hypothesis that these two variables are not associated. Use an alpha value of .05, two-tailed.

Facebook Friends	Satisfaction With Life Scale
5	11
6	10
2	5
8	9
6	6
4	8
5	12
3	9
8	10
5	7

20. Create a scatterplot of these data.

21. Which statistic is appropriate to determine if these two variables are associated?

22. Write the null hypothesis and research hypothesis of this study using population parameters.

23. What is the critical value for this two-tailed test?

24. Compute the test statistic.

25. Compute the effect size.

26. Write an APA-style summary of this analysis.

27. Enter the above data into SPSS, and run the appropriate correlation analysis. Confirm that the obtained r value you computed by hand is the same as that produced by SPSS.

SCENARIO 3: CORRELATION AND REGRESSION

A researcher wanted to know if there was an association between the number of books a student reads during summer and that student's attitude toward school. The researcher asked eight students who were entering the sixth grade how many books they had read during summer and how much they liked school (1 = *I don't like school at all* to 10 = *I really like school*). The researcher expected that these variables would be positively associated. Use a one-tailed test with an alpha value of .05.

Number of Books Read During Summer	Attitude Toward School
0	1
2	3
4	5
6	9
5	6
7	8
4	7
2	4
3	4
8	7

28. Create a scatterplot of these data.

29. Which statistic is appropriate to determine if these two variables are associated?

30. Write the null and research hypotheses of this study using population parameters (one-tailed).

31. What is the critical value for this one-tailed test?

32. Compute the test statistic.

33. Compute the effect size.

34. Write an APA-style summary of this analysis.

35. Use the correlation you computed on the previous page to create a regression equation to predict school attitude from number of books read.

36. Use the regression equation to determine the predicted score for attitude toward school for someone who read one book.

Goodness-of-Fit and Independence Chi-Square Statistics

After reading this chapter, you should be able to perform the following:

- Describe the difference between a goodness-of-fit chi-square and a chi-square test of independence, and identify when to use each
- Describe the logic of the chi-square statistic
- Write the null and research hypotheses for goodness-of-fit chi-square and a chi-square test of independence
- Compute the chi-square statistic and determine if the null hypothesis should be rejected
- Summarize the results of a chi-square

OVERVIEW OF CHI-SQUARE

Most of the statistics you have learned in this course require you to compute one or more means before the results can be interpreted. However, there are many interesting research scenarios in which the data are nominal (e.g., *political affiliation*: Democrat, Republican, Independent) or ordinal (e.g., *highest level of education completed*: high school, some college, college, some postgraduate, graduate), and therefore, it is impossible to compute a mean. For example, suppose you wanted to know if voters' affiliation with political parties is significantly different today than it was 2 years ago. You could obtain a sample of voters and ask them with which political party they most often affiliate: Democrat, Republican, or Independent. Example data are presented in Table 15.1.

Table 15.1   Number of people identifying with each political affiliation.

Political Affiliation		
Democrat	Republican	Independent
22	22	12

In this case, it would be impossible to compute a mean response because the response options are nominal categories. The data are *frequency counts* for each political party (i.e., the number of people who said Democrat, Republican, or Independent). A chi-square statistic is used when the data to be analyzed are frequency counts for different categories.

Reading Question

1. When the data that a study produces is in the form of _____ the chi-square statistic is appropriate.

   a. means

   b. standard deviations

   c. interval/ratio data

   d. frequency counts for different categories

There are two different types of chi-square statistics, and they are each used in different research situations. A *goodness-of-fit chi-square* is used to analyze the relative frequencies of different categories within a single variable. The political affiliation study described above would be analyzed using a goodness-of-fit chi-square because the researchers want to compare the relative frequencies of Democrats, Republicans, and Independents, which are all different categories of the variable political affiliation. A *chi-square test of independence* is used to determine if the relative frequencies within the categories of one variable are associated with the relative frequencies within the categories of a second variable. For example, suppose you wanted to know if peoples' political affiliation (e.g., Democrat, Republican, or Independent) was associated with their opinion of a Democratic president's policies (e.g., Approve or Disapprove). In order to answer this question, you could obtain a sample of voters and ask them their political affiliation (i.e., Democrat, Republican, or Independent) and their opinion of the president's policies (i.e., Approve or Disapprove). All of the possible combinations of answers create six categories and the voters' actual answers determine the frequency counts in each of the six categories. Example data are presented in Table 15.2.

Table 15.2   Number of people identifying with each political affiliation by approval of the president's policies.

		Political Affiliation		
		Democrat	Republican	Independent
Policy opinion	Approve	15	2	6
	Disapprove	7	20	6

The chi-square for independence will determine if the two variables of political affiliation and policy opinion are independent (i.e., if there is no association between the two variables).

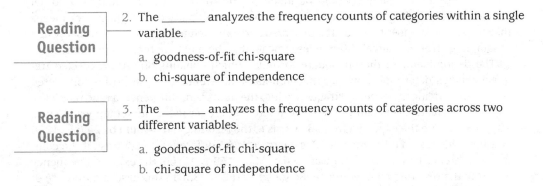

Reading Question

2. The _____ analyzes the frequency counts of categories within a single variable.

   a. goodness-of-fit chi-square

   b. chi-square of independence

Reading Question

3. The _____ analyzes the frequency counts of categories across two different variables.

   a. goodness-of-fit chi-square

   b. chi-square of independence

LOGIC OF THE CHI-SQUARE TEST

Both chi-square tests use the same logic. In fact, they both use the following formula.

$$\chi^2 = \Sigma \frac{(OF - EF)^2}{EF}$$

There are only two terms in the chi-square formula, the observed frequency (i.e., OF) and the expected frequency (i.e., EF), however each cell of the chi-square has its own observed and expected frequencies. The observed frequencies are the actual frequency counts collected from the sample; they are the actual data. The expected frequencies are defined by the null hypothesis and the study's sample size. The expected frequencies are the exact frequency counts expected *if the null hypothesis is true,* given the studies sample size. Studies based on more data will have higher expected frequencies than those based on less data. A very important limitation of both types of chi-squares is that if an expected frequency is less than 5, a chi-square should not be performed until after the sample size is increased.

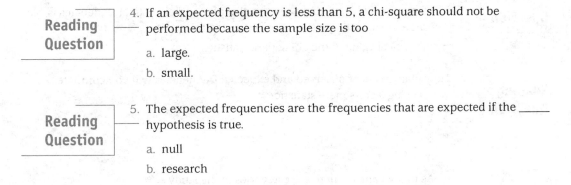

Reading Question

4. If an expected frequency is less than 5, a chi-square should not be performed because the sample size is too

   a. large.

   b. small.

Reading Question

5. The expected frequencies are the frequencies that are expected if the _____ hypothesis is true.

   a. null

   b. research

The numerator of the chi-square statistic computes the difference between the observed frequency (i.e., the actual data) and the expected frequency (i.e., what the data should be if the null is true). If the null is true and *there were no sampling error*, the observed frequency and the expected frequency would be identical and the numerator would be zero. Of course, some sampling error usually does occur. The possibility of sampling error means that "small" differences between the observed and expected frequencies are probably due to sampling error but "large" differences indicate that the null hypothesis is probably false.

The denominator of the chi-square formula, which contains only the expected frequency, helps determine how big the numerator difference must be to be considered "large." By dividing the expected frequency into the numerator difference, a ratio of *relative difference* is created. For example, if the computed difference in the numerator was 12 (i.e., $18 - 6 = 12$) and the expected frequency was 6, the resulting ratio would be 24 (i.e., $12^2/6 = 24$). In this case, a difference of 12 is a large *relative* difference. In contrast, if the computed difference in the numerator was 12 (i.e., $180 - 168 = 12$) but the expected frequency was 168, the resulting ratio would be .86 (i.e., $12^2/168 = .86$). In this case, a difference of 12 is a relatively small difference. When the expected frequency is large, it takes a larger difference between observed and expected frequencies to be "large."

The Σ symbol in the equation indicates that you must create a relative difference ratio for each category in the study and then sum all of them to create a final obtained chi-square value. If the null hypothesis is true, the final obtained chi-square value is likely to be close to zero. If the null hypothesis is false, the obtained chi-square value is likely to be far from zero. As with other statistics, if the obtained chi-square is greater than the critical value, you should reject the null hypothesis.

Reading Question

6. The numerator of the chi-square computes the difference between the observed and expected frequencies. If the null is true, the difference is likely to be close to

   a. 0.

   b. 1.

   c. 6.

   d. .25.

Reading Question

7. The denominator of the chi-square helps determine

   a. whether a difference between the observed and expected frequencies is "large," relative to the size of the expected frequency.

   b. the critical value of the chi-square statistic.

Reading Question

8. How many pairs of observed and expected frequencies will you compute when using a chi-square statistic?

   a. 2

   b. 6

   c. 0

   d. As many pairs as there are categories in the study.

Reading
Question

9. If the summed relative differences (called the obtained chi-square value) is greater than the critical value, you should

  a. reject the null.

  b. fail to reject the null.

COMPARING THE GOODNESS-OF-FIT CHI-SQUARE AND THE CHI-SQUARE FOR INDEPENDENCE

Both types of chi-squares (a) analyze frequency counts, (b) test a null hypothesis, (c) use the same formula, and (d) compare an obtained chi-square value with a critical value in order to determine if the null hypothesis should be rejected. However, as discussed above, the goodness of fit analyzes a single variable while the chi-square for independence analyzes the association between two variables. We will now work through a complete example of each type of chi-square starting with the goodness of fit.

GOODNESS-OF-FIT CHI-SQUARE EXAMPLE

We will now analyze the data introduced at the beginning of the chapter concerning the relative frequencies of voters' affiliations with different political parties. Suppose you collected the data in Table 15.3 from a sample of voters from your county.

Table 15.3	Number of people identifying with each political affiliation.	

Political Affiliation		
Democrat	Republican	Independent
22	22	12

You want to know if these frequency counts of political affiliation are different from the frequencies reported 2 years ago, specifically 50% Democrats, 30% Republicans, and 20% Independents.

Step 1: State the Null and Research Hypotheses

In this scenario, the null hypothesis is that the proportions of people affiliating with each party will be the same as they were 2 years ago. Specifically, *if the null hypothesis is true*, you would expect your sample to be 50% Democrats, 30% Republicans, and 20% Independents. The research hypothesis is that the proportions of people affiliating with each party will be different from what they were 2 years ago.

**Reading
Question**
10. The null hypothesis for the goodness-of-fit chi-square always states that the frequency counts in each category

    a. are the same.

    b. are similar to the expected frequency counts for each category.

Step 2: Define the Critical Regions

The chi-square is different from other statistics in that the df that determines the critical value is *not* based on sample size. Rather, in a chi-square, the df is based on the *number of categories* in the study. Specifically, the df for a goodness-of-fit chi-square is

$$df = \text{Categories} - 1.$$

In this case, there are three categories, and so the $df = 2$. When you look up the critical value for chi-square in Appendix G, you find that when the $df = 2$ and the $\alpha = .05$, the critical value is 5.99. Therefore, if the computed chi-square value is equal to or greater than 5.99, you should reject the null hypothesis.

**Reading
Question**
11. The df value for a chi-square is based on

    a. the number of participants.

    b. the number of categories being counted.

Step 3: Compute the Test Statistic

Step 3a: Determine the Expected Frequencies Defined by the Null Hypothesis

The expected frequencies are created by converting the percentages (or proportions) stated in the null hypothesis into the exact frequencies expected, given the study's sample size. If you collected a total of 56 responses (i.e., 22 + 22 + 12 = 56), the expected frequencies for each category of political affiliation would be as follows:

Percent Predicted by Null	Expected f
50% Democrats: 50% of 56 = .50(56) =	28
30% Republicans: 30% of 56 = .30(56) =	16.8
20% Independents: 20% of 56 = .20(56) =	11.2

**Reading
Question**
12. The expected frequencies in a goodness-of-fit chi-square

    a. can be different in every cell.

    b. will always be the same in every cell.

Step 3b: Compute the Obtained Value

The observed and expected frequencies are presented in Table 15.4.

Table 15.4	Observed frequencies (OF) and expected frequencies (EF) for each political affiliation.

Political Affiliation		
Democrat	Republican	Independent
OF = 22 EF = 28	OF = 22 EF = 16.8	OF = 12 EF = 11.2

The obtained chi-square value is calculated below by creating a squared relative difference ratio for each category in the study and then summing them.

$$\chi^2 = \Sigma \frac{(OF - EF)^2}{EF} \; = \; \frac{(22-28)^2}{28} + \frac{(22-16.8)^2}{16.8} + \frac{(12-11.2)^2}{11.2}$$

$$= 1.285 + 1.610 + 0.057$$

$$= \; 2.952$$

The obtained chi-square value of 2.952 is not greater than the critical chi-square value of 5.99. Therefore, you should not reject the null hypothesis. The differences between the observed and expected frequency counts were small enough that they could have resulted from sampling error.

Reading Question

13. If the obtained chi-square is less than the critical value, you should

   a. reject the null hypothesis.

   b. fail to reject the null hypothesis.

After computing the test statistic, the next step is usually computing an effect size. However, we will skip this step for goodness-of-fit chi-square tests. Unlike all other effect size statistics presented in this text, the measure of effect size for a goodness-of-fit chi-square is not a measure of association between two variables, and therefore, its interpretation is quite different from all other measures of effect size presented in this text. Refer to Cohen (1988) if you are interested in computing effect sizes for a goodness-of-fit chi-square.

Step 4: Interpret the Results

The results of this chi-square test are summarized below.

The political affiliations with the Democratic, Republican, and Independent parties reported by the sample of voters from this county are not significantly different from those reported 2 years ago, χ^2 (2, N = 56) = 2.952, p > .05.

CHI-SQUARE FOR INDEPENDENCE

We will now analyze the data introduced earlier concerning the association between voters' political affiliation and their opinion of a Democratic president's policies.

Step 1: State the Null and Research Hypotheses

The chi-square for independence helps determine whether two variables measured on nominal or ordinal scales of measurement are associated. In this case, the chi-square tests whether one's approval or disapproval of the president's policies is associated with one's political affiliation. Similar to the null hypotheses for the correlation, this chi-square's null hypothesis states that the two variables in the study are not associated (i.e., that the two variables are independent of each other). Specifically, the null hypothesis in this case would be "Policy opinion and political affiliation are not associated." The research hypothesis states that the two variables in the study are associated.

Reading Question

14. The null hypothesis for the chi-square for independence always states that the two variables being analyzed are

   a. associated.

   b. not associated.

Step 2: Define the Critical Regions

The df for a chi-square of independence is determined by the following formula:

$$df = (\text{Columns} - 1) \times (\text{Rows} - 1)$$

where Columns = number of categories in the columns and Rows = number of categories in the rows.

In this case, Columns = 3 and Rows = 2. The df is $(3 - 1) \times (2 - 1) = (2) \times (1) = 2$. The critical value for a chi-square when df = 2 and the α = .05 is 5.99. If the obtained chi-square is greater than 5.99, the null hypothesis should be rejected.

Table 15.5	Observed frequencies (OF) and expected frequencies (EF) for each political affiliation by approval of a Democratic president's policies.

		Political Affiliation			
		Democrat	*Republican*	*Independent*	*Column Total*
Policy opinion	Approve	15 *9.103*	2 *9.103*	7 *5.793*	24
	Disapprove	7 *12.897*	20 *12.897*	7 *8.207*	34
	Row total	22	22	14	*N* = 58

Reading Question	15. As with the goodness-of-fit chi-square, the *df* for the chi-square for independence is based on the

       a. number of participants in the study.

       b. number of categories being counted.

Step 3: Compute the Test Statistic

Step 3a: Determine the Expected Frequencies Defined by the Null Hypothesis

Each of the six categories (i.e., cells) created by the possible combinations of responses to political affiliation and policy opinion will have its own expected frequency. The expected frequencies are displayed in *italics* in each cell. Each cell's expected frequency is based on the total frequency count of the row (i.e., RT) and column (i.e., CT) of which it is a part. The total frequency counts for each row and column are presented in Table 15.5.

The formula used to compute the expected frequencies for each cell in the study is below.

$$EF = \frac{RT \times CT}{N},$$

where RT refers to the total frequency in a given row and CT refers to the total frequency in a given column.

For example, for the first cell in the design (Democrats/Approve) the RT is 24 and CT is 22 and *N* is the total number of people (*N* = 58).

Each expected frequencies are computed as follows:

The EF for the Democrat/Approve cell is $\qquad EF = \frac{(24)(22)}{58} = 9.103.$

The EF for the Republican/Approve cell is $\qquad EF = \frac{(24)(22)}{58} = 9.103.$

The EF for the Independent/Approve cell is

$$EF = \frac{(24)(14)}{58} = 5.793.$$

The EF for the Democrat/Disapprove cell is

$$EF = \frac{(34)(22)}{58} = 12.897.$$

The EF for the Republican/Disapprove cell is

$$EF = \frac{(34)(22)}{58} = 12.897.$$

The EF for the Independent/Disapprove cell is

$$EF = \frac{(34)(14)}{58} = 8.207.$$

Reading Question

16. An expected frequency is computed separately for each cell.

   a. True

   b. False

Step 3b: Compute the Obtained Value

The obtained chi-square value is calculated by finding the relative squared difference between the observed and expected frequencies for each cell in the study and then summing them. The obtained chi-square is computed as follows.

$$\chi^2 = \Sigma \frac{(OF - EF)^2}{EF} = \frac{(15 - 9.103)^2}{9.103} + \frac{(2 - 9.103)^2}{9.103} + \frac{(7 - 5.793)^2}{5.793} +$$

$$\frac{(7 - 12.897)^2}{12.897} + \frac{(20 - 12.897)^2}{12.897} + \frac{(7 - 8.207)^2}{8.207}$$

$$= 3.820 + 5.542 + 0.251 + 2.696 + 3.912 + 0.178 = 16.399$$

The obtained chi-square value of 16.40 is greater than the critical chi-square value of 5.99. Therefore, the null hypothesis should be rejected. The differences between the observed and expected frequency counts were large enough that they were unlikely to have been created due to sampling error, instead it is likely that voters' opinions of the president's policies and their political affiliation are associated.

Step 4: Compute the Effect Size, and Describe It

When computing the effect size for all of the other statistics discussed in this text, we provided a single statistic (i.e., d for t tests, η_p^2 for ANOVAs, and r^2 for correlations). However, when computing the effect size for a chi-square of independence, the statistic you should use depends on the size of the chi-square test you performed. If the chi-square was a 2×2 (i.e., both variables had exactly two categories), the phi (ϕ) coefficient is the correct measure of the study's effect size. If either variable has three or more categories, Cramer's ϕ is the correct measure of effect size. The formulas and effect size guidelines for phi and Cramer's ϕ are presented in Table 15.6. You should note that the effect size guidelines change for Cramer's ϕ as the df of the chi-square test increases.

Table 15.6 Effect sizes for chi-square and guidelines for interpretation.

Statistic	When It Is Used	Formula	Effect Size Guidelines
Phi coefficient (ϕ)	Both variables have two categories	$\varphi = \sqrt{\dfrac{\chi^2}{N}}$	.1 = small
			.3 = medium
			.5 = large
Cramer's phi (ϕ)	At least one variable has three or more categories	$\varphi' = \sqrt{\dfrac{\chi^2}{N(df*)}}$ $df*$ = (Columns − 1) or (Rows − 1), whichever is smaller	$df*$ = 1
			.1 = small
			.3 = medium
			.5 = large
			$df*$ = 2
			.07 = small
			.21 = medium
			.35 = large
			$df*$ = 3
			.06 = small
			.17 = medium
			.29 = large

In this case, Cramer's ϕ is the appropriate measure of effect size because one of the variables in the original chi-square has three categories. Cramer's ϕ is computed as follows.

$$\text{Cramer's } \phi = \sqrt{\frac{\chi^2}{N(df*)}} = \sqrt{\frac{16.399}{58(1)}} = 0.532$$

The first set of effect size guidelines are appropriate because $df*$ = (CT − 1) = 2 − 1 = 1. Therefore, the size of the association between voters' political affiliation and their opinion of the president's policies is large.

Reading Question	17. When both variables in a chi-square analysis have just two levels, _____ is the appropriate measure of effect size.

a. the phi coefficient

b. Cramer's phi

Reading Question	18. When at least one variable in a chi-square analysis has more than two levels, _____ is the appropriate measure of effect size.

a. the phi coefficient

b. Cramer's phi

Step 5: Interpret the Results

In this study, the null hypothesis was rejected meaning that the association between policy opinion and political affiliation is statistically significant. After rejecting a chi-square's null hypothesis, you must look at the differences between the observed and expected frequencies in each cell. Looking at these values reveals that four of the six cells had large differences, and four had only small differences. These four cells with the large differences were those in the Democrat and Republican columns. It is clear from these values that more Democrats approved of the president's policies than was expected by chance and that fewer Democrats disapproved of the president's policies than was expected by chance. The exact opposite pattern was found for Republicans. The following passage is an example of how the results of this study might be reported.

The voters' opinions of the president's policies were associated with the voters' political affiliations, χ^2 (2, N = 58) = 16.40, p < .05, ϕ = .53. More Democrats and fewer Republicans approved of the president's policies than would be expected by chance. More Republicans and fewer Democrats disapproved of the policies than would be expected by chance. The approval and disapproval of Independents were very close to what was expected by chance.

SPSS

Goodness-of-Fit Chi-Square

We will now analyze the political affiliation data using SPSS to perform a goodness-of-fit chi-square. The data are provided in Table 15.7.

Table 15.7   Data used for SPSS example for chi-square test of goodness of fit.

Political Affiliation		
Democrat	Republican	Independent
22	22	12

You want to know if these frequency counts of political affiliation are different from the frequencies reported 2 years ago. Two years ago your county consisted of 50% Democrats, 30% Republicans, and 20% Independents.

Data File

The data file for chi-square looks very different from the table of frequency counts shown above. The data file will have a single column labeled with the variable being measured (i.e., Political Affiliation) and then a list of each person's response (i.e., Democrat, Republican, or Independent).

As with previous data files, we will use codes to represent the nominal category that each participant identified as their political affiliation (i.e., 1 = Democrat, 2 = Republican, 3 = Independent). From the SPSS Statistics Data Editor screen, click on the Variable View tab at the bottom left. Type "Political_Affiliation" in the Name column. Then, click in the Values box across from "Political_Affiliation." In the Value box, enter a 1 and in the Label box, enter Democrat and click Add. Then type 2 and Republican, and click Add. Then, finally 3 and Independent, and click Add. Then, click OK. Now click on the Data View tab at the bottom left. Now enter the data. Given the frequency counts in the above table the data file will have one column with 22 Democrat entries, 22 Republican entries, and 12 Independent entries. This means your data file will have one column containing 22 "1s," 22 "2s," and 12 "3s." A screenshot (Figure 15.1) of part of the data file is shown here.

Obtaining a Goodness-of-Fit Chi-Square

To perform the chi-square analysis do the following:

- Click on the Analyze menu. Choose Non-parametric Tests, then click on Legacy Dialogs and select Chi-square.
- Move the variable label PoliticalAffiliation to the Test Variable List.
- Click on the Values button and enter the exact expected frequencies based on the null hypothesis.
   o   If all of the expected values were the same, you could click on the "All categories equal" button but in this case, you must compute the expected frequencies by hand and then enter them in the correct order (i.e., the expected frequency for value 1 (28), then value 2 (16.8), and finally value 3 (11.2)). You must click on the "Add" button after you enter each value. Then, click OK. Your screen should look like the one in Figure 15.2.

Annotated Output

For SPSS output, see Figures 15.3 and 15.4.

Reading Question

19. When entering data into SPSS for a goodness-of-fit chi-square you will have
   a. one column of data.
   b. one column of data for each category.

Figure 15.1   SPSS screenshot of data entry for chi-square test of goodness of fit.

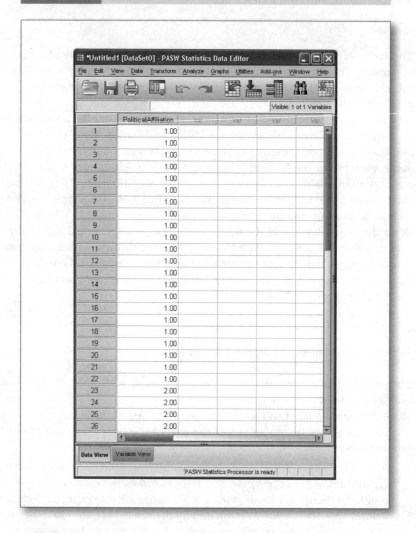

Reading Question

20. Use the "Test Statistics" output to determine if you should reject or fail to reject the null hypothesis. Based on the output the null hypothesis should

   a. be rejected.

   b. not be rejected.

| Figure 15.2 | SPSS screenshot for setting up the chi-square test of goodness of fit. |

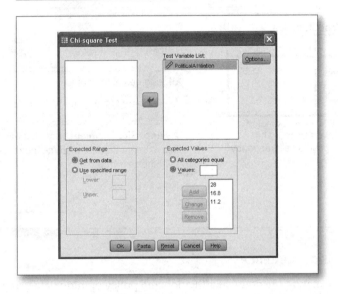

| Figure 15.3 | SPSS screenshot of observed and expected frequencies for chi-square test of goodness of fit. |

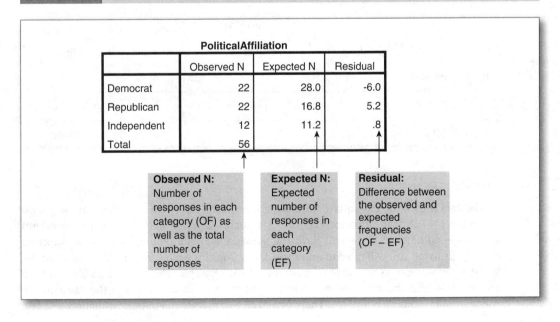

Figure 15.4 SPSS screenshot of chi-square for goodness of fit.

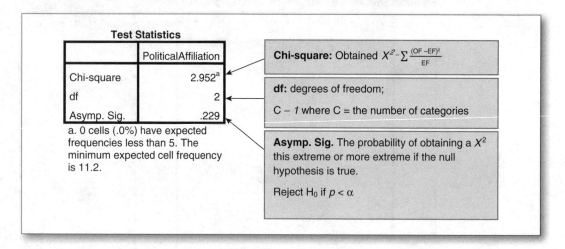

Test Statistics

	PoliticalAffiliation
Chi-square	2.952[a]
df	2
Asymp. Sig.	.229

a. 0 cells (.0%) have expected frequencies less than 5. The minimum expected cell frequency is 11.2.

Chi-square: Obtained $X^2 - \sum \frac{(OF - EF)^2}{EF}$

df: degrees of freedom;

$C - 1$ where C = the number of categories

Asymp. Sig. The probability of obtaining a X^2 this extreme or more extreme if the null hypothesis is true.

Reject H_0 if $p < \alpha$

Chi-Square for Independence

We will now analyze the political affiliation and policy opinion data using SPSS to perform a chi-square for independence. The data are shown in Table 15.8.

Table 15.8 Data used for SPSS example for chi-square test of independent.

		Political Affiliation			Total
		Democrat	Republican	Independent	
Policy opinion	Approve	15	2	7	24
	Disapprove	7	20	7	34
	Total	22	22	14	$N = 58$

Data File

The data file for the chi-square for independence will have two columns. One will have the values for Political Affiliation (i.e., 1 = Democrat, 2 = Republican, 3 = Independent) in a single column and one will have the values for Policy Opinion (i.e., 1 = Approve, 2 = Disapprove). You will need to enter the data values for each categorical variable on the Variable View screen as you did in the previous SPSS example. The actual data file will have 15 rows in which the value in the Political Affiliation column is a 1 and the value in the Policy Opinion column is also a 1. There would be two rows with Political Affiliation = 2 and

Policy Opinion = 1. Then 7 rows with Political Affiliation = 3 and Policy Opinion = 1. This coding system would be continued for the Disapprove row in the above table. After all of the data are entered into the SPSS Data Editor your data file will look similar to the screenshot in Figure 15.5.

| Figure 15.5 | SPSS screenshot of data entry for chi-square test of independence. |

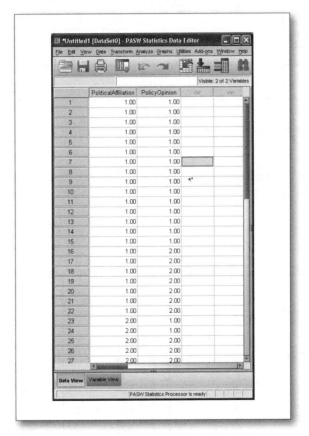

Obtaining a Chi-Square for Independence

To perform the chi-square:

- Click on the Analyze menu. Choose Descriptive Statistics and select Crosstabs.
- Move the variable labeled "PoliticalAffiliation" to the Rows box and the variable labeled "PolicyOpinion" to the Column(s) box.
- Click on the Statistics button and check the chi-square box and click Continue.
- Click the Cells button and make sure that the observed and expected boxes are both checked.
- Click Continue, then click OK.

Annotated Output

For SPSS output, see Figures 15.6 to 15.8.

| Figure 15.6 | SPSS screenshot of output with total number of responses. |

Case Processing Summary

	Cases					
	Valid		Missing		Total	
	N	Percent	N	Percent	N	Percent
Political_Affiliation * Policy_Opinion	58	100.0%	0	.0%	58	100.0%

Total N: The total number of responses

| Figure 15.7 | SPSS screenshot of output of observed frequencies, expected frequencies, row totals, and column totals. |

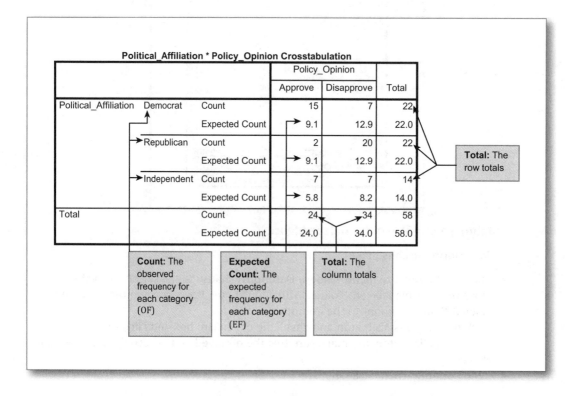

Political_Affiliation * Policy_Opinion Crosstabulation

			Policy_Opinion		Total
			Approve	Disapprove	
Political_Affiliation	Democrat	Count	15	7	22
		Expected Count	9.1	12.9	22.0
	Republican	Count	2	20	22
		Expected Count	9.1	12.9	22.0
	Independent	Count	7	7	14
		Expected Count	5.8	8.2	14.0
Total		Count	24	34	58
		Expected Count	24.0	34.0	58.0

Total: The row totals

Count: The observed frequency for each category (OF)

Expected Count: The expected frequency for each category (EF)

Total: The column totals

Figure 15.8	SPSS screenshot of chi-square test of independence.

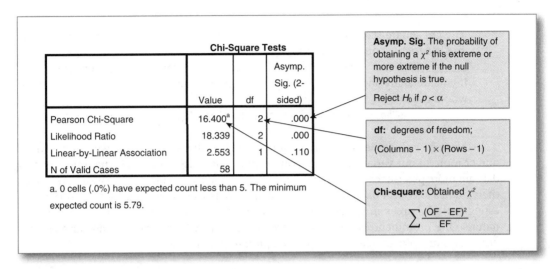

Chi-Square Tests

	Value	df	Asymp. Sig. (2-sided)
Pearson Chi-Square	16.400[a]	2	.000
Likelihood Ratio	18.339	2	.000
Linear-by-Linear Association	2.553	1	.110
N of Valid Cases	58		

a. 0 cells (.0%) have expected count less than 5. The minimum expected count is 5.79.

Asymp. Sig. The probability of obtaining a χ^2 this extreme or more extreme if the null hypothesis is true.

Reject H_0 if $p < \alpha$

df: degrees of freedom;

(Columns – 1) × (Rows – 1)

Chi-square: Obtained χ^2

$$\sum \frac{(OF - EF)^2}{EF}$$

Reading Question

21. Should the null hypothesis be rejected for this analysis?

   a. Yes

   b. No

REFERENCE

Cohen, J. (1988). *Statistical power analyses for the behavioral sciences* (2nd ed.). Hillsdale, NJ: Lawrence Erlbaum.

Activity 15-1:   Goodness-of-Fit Chi-Square and Chi-Square for Independence

Learning Objectives

After reading the chapter and completing this activity, you should be able to do the following:

- Determine when to use a goodness-of-fit chi-square or a chi-square for independence
- Determine the expected frequencies for chi-square
- Compute a goodness-of-fit chi-square and a chi-square for independence
- Write one or two sentences that summarize the results of a chi-square analysis

WHEN TO USE THE GOODNESS-OF-FIT CHI-SQUARE VERSUS THE CHI-SQUARE FOR INDEPENDENCE

1. The chi-square statistic is used to analyze frequency counts. If you are analyzing a single variable you would use a _____ _____ (*Choose one*: goodness-of-fit chi-square/chi-square of independence). If you are analyzing the relationship between two nominal or ordinal variables you would use a _____ _____ (*Choose one*: goodness-of-fit chi-square/chi-square of independence).

In this text, we have devoted most of our time to learning statistics that we can use when one or more of our variables are interval or ratio. The reason for this is that interval/ratio data are more precise than nominal or ordinal data, and as a result, most researchers design their studies to collect data that are interval or ratio. However, there are several very interesting research areas in which many if not most of the data are nominal or ordinal in nature. One prominent example of a research area in which many of the variables are nominal is in political science and public opinion polling.

WHEN EXPECTED FREQUENCIES ARE TOO LOW

2. The chi-square statistic is appropriate for all of the research scenarios described in the following questions. You should remember however that if one or more computed expected frequencies for any chi-square analysis is less than _____ (*Choose one*: .01, .05, 5, 10) you should NOT perform a chi-square test. If an expected frequency is less than this number you should collect more data until all of the expected frequencies are greater than this number.

FOUR EXAMPLES

Between August 27 and 30, 2010, researchers called registered voters and asked them several questions and recorded their answers. One of the questions they asked was as follows:
"Now, thinking back on some of the major pieces of legislation Congress has passed in the last two years, would you say you approve or disapprove of the health care overhaul?" Of the 1,021 people who were asked this question, 970 responded by saying "Approve" or "Disapprove." The rest had "No opinion" and were excluded from the analysis. The observed frequency counts for each response option are provided below. Compute a chi-square to determine if the sample's responses were significantly different from a 50%/50% Approve/Disapprove split on the health care overhaul.

Approve	*Disapprove*
398	572

3. Compute the expected frequency for each cell. Write the expected frequency for each cell into the above cells.

4. Are all of the expected frequencies sufficiently large to proceed with the chi-square?

   a. Yes

   b. No

5. Determine the critical value for this chi-square analysis.

6. Compute the obtained chi-square value and determine if you should reject or fail to reject the null hypothesis.

7. Which measure of effect size should be used for this goodness-of-fit chi-square?

   a. the phi coefficient, ϕ

   b. Cramer's phi, ϕ'

   c. Neither, we will not compute an effect size for goodness-of-fit chi-square

8. Which of the following is the best summary of this chi-square analysis?

   a. Significantly more people approve of the health care overhaul than would be expected by chance, χ^2 (___ , $N =$ ___) = _____, $p < .05$.

   b. Significantly more people disapprove of the health care overhaul than would be expected by chance, χ^2 (___ , $N =$ ___) = _____, $p < .05$.

   c. The proportions of people who approve and disapprove of the health care overhaul are not significantly different from those that would be expected by chance, χ^2 (___, $N =$ ___) = _____, $p < .05$.

Another question that the researchers asked registered voters was "Now, thinking back on some of the major pieces of legislation Congress has passed in the last two years, would you say you approve or disapprove of increased government regulation of banks and major financial institutions? The observed frequency counts for the response categories of "Approve," "Disapprove," and "No opinion" are below. Test the null hypothesis that the responses will be 50% approve, 50% disapprove, and 0% no opinion.

Approve	Disapprove	No opinion
620	373	28

9. Compute the expected frequency for each cell. Write the expected frequency for each cell into the above cells.

10. Are all of the expected frequencies sufficiently large to proceed with the chi-square?

   c. Yes

   d. No

11. There are two ways you could deal with the expected frequency of the "no opinion" cell being too low. You could change your hypothesis so that the expected frequency would be higher or you could simply drop the respondents from the analysis. Which do you think would be the better choice in this case? Explain your reasoning.

12. Now drop the "no opinion" respondents and recompute the expected frequencies for the approve and disapprove cells. Write them in the respective cells.

13. Determine the critical value for this chi-square analysis.

14. Compute the obtained chi-square value and determine if you should reject or fail to reject the null hypothesis.

15. Write one or two sentences that summarize the results of this study.

16. In the study you just completed, the "no opinion" respondents were excluded because the expected frequency in that cell would have been 0. The only reason it would have been 0 was because the hypothesis was that 0% of the respondents would not have any opinion. It would have been okay to include the "no opinion" respondents if the hypothesis being tested had predicted some value greater than 0 for that cell. Suppose that researchers always expect about 5% of every population to have no opinion on any issue. If that were the case for the previous analysis what would have been the expected frequencies for each of the approve, disapprove, and no opinion cells?

Respondents were also asked what Congress should do about tax cuts. They were given three options: (1) keep them in place for all taxpayers, (2) keep them in place for those making less than 250K a year but end them for those making more than 250K a year, or (3) do nothing and allow the tax cuts to expire for all taxpayers. The observed frequencies for each of these categories are shown below. Test the hypothesis that respondents are *equally split across these three categories*.

Keep Tax Cuts for All	Keep Tax Cuts for Only Those Making Less Than 250K	Do Nothing and Allow Tax Cuts to Expire for All Taxpayers
378	449	153

17. Compute the expected frequency for each cell. Write the expected frequency for each cell into the above cells.

18. Are all of the expected frequencies sufficiently large to proceed with the chi-square?

    a. Yes

    b. No

19. Determine the critical value for this chi-square analysis.

20. Compute the obtained chi-square value and determine if you should reject or fail to reject the null hypothesis.

21. Write one or two APA sentences that summarize the results of this study.

Finally, it seems likely that a respondent's political identification as Republican, Democrat, or Independent will be associated with one's opinion on the tax cut issue. To test the hypothesis that political identification and opinion on the tax cuts are associated, run a chi-square on the data in the table below.

	Keep Tax Cuts for All	Keep Tax Cuts for Only Those Making Less Than 250k	Do Nothing and Allow Tax Cuts to Expire for All Taxpayers
Republican	204	121	42
Independent	111	116	43
Democrat	65	215	68

22. Compute the expected frequency for each cell. Write the expected frequency for each cell into the above cells.

23. Are all of the expected frequencies sufficiently large to proceed with the chi-square?

    a. Yes

    b. No

24. Determine the critical value for this chi-square analysis.

25. Compute the obtained chi-square value and determine if you should reject or fail to reject the null hypothesis.

26. Which measure of effect size should be used for this test for independence chi-square?

    a. the phi coefficient, ϕ

    b. Cramer's phi, ϕ'

27. Compute the appropriate measure of effect size for this study below, determine which set of effect size guidelines should be used and then determine if the effect is small, medium, or large.

28. Write one or two APA sentences that summarize the results of this study.

Activity 15-2: Choose the Correct Statistic

Learning Objectives

After reading the chapter and this activity, you should be able to do the following:

- Read a research scenario and determine which statistic should be used

Determine which statistic should be used in each of the following research scenarios: z for a single score, z for sample mean, single sample t, related samples t, independent samples t, one-way independent samples ANOVA, two-way independent samples ANOVA, Pearson correlation, Spearman correlation, chi-square goodness of fit, or chi-square test of independence.

    a. z for a single score
    b. z for a sample mean
    c. single sample t
    d. independent measures t
    e. repeated/related measures t
    f. independent measures ANOVA
    g. two-factor ANOVA
    h. Pearson correlation
    i. Spearman correlation
    j. chi-square goodness of fit
    k. chi-square test of independence

1. Is a male politician's height associated with his popularity with voters? A researcher randomly selected 20 male politicians and looked up their height on the Internet. The researcher then looked up each of their popularity ratings on the Internet (ratings were given as a percentage approval rating that ranged from 0% to 100%).

2. Chris earned a 92 on her geometry final. She wants to know how her score compares with those of her classmates. The problem is she only knows her own score, the mean score on the test, and the standard deviation on the test. What statistic should be used to determine what percent of her classmates had a lower score than she did?

3. Although the Internet provides access to a wealth of information, finding that information is not always easy. However, there are a number of skills that can greatly speed up the process. For example, "ctrl-f" can be used to find a particular word once you are on a web page. Unfortunately, a recent study revealed that 90% of people did not know this shortcut. A student wants to know if this is also true of college students. The student obtains a sample of 73 students and asks them what hitting the "ctrl-f" key combination does when you are on a web page. Each person's response was coded as either correct or incorrect. Fifty two students answered the question correctly while 21 answered the question incorrectly. What statistic should be used to determine if the proportion of college students who know the "ctrl-f" short cut is different from the proportion of people in the general population who know the short cut?

4. A neurologist has 20 patients all of whom suffered severe head trauma between 3 and 6 months ago. He wants to know if their ability to recall words is different from the general population. He gave all 20 patients a standardized memory test. The general population's mean score on this standardized test is 75 with a standard deviation of 10. His patients scored a mean of 60. What statistic should be used to determine if the recall scores of his patients are significantly different from the recall scores in the general population?

5. Are college students who attend religiously affiliated schools more religious than the general population? A national survey reports that on a 10-point religiosity scale (with 10 being the most religious rating) the average rating for Americans is 7 with a standard deviation of 3.2. A sample of 157 students who all attended religiously affiliated colleges had a mean religiosity rating of 7.75. Is the sample of students significantly more religious than the general American population?

6. Several researchers have found that the attitudes students have about learning are associated with their grades in college. Students who view classes as an opportunity to learn new things tend to perform better in college than students who view classes as obstacles that they must tolerate before they get to their careers. One of the studies classified students into one of these two groups and then compared the mean college GPAs of the two groups. What statistic should be used to determine if the GPAs of the two groups are significantly different?

7. A teacher gives a multiple choice test with 100 questions. Every question on the test has exactly one correct answer and three incorrect answers. The teacher wants to know how well his 37 students did compared with chance performance (i.e., compared with 25 correct answers). What statistic should be used to determine if his students did better than chance?

8. What is the association between years of formal education people completed and their income? A group of students used government survey data to answer this question. The years of education variable was measured as "through junior high," "through high school," "some college," "completed college," "some graduate school," and "completed graduate school." For the income variable, they classified each family into one of seven different income categories ranging from "below the poverty line" to "more than $1 million dollars a year."

9. Mr. Jackson was in a car accident and suffered a serious head injury. It is possible that an area of his brain that helps process visual images was severely damaged. A neurologist wants to give Mr. Jackson a visual imagery test in order to determine if his visual imagery ability is severely impaired compared with the visual imagery ability of other adult males his age. The mean visual imagery score for adult males of Mr. Jackson's age is $\mu = 46$ with $\sigma = 7$. What is Mr. Jackson's percentile rank for visual imagery?

10. Do the feeding practices at a certain zoo help make its gorillas healthy? At a certain zoo, the gorillas must "hunt and forage" for their food rather than finding it placed in the same location of their habitat every day. Is this practice beneficial to the gorillas? To address this question, a zoo worker hid the gorillas' food in a different location every day. After 3 years, the zoo veterinarian gave every gorilla a physical and used a standardized rating system to give each gorilla a rating for health which ranged from 1 = *very unhealthy* to 10 = *very healthy*. The minimal acceptable rating on this scale that is established by the National Zoological Society is 7. Are the gorillas at this zoo significantly healthier than the minimum national standard for gorilla health?

11. In an attempt to study attitude change, a group of students asked participants their opinion of a local sandwich shop by having them rate the shop's sandwiches on a scale from 1 (*terrible*) to 10 (*great*). The participants then had to write a persuasive speech in which they were to make the strongest argument they could to convince others that they should eat at the sandwich shop. A week after writing the persuasive speech, the participants were again asked to rate the shop's sandwiches on the same 1 to 10 scale. What statistic should be used to determine if writing a persuasive speech leads to higher ratings than prior to writing the speech?

12. A researcher studying problem solving presented "the candle problem" to two different groups. In order to solve the problem, participants had to discover a way to attach a burning candle to a wall. Both groups were given a candle, a small box of wooden matches, thumb tacks, and paper clips. The only difference between the two conditions was the starting position of the matches. For half of the participants, the matches were packaged in the box, and for half, the matches were presented outside of the box. The researcher marked what condition each participant was in (i.e., filled-box condition or empty-box condition) and whether each participant solved the problem or did not solve the problem. What statistic should be used to determine if the box-full and box-empty conditions differ in terms of the proportion of participants who successfully solved the problem?

13. A researcher taught one group of people to use the method of loci and then asked them to use it to study and then recall a list of 100 words. Another group of

people were given the same amount of time to study the same list of 100 words and were also asked to recall them. Did the method of loci group recall more words than the control group?

14. The testing effect illustrates that trying to retrieve information that you have learned (i.e., testing yourself over what you have learned) increases one's memory for that material on future tests. One of the studies that illustrates the testing effect had half of the participants study material for *four* 5-minute sessions before taking a final test while the other participants studied the same material for *one* 5-minute session and took 3 sample tests before taking the final test. Additionally, half of the participants in each group took the final test after a delay of several minutes while the other half took the final test after a delay of 1 week. The dependent variable in this study was the number of correct responses on the final test. (Incidentally, none of the questions on the final test appeared on any of the sample tests). What statistic should be used to determine if practice tests result in higher scores than studying without practice tests? Did the testing effect differ based on the length of the time delay before the final test?

15. Do speed reading classes really increase reading speed without a decline in comprehension? A researcher randomly assigned readers to one of two groups. One group completed a nationally advertised speed reading course. The other group received no speed reading training. Half of the people in each group were given as much time as they needed to read a book and then they took a test on the book. The other half of each group did not read the book but took the test on the book to function as two control conditions.

16. A group of students in a criminology course obtained government and police records to analyze the relationship between a family's income and the number of times that family had been burglarized. They classified each family into one of seven different income categories ranging from "below the poverty line" to "more than $1 million dollars a year." The number of times each family was burglarized was obtained from police records. What statistic should be used to determine if the number of times a family was burglarized is associated with their income level?

17. A group of undergraduate students performed a variation of a classic psychology experiment for a class project. In a series of trials, a participant had to say which of two lines was longer. In every trial, one of the lines was substantially longer than the other, so it was very obvious which line was longer. However, before the participant made the judgment on each trial, four confederates (i.e., people working with the experimenter that were pretending to be research participants) made their judgments. For several trials, all of the confederates made the correct judgment. On the critical trial, however, all four confederates intentionally chose the wrong line. The critical question was whether or not the one true participant would conform by also picking the wrong line or if the participant would go against the group and pick the line that was obviously longer. The undergraduate students predicted that only 25% of the participants would resist the social pressure to conform by choosing the correct line and 75% of the sample would conform by choosing the line that was obviously shorter. What statistic should be used to test their hypothesis?

18. Postpartum depression is quite common among new mothers, and recent research has shown that a significant proportion of men also experience depression with the addition of a child to the family. A researcher wonders if the level of depression experienced by the mother is associated with the level of depression experienced by the father. To test this, the researcher gives both the mother and the father the Inventory to Diagnose Depression (IDD). Scores on this inventory range from 0 to 88 with higher scores indicating greater levels of depression. What statistic should be used to determine if there is a relationship between the IDD scores of mothers and fathers?

19. The researcher discovers that IDD scores of the mother and father are significantly associated. However, she also wants to know if men and women have significantly different levels of depression. Thus, she runs a different analysis to compare the IDD scores of the mother and father. When setting up the data file she is careful to match each mother's IDD scores with her partner's IDD score. What statistic should be used to determine if mothers were significantly more depressed than fathers?

20. A clinician wonders if the socioeconomic status (SES) of a family is associated with levels of depression after having a new child. The clinician obtains a sample of 60 new mothers. Twenty have a low SES, 20 are middle class, and 20 have a high SES. Each mother completes the IDD. What statistic should be used to determine if mothers with low SES have higher levels of depression than mothers with a higher SES?

21. Does working outside of the home affect postpartum depression? To investigate this possibility, a researcher obtains a sample of 75 women: 25 who worked full time outside of the home, 25 who worked part time outside of the home, and 25 who stayed home. IDD scores were collected 6 months after the baby was born.

22. Postpartum depression affects men as well, and so another researcher decides to replicate the study above using both mothers and fathers. This time, 75 new mothers and 75 new fathers were recruited. Within each gender, 25 who worked full time outside of the home, 25 who worked part time outside of the home, and 25 who stayed home. What statistic should be used to determine if IDD scores depend upon gender and work status?

Activity 15-3: Practice Problems

SCENARIO 1: GOODNESS-OF-FIT PROBLEM

For a project in a statistics class, you must collect data and then analyze it using a chi-square statistic. You decide to collect data on how easily people could go 1 week without using various software/social media products. Specifically, you ask 60 of your fellow students which of the following three programs they would be most willing to NOT use for 1 week: (1) e-mail, (2) Facebook, or (3) Twitter. The obtained frequencies for each of these categories are shown below. Your *null hypothesis* is that each of the three categories will have the same frequencies ($N = 60$). Use $\alpha = .05$.

e-Mail	Facebook	Twitter
11	9	40

1. What is the *df* for this study?

2. What is the critical value for this study?

3. What is the expected frequency for each cell?

4. What is the obtained χ^2 value for this study?

5. Should the null hypothesis for this study be rejected?

6. Which of the following is the best summary of this study's results?

   a. Students in the study said that they were much more likely to give up using Twitter for 1 week than e-mail or Facebook, $\chi^2 (2, N = 60) = 5.99, p < .05$.

   b. Students in the study said that they were much more likely to give up using Twitter for 1 week than e-mail or Facebook, $\chi^2 (2, N = 60) = 30.1, p < .05$.

   c. Students in the study said that they were much more likely to give up using Twitter for 1 week than e-mail or Facebook, $\chi^2 (3, N = 60) = 7.81, p < .05$.

   d. Students in the study were equally likely to say that they would give up e-mail, Facebook, or Twitter, $\chi^2 (3, N = 60) = 7.81, p > .05$.

SCENARIO 2: INDEPENDENCE PROBLEM

Another student in your class collects data for her chi-square project by recording students' gender and asking students whether or not they were vegetarians. Her study had 15 males and 15 females. She wanted to know if the variables of Gender and Type of Diet (i.e., Vegetarian or Not Vegetarian) were associated. Her observed frequencies are shown in the following table. Use $\alpha = .05$.

	Vegetarian	Not Vegetarian
Male	3	12
Female	7	8

7. What is the *df* for this study?

8. What is the critical value for this study?

9. What is the expected frequency for each cell?

10. What is the obtained χ^2 value for this study?

11. Should the null hypothesis of this study be rejected?

12. Compute the effect size.

13. Which of the following is the best summary of this study's results?

    a. In the students participating in the study, there was an association between Diet (i.e., Vegetarian or Not Vegetarian) and Gender, χ^2 (1, $N = 30$) $= 2.4, p > .05$, $\phi' = .28$. More females were vegetarian than was expected by chance, and fewer males were vegetarian than was expected by chance.

    b. In the students participating in the study, there was an association between Diet (i.e., Vegetarian or Not Vegetarian) and Gender, χ^2 (1, $N = 30$) $= 3.8, p < .05, \phi' = .28$.

    c. In the students participating in the study, there was no association between Diet (i.e., Vegetarian or Not Vegetarian) and Gender, χ^2 (1, $N = 30$) $= 3.8, p < .05, \phi' = .28$.

    d. In the students participating in the study, there was no association between Diet (i.e., Vegetarian or Not Vegetarian) and Gender, χ^2 (1, $N = 30$) $= 2.4, p > .05, \phi' = .28$.

SCENARIO 3: INDEPENDENCE PROBLEM

As a class project, a group of students took turns waiting at a busy intersection and recorded the gender of each driver they saw and whether or not that driver was currently using a cell phone while driving. Use the data they collected below to test the null hypothesis that there is no association between gender and cell phone use while driving. Use $\alpha = .05$.

	Gender	
Using Cell Phone While Driving	*Male*	*Female*
Yes	16	19
No	10	11

14. Which chi-square should be used to test this null hypothesis?

15. What is the critical region for this chi-square test?

16. Are all of the expected frequencies sufficiently large to compute the chi-square test?

17. Compute the obtained chi-square for these data.

18. Is their sufficient evidence to reject the null hypothesis?

19. Compute and interpret the effect size for these data.

20. Write an APA-style summary of this analysis.

21. Enter the above data into SPSS and run the appropriate chi-square analysis. Confirm that the chi-square value you computed by hand is the same as that produced by SPSS.

SCENARIO 4: GOODNESS-OF-FIT PROBLEM

As a class project, a student asked 25 people what type of cell phone they currently used most frequently. She wanted to know which one type of cell phone was more commonly used than any other. Use the data she collected to test the null hypothesis that all of the cell phone types are equally common. Use $\alpha = .05$.

Cell Phone Types		
Blueberry	U Phone	Trak Phone
10	12	3

22. Which chi-square should be used to test this null hypothesis?

23. What is the critical region for this chi-square test?

24. Are all of the expected frequencies sufficiently large to compute the chi-square test?

25. Compute the obtained chi-square for these data.

26. Is their sufficient evidence to reject the null hypothesis?

27. Write an APA-style summary of this analysis.

28. Enter the above data into SPSS and run the appropriate chi-square analysis. Confirm that the chi-square value you computed by hand is the same as that produced by SPSS.

NOTES

C H A P T E R   1 6

Statistical Assumptions

PARAMETRIC AND NONPARAMETRIC STATISTICS

The inferential statistics covered in this book are classified as either parametric or nonparametric statistics. Parametric statistics include the z for a sample mean, all t tests, all ANOVAs, and the Pearson's correlation. Nonparametric statistics include the Spearman's correlation and both chi-square tests.

Reading Question

1. Which of the following statistics are nonparametric? (Choose 2)
   a. z for a sample mean
   b. all t tests
   c. all ANOVAs
   d. all chi-squares
   e. Pearson's correlation
   f. Spearman's correlation

Researchers use parametric tests whenever possible because they generally have more statistical power than nonparametric tests. The main reason for the enhanced statistical power of parametric tests is the more precise data required by parametric tests. For example, the parametric Pearson's correlation requires the actual raw scores while the Spearman's correlation requires only the rank order of the scores. Clearly, some measurement precision is lost when using ranks rather than scores. This reduction in measurement precision is akin to having more measurement error, which you now know reduces statistical power.

Reading Question

2. Which type of statistics typically results in greater statistical power and why?
   a. Parametric—the data are generally more precise.
   b. Nonparametric—the data are generally less precise.

Although parametric statistics typically have greater statistical power than nonparametric statistics, it is not always possible to use parametric statistics. All statistics are based on specific assumptions, and if these assumptions are violated, the statistic may yield misleading results. In general, parametric statistics have more stringent assumptions than nonparametric statistics. Therefore, if a given set of data does not meet the assumptions of a parametric test, researchers must resort to the less powerful, but still useful, nonparametric tests.

Reading Question

3. Which types of statistics typically have more stringent assumptions?
   a. Parametric
   b. Nonparametric

The parametric statistics that you have learned in this course share several, but not all, of the same assumptions. If you understand four basic assumptions, you will be able to safely run all of the parametric statistics discussed in this text. The four basic assumptions are (1) independence of data, (2) interval/ratio scale of measurement, (3) normality of distributions, and (4) homogeneity of variance.

ASSUMPTION 1: INDEPENDENCE OF DATA

All of the statistical tests in this book, parametric *and* nonparametric, share the first assumption of independence. This means that a given data point within a condition is independent of all other data points within that same condition. For example, suppose that a researcher stops people who are shopping together at the mall to assess their opinions of a political candidate. The researcher reads a question to the group and then each person states his or her response. This procedure would likely create data that violates the assumption of independence because it is very likely that hearing other group members respond will change the responses of subsequent group members. The responses (i.e., data) provided by each individual would not be independent of the responses provided by other individuals. For all of the statistical tests presented in this book, the data must be collected in ways that maximize the independence of the data. If you take a research methods course, you will learn the many procedures that researchers use to collect individual responses or scores that are independent.

The assumption of independence does not mean that there can be no dependence in the entire data set. For example, a researcher could measure a person's political attitudes before a televised speech and then again after the speech. It is perfectly acceptable (and even desirable) to measure the same person under two different conditions. You may have dependence *between* conditions, just not dependence *within* the conditions.

Reading Question

4. Which of the following would violate the assumption of independence?
   a. Measuring the same students' attitudes toward statistics at the beginning and end of a statistics course.
   b. Comparing the exam scores of students across different sections of a course when several students in one section copied answers from each other.

Reading Question

5. Only parametric statistics require that data be independent.
   a. True
   b. False

ASSUMPTION 2: INTERVAL/RATIO DATA

In addition to independence, parametric tests also require that the data must be measured on an interval or ratio scale of measurement. The specific details of this assumption vary based on the statistic.

CORRELATION: You may use the parametric Pearson's correlation test if both variables are measured on an interval or ratio scale. However, if *either* variable is measured on an ordinal scale, you must use the nonparametric Spearman's correlation test.

t TESTS AND ANOVAS: You may use *t* tests or ANOVAs if the dependent variable (DV) in the study is measured on an interval or ratio scale. The independent variable (IV) (i.e., the grouping variable) for *t* tests and ANOVAs can be either nominal or ordinal.

Reading Question

6. A school psychologist compares the academic rank (e.g., 1st, 2nd, 3rd) of a sample of student athletes and a sample of students who are not athletes. Why can't he use a parametric *t* test to analyze these data?
   a. The DV is not measured on an interval or ratio scale.
   b. Both variables are measured on an ordinal scale.

Reading Question

7. A sports psychologist tests for an association between finishing position in a race and satisfaction with one's race performance. Why can't she use a Pearson's correlation?

   a. At least one variable is not measured on an interval or ratio scale.

   b. Both variables are measured on an interval/ratio scale.

ASSUMPTION 3: NORMALITY

For the parametric statistics, the distribution of sample means of interval or ratio scores must have a normal shape. As you know from previous chapters, we use the distribution of sample means to determine if a particular outcome is unlikely if the null hypothesis is true. However, if the distribution of sample means is not normally shaped, our decisions about the null hypothesis are more likely to be wrong.

As was the case with the interval/ratio data assumption, the assumption of normality varies based on the statistic.

PEARSON'S CORRELATION: You may use the parametric Pearson's correlation if both variables are normally distributed.

t TESTS AND ANOVAS: You may use *t* tests or ANOVAs if the DV in the study is normally distributed within each condition. In the case of related samples *t* tests, remember that the DV is the difference between the scores from each condition, not the raw scores. Therefore, the distribution of difference scores must have a normal shape.

Fortunately, if the original population is normally shaped, the distribution of sample means is very likely to be normally shaped. For example, research has shown that population IQ scores are frequently normally distributed. Therefore, the distributions of sample means for IQ scores are very likely to be normally distributed. Unfortunately, for many variables that are less commonly researched, the shape of a population distribution is unknown. Therefore, in many cases, we must rely on the central limit theorem to determine if the distribution of sample means is likely to have a normal shape.

The central limit theorem tells us that a distribution of sample means approaches a normal shape as the sample size increases. Thus, if you have a large sample ($N > 30$), the distribution of sample means will likely be normally distributed even if the population distribution *does not* have a normal shape. However, if the population distribution is *severely* skewed, a larger sample size may be required for the distribution of sample means to be normally shaped.

If you have a relatively small sample size (i.e., $N < 30$) and you do not know the shape of the population distribution, you must look at your data more closely. Specifically, you must look at the shape of each sample distribution. If each sample of scores is approximately normally distributed, researchers commonly infer that the population distribution is also normally distributed and, therefore, the distribution of sample means is similarly normally distributed. There are statistical tests that can be done to determine if sample distributions deviate significantly from normal (e.g., Kolmogorov–Smirnov and Shapiro–Wilk). Field (2009) provides an excellent discussion of these statistics.

It is important to note that minimum sample sizes (e.g., $N > 30$) refer to the minimum number of people within each cell of the design. Thus, if you are comparing the scores for two different groups of people, you need 30 people per group, for a total of 60 people. If you are conducting a 2 × 2 independent measures ANOVA, you have 4 cells and need 30 people per cell, for a total of 120 people. The advantages of repeated measures designs become far more obvious in this context. While an independent measures design with 4 cells requires 120 people, a repeated measures design of the same size requires just 30 people.

Reading Question

8. Which of the following will typically lead to a distribution of sample means with a normal shape? Choose all that apply.

   a. A normally distributed population of scores.

   b. A sample size that is less than 20.

   c. A sample size that is greater than 30.

Reading Question

9. If your sample size is less than 30, and you do not know what the underlying population distribution looks like, how do you determine if the distribution of sample means is likely to be normally distributed?

   a. Hypothesis tests are not possible with sample sizes below 30.

   b. If the scores in each sample are normally distributed, you can infer that the population and the distribution of sample means are similarly normal.

   c. Create a distribution of sample means for your study; if it is normal, you can infer that the population is also normal.

Reading Question

10. If you suspect that the distribution of sample means is not normally distributed, you should not conduct a parametric hypothesis test.

    a. True

    b. False

Reading Question

11. If a study includes three conditions and there are only 15 people in each condition, what must the researcher check to assess the normality assumption?

    a. That all three means are similar.

    b. The shape of the distributions of scores within each condition.

ASSUMPTION 4: HOMOGENEITY OF VARIANCE

Another important assumption for hypothesis testing with *t* tests and ANOVAs is *homogeneity of variance*. Very broadly, this means that when you have multiple samples, they should come from populations with similar variances. For example, suppose that you wanted to compare the SAT scores of males and females. The independent *t* test assumes that the two populations (i.e., men and women) have similar amounts of variability (i.e., similar variances/standard deviations) in SAT scores. As with the previous assumptions, the details are a bit different for the different statistics.

t TESTS AND ANOVAS: When comparing two or more means, the standard deviations associated with each mean should be similar. This is not an assumption for the related samples *t*, only the independent samples and single sample *t* tests.

PEARSON'S CORRELATION: Does not assume homogeneity of variance.

Reading Question	12. The homogeneity of variance assumption states that, if more than one group is used, the
	
	    a. sample standard deviations for the groups should be exactly equal.
	
	    b. samples should come from populations with similar amounts of variability.
	
	    c. samples should have homogeneous means and standard deviations.

We rarely have access to population data and so we cannot just look at two population standard deviations (or variances) to determine if they are equivalent. Instead, we must rely on the sample standard deviation (*SD*) to estimate the population variability (σ). If comparing two sample means, you need to determine if the two sample *SD*s are similar. Although there are statistical tests for this purpose (e.g., Levene test discussed in Chapter 10), we often use *the rule of thumb that the smallest standard deviation should not be less than half the size of the largest standard deviation*. You should conduct a formal test of the homogeneity of variance assumption if this rule of thumb is violated.

Reading Question	13. A researcher administers Drug A, Drug B, and Drug C to three different samples, then records the number of anxiety symptoms displayed by each sample. The *SD*s were 4.2, 6.2, and 3.0, respectively. Should the researcher perform a formal homogeneity of variance test?
	
	    a. Yes, the rule of thumb is violated. The smallest *SD* is less than half the size of the largest *SD*.
	
	    b. No, the rule of thumb is not violated. The smallest *SD* is more than half the size of the largest *SD*.

We have simplified the assumption assessment process for homogeneity of variance in this introductory text. Rather than using a rule of thumb, researchers can use SPSS to test for homogeneity of variance. Very briefly, Levene's test assesses homogeneity of variance for independent samples *t* and independent samples ANOVA. The related measures ANOVA does not assume homogeneity of variance, but rather makes a closely related assumption of Sphericity, which is tested using Mauchly's test. We refer you to Field (2009) for an in depth (yet very readable) discussion of these topics.

WHEN ASSUMPTIONS ARE VIOLATED

If your data violates one or more of these assumptions, you should not compute parametric statistics; instead you must use nonparametric statistics. While this course covered only three nonparametric statistics (e.g., Spearman's correlation, chi-square goodness of fit, and chi-square test of independence), most parametric statistics do have nonparametric counterparts. Below, we list the nonparametric counterparts for each of the parametric statistics in this book. These tests do have some assumptions, but they are far less stringent than for the parametric tests. As mentioned previously, nonparametric tests are less powerful than parametric tests and therefore they are only used when assumptions are violated. Whenever possible, researchers design their studies so they can use parametric statistics.

CONCLUDING NOTES

Some of the data you analyzed in previous activities violated the parametric assumptions you now understand. While this was not ideal, we wanted you to work with small sample sizes when doing computations. As you now know, small samples are likely to violate statistical assumptions. We sacrificed statistical purity for pedagogical clarity.

Table 16.1 Parametric tests and their nonparametric counterparts.

Parametric Test	Nonparametric Counterpart
Single sample *t* test	No comparable test
Related measures *t* test	Wilcoxon test
Independent measures *t* test	Mann–Whitney *U*
One-way independent measures ANOVA	Kruskal–Wallis test or chi-square goodness of fit
One-way repeated measures ANOVA	Friedman test
Two-factor independent measures ANOVA	Friedman test
Pearson's correlation	Spearman's correlation

Throughout this course, we consistently presented five steps for statistical hypothesis testing. Now that you understand the basic statistical assumptions, we recommend that you check statistical assumptions first. Therefore, the six-step hypothesis testing process is (1) evaluating statistical assumptions, (2) stating null and research hypotheses, (3) identifying critical region(s), (4) computing the test statistic, (5) computing the effect size, and (6) writing a summary of the results.

Reading Question

14. When conducting a hypothesis test you should begin by
    a. determining if the statistical assumptions of the test are met.
    b. stating the null and research hypotheses.

For further information on assumptions for each test and how to test the assumptions in SPSS, we highly recommend Field (2009), *Discovering Statistics Using SPSS*. Field also discusses each of the nonparametric tests in the table above.

REFERENCE

Field, A. (2009). *Discovering statistics using SPSS*. Thousand Oaks, CA: Sage.

Activity 16-1: Evaluating Statistical Assumptions

Learning Objectives

After reading the chapter and completing this activity, you should be able to do the following.

- Describe the four basic assumptions for parametric null hypothesis significance testing: (1) independence, (2) interval/ratio data, (3) normality, and (4) homogeneity of variance
- Determine if a given data set violates the assumptions of a given parametric statistic

1. Briefly describe the four assumptions for parametric statistics discussed in the reading. (*Note*: They are listed in the first learning objective above.)

EVALUATE ASSUMPTIONS FOR AN INDEPENDENT SAMPLES ANOVA

A psychologist compares the effectiveness of cognitive behavioral therapy (CBT) and psychodynamic therapy (PDT) for treating anxiety disorder. The psychologist identifies a sample with anxiety disorder and randomly divides them into three different groups. Each group undergoes CBT, PDT, or receives no treatment (NT) for 6 months. Levels of anxiety are assessed using a survey, which yields interval scale scores ranging from 0 to 10, with higher scores indicating greater anxiety. In this study, the IV is the type of treatment and the DV is each person's anxiety score.

2. Are the data independent?

3. Is anxiety measured on an interval/ratio scale?

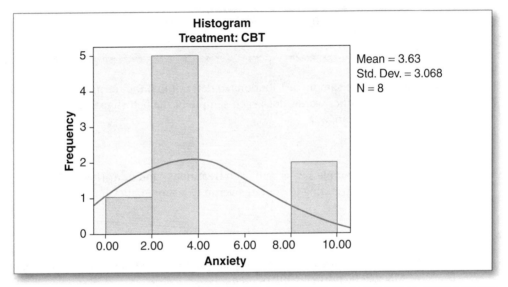

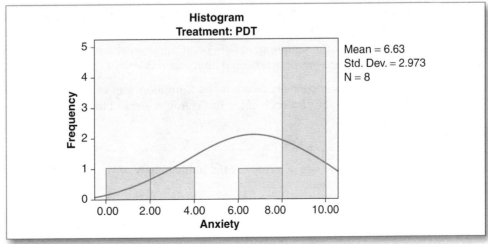

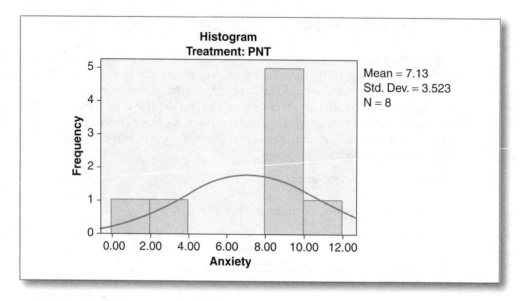

4. Use the above sample distributions to determine if the normality assumption is violated. In other words, does each sample fit the bell-shaped curve fairly well? Explain your answer.

5. What is the sample size within each treatment condition? How is the sample size probably contributing to your answer in Question 4 above?

6. Should the researcher be relatively confident that the distribution of sample means will be normally distributed?

   a. Yes, because the sample scores are normally distributed so the population is probably normally distributed.

   b. No, because the sample scores are not normally distributed and the sample size is too small to rely on the central limit theorem.

7. To assess the homogeneity of variance assumption, you will need to compare the standard deviations for each of the three groups. Record the three standard deviations below:

   CBT: _____   PDT: _____   NT: _____

8. Explain how you can determine if the homogeneity of variance assumption is likely to be violated.

9. Based on your evaluation of the assumptions, should the researcher use an independent ANOVA to analyze these data?

10. What can the researcher do as a next step in this research?
    a. Increase the sample size in each condition to $n > 30$.
    b. Give up.

EVALUATE ASSUMPTIONS FOR A RELATED SAMPLES *t*

Researchers want to determine if viewing a documentary on the dangers of cell phone use while driving *decreases* the frequency of cell phone use while driving. They asked 15 teenage drivers to indicate the extent to which they agreed with the statement "I am likely to use my cell phone while driving" using a Likert scale where 1 = *strongly disagree* and 7 = *strongly agree*. Then, each driver watched a video on the dangers of driving while using a cell phone. After watching the video, the drivers responded to the same statement again. The data are graphed below.

11. Are the data within each condition independent?

12. Is the DV measured on an interval/ratio scale?

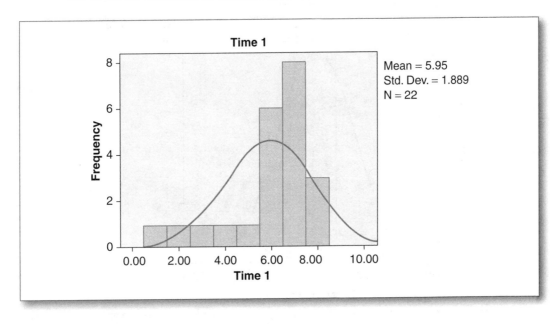

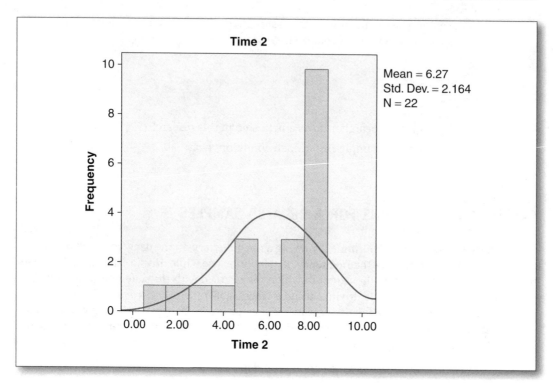

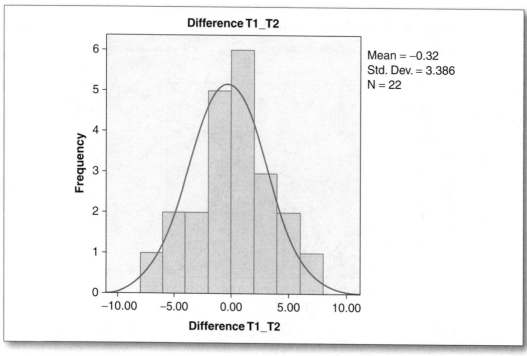

13. Should the researcher be relatively confident that the normality assumption was met? (*Hint:* Which one of the above three figures should you use?) Explain your rationale.

14. Based on your evaluation of the assumptions, can the researcher use a related samples *t* test to analyze these data?

EVALUATE ASSUMPTIONS FOR A PEARSON'S CORRELATION

Every 2 years the National Opinion Research Center collects data from a random sample of adults (18 years and older) in the United States. In 2010, respondents were asked to indicate how many years of school they have completed as well as their age when their first child was born (respondent's without children were excluded from this analysis). Data from 312 people are represented in the graphs below.

15. Are the data independent?

16. Are the data measured on an interval/ratio scale?

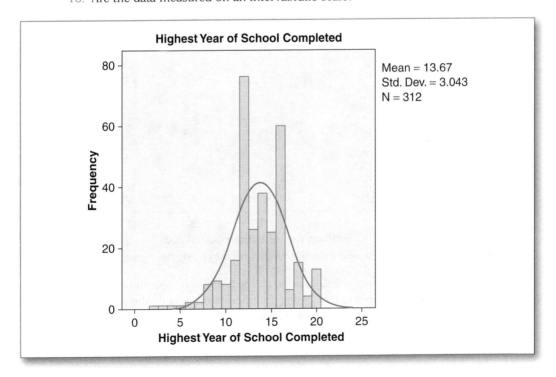

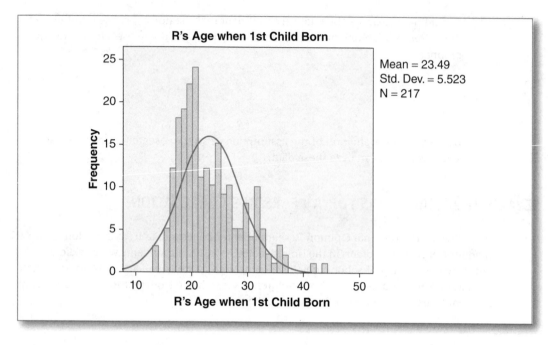

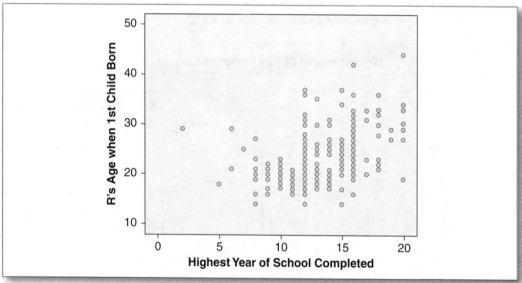

17. Use the above sample distributions and scatterplot to determine if the normality assumption is likely to be violated. In other words, should the researcher run a Pearson's correlation or a Spearman's correlation. Explain your answer.

Appendix A

Unit Normal Table (z Table)

z score	Body	Tail	z score	Body	Tail	z score	Body	Tail	z score	Body	Tail
0.00	0.5000	0.5000	0.25	0.5987	0.4013	0.50	0.6915	0.3085	0.75	0.7734	0.2266
0.01	0.5040	0.4960	0.26	0.6026	0.3974	0.51	0.6950	0.3050	0.76	0.7764	0.2236
0.02	0.5080	0.4920	0.27	0.6064	0.3936	0.52	0.6985	0.3015	0.77	0.7794	0.2206
0.03	0.5120	0.4880	0.28	0.6103	0.3897	0.53	0.7019	0.2981	0.78	0.7823	0.2177
0.04	0.5160	0.4840	0.29	0.6141	0.3859	0.54	0.7054	0.2946	0.79	0.7852	0.2148
0.05	0.5199	0.4801	0.30	0.6179	0.3821	0.55	0.7088	0.2912	0.80	0.7881	0.2119
0.06	0.5239	0.4761	0.31	0.6217	0.3783	0.56	0.7123	0.2877	0.81	0.7910	0.2090
0.07	0.5279	0.4721	0.32	0.6255	0.3745	0.57	0.7157	0.2843	0.82	0.7939	0.2061
0.08	0.5319	0.4681	0.33	0.6293	0.3707	0.58	0.7190	0.2810	0.83	0.7967	0.2033
0.09	0.5359	0.4641	0.34	0.6331	0.3669	0.59	0.7224	0.2776	0.84	0.7995	0.2005
0.10	0.5398	0.4602	0.35	0.6368	0.3632	0.60	0.7257	0.2743	0.85	0.8023	0.1977
0.11	0.5438	0.4562	0.36	0.6406	0.3594	0.61	0.7291	0.2709	0.86	0.8051	0.1949
0.12	0.5478	0.4522	0.37	0.6443	0.3557	0.62	0.7324	0.2676	0.87	0.8078	0.1922
0.13	0.5517	0.4483	0.38	0.6480	0.3520	0.63	0.7357	0.2643	0.88	0.8106	0.1894
0.14	0.5557	0.4443	0.39	0.6517	0.3483	0.64	0.7389	0.2611	0.89	0.8133	0.1867
0.15	0.5596	0.4404	0.40	0.6554	0.3446	0.65	0.7422	0.2578	0.90	0.8159	0.1841
0.16	0.5636	0.4364	0.41	0.6591	0.3409	0.66	0.7454	0.2546	0.91	0.8186	0.1814
0.17	0.5675	0.4325	0.42	0.6628	0.3372	0.67	0.7486	0.2514	0.92	0.8212	0.1788
0.18	0.5714	0.4286	0.43	0.6664	0.3336	0.68	0.7517	0.2483	0.93	0.8238	0.1762
0.19	0.5753	0.4247	0.44	0.6700	0.3300	0.69	0.7549	0.2451	0.94	0.8264	0.1736
0.20	0.5793	0.4207	0.45	0.6736	0.3264	0.70	0.7580	0.2420	0.95	0.8289	0.1711
0.21	0.5832	0.4168	0.46	0.6772	0.3228	0.71	0.7611	0.2389	0.96	0.8315	0.1685
0.22	0.5871	0.4129	0.47	0.6808	0.3192	0.72	0.7642	0.2358	0.97	0.8340	0.1660
0.23	0.5910	0.4090	0.48	0.6844	0.3156	0.73	0.7673	0.2327	0.98	0.8365	0.1635
0.24	0.5948	0.4052	0.49	0.6879	0.3121	0.74	0.7704	0.2296	0.99	0.8389	0.1611

(Continued)

(Continued)

z score	Body	Tail	z score	Body	Tail	z score	Body	Tail	z score	Body	Tail
1.00	0.8413	0.1587	1.33	0.9082	0.0918	1.66	0.9515	0.0485	1.99	0.9767	0.0233
1.01	0.8438	0.1562	1.34	0.9099	0.0901	1.67	0.9525	0.0475	2.00	0.9772	0.0228
1.02	0.8461	0.1539	1.35	0.9115	0.0885	1.68	0.9535	0.0465	2.01	0.9778	0.0222
1.03	0.8485	0.1515	1.36	0.9131	0.0869	1.69	0.9545	0.0455	2.02	0.9783	0.0217
1.04	0.8508	0.1492	1.37	0.9147	0.0853	1.70	0.9554	0.0446	2.03	0.9788	0.0212
1.05	0.8531	0.1469	1.38	0.9162	0.0838	1.71	0.9564	0.0436	2.04	0.9793	0.0207
1.06	0.8554	0.1446	1.39	0.9177	0.0823	1.72	0.9573	0.0427	2.05	0.9798	0.0202
1.07	0.8577	0.1423	1.40	0.9192	0.0808	1.73	0.9582	0.0418	2.06	0.9803	0.0197
1.08	0.8599	0.1401	1.41	0.9207	0.0793	1.74	0.9591	0.0409	2.07	0.9808	0.0192
1.09	0.8621	0.1379	1.42	0.9222	0.0778	1.75	0.9599	0.0401	2.08	0.9812	0.0188
1.10	0.8643	0.1357	1.43	0.9236	0.0764	1.76	0.9608	0.0392	2.09	0.9817	0.0183
1.11	0.8665	0.1335	1.44	0.9251	0.0749	1.77	0.9616	0.0384	2.10	0.9821	0.0179
1.12	0.8686	0.1314	1.45	0.9265	0.0735	1.78	0.9625	0.0375	2.11	0.9826	0.0174
1.13	0.8708	0.1292	1.46	0.9279	0.0721	1.79	0.9633	0.0367	2.12	0.9830	0.0170
1.14	0.8729	0.1271	1.47	0.9292	0.0708	1.80	0.9641	0.0359	2.13	0.9834	0.0166
1.15	0.8749	0.1251	1.48	0.9306	0.0694	1.81	0.9649	0.0351	2.14	0.9838	0.0162
1.16	0.8770	0.1230	1.49	0.9319	0.0681	1.82	0.9656	0.0344	2.15	0.9842	0.0158
1.17	0.8790	0.1210	1.50	0.9332	0.0668	1.83	0.9664	0.0336	2.16	0.9846	0.0154
1.18	0.8810	0.1190	1.51	0.9345	0.0655	1.84	0.9671	0.0329	2.17	0.9850	0.0150
1.19	0.8830	0.1170	1.52	0.9357	0.0643	1.85	0.9678	0.0322	2.18	0.9854	0.0146
1.20	0.8849	0.1151	1.53	0.9370	0.0630	1.86	0.9686	0.0314	2.19	0.9857	0.0143
1.21	0.8869	0.1131	1.54	0.9382	0.0618	1.87	0.9693	0.0307	2.20	0.9861	0.0139
1.22	0.8888	0.1112	1.55	0.9394	0.0606	1.88	0.9699	0.0301	2.21	0.9864	0.0136
1.23	0.8907	0.1093	1.56	0.9406	0.0594	1.89	0.9706	0.0294	2.22	0.9868	0.0132
1.24	0.8925	0.1075	1.57	0.9418	0.0582	1.90	0.9713	0.0287	2.23	0.9871	0.0129
1.25	0.8944	0.1056	1.58	0.9429	0.0571	1.91	0.9719	0.0281	2.24	0.9875	0.0125
1.26	0.8962	0.1038	1.59	0.9441	0.0559	1.92	0.9726	0.0274	2.25	0.9878	0.0122
1.27	0.8980	0.1020	1.60	0.9452	0.0548	1.93	0.9732	0.0268	2.26	0.9881	0.0119
1.28	0.8997	0.1003	1.61	0.9463	0.0537	1.94	0.9738	0.0262	2.27	0.9884	0.0116
1.29	0.9015	0.0985	1.62	0.9474	0.0526	1.95	0.9744	0.0256	2.28	0.9887	0.0113
1.30	0.9032	0.0968	1.63	0.9484	0.0516	1.96	0.9750	0.0250	2.29	0.9890	0.0110
1.31	0.9049	0.0951	1.64	0.9495	0.0505	1.97	0.9756	0.0244	2.30	0.9893	0.0107
1.32	0.9066	0.0934	1.65	0.9505	0.0495	1.98	0.9761	0.0239	2.31	0.9896	0.0104

z score	Body	Tail	z score	Body	Tail	z score	Body	Tail	z score	Body	Tail
2.32	0.9898	0.0102	2.62	0.9956	0.0044	2.92	0.9982	0.0018	3.22	0.9994	0.0006
2.33	0.9901	0.0099	2.63	0.9957	0.0043	2.93	0.9983	0.0017	3.23	0.9994	0.0006
2.34	0.9904	0.0096	2.64	0.9959	0.0041	2.94	0.9984	0.0016	3.24	0.9994	0.0006
2.35	0.9906	0.0094	2.65	0.9960	0.0040	2.95	0.9984	0.0016	3.25	0.9994	0.0006
2.36	0.9909	0.0091	2.66	0.9961	0.0039	2.96	0.9985	0.0015	3.26	0.9994	0.0006
2.37	0.9911	0.0089	2.67	0.9962	0.0038	2.97	0.9985	0.0015	3.27	0.9995	0.0005
2.38	0.9913	0.0087	2.68	0.9963	0.0037	2.98	0.9986	0.0014	3.28	0.9995	0.0005
2.39	0.9916	0.0084	2.69	0.9964	0.0036	2.99	0.9986	0.0014	3.29	0.9995	0.0005
2.40	0.9918	0.0082	2.70	0.9965	0.0035	3.00	0.9987	0.0013	3.30	0.9995	0.0005
2.41	0.9920	0.0080	2.71	0.9966	0.0034	3.01	0.9987	0.0013	3.31	0.9995	0.0005
2.42	0.9922	0.0078	2.72	0.9967	0.0033	3.02	0.9987	0.0013	3.32	0.9995	0.0005
2.43	0.9925	0.0075	2.73	0.9968	0.0032	3.03	0.9988	0.0012	3.33	0.9996	0.0004
2.44	0.9927	0.0073	2.74	0.9969	0.0031	3.04	0.9988	0.0012	3.34	0.9996	0.0004
2.45	0.9929	0.0071	2.75	0.9970	0.0030	3.05	0.9989	0.0011	3.35	0.9996	0.0004
2.46	0.9931	0.0069	2.76	0.9971	0.0029	3.06	0.9989	0.0011	3.36	0.9996	0.0004
2.47	0.9932	0.0068	2.77	0.9972	0.0028	3.07	0.9989	0.0011	3.37	0.9996	0.0004
2.48	0.9934	0.0066	2.78	0.9973	0.0027	3.08	0.9990	0.0010	3.38	0.9996	0.0004
2.49	0.9936	0.0064	2.79	0.9974	0.0026	3.09	0.9990	0.0010	3.39	0.9997	0.0003
2.50	0.9938	0.0062	2.80	0.9974	0.0026	3.10	0.9990	0.0010	3.40	0.9997	0.0003
2.51	0.9940	0.0060	2.81	0.9975	0.0025	3.11	0.9991	0.0009	3.41	0.9997	0.0003
2.52	0.9941	0.0059	2.82	0.9976	0.0024	3.12	0.9991	0.0009	3.42	0.9997	0.0003
2.53	0.9943	0.0057	2.83	0.9977	0.0023	3.13	0.9991	0.0009	3.43	0.9997	0.0003
2.54	0.9945	0.0055	2.84	0.9977	0.0023	3.14	0.9992	0.0008	3.44	0.9997	0.0003
2.55	0.9946	0.0054	2.85	0.9978	0.0022	3.15	0.9992	0.0008	3.45	0.9997	0.0003
2.56	0.9948	0.0052	2.86	0.9979	0.0021	3.16	0.9992	0.0008	3.46	0.9997	0.0003
2.57	0.9949	0.0051	2.87	0.9979	0.0021	3.17	0.9992	0.0008	3.47	0.9997	0.0003
2.58	0.9951	0.0049	2.88	0.9980	0.0020	3.18	0.9993	0.0007	3.48	0.9997	0.0003
2.59	0.9952	0.0048	2.89	0.9981	0.0019	3.19	0.9993	0.0007	3.49	0.9998	0.0002
2.60	0.9953	0.0047	2.90	0.9981	0.0019	3.20	0.9993	0.0007	3.50	0.9998	0.0002
2.61	0.9955	0.0045	2.91	0.9982	0.0018	3.21	0.9993	0.0007	3.51	0.9998	0.0002

Appendix B

One-Tailed Probabilities t Table

df	α = .05	α = .01	df	α = .05	α = .01	df	α = .05	α = .01	df	α = .05	α = .01
1	6.3138	31.8205	32	1.6939	2.4487	63	1.6694	2.3870	94	1.6612	2.3667
2	2.9200	6.9646	33	1.6924	2.4448	64	1.6690	2.3860	95	1.6611	2.3662
3	2.3534	4.5407	34	1.6909	2.4411	65	1.6686	2.3851	96	1.6609	2.3658
4	2.1318	3.7469	35	1.6896	2.4377	66	1.6683	2.3842	97	1.6607	2.3654
5	2.0150	3.3649	36	1.6883	2.4345	67	1.6679	2.3833	98	1.6606	2.3650
6	1.9432	3.1427	37	1.6871	2.4314	68	1.6676	2.3824	99	1.6604	2.3646
7	1.8946	2.9980	38	1.6860	2.4286	69	1.6672	2.3816	100	1.6602	2.3642
8	1.8595	2.8965	39	1.6849	2.4258	70	1.6669	2.3808	101	1.6601	2.3638
9	1.8331	2.8214	40	1.6839	2.4233	71	1.6666	2.3800	102	1.6599	2.3635
10	1.8125	2.7638	41	1.6829	2.4208	72	1.6663	2.3793	103	1.6598	2.3631
11	1.7959	2.7181	42	1.6820	2.4185	73	1.6660	2.3785	104	1.6596	2.3627
12	1.7823	2.6810	43	1.6811	2.4163	74	1.6657	2.3778	105	1.6595	2.3624
13	1.7709	2.6503	44	1.6802	2.4141	75	1.6654	2.3771	106	1.6594	2.3620
14	1.7613	2.6245	45	1.6794	2.4121	76	1.6652	2.3764	107	1.6592	2.3617
15	1.7531	2.6025	46	1.6787	2.4102	77	1.6649	2.3758	108	1.6591	2.3614
16	1.7459	2.5835	47	1.6779	2.4083	78	1.6646	2.3751	109	1.6590	2.3610
17	1.7396	2.5669	48	1.6772	2.4066	79	1.6644	2.3745	110	1.6588	2.3607
18	1.7341	2.5524	49	1.6766	2.4049	80	1.6641	2.3739	111	1.6587	2.3604
19	1.7291	2.5395	50	1.6759	2.4033	81	1.6639	2.3733	112	1.6586	2.3601
20	1.7247	2.5280	51	1.6753	2.4017	82	1.6636	2.3727	113	1.6585	2.3598
21	1.7207	2.5176	52	1.6747	2.4002	83	1.6634	2.3721	114	1.6583	2.3595
22	1.7171	2.5083	53	1.6741	2.3988	84	1.6632	2.3716	115	1.6582	2.3592
23	1.7139	2.4999	54	1.6736	2.3974	85	1.6630	2.3710	116	1.6581	2.3589
24	1.7109	2.4922	55	1.6730	2.3961	86	1.6628	2.3705	117	1.6580	2.3586
25	1.7081	2.4851	56	1.6725	2.3948	87	1.6626	2.3700	118	1.6579	2.3584
26	1.7056	2.4786	57	1.6720	2.3936	88	1.6624	2.3695	119	1.6578	2.3581
27	1.7033	2.4727	58	1.6716	2.3924	89	1.6622	2.3690	120	1.6577	2.3578
28	1.7011	2.4671	59	1.6711	2.3912	90	1.6620	2.3685	∞	1.6450	2.3260
29	1.6991	2.4620	60	1.6706	2.3901	91	1.6618	2.3680			
30	1.6973	2.4573	61	1.6702	2.3890	92	1.6616	2.3676			
31	1.6955	2.4528	62	1.6698	2.3880	93	1.6614	2.3671			

Two-Tailed Probabilities t Table

df	α = .05	α =.01	df	α = .05	α =.01	df	α = .05	α =.01	df	α = .05	α =.01
1	12.7062	63.6567	32	2.0369	2.7385	63	1.9983	2.6561	94	1.9855	2.6291
2	4.3027	9.9248	33	2.0345	2.7333	64	1.9977	2.6549	95	1.9853	2.6286
3	3.1824	5.8409	34	2.0322	2.7284	65	1.9971	2.6536	96	1.9850	2.6280
4	2.7764	4.6041	35	2.0301	2.7238	66	1.9966	2.6524	97	1.9847	2.6275
5	2.5706	4.0321	36	2.0281	2.7195	67	1.9960	2.6512	98	1.9845	2.6269
6	2.4469	3.7074	37	2.0262	2.7154	68	1.9955	2.6501	99	1.9842	2.6264
7	2.3646	3.4995	38	2.0244	2.7116	69	1.9949	2.6490	100	1.9840	2.6259
8	2.3060	3.3554	39	2.0227	2.7079	70	1.9944	2.6479	101	1.9837	2.6254
9	2.2622	3.2498	40	2.0211	2.7045	71	1.9939	2.6469	102	1.9835	2.6249
10	2.2281	3.1693	41	2.0195	2.7012	72	1.9935	2.6459	103	1.9833	2.6244
11	2.2010	3.1058	42	2.0181	2.6981	73	1.9930	2.6449	104	1.9830	2.6239
12	2.1788	3.0545	43	2.0167	2.6951	74	1.9925	2.6439	105	1.9828	2.6235
13	2.1604	3.0123	44	2.0154	2.6923	75	1.9921	2.6430	106	1.9826	2.6230
14	2.1448	2.9768	45	2.0141	2.6896	76	1.9917	2.6421	107	1.9824	2.6226
15	2.1314	2.9467	46	2.0129	2.6870	77	1.9913	2.6412	108	1.9822	2.6221
16	2.1199	2.9208	47	2.0117	2.6846	78	1.9908	2.6403	109	1.9820	2.6217
17	2.1098	2.8982	48	2.0106	2.6822	79	1.9905	2.6395	110	1.9818	2.6213
18	2.1009	2.8784	49	2.0096	2.6800	80	1.9901	2.6387	111	1.9816	2.6208
19	2.0930	2.8609	50	2.0086	2.6778	81	1.9897	2.6379	112	1.9814	2.6204
20	2.0860	2.8453	51	2.0076	2.6757	82	1.9893	2.6371	113	1.9812	2.6200
21	2.0796	2.8314	52	2.0066	2.6737	83	1.9890	2.6364	114	1.9810	2.6196
22	2.0739	2.8188	53	2.0057	2.6718	84	1.9886	2.6356	115	1.9808	2.6193
23	2.0687	2.8073	54	2.0049	2.6700	85	1.9883	2.6349	116	1.9806	2.6189
24	2.0639	2.7969	55	2.0040	2.6682	86	1.9879	2.6342	117	1.9804	2.6185
25	2.0595	2.7874	56	2.0032	2.6665	87	1.9876	2.6335	118	1.9803	2.6181
26	2.0555	2.7787	57	2.0025	2.6649	88	1.9873	2.6329	119	1.9801	2.6178
27	2.0518	2.7707	58	2.0017	2.6633	89	1.9870	2.6322	120	1.9799	2.6174
28	2.0484	2.7633	59	2.0010	2.6618	90	1.9867	2.6316	∞	1.9600	2.5760
29	2.0452	2.7564	60	2.0003	2.6603	91	1.9864	2.6309			
30	2.0423	2.7500	61	1.9996	2.6589	92	1.9861	2.6303			
31	2.0395	2.7440	62	1.9990	2.6575	93	1.9858	2.6297			

Appendix C

F *Table* ($\alpha = .05$)

df denominator	*df* numerator									
	1	2	3	4	5	6	7	8	9	10
1	161.45	199.50	215.71	224.58	230.16	233.99	236.77	238.88	240.54	241.88
2	18.51	19.00	19.16	19.25	19.30	19.33	19.35	19.37	19.38	19.40
3	10.13	9.55	9.28	9.12	9.01	8.94	8.89	8.85	8.81	8.79
4	7.71	6.94	6.59	6.39	6.26	6.16	6.09	6.04	6.00	5.96
5	6.61	5.79	5.41	5.19	5.05	4.95	4.88	4.82	4.77	4.74
6	5.99	5.14	4.76	4.53	4.39	4.28	4.21	4.15	4.10	4.06
7	5.59	4.74	4.35	4.12	3.97	3.87	3.79	3.73	3.68	3.64
8	5.32	4.46	4.07	3.84	3.69	3.58	3.50	3.44	3.39	3.35
9	5.12	4.26	3.86	3.63	3.48	3.37	3.29	3.23	3.18	3.14
10	4.96	4.10	3.71	3.48	3.33	3.22	3.14	3.07	3.02	2.98
11	4.84	3.98	3.59	3.36	3.20	3.09	3.01	2.95	2.90	2.85
12	4.75	3.89	3.49	3.26	3.11	3.00	2.91	2.85	2.80	2.75
13	4.67	3.81	3.41	3.18	3.03	2.92	2.83	2.77	2.71	2.67
14	4.60	3.74	3.34	3.11	2.96	2.85	2.76	2.70	2.65	2.60
15	4.54	3.68	3.29	3.06	2.90	2.79	2.71	2.64	2.59	2.54
16	4.49	3.63	3.24	3.01	2.85	2.74	2.66	2.59	2.54	2.49
17	4.45	3.59	3.20	2.96	2.81	2.70	2.61	2.55	2.49	2.45
18	4.41	3.55	3.16	2.93	2.77	2.66	2.58	2.51	2.46	2.41
19	4.38	3.52	3.13	2.90	2.74	2.63	2.54	2.48	2.42	2.38
20	4.35	3.49	3.10	2.87	2.71	2.60	2.51	2.45	2.39	2.35
21	4.32	3.47	3.07	2.84	2.68	2.57	2.49	2.42	2.37	2.32
22	4.30	3.44	3.05	2.82	2.66	2.55	2.46	2.40	2.34	2.30
23	4.28	3.42	3.03	2.80	2.64	2.53	2.44	2.37	2.32	2.27
24	4.26	3.40	3.01	2.78	2.62	2.51	2.42	2.36	2.30	2.25
25	4.24	3.39	2.99	2.76	2.60	2.49	2.40	2.34	2.28	2.24
26	4.23	3.37	2.98	2.74	2.59	2.47	2.39	2.32	2.27	2.22

df denominator	1	2	3	4	5	6	7	8	9	10
					df numerator					
27	4.21	3.35	2.96	2.73	2.57	2.46	2.37	2.31	2.25	2.20
28	4.20	3.34	2.95	2.71	2.56	2.45	2.36	2.29	2.24	2.19
29	4.18	3.33	2.93	2.70	2.55	2.43	2.35	2.28	2.22	2.18
30	4.17	3.32	2.92	2.69	2.53	2.42	2.33	2.27	2.21	2.16
31	4.16	3.30	2.91	2.68	2.52	2.41	2.32	2.25	2.20	2.15
32	4.15	3.29	2.90	2.67	2.51	2.40	2.31	2.24	2.19	2.14
33	4.14	3.28	2.89	2.66	2.50	2.39	2.30	2.23	2.18	2.13
34	4.13	3.28	2.88	2.65	2.49	2.38	2.29	2.23	2.17	2.12
35	4.12	3.27	2.87	2.64	2.49	2.37	2.29	2.22	2.16	2.11
36	4.11	3.26	2.87	2.63	2.48	2.36	2.28	2.21	2.15	2.11
37	4.11	3.25	2.86	2.63	2.47	2.36	2.27	2.20	2.14	2.10
38	4.10	3.24	2.85	2.62	2.46	2.35	2.26	2.19	2.14	2.09
39	4.09	3.24	2.85	2.61	2.46	2.34	2.26	2.19	2.13	2.08
40	4.08	3.23	2.84	2.61	2.45	2.34	2.25	2.18	2.12	2.08
45	4.06	3.20	2.81	2.58	2.42	2.31	2.22	2.15	2.10	2.05
50	4.03	3.18	2.79	2.56	2.40	2.29	2.20	2.13	2.07	2.03
55	4.02	3.16	2.77	2.54	2.38	2.27	2.18	2.11	2.06	2.01
60	4.00	3.15	2.76	2.53	2.37	2.25	2.17	2.10	2.04	1.99
65	3.99	3.14	2.75	2.51	2.36	2.24	2.15	2.08	2.03	1.98
70	3.98	3.13	2.74	2.50	2.35	2.23	2.14	2.07	2.02	1.97
75	3.97	3.12	2.73	2.49	2.34	2.22	2.13	2.06	2.01	1.96
80	3.96	3.11	2.72	2.49	2.33	2.21	2.13	2.06	2.00	1.95
85	3.95	3.10	2.71	2.48	2.32	2.21	2.12	2.05	1.99	1.94
90	3.95	3.10	2.71	2.47	2.32	2.20	2.11	2.04	1.99	1.94
95	3.94	3.09	2.70	2.47	2.31	2.20	2.11	2.04	1.98	1.93
100	3.94	3.09	2.70	2.46	2.31	2.19	2.10	2.03	1.97	1.93
105	3.93	3.08	2.69	2.46	2.30	2.19	2.10	2.03	1.97	1.92
110	3.93	3.08	2.69	2.45	2.30	2.18	2.09	2.02	1.97	1.92
115	3.92	3.08	2.68	2.45	2.29	2.18	2.09	2.02	1.96	1.91
120	3.92	3.07	2.68	2.45	2.29	2.18	2.09	2.02	1.96	1.91

F *Table* (α = .01)

df denominator	|| *df* numerator									
	1	2	3	4	5	6	7	8	9	10
1	4052.18	4999.50	5403.35	5624.58	5763.65	5858.99	5928.36	5981.07	6022.47	6055.85
2	98.50	99.00	99.17	99.25	99.30	99.33	99.36	99.37	99.39	99.40
3	34.12	30.82	29.46	28.71	28.24	27.91	27.67	27.49	27.35	27.23
4	21.20	18.00	16.69	15.98	15.52	15.21	14.98	14.80	14.66	14.55
5	16.26	13.27	12.06	11.39	10.97	10.67	10.46	10.29	10.16	10.05
6	13.75	10.92	9.78	9.15	8.75	8.47	8.26	8.10	7.98	7.87
7	12.25	9.55	8.45	7.85	7.46	7.19	6.99	6.84	6.72	6.62
8	11.26	8.65	7.59	7.01	6.63	6.37	6.18	6.03	5.91	5.81
9	10.56	8.02	6.99	6.42	6.06	5.80	5.61	5.47	5.35	5.26
10	10.04	7.56	6.55	5.99	5.64	5.39	5.20	5.06	4.94	4.85
11	9.65	7.21	6.22	5.67	5.32	5.07	4.89	4.74	4.63	4.54
12	9.33	6.93	5.95	5.41	5.06	4.82	4.64	4.50	4.39	4.30
13	9.07	6.70	5.74	5.21	4.86	4.62	4.44	4.30	4.19	4.10
14	8.86	6.51	5.56	5.04	4.69	4.46	4.28	4.14	4.03	3.94
15	8.68	6.36	5.42	4.89	4.56	4.32	4.14	4.00	3.89	3.80
16	8.53	6.23	5.29	4.77	4.44	4.20	4.03	3.89	3.78	3.69
17	8.40	6.11	5.18	4.67	4.34	4.10	3.93	3.79	3.68	3.59
18	8.29	6.01	5.09	4.58	4.25	4.01	3.84	3.71	3.60	3.51
19	8.18	5.93	5.01	4.50	4.17	3.94	3.77	3.63	3.52	3.43
20	8.10	5.85	4.94	4.43	4.10	3.87	3.70	3.56	3.46	3.37
21	8.02	5.78	4.87	4.37	4.04	3.81	3.64	3.51	3.40	3.31
22	7.95	5.72	4.82	4.31	3.99	3.76	3.59	3.45	3.35	3.26
23	7.88	5.66	4.76	4.26	3.94	3.71	3.54	3.41	3.30	3.21
24	7.82	5.61	4.72	4.22	3.90	3.67	3.50	3.36	3.26	3.17
25	7.77	5.57	4.68	4.18	3.85	3.63	3.46	3.32	3.22	3.13
26	7.72	5.53	4.64	4.14	3.82	3.59	3.42	3.29	3.18	3.09

	df numerator									
df denominator	1	2	3	4	5	6	7	8	9	10
27	7.68	5.49	4.60	4.11	3.78	3.56	3.39	3.26	3.15	3.06
28	7.64	5.45	4.57	4.07	3.75	3.53	3.36	3.23	3.12	3.03
29	7.60	5.42	4.54	4.04	3.73	3.50	3.33	3.20	3.09	3.00
30	7.56	5.39	4.51	4.02	3.70	3.47	3.30	3.17	3.07	2.98
31	7.53	5.36	4.48	3.99	3.67	3.45	3.28	3.15	3.04	2.96
32	7.50	5.34	4.46	3.97	3.65	3.43	3.26	3.13	3.02	2.93
33	7.47	5.31	4.44	3.95	3.63	3.41	3.24	3.11	3.00	2.91
34	7.44	5.29	4.42	3.93	3.61	3.39	3.22	3.09	2.98	2.89
35	7.42	5.27	4.40	3.91	3.59	3.37	3.20	3.07	2.96	2.88
36	7.40	5.25	4.38	3.89	3.57	3.35	3.18	3.05	2.95	2.86
37	7.37	5.23	4.36	3.87	3.56	3.33	3.17	3.04	2.93	2.84
38	7.35	5.21	4.34	3.86	3.54	3.32	3.15	3.02	2.92	2.83
39	7.33	5.19	4.33	3.84	3.53	3.30	3.14	3.01	2.90	2.81
40	7.31	5.18	4.31	3.83	3.51	3.29	3.12	2.99	2.89	2.80
45	7.23	5.11	4.25	3.77	3.45	3.23	3.07	2.94	2.83	2.74
50	7.17	5.06	4.20	3.72	3.41	3.19	3.02	2.89	2.78	2.70
55	7.12	5.01	4.16	3.68	3.37	3.15	2.98	2.85	2.75	2.66
60	7.08	4.98	4.13	3.65	3.34	3.12	2.95	2.82	2.72	2.63
65	7.04	4.95	4.10	3.62	3.31	3.09	2.93	2.80	2.69	2.61
70	7.01	4.92	4.07	3.60	3.29	3.07	2.91	2.78	2.67	2.59
75	6.99	4.90	4.05	3.58	3.27	3.05	2.89	2.76	2.65	2.57
80	6.96	4.88	4.04	3.56	3.26	3.04	2.87	2.74	2.64	2.55
85	6.94	4.86	4.02	3.55	3.24	3.02	2.86	2.73	2.62	2.54
90	6.93	4.85	4.01	3.53	3.23	3.01	2.84	2.72	2.61	2.52
95	6.91	4.84	3.99	3.52	3.22	3.00	2.83	2.70	2.60	2.51
100	6.90	4.82	3.98	3.51	3.21	2.99	2.82	2.69	2.59	2.50
105	6.88	4.81	3.97	3.50	3.20	2.98	2.81	2.69	2.58	2.49
110	6.87	4.80	3.96	3.49	3.19	2.97	2.81	2.68	2.57	2.49
115	6.86	4.79	3.96	3.49	3.18	2.96	2.80	2.67	2.57	2.48
120	6.85	4.79	3.95	3.48	3.17	2.96	2.79	2.66	2.56	2.47

Appendix D

The Studentized Range Statistic (q) Table

alpha = .05 (*top*)
alpha = .01 (*bottom*)

df for error term	Number of treatment conditions					
	2	3	4	5	6	7
5	3.64	4.60	5.22	5.67	6.03	6.33
	5.70	6.98	7.80	8.42	8.91	9.32
6	3.46	4.34	4.90	5.30	5.63	5.90
	5.24	6.33	7.03	7.56	7.97	8.32
7	3.34	4.16	4.68	5.06	5.36	5.61
	4.95	5.92	6.54	7.01	7.37	7.68
8	3.26	4.04	4.53	4.89	5.17	5.40
	4.75	5.64	6.20	6.62	6.96	7.24
9	3.20	3.95	4.41	4.76	5.02	5.24
	4.60	5.43	5.96	6.35	6.66	6.91
10	3.15	3.88	4.33	4.65	4.91	5.12
	4.48	5.27	5.77	6.14	6.43	6.67
11	3.11	3.82	4.26	4.57	4.82	5.03
	4.39	5.15	5.62	5.97	6.25	6.48
12	3.08	3.77	4.20	4.51	4.75	4.95
	4.32	5.05	5.50	5.84	6.10	6.32
13	3.06	3.73	4.15	4.45	4.69	4.88
	4.26	4.96	5.40	5.73	5.98	6.19
14	3.03	3.70	4.11	4.41	4.64	4.83
	4.21	4.89	5.32	5.63	5.88	6.08
15	3.01	3.67	4.08	4.37	4.59	4.78
	4.17	4.84	5.25	5.56	5.80	5.99
16	3.00	3.65	4.05	4.33	4.56	4.74
	4.13	4.79	5.19	5.49	5.72	5.92

df for error term	Number of treatment conditions					
	2	3	4	5	6	7
17	2.98 4.10	3.63 4.74	4.02 5.14	4.30 5.43	4.52 5.66	4.70 5.85
18	2.97 4.07	3.61 4.70	4.00 5.09	4.28 5.38	4.49 5.60	4.67 5.79
19	2.96 4.05	3.59 4.67	3.98 5.05	4.25 5.33	4.47 5.55	4.65 5.73
20	2.95 4.02	3.58 4.64	3.96 5.02	4.23 5.29	4.45 5.51	4.62 5.69
30	2.89 3.89	3.49 4.45	3.85 4.80	4.10 5.05	4.30 5.24	4.46 5.40
40	2.86 3.82	3.44 4.37	3.79 4.70	4.04 4.93	4.23 5.11	4.39 5.26
60	2.83 3.76	3.40 4.28	3.74 4.59	3.98 4.82	4.16 4.99	4.31 5.13
120	2.80 3.70	3.36 4.20	3.68 4.50	3.92 4.71	4.10 4.87	4.24 5.01
∞	2.77 3.64	3.31 4.12	3.63 4.40	3.86 4.60	4.03 4.76	4.17 4.88

Source: Adapted from http://www.stat.duke.edu/courses/Spring98/sta110c/qtable.html

Appendix E

One-Tailed Pearson's Correlation Table

df	α = .05	α = .01	df	α = .05	α = .01	df	α = .05	α = .01	df	α = .05	α = .01
1	0.988	1.000	31	0.291	0.403	61	0.209	0.293	91	0.172	0.241
2	0.900	0.980	32	0.287	0.397	62	0.207	0.290	92	0.171	0.240
3	0.805	0.934	33	0.283	0.392	63	0.206	0.288	93	0.170	0.238
4	0.729	0.882	34	0.279	0.386	64	0.204	0.286	94	0.169	0.237
5	0.669	0.833	35	0.275	0.381	65	0.203	0.284	95	0.168	0.236
6	0.621	0.789	36	0.271	0.376	66	0.201	0.282	96	0.167	0.235
7	0.582	0.750	37	0.267	0.371	67	0.200	0.280	97	0.166	0.234
8	0.549	0.715	38	0.264	0.367	68	0.198	0.278	98	0.165	0.232
9	0.521	0.685	39	0.260	0.362	69	0.197	0.276	99	0.165	0.231
10	0.497	0.658	40	0.257	0.358	70	0.195	0.274	100	0.164	0.230
11	0.476	0.634	41	0.254	0.354	71	0.194	0.272	101	0.163	0.229
12	0.458	0.612	42	0.251	0.350	72	0.193	0.270	102	0.162	0.228
13	0.441	0.592	43	0.248	0.346	73	0.191	0.268	103	0.161	0.227
14	0.426	0.574	44	0.246	0.342	74	0.190	0.266	104	0.161	0.226
15	0.412	0.558	45	0.243	0.338	75	0.189	0.265	105	0.160	0.225
16	0.400	0.543	46	0.240	0.335	76	0.188	0.263	106	0.159	0.224
17	0.389	0.529	47	0.238	0.331	77	0.186	0.261	107	0.158	0.223
18	0.378	0.516	48	0.235	0.328	78	0.185	0.260	108	0.158	0.222
19	0.369	0.503	49	0.233	0.325	79	0.184	0.258	109	0.157	0.221
20	0.360	0.492	50	0.231	0.322	80	0.183	0.257	110	0.156	0.220
21	0.352	0.482	51	0.228	0.319	81	0.182	0.255	111	0.156	0.219
22	0.344	0.472	52	0.226	0.316	82	0.181	0.253	112	0.155	0.218
23	0.337	0.462	53	0.224	0.313	83	0.180	0.252	113	0.154	0.217
24	0.330	0.453	54	0.222	0.310	84	0.179	0.251	114	0.153	0.216
25	0.323	0.445	55	0.220	0.307	85	0.178	0.249	115	0.153	0.215
26	0.317	0.437	56	0.218	0.305	86	0.176	0.248	116	0.152	0.214
27	0.311	0.430	57	0.216	0.302	87	0.175	0.246	117	0.152	0.213
28	0.306	0.423	58	0.214	0.300	88	0.174	0.245	118	0.151	0.212
29	0.301	0.416	59	0.213	0.297	89	0.174	0.244	119	0.150	0.211
30	0.296	0.409	60	0.211	0.295	90	0.173	0.242	120	0.150	0.210

Two-Tailed Pearson's Correlation Table

df	α = .05	α = .01	df	α = .05	α = .01	df	α = .05	α = .01	df	α = .05	α = .01
1	0.997	1.000	31	0.344	0.978	61	0.248	0.983	91	0.204	0.986
2	0.950	0.995	32	0.339	0.978	62	0.246	0.983	92	0.203	0.986
3	0.878	0.987	33	0.334	0.978	63	0.244	0.983	93	0.202	0.986
4	0.811	0.981	34	0.329	0.979	64	0.242	0.983	94	0.201	0.986
5	0.754	0.978	35	0.325	0.979	65	0.240	0.983	95	0.200	0.986
6	0.707	0.975	36	0.320	0.979	66	0.239	0.983	96	0.199	0.986
7	0.666	0.974	37	0.316	0.979	67	0.237	0.984	97	0.198	0.986
8	0.632	0.973	38	0.312	0.979	68	0.235	0.984	98	0.197	0.986
9	0.602	0.973	39	0.308	0.980	69	0.234	0.984	99	0.196	0.986
10	0.576	0.973	40	0.304	0.980	70	0.232	0.984	100	0.195	0.986
11	0.553	0.973	41	0.301	0.980	71	0.230	0.984	101	0.194	0.986
12	0.532	0.973	42	0.297	0.980	72	0.229	0.984	102	0.193	0.986
13	0.514	0.973	43	0.294	0.980	73	0.227	0.984	103	0.192	0.986
14	0.497	0.973	44	0.291	0.981	74	0.226	0.984	104	0.191	0.986
15	0.482	0.973	45	0.288	0.981	75	0.224	0.984	105	0.190	0.986
16	0.468	0.974	46	0.285	0.981	76	0.223	0.984	106	0.189	0.987
17	0.456	0.974	47	0.282	0.981	77	0.221	0.985	107	0.188	0.987
18	0.444	0.974	48	0.279	0.981	78	0.220	0.985	108	0.187	0.987
19	0.433	0.975	49	0.276	0.981	79	0.219	0.985	109	0.187	0.987
20	0.423	0.975	50	0.273	0.981	80	0.217	0.985	110	0.186	0.987
21	0.413	0.975	51	0.271	0.982	81	0.216	0.985	111	0.185	0.987
22	0.404	0.975	52	0.268	0.982	82	0.215	0.985	112	0.184	0.987
23	0.396	0.976	53	0.266	0.982	83	0.213	0.985	113	0.183	0.987
24	0.388	0.976	54	0.263	0.982	84	0.212	0.985	114	0.182	0.987
25	0.381	0.976	55	0.261	0.982	85	0.211	0.985	115	0.182	0.987
26	0.374	0.977	56	0.259	0.982	86	0.210	0.985	116	0.181	0.987
27	0.367	0.977	57	0.256	0.982	87	0.208	0.985	117	0.180	0.987
28	0.361	0.977	58	0.254	0.983	88	0.207	0.985	118	0.179	0.987
29	0.355	0.977	59	0.252	0.983	89	0.206	0.985	119	0.179	0.987
30	0.349	0.978	60	0.250	0.983	90	0.205	0.986	120	0.178	0.987

Appendix F

Spearman's Correlation Table

1-tail α levels	0.05	0.025	0.01	0.005		0.05	0.025	0.01	0.005
2-tail α levels	0.1	0.05	0.02	0.01		0.1	0.05	0.02	0.01
N = 4	1.000				N = 30	0.306	0.362	0.425	0.467
5	0.900	1.000	1.000		31	0.301	0.356	0.418	0.459
6	0.829	0.886	0.943	1.000	32	0.296	0.350	0.412	0.452
7	0.714	0.786	0.893	0.929	33	0.291	0.345	0.405	0.446
8	0.643	0.738	0.833	0.881	34	0.278	0.340	0.399	0.439
9	0.600	0.700	0.783	0.833	35	0.283	0.335	0.394	0.433
10	0.564	0.648	0.745	0.794	36	0.279	0.330	0.388	0.427
11	0.536	0.618	0.709	0.755	37	0.275	0.325	0.383	0.421
12	0.503	0.587	0.671	0.727	38	0.271	0.321	0.378	0.415
13	0.484	0.560	0.648	0.703	39	0.267	0.317	0.373	0.410
14	0.464	0.538	0.622	0.675	40	0.264	0.313	0.368	0.405
15	0.443	0.521	0.604	0.654	41	0.261	0.309	0.364	0.400
16	0.429	0.503	0.582	0.635	42	0.257	0.305	0.359	0.395
17	0.414	0.485	0.566	0.615	43	0.254	0.301	0.355	0.391
18	0.401	0.472	0.550	0.600	44	0.251	0.298	0.351	0.386
19	0.391	0.460	0.535	0.584	45	0.248	0.294	0.347	0.382
20	0.380	0.447	0.520	0.570	46	0.246	0.291	0.343	0.378
21	0.370	0.435	0.508	0.556	47	0.243	0.288	0.340	0.374
22	0.361	0.425	0.496	0.544	48	0.240	0.285	0.336	0.370
23	0.353	0.415	0.486	0.532	49	0.238	0.282	0.333	0.366
24	0.344	0.406	0.476	0.521	50	0.235	0.279	0.329	0.363
25	0.337	0.398	0.466	0.511	60	0.214	0.255	0.300	0.331
26	0.331	0.390	0.457	0.501	70	0.190	0.235	0.278	0.307
27	0.324	0.382	0.448	0.491	80	0.185	0.220	0.260	0.287
28	0.317	0.375	0.440	0.483	90	0.174	0.207	0.245	0.271
29	0.312	0.368	0.433	0.475	100	0.165	0.197	0.233	0.257

Source: Adapted from http://www.oup.com/uk/orc/bin/9780199265152/01student/04calculation/chapter_11_spearman.xls

Appendix G

Critical Values for Chi-Square

df	α = 0.05	α = 0.01
1	3.841	6.635
2	5.991	9.210
3	7.815	11.345
4	9.488	13.277
5	11.070	15.086
6	12.592	16.812
7	14.067	18.475
8	15.507	20.090
9	16.919	21.666
10	18.307	23.209
11	19.675	24.725
12	21.026	26.217
13	22.362	27.688
14	23.685	29.141
15	24.996	30.578
16	26.296	32.000
17	27.587	33.409
18	28.869	34.805
19	30.144	36.191
20	31.410	37.566
21	32.671	38.932
22	33.924	40.289
23	35.172	41.638
24	36.415	42.980
25	37.652	44.314
26	38.885	45.642
27	40.113	46.963
28	41.337	48.278
29	42.557	49.588
30	43.773	50.892

Appendix H

Computing SSs for Factorial ANOVA

Low Body Temperature		High Body Temperature	
Beer	Placebo	Beer	Placebo
10	5	14	11
8	8	17	8
7	6	12	9
8	7	19	13
9	4	18	8
7	10	15	12
12	7	12	10
11	9	21	9
$\Sigma X = 72$; $\Sigma X^2 = 672$	$\Sigma X = 56$; $\Sigma X^2 = 420$	$\Sigma X = 128$; $\Sigma X^2 = 2124$	$\Sigma X = 80$; $\Sigma X^2 = 824$

The above table displays the scores within each of the four conditions in this study. The ΣX and the ΣX^2 within each condition are displayed in each column of the table.

We will start by computing the SS for all of the scores by summing all of the scores to find $\Sigma X_{total} = 72 + 56 + 128 + 80 = 336$. Then, the sum of all the squared scores is $\Sigma X^2 = 672 + 420 + 2124 + 824 = 4040$. Use the SS formula to find the SS_{total}, where $N =$ the total number of scores or 32.

$$SS_{total} = \Sigma X^2 - \frac{(\Sigma X)^2}{N} = 4040 - \frac{(336)^2}{32} = 512$$

Then, compute the SS_{within} (also called the SS_{error}) by computing the individual SSs within each of the four conditions. The SS for the Low Body Temperature, Beer condition is computed below:

$$SS = \Sigma X^2 - \frac{(\Sigma X)^2}{N} = 672 - \frac{(72)^2}{8} = 24$$

By using the same procedure for the other three conditions, we find the other condition SSs to be: 28, 76, and 24. The SS_{within} is the sum of the individual condition SSs, or 152.

$$SS_{within} = 24 + 28 + 76 + 24 = 152$$

The next step is to compute the SSs for each of the three effects we are interested in, namely the main effect of Body Temperature, the main effect of Alcohol, and the Interaction. First, we compute the SS for all of these effects combined called the $SS_{between}$. This is done by simply subtracting the SS_{within} from the SS_{total}.

$$SS_D = SS_T - SS_W$$

$$SS_{between} = 512 - 152 = 360$$

Next, we must determine how much of the $SS_{between}$ variability was due to the main effect of Factor A; in this case, how much of the 360 variability was due to differences in Body Temperature. This is done by using the following formula:

$$SS_{body\ temp} = \Sigma \frac{A^2_{level}}{n_{level}} - \frac{T^2}{N}$$

$$= \frac{(72+56)^2}{16} + \frac{(128+80)^2}{16} - \frac{(72+56+128+80)^2}{32}$$

$$= 1024 + 2704 - 3528 = 200.$$

A_{level} represents the sum of the scores in a given condition of Factor A. In the present case, Factor A is Body Temperature, which has two levels so that there will be two A_{level} terms in the equation. For example, the sums of the scores in the Low Body Temperature conditions were 72 and 56, from the Low Body Temperature with Beer and Low Body Temperature with Placebo conditions, respectively. The sums of the scores in the High Body Temperature conditions were 128 and 80, respectively. In the above equation, T represents the sum of all the scores in the design; n_{level} represents the number of scores in a given level of Factor A, and N represents the number of scores in the entire study. So, the $SS_{body\ temp}$ accounts for 200 of the 360 between-treatment variability. A similar procedure yields the SS for Alcohol.

$$SS_{alcohol} = \Sigma \frac{A^2_{level}}{n_{level}} - \frac{T^2}{N} = \frac{(72+128)^2}{16} + \frac{(56+80)^2}{16} - \frac{(72+56+128+80)^2}{32}$$

$$= 2500 + 1156 - 3528 = 128.$$

So the $SS_{alcohol}$ accounts for another 128 of the 360 between-treatment variability.

The final SS we need is the $SS_{interaction}$. As stated above, the three effects all created an $SS_{between}$ of 360. If the $SS_{body\ temp}$ was 200 and the $SS_{alcohol}$ was 128, the $SS_{interaction}$ must be 32.

$$SS_{interaction} = SS_{between} - SS_{body\ temp} - SS_{alcohol} = 360 - 200 - 128 = 32$$

Appendix I

Computing Simple Effects for Factorial ANOVA

After discovering a significant interaction between two variables, simple effects are computed to interpret the interaction. You can compute simple effects by hand, but doing them in SPSS is far easier. Unfortunately, you cannot compute simple effects using the point and click menus in SPSS. Instead, you must use the syntax window in SPSS. Fortunately, you can get SPSS to do part of the work for you.

For this example, we use the data from Activity 13-1.

- Set up the ANOVA as usual.
  - Click on the Analyze menu, select General Linear Model, then choose Univariate.
  - Move the IVs (in this case, Gender and Exercise Type) into the Fixed Factors box and the DV (in this case, Muscle Gained) into the DV box.
- Click on the Options button.
- Move one IV (in this case, Gender) into the Display Means for box.
- Select Bonferroni from the Confidence Interval Adjustment drop-down box.
- Click on Continue.
- Click on the Paste button.
- A syntax window will open up with the following syntax:

UNIANOVA MuscleGained BY Exercise Gender
/METHOD = SSTYPE(3)
/INTERCEPT = INCLUDE
/EMMEANS = TABLES(Gender) COMPARE ADJ(BONFERRONI)
/CRITERIA = ALPHA(.05)
/DESIGN = Exercise Gender Exercise*Gender.

If you ran this analysis, you would simply be running a factorial ANOVA. To change the syntax so that it will run simple effects, only one line (the /EMMEANS line) needs to be edited. The original syntax refers to just one IV (Gender). You need to edit it such that it includes both IVs (Gender and Exercise) as follows:

Original syntax:

/EMMEANS = TABLES(Gender) COMPARE ADJ(BONFERRONI)

Edited syntax:

/EMMEANS = TABLES(Gender*Exercise) COMPARE(Exercise) ADJ(BONFERRONI)

Thus, the complete syntax will read as follows:

UNIANOVA MuscleGained BY Exercise Gender

/METHOD = SSTYPE(3)

/INTERCEPT = INCLUDE

/EMMEANS = TABLES(Gender*Exercise) COMPARE(Exercise) ADJ(BONFERRONI)

/CRITERIA = ALPHA(.05)

/DESIGN = Exercise Gender Exercise*Gender.

After editing the syntax, click Run and then click All.

The output will include an ANOVA summary table that is not relevant for the simple effects (it simply replicates the summary table you generated previously). The simple effects analysis is in the following three tables:

For this particular analysis, two simple effects are being tested. One is the difference in mean muscle gain for men in the weight training and yoga conditions. The other is a

Estimates

Dependent Variable: MuscleGained

Gender	Exercise	Mean	Std. Error	95% Confidence Interval Lower Bound	Upper Bound
male	weight training	6.900	.592	5.699	8.101
	yoga	4.000	.592	2.799	5.201
female	weight training	3.500	.592	2.299	4.701
	yoga	3.100	.592	1.899	4.301

The means in this table are the cell means used to generate the mean differences in the table below. These are the same cell means generated by the original factorial ANOVA.

Pairwise Comparisons

Dependent Variable: MuscleGained

Gender	(I) Exercise	(J) Exercise	Mean Difference (I-J)	Std. Error	Sig.[b]	95% Confidence Interval for Difference[b] Lower Bound	Upper Bound
male	weight training	yoga	2.900*	.838	.001	1.201	4.599
	yoga	weight training	-2.900*	.838	.001	-4.599	-1.201
female	weight training	yoga	.400	.838	.636	-1.299	2.099
	yoga	weight training	-.400	.838	.636	-2.099	1.299

Based on estimated marginal means

*. The mean difference is significant at the .05 level.

b. Adjustment for multiple comparisons: Bonferroni.

Mean Difference: The mean differences being compared for each simple effect.

Sig.: Displays the p values for the simple effects. Reject H_0, if p value < α.

Univariate Tests

Dependent Variable: MuscleGained

Gender		Sum of Squares	df	Mean Square	F	Sig.
male	Contrast	42.050	1	42.050	11.986	.001
	Error	126.300	36	3.508		
female	Contrast	.800	1	.800	.228	.636
	Error	126.300	36	3.508		

Each F tests the simple effects of Exercise within each level combination of the other effects shown. These tests are based on the linearly independent pairwise comparisons among the estimated marginal means.

This table provides the statistical information necessary for reporting simple effects. For example, the following information would be included in a report of the simple effect for males:

$F(1,36) = 11.96, p = .001$

similar comparison for women. Males who weight trained gained $M = 6.90$ pounds of muscle while men who did yoga gained $M = 4.00$ pounds of muscle, resulting in a difference of 2.90 pounds of muscle. This difference was significant, $F(1, 36) = 11.96, p = .001$, indicating that for men weight training led to significantly more muscle gain than doing yoga.

A different pattern of results emerged for women. Specifically, women who weight trained gained $M = 3.50$ pounds of muscle while women who did yoga gained $M = 3.10$ pounds of muscle, resulting in a difference of .40 between the two conditions. This difference was not significant, $F(1, 36) = .23, p = .64$, indicating that for women weight training and yoga were equally effective in terms of muscle gain.

For this particular study, we ran the simple effects comparing the two exercise conditions within gender. We could have also run the analyses by comparing men and women within each exercise condition. It is up to you to choose the analysis that makes the most sense given your data and hypotheses.

Index

Note: A *t* following a page number refers to a table on that page.

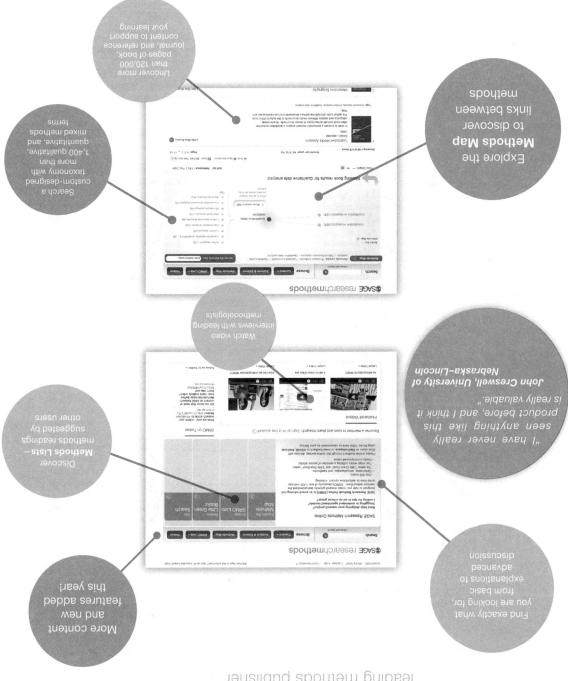